Fodor's 94
Los Angeles

Fodor's Travel Publications, Inc.
New York • Toronto • London • Sydney • Auckland

Copyright © 1993
by Fodor's Travel Publications, Inc.

ISBN 0–679–02526–X

Fodor's Los Angeles

Editor: Holly Hughes
Contributors: William P. Brown, Bruce David Colen, Rosemary Freskos, Mary Jane Horton, Jane E. Lasky, Ellen Melinkoff, Marcy Pritchard, Linda K. Schmidt, Aaron Sugarman, Bobbi Zane
Creative Director: Fabrizio La Rocca
Cartographer: David Lindroth
Illustrator: Karl Tanner
Cover Photograph: Alan Becker/Image Bank

Design: Vignelli Associates

Special Sales

Contents

Foreword

While every care has been taken to ensure the accuracy of the information in this guide, the passage of time will always bring change and, consequently, the publisher cannot accept responsibility for errors that may occur.

All prices and opening times quoted here are based on information supplied to us at press time. Hours and admission fees may change, however, and the prudent traveler will avoid inconvenience by calling ahead.

Fodor's wants to hear about your travel experiences, both pleasant and unpleasant. When a hotel or restaurant fails to live up to its billing, let us know, and we will investigate the complaint and revise our entries where the facts warrant it.

Send your letters to the editors of Fodor's Travel Publications, 201 E. 50th Street, New York, NY 10022.

Highlights '94 and Fodor's Choice

Highlights '94

West L.A. awaits the arrival of the **J. Paul Getty Center,** set to occupy some 110 acres atop a hill that allows panoramic views of the Pacific and the Los Angeles basin. All this is scheduled to happen sometime in 1996 or 1997. Elsewhere on the west side, the posh Beverly Hills Hotel has shut down for renovations but will reopen in early 1995.

In Downtown L.A., construction continues on the **Walt Disney Concert Hall,** future home of the Los Angeles Philharmonic. Scheduled for completion in 1997, the hall is being designed by local architectural hero Frank Gehry. Word is that this structure will be more conservative than typical Gehry creations.

Down the coast, the *Spruce Goose* has successfully relocated to Oregon, but the *Queen Mary* still resides in Long Beach. Now called the *Queen Mary* **Seaport,** the complex includes the famous ship, the Queen's Marketplace (for shopping and eating), and a mini amusement park called the Queen's Playland. At press time, plans had yet to be finalized for the use of the space, referred to as the Dome at the *Queen Mary,* which Howard Hughes's famous giant plane once occupied. The Hotel *Queen Mary* is in full swing, with more than 300 staterooms and suites. Fans of the *Queen Mary* will be happy to learn that there is no longer an admission fee to board the incredible Art Deco ship for a self-guided tour. Guided tours are $5 for adults and $3 for children under 12. Should you care to take an audio tour of the upper decks in English, Spanish, German, or Japanese, you can purchase one for $3.50.

Meanwhile, in Anaheim, **Disneyland** is considering an expansion, although at press time there were no firm plans. The proposal is that the famous theme park will sprout an addition (akin to Orlando's Epcot and tentatively called Westcot) that will include more hotels, as well as more amusements.

Generally, 1993 was a good year for Los Angeles. A **new mayor,** the first in two decades, was elected, and the feeling among residents is that Mayor Richard Riordan, a successful businessman (among his many holdings is the landmark Pantry Restaurant downtown) will enable the city to thrive economically. Word has it that he intends to run the city as a big business.

The Southland gained a new hockey team, called the Mighty Ducks after the Disney movie of the same name (for obvious reasons as the team is sponsored by Disney). The Ducks push the puck in a new stadium in Anaheim.

This has been a banner year for new hotels, with the opening of two major players: the Hotel Inter-Continental and the Beverly Prescott. It seems that interest in the city has finally grown to fill the glut of hotel rooms created in 1984 for the Olympics.

Fodor's Choice

No two people will agree on what makes a perfect vacation, but it's fun and helpful to know what others think. We hope you'll have a chance to experience some of Fodor's Choices yourself while visiting Los Angeles. For detailed information about each entry, refer to the appropriate chapters within this guidebook.

Postcard Sights

Griffith Park Observatory

Capitol Records Building

Malibu Beach seen from the Getty Museum

The Blue Whale, a.k.a. the Pacific Design Center

Melrose Avenue

Museums

Gene Autry Western Heritage Museum

J. Paul Getty Museum

Museum of Contemporary Art

Natural History Museum of Los Angeles

Norton Simon Museum

Parks and Gardens

Descanso Gardens

Eaton Canyon Park and Nature Center

Huntington Library and Botanical Garden

Will Rogers State Park

William S. Hart County Park

Hotels

Century Plaza Hotel *(Very Expensive)*

Hotel Bel-Air *(Very Expensive)*

The Regent Beverly Wilshire *(Very Expensive)*

The Ritz-Carlton, Marina del Rey *(Very Expensive)*

Restaurants

Rex Il Ristorante *(Very Expensive)*

Arnie Morton's of Chicago *(Expensive–Very Expensive)*

L'Orangerie *(Expensive–Very Expensive)*

The Dining Room *(Expensive)*

Spago *(Moderate–Expensive)*

Citrus *(Moderate)*

Il Fornaio Cucina Italiana *(Inexpensive–Moderate)*

Mon Kee Seafood *(Inexpensive–Moderate)*

Art's Delicatessen *(Inexpensive)*

Special Moments

Christmas Boat Parade, Marina del Rey

Entering the Santa Monica Kite Festival

A walk in the Hollywood Hills, with view of Los Angeles and the ocean

Watching the filming of a live TV show

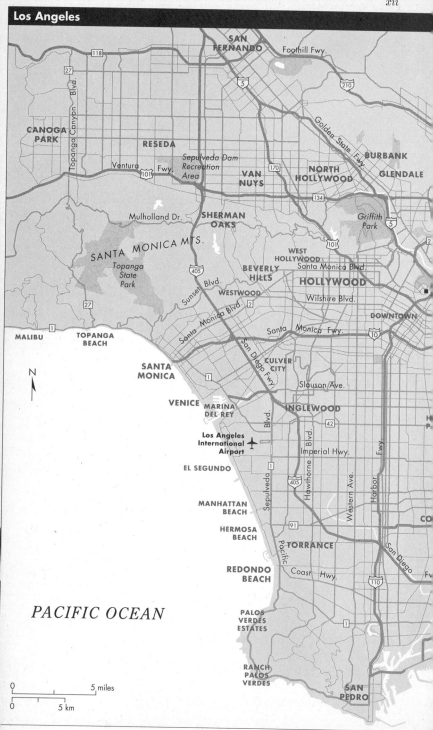

Los Angeles

PACIFIC OCEAN

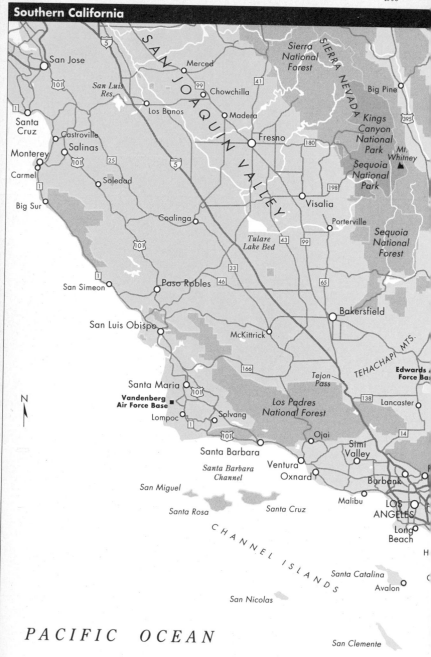

Southern California

San Jose

San Luis Res.

Merced

Sierra National Forest

SIERRA NEVADA

Big Pine

Chowchilla

Santa Cruz

Castroville

Salinas

Los Banos

Madera

Fresno

Kings Canyon National Park

Mt. Whitney

Monterey

Carmel

Soledad

Sequoia National Park

Big Sur

Coalinga

Visalia

Porterville

Sequoia National Forest

San Simeon

Tulare Lake Bed

Paso Robles

San Luis Obispo

McKittrick

Bakersfield

TEHACHAPI MTS.

Edwards Force Ba

Santa Maria

Vandenberg Air Force Base

Lompoc

Solvang

166

Tejon Pass

Lancaster

N

Los Padres National Forest

Ojai

Simi Valley

Santa Barbara

Ventura

Burbank

Santa Barbara Channel

Oxnard

San Miguel

Malibu

LOS ANGELES

Santa Rosa

Santa Cruz

Long Beach

CHANNEL ISLANDS

H

Santa Catalina

Avalon

San Nicolas

San Clemente

PACIFIC OCEAN

0   50 miles

0   75 km

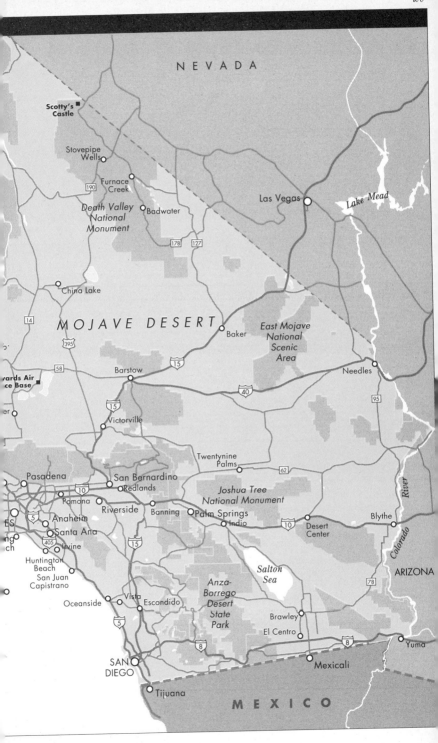

World Time Zones

Numbers below vertical bands relate each zone to Greenwich Mean Time (0 hrs.).
Local times frequently differ from these general indications,
as indicated by light-face numbers on map.

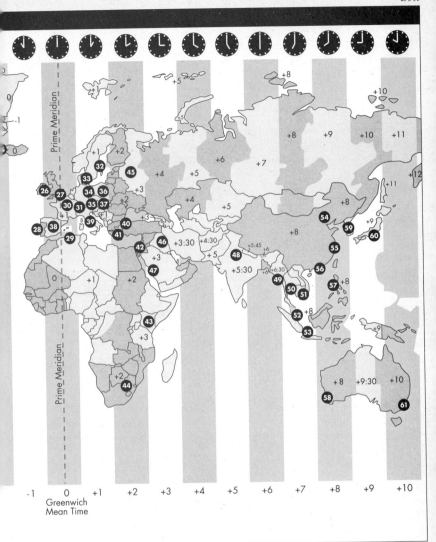

-1 +0 +1 +2 +3 +4 +5 +6 +7 +8 +9 +10

-1 0 +1 +2 +3 +4 +5 +6 +7 +8 +9 +10
Greenwich
Mean Time

Mecca, **47**
Mexico City, **12**
Miami, **18**
Montréal, **15**
Moscow, **45**
Nairobi, **43**
New Orleans, **11**
New York City, **16**

Ottawa, **14**
Paris, **30**
Perth, **58**
Reykjavík, **25**
Rio de Janeiro, **23**
Rome, **39**
Saigon (Ho Chi Minh City), **51**

San Francisco, **5**
Santiago, **21**
Seoul, **59**
Shanghai, **55**
Singapore, **52**
Stockholm, **32**
Sydney, **61**
Tokyo, **60**

Toronto, **13**
Vancouver, **4**
Vienna, **35**
Warsaw, **36**
Washington, D.C., **17**
Yangon, **49**
Zürich, **31**

Introduction

By Jane E. Lasky

A syndicated newspaper columnist, television producer, and author of several travel books, Jane Lasky also publishes articles in many national magazines, such as Vogue, Connoisseur, Los Angeles, Travel & Leisure, *and* Esquire.

You're preparing for your trip to Los Angeles. You're psyching up with Beach Boys CDs, and some Hollywood epics on the laser-disc player. You've pulled out your Hawaiian shirts and tennis shorts. You've studied the menu at Taco Bell. You're even doing a crash regimen at your local tanning salon and aerobics studio so you won't *look* so much like a tourist when you hit the coast.

Well, relax. *Everybody's* a tourist in LaLa Land. Even the stars are star-struck (as evidenced by the celebrities watching the other celebrities at Spago). Los Angeles is a city of ephemerals, of transience, and above all, of illusion. Nothing here is quite real, and that's the reality of it all. That air of anything-can-happen—as it often does—is what motivates thousands to move to and millions to vacation in this promised land each year. Visitors don't just come from the East or Midwest, mind you, but from the Far East, Down Under, Europe, and South America. It's this influx of cultures that's been the lifeblood of Los Angeles since its Hispanic beginning.

We cannot predict what *your* Los Angeles will be like. You can laze on a beach or soak up some of the world's greatest art collections. You can tour the movie studios and stars' homes or take the kids to Disneyland, Magic Mountain, or Knott's Berry Farm. You can shop luxurious Beverly Hills' Rodeo Drive or browse for hipper novelties on boutique-lined Melrose Avenue. The possibilities are endless—rent a boat to Catalina Island, watch the floats in Pasadena's Rose Parade, or dine on tacos, sushi, goat cheese pizza, or just plain hamburgers, hot dogs, and chili.

No matter how fast-forward Los Angeles seems to spin, the heart of the city—or at least its stomach—is still deep in the 1950s. Sure, the lighter, nouvelle-inspired California cuisine has made a big splash (no one here has ever been ridiculed as a "health-food nut" for preferring a healthier diet), but nothing is more quintessentially Californian than Johnny Rockets (a chrome-and-fluorescent burger paradise on Melrose) or Pink's (a beloved greasy spoon of a chili-dog dive on La Brea).

None of this was imagined when Spanish settlers founded their Pueblo de la Reina de Los Angeles in 1781. In fact, no one predicted a golden future for desert-dry southern California until well after San Francisco and northern California had gotten a head start with their own gold rush. The dusty outpost of Los Angeles eventually had oil and oranges, but the golden key to its success came on the silver screen: the movies. Although, if the early pioneers of Hollywood—religiously conservative fruit farmers—had gotten their way, their town's name would never have become synonymous with cinema and entertainment.

The same sunshine that draws today's visitors and new residents drew Cecil B. DeMille and Jesse Lasky in 1911 while searching for a place to make movies besides New York City. Lesser filmmakers had been shooting reels for the nickelodeons of the day in Hollywood, but DeMille and Lasky were the first to make a feature-length movie here. It took another 15 years to break through the sound barrier in cinema, but the silent-film era made Hollywood's name synonymous with fantasy, glamour, and, as the first citizens would snicker in disgust, with sin.

Outrageous partying, extravagant homes, eccentric clothing, and money, money, money have been symbols of life in Los Angeles ever since. Even the more conservative oil, aerospace, computer, banking, and import/export industries on the booming Pacific Rim have enjoyed the prosperity that leads inevitably to fun living. But even without piles of bucks, many people have found a kindred spirit in Los Angeles for their colorful lifestyles, be they spiritually, socially, or sexually unusual. Tolerance reigns; live and let live—which explains why you, too, will fit in.

When you arrive in Los Angeles, turn your car radio to 94.7 FM. "Ninety-four-seven, the Way-ee-yave," as this station's identifiers croon it, plays New Age, mellow modern, and a synthesizer blend of soft jazz, gentle rock, and cosmic chords not easily found anywhere else on your dial. The mix makes for the perfect freeway-driving soundtrack. It's Muzak for tomorrow's world—the '60s recycled into the '90s; the tempo of Tinseltown, laid back and out there.

If cosmic music sounds corny to you, there are classical, contemporary, blues, soul, and rock stations here— and, believe us, with "drive time" what it is in Los Angeles, you'll have plenty of time to find them. Disc jockey Jay Thomas plays the latest dance, rock, and pop hits on KPWR 106 FM, better known as The Power, and jazz and blues can be heard on KLON, 88.1 FM, featuring such artists as Wynton Marsalis and Ray Charles. For the latest traffic update, tune in KFWB, 98 AM, the 24-hour news station ("You give us 22 minutes, we'll give you the world") offers traffic updates every 10 minutes. Dr. David Viscott has a radio show on KABC AM Talkradio, weekdays from 1 PM to 3 PM, offering free psychiatric help to callers.

No matter what you turn on and what turns you on while you drive the infamous freeways, these asphalt ribbons are your passage to the far-flung pleasures of Los Angeles. Getting there *can* be half the fun, outside of rush-crush hours (7–9 AM and 3–7 PM), but when the freeway bogs down with bumper-to-bumper Japanese imports, minipickups, and sleek Mercedes, blame Detroit. It was the U.S.

automakers and oil companies that, earlier this century, lobbied successfully to replace an electric mass transit system in Southern California with a diesel bus system. Free-spirited Californians drove blithely on, indulging their independence until one day, sometime in the mid-1950s, the smog got thick enough to kill. Mandatory emission controls have helped clear up that problem. Nevertheless, check the papers daily to ascertain the air quality.

No city has embraced the romance of the automobile as has Los Angeles. Cars are not only essential transportation but essential fashion accessories. They announce the wealth, politics, and taste of their drivers. Vanity license plates, a California innovation, condense the meaning of one's life into seven letters (MUZKBIZ). Sun roofs, ski racks, and cardboard windshield visors sell better here than anywhere else. You are what you drive—a thought worth remembering when you rent a car. Yes, Lamborghinis are available, even by the hour.

The distance between places in Los Angeles explains why the ethnic enclaves have not merged, regardless of the melting-pot appearance of the city. Especially since the rioting in the spring of 1992, which—among other things—brought to the surface much long-simmering tension between various ethnic groups, it is imposssible to gloss over the disparities of race, economics, and social mobility between neighborhoods. Nonetheless, at its best, and most notable for visitors, is the rich cultural and culinary diversity this mix of peoples creates.

There's something about a shiny, better world that beckons so many diverse people to Los Angeles. For some, a better world is self-enhancing—the building of the body beautiful, a personal fortune, or the hottest hotrod. Others try to better their world through the arts, politics, or spiritual exploration. For some it is enough just to surf and sun.

Set off from the rest of the continent by mountains and desert, and from the rest of the world by an ocean, this incredible corner of creation has evolved its own identity that conjures envy, fascination, ridicule, and scorn—often all at once. Those from purportedly more sophisticated cities note what Los Angeles lacks. Others from more provincial towns raise an eyebrow at what it has. Yet 12.5 million people visit the city annually, and three-quarters of them come back for more. Indeed, you cannot do Los Angeles in a day or a week or even two. This second largest city in America holds too many choices between its canyons and its coast to be exhausted in one trip; it will exhaust you first.

1 Essential Information

Before You Go

Visitor Information

The **Los Angeles Visitors and Convention Bureau** (633 W. Fifth St., Suite 6000, Los Angeles 90071, tel. 213/624–7300) will provide you with extensive free information about the region, including the quarterly calendar of entertainment and special events titled "Datelines." Los Angeles also maintains a 24-hour toll-free multilingual line for information about community services (tel. 800/339–6993).

In addition, there are visitors centers and chambers of commerce in many of the communities in the Los Angeles area, including **Beverly Hills** (239 S. Beverly Dr., Beverly Hills 90212, tel. 310/271–8174 or 800/345–2210), **Glendale** (200 S. Louise St., Box 112, Glendale 91209, tel. 818/240–7870), **Hollywood** (7000 Hollywood Blvd., Suite 911, Hollywood 90028, tel. 213/469–8311), **Long Beach** (1 World Trade Center, Suite 300, Long Beach 90831, tel. 310/436–3645), **Oxnard** (815 S. A St., Oxnard 93030, tel. 805/483–3921), and **Pasadena** (171 S. Los Robles Ave., Pasadena 91101, tel. 818/795–9311).

The **California Office of Tourism** (801 K St., Suite 1600, Sacramento, CA 95814, tel. 916/322–2881) can answer many questions about travel in the state. You can also order a detailed 208-page book, *Discover the Californias,* which includes an informative section on the Los Angeles area (free; tel. 800/862–2543).

Tours and Packages

Should you buy your travel arrangements to Los Angeles packaged or do it yourself? There are advantages either way. Buying packaged arrangements saves you money, particularly if you can find a program that includes exactly the features you want. You also get a pretty good idea of what your trip will cost from the outset. Generally, you have two options: fully escorted tours and independent packages. Escorted tours mean having limited free time and traveling with strangers. Travel is most often via motorcoach, with a tour director in charge. Your baggage is handled, your time rigorously scheduled, and most meals planned. Escorted tours are usually sold in three categories: deluxe, first-class, and tourist or budget class, the most important difference among them being the level of accommodations. Independent packages allow plenty of flexibility. They generally include airline travel and hotels, with certain options available, such as sightseeing, car rental, and excursions. Independent packages are usually more expensive than escorted tours, but your time is your own.

While you can book directly through tour operators, you will pay no more to go through a travel agent, who will be able to tell you about tours and packages from a number of operators. Whatever program you ultimately choose, be sure to find out exactly what is included: taxes, tips, transfers, meals, baggage handling, ground transportation, entertainment, excursions, sports or recreation (and rental equipment if necessary). Ask about the level of hotel used, its location, the size of its rooms, the kind of beds, and its amenities, such as pool, room service, or programs for children, if they're important to you. Find out the operator's cancellation penalties. Nearly everyone charges them, and the only way to avoid them is to buy trip- cancellation insurance (available from your travel agent). Also ask about the single supplement, a surcharge assessed to solo travelers. Some operators do not make you pay it if you agree to be matched up with a roommate of the same sex, even if one is not found by departure time.

Fully Escorted Tours On most escorted tours, Los Angeles is just one stop on a multi-day tour that includes all of California. Look into **Tauck Tours** (11 Wilton Rd., Westport, CT 06881, tel. 203/226–6911 or 800/468–2825) and **Maupintour** (Box 807, Lawrence, KS 66044, tel. 913/843–1211 or 800/255–4266) in the deluxe category; **Gadabout Tours** (700 E. Tahquitz Way, Palm Springs, CA 92262, tel. 619/325–5556 or 800/952–5068), **Domenico Tours** (751 Broadway, Bayonne, NJ 07002, tel. 201/823–8687 or 800/554–8687), and **Globus-Gateway** (95-25 Queens Blvd., Rego Park, NY 11374, tel. 718/268–7000 or 800/221–0090) in the first-class category.

Independent Packages Independent packages that feature Los Angeles often include visits to such top attractions as Disneyland. Try **American Airlines Fly AAway Vacations** (tel. 800/321–2121), **Continental Airlines' Grand Destinations** (tel. 800/634–555), **Delta Dream Vacations** (tel. 800/872–7786), **United Airlines' Vacation Planning Center** (tel. 800/328–6877). Also look into **SuperCities** (11330 Blondo St., Omaha, NE 68164, tel. 402/498–8999 or 800/333–1234).

Special-interest Travel Special-interest programs focus on everything from flora and fauna surrouding the city to nearby wineries and the Rose Bowl. Such programs may be fully escorted or independent. Some require a certain amount of expertise, but most are for the average traveler with an interest and are usually hosted by experts in the subject matter. The price range is wide, but the cost is usually higher—sometimes a lot higher—than for ordinary escorted tours and packages, because of the expert guiding and special activities.

Rose Bowl **Cartan Tours** (2809 Butterfield Road, Oak Brook, IL 60521, tel. 708/571–1400 or 800/422–7826) offers packages that include tickets to the game plus seats for the parade and post-parade admission to Vistory Park, where all the floats line up for viewing.

Nature **Sierra Club** (730 Polk St., San Francisco, CA 94109, tel. 415/776–2211) offers guided tours of the desert regions at the edge of the city, and the **Wilderness Institute** (28118 Agoura Rd., Agoura Hills, CA 91301, tel. 818/991–7327) offers guided tours of the scenic Santa Monica Mountains National Park.

Tips for British Travelers

Passports and Visas You need a valid 10-year passport to enter the United States. A visa is not necessary unless 1) you are planning to stay more than 90 days; 2) your trip is for purposes other than vacation; 3) you have at some time been refused a visa, or refused admission to, the United States, or have been required to leave by the U.S. Immigration and Naturalization Service; or 4) you do not have a return or onward ticket. You will need to fill out the Visa Waiver Form, 1–94W, supplied by the airline.

To apply for a visa or for more information, call the U.S. Embassy's Visa Information Line (tel. 0891/200–290; calls cost 48p per minute or 36p per minute cheap rate).

Customs British visitors aged 21 or over may import the following into the United States: 200 cigarettes or 50 cigars or 2 kilograms of tobacco; one U.S. liter of alcohol; gifts to the value of $100. Restricted items include meat products, seeds, plants, and fruits. Never carry illegal drugs.

Returning to Britain from countries outside the EC such as the United States, you may import duty-free 200 cigarettes, 100 cigarillos, 50 cigars or 250 grams of tobacco; 1 liter of spirits or 2 liters of fortified or sparkling wine; 2 liters of still table wine; 60 millileters of perfume; 250 millileters of toilet water; plus £36 worth of other goods, including gifts and souvenirs.

Insurance The **Association of British Insurers,** a trade association representing 450 insurance companies, advises extra medical coverage for visitors to the United States.

For advice by phone or a free booklet, "Holiday Insurance," that sets out what to expect from a holiday-insurance policy and gives price guidelines, contact the Association of British Insurers (51 Gresham St., London EC2V 7HQ, tel. 071/600–3333; 30 Gordon St., Glasgow G1 3PU, tel. 041/226–3905; Scottish Provincial Bldg., Donegall Sq. W, Belfast BT1 6JE, tel. 0232/249176; call for other locations).

Tour Operators Tour operators offering packages to the Los Angeles area include **British Airways Holidays** (Atlantic House, Hazelwick Ave., Three Bridges, Crawley, West Sussex RH10 1NP, tel. 0293/611611), **Jetsave** (Sussex House, London Rd., East Grinstead, W. Sussex RH19 1LD, tel. 0342/312033), **Key to America** (15 Feltham Rd., Ashford, Middlesex TW15 1DQ), tel. 0784/248777), **Kuoni Travel Ltd.** (Kuoni House, Dorking, Surrey RH5 4AZ, tel. 0306/742222), **Premier Holidays** (Premier Travel Center, Westbrook, Milton Rd., Cambridge CB4 1YQ, tel. 0223/355977), and **Trailfinders** (194 Kensington High St., London W8 7RG, tel. 071/937–5400; 58 Deansgate, Manchester M3 2Ff, tel. 061/839–6969).

Travelers with Disabilities Main information sources include the **Royal Association for Disability and Rehabilitation** (RADAR, 25 Mortimer St., London W1N 8AB, tel. 071/637–5400), which publishes travel information for the disabled in Britain, and **Mobility International** (228 Borough High St., London SE1 1JX, tel. 071/403–5688), the headquarters of an international membership organization that serves as a clearinghouse of travel information for people with disabilities.

When to Go

Almost any time of the year is the right time to go to Los Angeles; the climate is mild and pleasant year-round. However, there is a rainy season from November through March, with the heaviest downpours usually coming in January; and summer, while virtually rainless, usually sees the famous Los Angeles smog at its worst, sometimes causing problems for those with respiratory ailments. It will be much too hot to enjoy Palm Springs in summer.

Climate Seasons in Los Angeles and in Southern California generally are not as defined as in most other temperate areas of the world. The Pacific Ocean is the primary moderating influence. In addition, mountains along the north and east sides of the Los Angeles coastal basin act as buffers against the extreme summer heat and winter cold of the desert and plateau regions.

However, mild sea breezes and winds from the interior can mix to produce a variety of weather conditions; an unusual aspect of the Los Angeles climate is the pronounced difference in temperature, humidity, cloudiness, fog, rain, and sunshine over short distances.

The following are average daily maximum and minimum temperatures for Los Angeles.

Jan.	64F	18C	May	69F	21C	Sept.	75F	24C
	44	7		53	12		60	16
Feb.	64F	18C	June	71F	22C	Oct.	73F	23C
	46	8		57	14		55	13
Mar.	66F	19C	July	75F	24C	Nov.	71F	22C
	48	9		60	16		48	9
Apr.	66F	19C	Aug.	75F	24C	Dec.	66F	19C
	51	11		62	17		46	8

For current weather conditions for cities in the United States and abroad, plus the local time and helpful travel tips, call the **Weather Channel Connection** (tel. 900/WEATHER; 95¢ per minute) from a touch-tone phone.

Festivals and Seasonal Events

Some of the major festivities scheduled for the greater Los Angeles area this year are listed here, month by month. "Datelines," a quarterly calendar of events, is available free of charge from the Los Angeles Visitors and Convention Bureau (*see* Visitor Information, *above*).

January **Tournament of Roses Parade and Game,** Pasadena. The 104th annual parade took place on New Year's Day 1993, with lavish floral floats, marching bands, and equestrian teams moving down Colorado Boulevard in Pasadena, followed by the Rose Bowl Game. You can take a close-up look at the floats for two days after the parade at Victory Park. *391 S. Orange Grove Blvd., Pasadena 91184, tel. 818/449–4100.*
Los Angeles City Metropolitan Tennis Tournament. For three consecutive weekends, the city's best battle it out on the courts of Vermont Canyon Courts and Arroyo Seco Park. *Tel. 818/246–5614.*
Southland Snowboard, Big Bear. Less than two hours' drive from downtown Los Angeles, daredevil snowboarders race against each other and the clock. *Bear Mountain Ski Resort, Box 6812, Big Bear Lake 92315, tel. 909/585–2519.*
Martin Luther King Parade, Long Beach. This event begins with a parade down 7th and Alameda streets and ends with a festival in Martin Luther King Park. Local community leaders speak on civil rights, while ethnic foods and music make the celebration. It's usually held the Saturday preceding the third Monday in January. *Office of Special Events, 333 W. Ocean Ave., Long Beach 90802, tel. 310/436–7703.*

Whale-watching, California coast. Hundreds of gray whales migrate from January through April and may be observed along the California coast from San Diego to the Oregon border. *California Office of Tourism, 801 K St., Suite 1600, Sacramento 95814, tel. 916/322–1396.*

February **Bob Hope Chrysler Classic,** Indian Wells, Palmer Course PGA, La Quinta, and Bermuda Dunes. This PGA golf tournament, a celebrity-packed pro-am, has been held in the desert in late January for the past 30 years. *Box 865, Rancho Mirage 92270, tel. 619/341–2299 or 619/346–8184.*

Chinese New Year and Golden Dragon Parade, Los Angeles. Floats, bands, and dragon dancers move through the streets of Chinatown. *Chinese Chamber of Commerce, 977 N. Broadway, Suite E, Los Angeles 90012, tel. 213/617–0396.*

National Date Festival, Indio. One of the country's more unusual expositions, this 10-day affair in mid-February includes an Arabian Nights pageant, a horse show, and camel and ostrich races. *46350 Arabia St., Indio 92202, tel. 619/863–8247 or 619/347–0676.*

March **Gulfstream Aerospace Invitational,** Indian Wells. The legends of golf compete for a $350,000 purse at this early March stop on the PGA Senior Tour. *Box 1816, Palm Desert 92261, tel. 619/568–3579.*

Santa Barbara International Film Festival, Santa Barbara. This early March festival has it all: premieres of international and U.S. films, a tribute to a film actor, documentaries and archival films, workshops and seminars headed by film-industry professionals, and a gala opening premiere. *1216 State St., Suite 710, Santa Barbara 93101, tel. 805/963–0023.*

Los Angeles Marathon, Los Angeles. Early in March, you can take part in this 26.2-mile run through the neighborhood streets, or watch others going for the finish. *11110 W. Ohio Ave., Suite 100, Los Angeles, tel. 310/444–5544.*

Santa Barbara International Cymbidium Orchid Show, Santa Barbara. This horticultural spectacular staged the second weekend in March features displays and demonstrations. *Box 3006, Santa Barbara 93130, tel. 805/687–0766.*

Fiesta de Las Golondrinas, San Juan Capistrano. Each year, in mid-March, there's a celebration of the arrival of the swallows on their journey from Argentina. *Mission San Juan Capistrano, 31882 Camino Capistrano, Suite 107, San Juan Capistrano 92675, tel. 714/248–2048.*

The Congressional Cup, Long Beach. This annual four-day yacht race takes place toward the end of the month at the Long Beach Yacht Club. *6201 Appian Way, Long Beach, 90803, tel. 310/598–9401.*

The Redondo Beach Kite Festival, Redondo Beach. On the second Sunday in March, weather permitting, this noncompetitive contest sends up hundreds of homemade kites on the south side of the pier. The third Sunday of March is reserved for a manufacturer's display of—you guessed it—kites. *The Sunshine Kite Co., 101 Fisherman's Wharf, Redondo Beach 90277, tel. 310/372–0308.*

Nabisco Dinah Shore Invitational, Rancho Mirage. At the end of March, the finest women golfers in the world compete for the richest purse on the LPGA circuit. *2 Racquet Club Dr., Rancho Mirage 92270, tel. 619/324–4546.*

April **Long Beach Grand Prix,** Long Beach. There is world-c
racing on a mid-April weekend, with five races, entert.
and celebrities. *3000 Pacific Ave., Long Beach 90806, tel.
310/981–2600.*

The Ramona Pageant, Hemet. On three weekends, from mid-
April until the end of the month, the poignant love story of
Ramona is presented by a large cast on a mountainside outdoor
stage. *Ramona Pageant Association, 27400 Ramona Bowl Rd.,
Hemet 92544, tel. 909/658–3111.*

Conejo Valley Days, Thousand Oaks. Held at the end of April,
this festival features a chili cook-off, picnic, parade, rodeo,
whisker contest, carnival rides and games. *Conejo Valley
Chamber of Commerce, 625 W. Hillcrest Dr., Thousand Oaks
91360, tel. 805/499–1993.*

May **Cinco de Mayo,** Los Angeles. One of Mexico's most important
holidays is celebrated with a fiesta in early May at El Pueblo
de Los Angeles State Historic Park in downtown Los Angeles.
845 N. Alameda St., Los Angeles, 90012, tel. 213/628–1274.

Wine Expo, Redondo Beach. Southern California's largest outdoor wine tasting takes place early in the month of May. Along
with the wine, there is entertainment, and tasting of food from
local restaurants. *Redondo Beach Chamber of Commerce, 1215
N. Catalina Ave., Redondo Beach 90277, tel. 310/376–6912.*

June **Mariachi USA,** Hollywood. A four-hour evening festival features the requisite mariachis and folklorico dancing, from both
sides of the border, at the Hollywood Bowl. The show ends with
a spectacular fireworks display. *Hollywood Bowl, 2301 N. Highland Ave., Hollywood, tel. 310/451-5044.*

July **Semana Nautica Summer Sports Festival,** Santa Barbara. This
festival, held from the latter part of June through the first of
July, is over 50 years old, and includes some three dozen ocean,
beach, and land events, most of them open to amateurs. *Semana Nautica Association, 5101 University Dr., Santa Barbara
93111, tel. 805/564–2052.*

Fourth of July Celebration, Pasadena. The famous Rose Bowl
is the site for an old-fashioned circus and a first-class fireworks
show. *Rose Bowl, 1001 Rose Bowl Dr., Pasadena 91103, tel.
818/577–3100.*

Orange County Fair, Costa Mesa. During its 10-day run from
early to mid-July, there is top-name entertainment, a rodeo,
food, music, arts and crafts, and hundreds of exhibits. *88 Fair
Dr., Costa Mesa 92626, tel. 714/751–3247.*

Santa Barbara National Horse Show, Santa Barbara. In mid-
July horses and riders compete in one of the nation's top horse
shows, and at the same time, at the same showgrounds, a flower
show features gardens, landscapes, and arrangements. *Santa
Barbara National Horse Show, 19th District Agricultural Association, Santa Barbara Showgrounds, Box 3006, Santa Barbara 93130, tel. 805/687–0766.*

International Surf Festival, Hermosa Beach, Manhattan
Beach, Redondo Beach, and Torrance. July winds up with a
three-day multicity celebration that includes lifeguard competitions, volleyball and body surfing tournaments, sand castle
sculptures, and sand runs. *International Surf Festival Com-
mittee, 2600 Strand, Manhattan Beach 90266, tel. 310/546–8843.*

August **Old Spanish Fiesta Days,** Santa Barbara. In the first week of
August the community celebrates the city's Hispanic heritage

with costumes, parades, *mercados* (marketplaces), and a rodeo. *Old Spanish Days in Santa Barbara, Inc., 1122 N. Milpas St., Santa Barbara 93103, tel. 805/962–8101.*

Nisei Week Japanese Festival, Los Angeles. The rich Japanese cultural heritage is celebrated mid-month with parades, street dancing, and a carnival in Little Tokyo. *244 S. San Pedro St., Suite 501, Los Angeles 90012, tel. 213/687–7193.*

September **Los Angeles County Fair,** Pomona. This is the largest county fair in the world. It runs for more than two weeks, from mid-September into the first days of October. Horse racing, entertainment, fine arts, home arts, horse shows, agricultural displays, wine judging, and flower and garden shows are among the attractions. *Los Angeles County Fair Association, Box 2250, Pomona 91769, tel. 909/623–3111.*

October **Southern California Grand Prix at Del Mar,** Del Mar. This event on a mid-October weekend includes vintage grand prix races, an auto exposition, and national sports car championships. *3000 Pacific Ave., Long Beach 90806, tel. 310/981–2600.*

November **The Skins Game,** Palm Desert. In the latter part of the month, four of the PGA's top golfing pros compete in a high-stakes hole-by-hole challenge. *Big Horn Golf Club, 51005 Hwy. 74, Palm Desert 92260, tel. 619/568–4038.*

Hollywood Christmas Parade, Hollywood. Right after Thanksgiving comes this celebrity-studded parade. *Hollywood Chamber of Commerce, 7000 Hollywood Blvd., Hollywood 90028, tel. 213/469–2337.*

December **Christmas Boat Parade of Lights,** Newport Beach. For six nights before Christmas, 200 decorated boats parade through the harbor. *1470 Jamboree Rd., Newport Beach 92660, tel. 714/644–8211.*

What to Pack

Clothing The most important rule to bear in mind in packing for a Southern California vacation is to prepare for changes in temperature. An hour's drive can take you up or down many degrees, and there can be a marked drop in temperature from daytime to nighttime. Clothes that can be layered are your best insurance—take along a sweater or jacket but also bring some shorts and cool cottons. Always tuck in a bathing suit; most lodgings have a pool, a spa, or sauna.

While casual dressing is a hallmark of the California lifestyle, men will need a jacket and tie for many good restaurants in the evening, and women will be more comfortable in something dressier than the regulation sightseeing garb of cotton dresses, walking shorts, or jeans and T-shirts.

It's also important to pack light—at least, don't take more luggage than you can handle. Porters and luggage trolleys are not always easy to find.

Be sure you take comfortable walking shoes. Even if you're not much of a walker at home, you're bound to find many occasions on a Southern California vacation when you'll want to hoof it, and nothing ruins the pleasures of sightseeing like sore feet.

Miscellaneous Although you can buy film, sunscreen lotion, aspirin, and most other necessities almost anywhere in Southern California, it's a good idea to take along a reasonable supply of the things you know you will be using routinely, to spare yourself the bother of stocking up. An extra pair of glasses, contact lenses, or prescription sunglasses is always a good idea. Also pack any prescription medications you need regularly.

Luggage Free baggage allowances on an airline depend on the airline, *Regulations* the route, and the class of your ticket. In general, on domestic flights and on international flights between the United States and foreign destinations, you are entitled to check two bags—neither exceeding 62 inches, or 158 centimeters (length + width + height), or weighing more than 70 pounds (32 kilograms). A third piece may be brought aboard as a carryon; its total dimensions are generally limited to less than 45 inches (114 centimeters), so it will fit easily under the seat in front of you or in the overhead compartment.

Safeguarding Your Before leaving home, itemize your bags' contents and their *Luggage* worth and then tag your luggage inside and out with your name, address, and phone number. (If you use your home address, cover it so that potential thieves can't see it.) At check-in, make sure that the tag attached by baggage handlers bears the correct three-letter code for your destination. If your bags do not arrive with you, or if you detect damage, do not leave the airport until you've filed a written report with the airline.

Insurance In the event of loss, damage, or theft on international flights, airlines limit their liability to $20 per kilogram for checked baggage (roughly about $640 per 70-pound bag) and $400 per passenger for unchecked baggage. On domestic flights, the ceiling is $1,250 per passenger. Excess-valuation insurance can be bought directly from the airline at check-in but leaves your bags vulnerable on the ground. Your own homeowner's policy may fill the gap; or you may want special luggage insurance. Sources include **The Travelers Companies** (1 Tower Sq., Hartford, CT 06183, tel. 203/277–0111 or 800/243- -3174) and **Wallach and Company, Inc.** (107 W. Federal St., Box 480, Middleburg, VA 22117, tel. 703/687–3166 or 800/237–6615).

Cash Machines

Automated-teller machines (ATMs) are proliferating; many are tied to international networks such as **Cirrus** and **Plus.** You can use your bank card at ATMs away from home to withdraw money from your accounts and get cash advances on a credit-card account (providing your card has been programmed with a personal identification number, or PIN). Check in advance on limits on withdrawals and cash advances within specified periods. Remember that finance charges apply on credit-card cash advances from ATMs just as on those from tellers. And note that transaction fees for ATM withdrawals outside your home turf will probably be higher than for withdrawals at home.

For specific Cirrus locations in the United States and Canada, call 800/424–7787 (for U.S. Plus locations, 800/843–7587), and press the area code and first three digits of the number you're calling from (or the calling area where you want an ATM).

Traveling with Cameras, Camcorders, and Laptops

Film and Cameras If your camera is new or if you haven't used it for a while, shoot and develop a few rolls of film before leaving home. Pack some lens tissue and an extra battery for your built-in light meter, and invest in an inexpensive skylight filter, to both protect your lens and provide some definition in hazy shots. Store film in a cool, dry place—never in the car's glove compartment or on the shelf under the rear window.

Films above ISO 400 are more sensitive to damage from airport security X-rays than others; very high speed films, ISO 1,000 and above, are exceedingly vulnerable. To protect your film, carry it with you in a plastic bag and ask for a hand inspection. Such requests are honored at American airports. Don't depend on a lead-lined bag to protect film in checked luggage—the airline may very well turn up the dosage of radiation to see what you've got in there. Airport metal detectors do not harm film, although you'll set off the alarm if you walk through one with a roll in your pocket. Call the Kodak Information Center (tel. 800/242–2424) for details.

Camcorders   Before your trip, put new or long-unused camcorders through their paces, and practice panning and zooming. Invest in a skylight filter to protect the lens, and check the lithium battery that lights up the LCD (liquid crystal display) modes. As for the rechargeable nickel-cadmium batteries that are the camera's power source, take along an extra pair, so while you're using your camcorder you'll have another battery recharging.

Unlike still-camera film, videotape is not damaged by X-rays. However, it may well be harmed by the magnetic field of a walk-through metal detector.

Laptops   Security X-rays do not harm hard-disk or floppy-disk storage. Most airlines allow you to use your laptop aloft but request that you turn it off during takeoff and landing so as not to interfere with navigation equipment. If you're a heavy computer user, consider traveling with a backup battery.

Traveling with Children

Publications   ***L.A. Parent*** (Box 3204, Burbank 91504, tel. 818/846–0400) is a
Local Guides   monthly newspaper filled with events listings and resources; it is available free at such places as libraries, supermarkets, museums, and toy stores. For a small fee, you can have an issue sent to you before your trip.

Places to Go with Children in Southern California, by Stephanie Kegan, is published by Chronicle Books; $9.95. ***Parents' Guide 1993,*** edited by Karen Mani (Paul Flattery Productions, $22.95), has 500 pages listing shopping, goods, recreation, and entertainment for kids. ***Kids Connection,*** by Elizabeth Topper, is another Los Angeles information guide for parents.

Newsletter   ***Family Travel Times,*** published 10 times a year by **Travel With Your Children** (TWYCH, 45 W. 18th St., 7th Floor Tower, New York, NY 10011, tel. 212/206–0688; annual subscription $55), covers destinations, types of vacations, and modes of travel; an airline issue comes out every other year (the last one, February/March 1993, is sold to nonsubscribers for $10). On Wednesday, the staff answers subscribers' questions on specific destinations.

Books   *Great Vacations with Your Kids,* by Dorothy Jordan and Marjorie Cohen ($13; Penguin USA, 120 Woodbine St., Bergenfield, NJ 07621, tel. 800/253–6476), helps you plan your trip with children, from toddlers to teens. *Traveling with Children—And*

Enjoying It, by Arlene K. Butler ($11.95 plus $3 shipping per book; Globe Pequot Press, Box 833, Old Saybrook, CT 06475, tel. 800/243–0495; in CT, 800/962–0973), discusses car, plane, and train travel, has useful pretrip checklists, and offers tips on how to cuts costs and keep kids healthy and happy en route.

Tour Operators **GrandTravel** (6900 Wisconsin Ave., Suite 706, Chevy Chase, MD 20815, tel. 301/986–0790 or 800/247–7651) offers international and domestic tours for grandparents traveling with their grandchildren. **Rascals in Paradise** (650 5th St., Suite 505, San Francisco, CA 94107, tel. 415/978–9800 or 800/872–7225) specializes in programs for families.

Getting There On domestic flights, children under 2 not occupying a seat
Air Fares travel free, and older children currently travel on the "lowest applicable" adult fare.

Baggage The adult baggage allowance applies for children paying half or more of the adult fare. Check with the airline for particulars.

Safety Seats The FAA recommends the use of safety seats aloft and details approved models in the free leaflet "**Child/Infant Safety Seats Recommended for Use in Aircraft**" (available from the Federal Aviation Administration, APA–200, 800 Independence Ave. SW, Washington, DC 20591, tel. 202/267–3479). Airline policy varies. U.S. carriers must allow FAA-approved models, but because these seats are strapped into a regular passenger seat, they may require that parents buy a ticket even for an infant under 2 who would otherwise ride free.

Facilities Aloft Airlines do provide other facilities and services for children, such as children's meals and freestanding bassinets (to those sitting in seats on the bulkhead, where there's enough legroom to accommodate them). Make your request when reserving. The annual February/March issue of *Family Travel Times* gives details of the children's services of dozens of airlines (*see above*). "Kids and Teens in Flight" (free from the U.S. Department of Transportation, tel. 202/366–2220) offers tips for children flying alone.

Lodgings Many hotels and motels let children under a certain age stay free in the same room with their parents; be sure to find out the cut-off age when you book. Some make nominal charges for cribs and $5–$10 charges for extra beds. For instance, the **Westin Bonaventure** (404 S. Figueroa St., Los Angeles 90071, tel. 213/624–1000) allows one child under 18 to stay free with parents. Other packages are available at the **Sheraton Grande** in Los Angeles and **Sheraton Universal Hotel** on the lot of Universal Studios (333 Universal Terrace Parkway, Universal City 91608, tel. 800/325–3535). Some area hotels, especially those in the vicinity of Disneyland, have children's programs: The **Anaheim Hilton** (777 Convention Way, Anaheim 92802, tel. 800/445–8667) has a free summer Kids Klub for children aged 5–15, with several counselors and a Kids Klub Corner in its restaurant.

Baby-sitting First check with the hotel concierge. **Sitters Unlimited** has
Services franchises in Los Angeles County, Huntington Beach, and Long Beach (tel. 310/596–0550), and Irvine, Tustin, and Santa Ana (tel. 714/559–5360).

Hints for Travelers with Disabilities

California is a national leader in making attractions and facilities accessible to travelers with disabilities. Since 1982 the state building code has required that all construction for public use include access for the disabled. State laws more than a decade old provide special privileges, such as license plates allowing special parking spaces, unlimited parking in time- limited spaces, and free parking in metered spaces. I.D. from states other than California is honored.

"Round the Town with Ease" is distributed by the Junior League of Los Angeles (Farmers' Market, 3rd and Fairfax Sts., Gate 12, Los Angeles 90036, tel. 213/937–5566; free to disabled travelers, $2 to all others). The **"Los Angeles Visitors Guide"** and the **"Los Angeles Lodging Guide,"** both published by the Los Angeles Visitor and Convention Bureau (*see* Visitor Information, *above*), use symbols to indicate attractions and accommodations with facilities for disabled travelers.

Organizations The **Information Center for Individuals with Disabilities** (Fort Point Pl., 27–43 Wormwood St., Boston, MA 02210, tel. 617/727–5540 or in MA 800/462–5015 between 11 and 4, or leave message; TDD/TTY, 617/345–9743) helps with problem-solving and publishes a monthly newsletter and numerous fact sheets, including the 10-page "Tips for Planning a Vacation" and the state-by-state list of "Tour Operators, Travel Agencies, and Travel Resources for People with Disabilities". On out-of-state orders, enclose $2 per sheet for postage. **Mobility International USA** (Box 3551, Eugene, OR 97403, voice and TDD tel. 503/343–1284) is the U.S. branch of an international organization based in Britain and present in 30 countries. It coordinates exchange programs for disabled people, especially programs with an educational, work, or community-service component; provides travel information; and publishes and sells *A World of Options for the '90s,* a guide to travel for people with disabilities ($16). Annual membership costs $20 and includes a quarterly newsletter and access to a referral service. **MossRehab Hospital Travel Information Service** (1200 W. Tabor Rd., Philadelphia, PA 19141, tel. 215/456–9603; TDD, 215/456–9602) tries to get people started with their travel plans; for a nominal postage and handling fee, it will send information on tourist sights, transportation, and accommodations in destinations around the world. The **Society for the Advancement of Travel for the Handicapped** (SATH, 347 5th Ave., Suite 610, New York, NY 10016, tel. 212/447–7284, fax 212/725–8253) provides lists of tour operators specializing in travel for the disabled, information sheets on traveling with specific disabilities and to specific countries, and a quarterly newsletter. Annual membership is $45, $25 for students and senior citizens. Nonmembers may send $3 and an SASE for information on specific destinations. **Travel Industry and Disabled Exchange** (TIDE, 5435 Donna Ave., Tarzana, CA 91356, tel. 818/368–5648) supplies travel information and publishes a quarterly newsletter. Annual membership is $15. **Travelin' Talk** (Box 3534, Clarksville, TN 37043, tel. 615/552–6670) is a network of disabled people worldwide ready to provide the lowdown on accessibility in their area. To join, there is a onetime registration fee (on a sliding scale of $1–$10 for individuals, $15–$50 for organizations) that also entitles you to a quarterly newsletter.

Travel Agencies and Tour Operators **Directions Unlimited** (720 N. Bedford Rd., Bedford Hills, NY 10507, tel. 914/241–1700), a travel agency, has expertise in tours and cruises for the disabled. **Evergreen Travel Service** (4114 198th St. SW, Suite 13, Lynnwood, WA 98036, tel. 206/776–1184 or 800/435–2288) operates Wings on Wheels Tours for those in wheelchairs, White Cane Tours for the blind, and tours for the deaf and makes group and independent arrangements for travelers with any disability. **Flying Wheels Travel** (143 W. Bridge St., Box 382, Owatonna, MN 55060, tel. 800/535–6790; in MN, 800/722–9351), arranges international tours, cruises, and independent travel itineraries for people with mobility disabilities.

Publications In addition to the fact sheets, newsletters, and books mentioned above are several free publications available from the Consumer Information Center (Pueblo, CO 81009): "New Horizons for the Air Traveler with a Disability," a U.S. Department of Transportation booklet (include Department 608Y in the address), and the Airport Operators Council's *Access Travel: Airports* (Dept. 5804), which describes facilities and services for the disabled at more than 500 airports worldwide.

Twin Peaks Press (Box 129, Vancouver, WA 98666, tel. 206/694–2462 or 800/637–2256) publishes the *Directory of Travel Agencies for the Disabled* ($19.95), listing more than 370 agencies worldwide; *Travel for the Disabled* ($19.95), listing some 500 access guides and accessible places worldwide; the *Directory of Accessible Van Rentals* ($9.95) for campers and RV travelers worldwide; and *Wheelchair Vagabond* ($14.95), a collection of personal travel tips. Add $2 per book for shipping. The Sierra Club publishes *Easy Access to National Parks* ($16 plus $3 shipping; 730 Polk St., San Francisco, CA 94109, tel. 415/776–2211).

Hints for Older Travelers

Discounts are available for meals, lodging, entry to various attractions, car rentals, tickets for buses and trains, campsites, and so on. The age that qualifies you for these senior discounts varies considerably. Our advice, if you are 50 or older, is to ask about senior discounts, even if there is no posted notice. Carry proof of your age, such as a driver's license, and of course any membership cards in organizations that provide discounts for seniors. Many discounts are given solely on the basis of your age, without any sort of membership requirement. A 10% cut on a bus ticket or a 10% cut on a pizza may not seem like a major saving, but they add up.

Organizations The **American Association of Retired Persons** (AARP, 601 E St. NW, Washington, DC 20049, tel. 202/434–2277) provides independent travelers the Purchase Privilege Program, which offers discounts on hotels, car rentals, and sightseeing. AARP also arranges group tours, cruises, and apartment living through AARP Travel Experience from American Express (400 Pinnacle Way, Suite 450, Norcross, GA 30071, tel. 800/927–0111); these can be booked through travel agents, except for the cruises, which must be booked directly (tel. 800/745–4567). AARP membership is open to those 50 and over; annual dues are $8 per person or couple.

Two other membership organizations offer discounts on lodgings, car rentals, and other travel products, along with such nontravel perks as magazines and newsletters. The **National Council of Senior Citizens** (1331 F St. NW, Washington,

DC 20004, tel. 202/347–8800) is a nonprofit advocacy group with some 5,000 local clubs across the United States; membership costs $12 per person or couple annually. **Mature Outlook** (6001 N. Clark St., Chicago, IL 60660, tel. 800/336–6330), a Sears Roebuck & Co. subsidiary with 800,000 members, charges $9.95 for an annual membership.

Note: When using any senior-citizen identification card for reduced hotel rates, mention it when booking, not when checking out. At restaurants, show your card before you're seated; discounts may be limited to certain menus, days, or hours. If you are renting a car, ask about promotional rates that might improve on your senior-citizen discount.

Educational Travel **Elderhostel** (75 Federal St., 3rd floor, Boston, MA 02110, tel. 617/426–7788) is a nonprofit organization that has inexpensive study programs for people 60 and older. Programs take place at more than 1,800 educational institutions in the United States, Canada, and 45 countries overseas, and courses cover everything from marine science to Greek myths and cowboy poetry. Participants generally attend lectures in the morning and spend the afternoon sightseeing or on field trips; they live in dorms on the host campuses.

Tour Operators **Saga International Holidays** (222 Berkeley St., Boston, MA 02116, tel. 800/343–0273), which specializes in group travel for people over 60, offers a selection of variously priced tours and cruises. If you want to take your grandchildren, look into **GrandTravel** (*see* Traveling with Children, *above*).

Publications The ***International Health Guide for Senior Citizen Travelers,*** by W. Robert Lange MD ($4.95 plus $1.50 for shipping; Pilot Books, 103 Cooper St., Babylon, NY 11702, tel. 516/422–2225), advises on pretrip planning and on traveling with specific medical conditions. It includes a list of what to pack in a basic medical travel kit and a chart showing how to adjust insulin dosages when flying across multiple time zones. ***Get Up and Go*** ($10.95 plus $1.75 postage, Gem Publishing Group, Box 50820, Reno, NV 89513, tel. 702/786–7419) is a 325-page handbook of travel tips and deals for Americans over 49; the same organization publishes the monthly ***Mature Traveler*** newsletter ($24.50 annually), covering senior travel bargains and programs.

Further Reading

Much has been written about the fascinating city of Los Angeles. *Los Angeles: The Enormous Village, 1781–1981,* by John D. Weaver, and *Los Angeles: Biography of a City,* by John and LaRee Caughey, will give you a fine background in how it came to be the city it is today. The unique social and cultural life of the whole Southern California area is explored in *Southern California: An Island on the Land* by Carey McWilliams.

One of the most outstanding features of Los Angeles is its architecture. *Los Angeles: The Architecture of Four Ecologies,* by Reyner Banham, relates the physical environment to the architecture. *Architecture in Los Angeles: A Compleat Guide,* by David Gebhard and Robert Winter, is exactly what the title promises, and very useful.

Many novels have been written with Los Angeles as the setting. One of the very best, Nathanael West's *Day of the Locust,* was first published in 1939, but still rings true. Budd Schulberg's *What Makes Sammy Run?*, Evelyn Waugh's *The Loved One*, and Joan Didion's *Play It as It Lays* are unforgettable. Other novels that give a sense of contemporary life in Los Angeles are *Sex and Rage* by Eve Babitz and *Less Than Zero* by Bret Easton Ellis. Raymond Chandler and Ross Macdonald have written many suspense novels with a Los Angeles background.

Arriving and Departing

Trains, planes, buses, and even luxury ocean liners all converge on the city with great frequency. But a car is virtually a necessity in Los Angeles, so if you drive here you can expect to save a good deal of time and money.

By Plane

Flights are either nonstop, direct, or connecting. A **nonstop** flight requires no change of plane and makes no stops. A **direct** flight stops at least once and can involve a change of plane, although the flight number remains the same; if the first leg is late, the second waits. This is not the case with a **connecting** flight, which involves a different plane and a different flight number.

Airports and Airlines **Los Angeles International Airport,** commonly called LAX (tel. 310/646–5252) is the largest airport in the area. Departures are from the upper level and arrivals on the lower level. Over 85 major airlines are serviced by LAX, the third largest airport in the world in terms of passenger traffic.

Among the major carriers that serve LAX are Air Canada (tel. 800/776–3000), America West (tel. 800/228–7862), American (tel. 800/433–7300), British Airways (tel. 800/247–9297), Continental (tel. 800/525–0280), Delta (tel. 800/221–1212), Japan Air Lines (tel. 800/525–3663), Northwest (tel. 800/225–2525), Southwest (tel. 800/531–5601), TWA (tel. 800/221–2000), United (tel. 800/241–6522), and USAir (tel. 800/428–4322).

Enjoying the Flight Because the air aloft is dry, drink plenty of beverages while on board; remember that drinking alcohol contributes to jet lag, as do heavy meals. Sleepers usually prefer window seats to curl up against; restless passengers ask to be on the aisle. Bulkhead seats, in the front row of each cabin, have more legroom, but since there's no seat ahead, trays attach awkwardly to the arms of your seat, and you must stow all possessions overhead. Bulkhead seats are usually reserved for the disabled, the elderly, and people traveling with babies.

Smoking Since February 1990, smoking has been banned on all domestic flights of less than six hours' duration; the ban also applies to domestic segments of international flights aboard U.S. and foreign carriers.

Cutting Flight Costs The Sunday travel section of most newspapers is a good source of deals. When booking, particularly through an unfamiliar company, call the Better Business Bureau to find out whether any complaints have been registered against the company, pay with a credit card if you can, and consider trip-cancellation and default insurance (available from your travel agent). *The Airline Passenger's Guerrilla Handbook*, by George Albert Brown ($14.95; Slawson Communications, Inc., 165 Vallecitos de Oro,

San Marcos, CA 92069, tel. 619/744–2299 or 800/752–9766), may be out of date in a few areas but remains a solid source of information on every aspect of air travel, including finding the cheapest fares.

Promotional Airfares To ride in the economy or coach section of the plane, you pay a confusing variety of fares. Most expensive is full-fare economy or unrestricted coach, which can be bought one-way or round-trip and can be changed and turned in for a refund. All the less expensive fares, called promotional or discount fares, are round-trip and involve restrictions. You must usually buy the ticket—commonly called an APEX (advance purchase excursion) when it's for international travel—in advance (seven, 14, or 21 days are usual). You must also respect certain minimum- and maximum-stay requirements and you must pay penalties for changes. Airlines generally allow some changes for a fee. But the cheaper the fare, the more likely the ticket is nonrefundable; it would take a death in the family for the airline to give you any of your money back if you had to cancel. The cheapest fares are also sold out quickly.

Consolidators Consolidators or bulk-fare operators—also known as bucket shops—buy blocks of seats on scheduled flights that airlines anticipate they won't be able to sell. They pay wholesale prices, add a markup, and resell the seats to travel agents or directly to the public at prices that still undercut the airline's promotional or discount fares. You pay more than on a charter but ordinarily less than for an APEX ticket, and usually without the advance-purchase restriction. Moreover, although tickets are marked nonrefundable so you can't turn them in to the airline for a full-fare refund, some consolidators sometimes give you your money back. If you doubt the reliability of a company, call the airline once you've made your booking and confirm that you do, indeed, have a reservation on the flight.

The biggest U.S. consolidator, C.L. Thomson Express, sells only to travel agents. Well-established consolidators selling to the public include **UniTravel** (Box 12485, St. Louis, MO 63132, tel. 314/569–0900 or 800/325–2222); **Council Charter** (205 E. 42nd St., New York, NY 10017, tel. 212/661–0311 or 800/800–8222), a division of the Council on International Educational Exchange; and **Travac** (989 6th Ave., New York, NY 10018, tel. 212/563–3303 or 800/872–8800).

Charter Flights Charters usually have the lowest fares and the most restrictions. Departures are limited and seldom on time, and you can lose all or most of your money if you cancel. (Generally, the closer to departure you cancel, the more you lose, although sometimes you will be charged only a small fee if you supply a substitute passenger.) The charterer, on the other hand, may legally cancel the flight for any reason up to 10 days before departure; within 10 days of departure, the flight may be canceled only if it becomes physically impossible to operate it. The charterer may also revise the itinerary or increase the price after you have bought the ticket, but if the new arrangement constitutes a "major change," you have the right to a refund. Before buying a charter ticket, read the fine print for the company's refund policy and details on major changes. Money for charter flights is usually be paid into a bank escrow account, the name of which should be on the contract. If you don't pay by credit card, make your check payable to the escrow account. The Department of Transportation's Consumer Affairs Office

(I–25, Washington, DC 20590, tel. 202/366–2220) can answer questions on charters and send you its "Plane Talk: Public Charter Flights" information sheet.

Charter operators may offer flights alone or with ground arrangements that constitute a charter package. Well-established charter operators include **Council Charter** (205 E. 42nd St., New York, NY 10017, tel. 212/661–0311 or 800/800–8222), and **Travel Charter** (1120 E. Long Lake Rd., Troy, MI 48098, tel. 313/528–3570 or 800/521–5267), with Midwestern departures. **DER Tours** (Box 1606, Des Plains, IL 60017, tel. 800/782–2424), a charterer and consolidator, sells through travel agents.

Discount Travel Clubs Travel clubs offer their members unsold space on airplanes, cruise ships, and package tours at nearly the last minute and at well below the original cost. Membership generally includes a regular bulletin or access to a toll-free telephone hot line giving details of available trips. Packages tend to be more common than flights alone. Reductions on hotels are also available. Clubs include **Discount Travel International** (114 Forrest Ave., Suite 203, Narberth, PA 19072, tel. 215/668–7184; $45 annually, single or family), **Moment's Notice** (425 Madison Ave., New York, NY 10017, tel. 212/486–0503; $45 annually, single or family), **Travelers Advantage** (CUC Travel Service, 49 Music Sq. W, Nashville, TN 37203, tel. 800/548–1116; $49 annually, single or family), and **Worldwide Discount Travel Club** (1674 Meridian Ave., Miami Beach, FL 33139, tel. 305/534–2082; $50 annually for family, $40 single).

Between the Airport and Hotels A dizzying array of ground transportation is available from LAX to all parts of Los Angeles and its environs. A taxi ride to downtown Los Angeles can take 20 minutes—*if* there is no traffic. But in Los Angeles, that's a big if. Visitors should request the flat fee ($24 at press time) to downtown or choose from the several ground transportation companies that offer set rates.

SuperShuttle (tel. 310/338–1111) offers direct service between the airport and hotels. The trip to or from downtown hotels runs about $12. The seven-passenger vans operate 24 hours a day. In the airport, phone 310/417–8988 or use the SuperShuttle courtesy phone in the luggage area; the van should arrive within 15 minutes. **L.A. Top Shuttle** (9100 S. Sepulveda Blvd., No. 128, tel. 310/670–6666) features door-to-door service and low rates ($10 per person from LAX to hotels in the Disneyland/Anaheim area). **Airport Coach** (tel. 714/491–3500 or 800/772–5299) provides regular service between LAX and the Pasadena and Anaheim areas.

The following limo companies charge a flat rate for airport service, ranging from $65 to $75: **Jackson Limousine** (tel. 213/734–9955), **West Coast Limousine** (tel. 213/756–5466), and **Dav-El Livery** (tel. 310/550–0070). Many of the cars have bars, stereos, televisions, and cellular phones.

Flyaway Service (tel. 818/994–5554) offers transportation between LAX and the central San Fernando Valley for around $6. For the western San Fernando Valley and Ventura area, contact the **Great American Stage Lines** (tel. 800/287–8659). **RTD** (tel. 213/626–4455) also offers limited airport service.

If you're driving, leave time for heavy traffic; it really can't be predicted.

Other Airports The greater Los Angeles area is served by several other local airports. **Ontario Airport** (tel. 909/988–2700), located about 35 miles east of Los Angeles, serves the San Bernardino–Riverside area. Domestic flights are offered by Alaska Airlines, American, American Eagle, America West, Continental, Delta, Northwest, SkyWest, Southwest, United, and United Express. Ground transportation possibilities include SuperShuttle as well as Inland Express (tel. 909/626–6599), Empire Airport Transportation (tel. 909/884–0744), Airport Coach (tel. 800/772–5299), and Southern California Coach (tel. 714/978–6415). **Long Beach Airport** (tel. 310/421–8295), at the southern tip of Los Angeles County, is served by Alaska, America West, American, Delta, and United airlines.

Burbank Airport (tel. 818/840–8847) serves the San Fernando Valley with commuter, and some longer, flights. Alaska Airlines, Alpha Air, American, American Eagle, America West, Delta, SkyWest, Southwest, and United Airlines are represented.

John Wayne Airport, in Orange County (tel. 714/252–5006), is served by TWA, SkyWest, American, Northwest, Alaska, American West, Continental, Delta, United, USAir, and Morris Airlines. Airport Coach (tel. 800/772–5299) provides ground transportation.

Car Rentals

In Los Angeles, it's not a question of whether wheels are a hindrance or a convenience: They're a necessity. More than 35 major companies and dozens of local rental companies serve a steady demand for cars at Los Angeles International Airport and various city locations.

All major car-rental companies are represented in the area, including **Avis** (tel. 800/331–1212; in Canada, 800/879–2847); **Budget** (tel. 800/527–0700); **Dollar** (tel. 800/800–4000); **Hertz** (tel. 800/654–3131; in Canada, 800/263– 0600); **National** (tel. 800/227–7368), known internationally as InterRent and Europcar (tel. 800/227–7368); and **Thrifty** (tel. 800/367–2277). Major budget car-rental agencies are **Alamo** (tel. 800/327–9633), **General** (tel. 800/327–7607), and **Ugly Duckling** (tel. 800/843–3825).

If expense is no object, **Luxury Line** (300 S. La Cienega, Beverly Hills, tel. 310/659–5555 or 310/657–2800) can rent you everything from Toyota Tercels to Rolls Royces, Jaguars, and Ferraris. Ironically, the Marina del Rey branch of **Budget** (tel. 310/821–8200) also rents upscale vehicles, like Jags, Mercedes, BMWs, and Saab convertibles.

Because Los Angeles is such a car-rental hub, rates are highly competitive; a little research pays off. The larger companies charge $35–$45 per day for a subcompact, with, typically, 75–100 miles free. That's not a lot of miles for sprawling Los Angeles, and it might make sense to find a weekly rate offering more free miles.

Extra Charges Picking up the car in one city or country and leaving it in another may entail drop-off charges or one-way service fees, which can be substantial. The cost of a collision or loss-damage waiver (*see below*) can be high, also.

Cutting Costs Major international companies have programs that discount their standard rates by 15%–30% if you make the reservation before departure (anywhere from two to 14 days), rent for a minimum number of days (typically three or four), and prepay the rental. More economical rentals are those that come as part of fly/drive or other packages, even those as bare-bones as the rental plus an airline ticket (*see* Tours and Packages, *above*).

One last tip: Remember to fill the tank when you turn in the vehicle, to avoid being charged for refueling at what you'll swear is the most expensive pump in town.

Insurance and Collision Damage Waiver The standard rental contract includes liability coverage (for damage to public property, injury to pedestrians, etc.) and coverage for the car against fire, theft (not included in certain countries), and collision damage with a deductible—most commonly $2,000–$3,000, occasionally more. In the case of an accident, you are responsible for the deductible amount unless you've purchased the collision damage waiver (CDW), which costs an average $12 a day.

Because this adds up quickly, you may be inclined to say "no thanks"—and that's certainly your option, although the rental agent may not tell you so. Find out if your own insurance covers damage to a rental car while traveling (not simply a car to drive when yours is in for repairs). And check whether charging car rentals to any of your credit cards will get you a CDW at no charge.

By Train

Los Angeles can be reached by **Amtrak** (tel. 800/USA–RAIL). The *Coast Starlight,* a superliner, travels along the spectacular California coast. It offers service from Seattle-Portland and Oakland–San Francisco down to Los Angeles. Amtrak's *San Joaquin* train runs through the Central Valley from Oakland to Bakersfield, where passengers transfer to a bus to Los Angeles. The *Sunset Limited* goes to Los Angeles from New Orleans, the *Eagle* from San Antonio, and the *Southwest Chief* and the *Desert Wind* from Chicago.

Union Station (800 N. Alameda St.) in Los Angeles is one of the grande dames of railroad stations, and is a remnant of the glory days of the railroads.

By Bus

The Los Angeles **Greyhound** terminal (tel. 213/620–1200) is at 208 East 6th Street, on the corner of Los Angeles Street.

Staying in Los Angeles

Important Addresses and Numbers

Tourist Information There is a **Visitor Information Center** at 685 S. Figueroa St. (tel. 213/689–8822). It is open Monday through Saturday 8–5. Or you can stop in at the **Los Angeles Convention and Visitors Bureau** (633 W. Fifth St., Suite 6000, tel. 213/624–7300).

Area communities also have information centers, including the **Beverly Hills Visitors Bureau** at 239 South Beverly Drive (tel.

310/271–8174; open weekdays 8:30–5), the **Long Beach Area Convention and Visitors Council** in Suite 300 at 1 World Trade Center (tel. 310/436–3645), the **Santa Monica Visitors Center,** in Palisades Park at 1400 Ocean Avenue (tel. 310/393–7593; open daily 10–4), the **Hollywood Visitors Center** at 6541 Hollywood Boulevard (tel. 213/461–4213; open Mon.–Sat. 9–5), and the **Pasadena Convention and Visitors Bureau** at 171 South Los Robles Avenue (tel. 818/795–9311; open weekdays 9–5, Sat. 10–4).

Information **Surf and Weather Report,** tel. 310/451–8761.

Community Services, tel. 800/339–6993 (24 hours).

Emergencies Dial 911 for **police** and **ambulance** in an emergency.

Doctors The **Los Angeles Medical Association Physicians Referral Service** (tel. 213/483–6122) is open weekdays 8:45–4:45. Most larger hospitals in Los Angeles have 24-hour emergency rooms. A few are: **St. John's Hospital and Health Center** (1328 22nd St., tel. 310/829–5511), **Cedar-Sinai Medical Center** (8700 Beverly Blvd., tel. 310/855–5000), and **Queen of Angels Hollywood Presbyterian Medical Center** (1300 N. Vermont Ave., tel. 213/413–3000).

24-hour The **Bellflower Pharmacy** (9400 E. Rosecrans Ave., Bellflower, *Pharmacies* tel. 310/920–4213) is open around the clock. The **Horton and Converse** pharmacies at 6625 Van Nuys Boulevard (Van Nuys, tel. 818/782–6251) and at 11600 Wilshire Boulevard (W. Los Angeles, tel. 310/478–0801) are open until 2 AM.

Getting Around Los Angeles

By Bus A bus ride on the **Southern California Rapid Transit District (RTD)** (tel. 213/626–4455) costs $1.10, with 25¢ for each transfer.

DASH (Downtown Area Short Hop) minibuses travel in a loop around the downtown area, stopping every two blocks or so. You pay 25¢ every time you get on, no matter how far you go. DASH (tel. 213/689–8822) runs weekdays and Saturday 6:30 AM–10 PM.

By Train The **Metrorail Blue Line** runs daily, 5 AM–10 PM, from downtown Los Angeles (corner of Flower and 7th streets) to Long Beach (corner of 1st Street and Long Beach Avenue), with 18 stops en route, most of them in Long Beach. The fare is $1.10 one way.

By Subway The **Metro Red Line,** opened in January 1993, runs 4.4 miles through downtown, from Union Station to MacArthur Park, making five stops. The fare is $1.10. The line will extend to Hollywood by 1998.

By Taxi You probably won't be able to hail a cab on the street in Los Angeles. Instead, you should phone one of the many taxi companies. The metered rate is $1.60 per mile. Two of the more reputable companies are **Independent Cab Co.** (tel. 213/385–8294 or 213/385–8294) and **United Independent Taxi** (tel. 213/653–5050). United accepts MasterCard and Visa.

By Limousine Limousines come equipped with everything from a full bar and telephone to a hot tub and a double bed. Reputable companies include **Dav-El Livery** (tel. 310/550–0070), **First Class** (tel.

310/476–1960), and **Le Monde Limousine** (tel. 310/474–6622 or 818/887–7878).

By Car   A car is a must. The freeway map *below* should help. If you plan to drive extensively, consider buying a *Thomas Guide*, which contains detailed maps of the entire county. Despite what you've heard, traffic is not always a major problem outside of rush hours (7 AM–9 PM and 3 AM–7 PM). Seat belts must be worn by all passengers at all times, as of January 1993.

Guided Tours

Orientation Tours   Los Angeles is so spread out and has such a wealth of sightseeing possibilities that an orientation bus tour may prove useful. The cost is about $25. All tours are fully narrated by a driver-guide. Reservations must be made in advance. Many hotels can book them for you.

Gray Line (1207 W. 3rd St., 90017, tel. 213/933–1475), one of the best-known tour companies in the country, picks passengers up from more than 140 hotels. There are more than 24 tours to Disneyland, Universal Studios, the *Queen Mary,* Catalina Island, and other attractions.

L.A. Tours and Sightseeing (6333 W. 3rd St., at the Farmers' Market, tel. 213/937–3361) covers places of interest in various parts of the city, including downtown, Hollywood, and Beverly Hills. For $36, this tour serves as a good orientation to vast Los Angeles. The company also operates tours to Disneyland and Universal City.

StarLine Sightseeing Tours (6845 Hollywood Blvd., Hollywood 90028, tel. 213/463–3131) has been showing people around Los Angeles since 1935. Like Gray Line, StarLine uses large tour buses and picks up at most area hotels. There are tours to Knott's Berry Farm, Disneyland, and other "musts"; but the company gets much of its business from its four-hour Stars' Home Tour, which takes visitors to more than 60 estates in Beverly Hills, Holmby Hills, and Bel Air. The tour departs from StarLine's Hollywood terminal at Mann's Chinese Theater hourly in the winter and every half hour in the summer. Hotel pickup can be arranged.

A more personalized look at the city can be had by planning a tour with **Casablanca Tours** (Roosevelt Hotel, 7000 Hollywood Blvd., Cabana 4, Hollywood 90028, tel. 213/461–0156), which offers an insider's look at Hollywood and Beverly Hills. The four-hour tour, which can be taken in the morning or afternoon, starts in Hollywood or in centrally located hotels. Tours are in minibuses with a maximum of people, and prices are equivalent to the large bus tours—about $29. Guides are college students with a high-spirited view of the city. The tour takes in the usual tourist spots—Hollywood Bowl, Mann's Chinese Theater, the Walk of Fame, and the homes of such stars as Jimmy Stewart and Neil Diamond. It also includes a visit to the posh shops along Rodeo Drive.

Special-interest Tours   So much of Los Angeles is known to the world through Hollywood, it is fitting that many of the special-interest tours feature Hollywood and its lore.

Grave Line Tours (Box 931694, Hollywood 90093, tel. 213/469–3127) is a clever, off-the-beaten-track tour that digs up the dirt

Los Angeles Freeways

SAN FERNANDO

Foothill Fwy.

118

5

Golden State Fwy.

210

Angeles Crest Hwy.

2

LA CANADA FLINTRIDGE

Hollywood Fwy.

BURBANK

GLENDALE

VAN NUYS

NORTH HOLLYWOOD

170

2

PASADENA
Foothill Fwy.

210

101

Ventura Fwy.

134

SHERMAN OAKS

Griffith Park

5

Huntington Dr.

SAN MARINO

101

Pasadena Fwy.

110

WEST HOLLYWOOD

BEVERLY HILLS

Santa Monica Blvd.

2

ALHAMBRA

SAN GABRIEL

405

Sunset Blvd.

WESTWOOD

HOLLYWOOD

San Bernardino Fwy.

Wilshire Blvd.

DOWNTOWN

MONTEREY PARK

Santa Monica Blvd.

10

60

2

Santa Monica Fwy.

10

Pomona Fwy.

SANTA MONICA

La Cienega Blvd.

La Brea Blvd.

Western Ave.

72

Rosemead Blvd.

1

San Diego Fwy.

CULVER CITY

Santa Ana Fwy.

Lincoln Blvd.

Slauson Ave.

VENICE

MARINA DEL REY

INGLEWOOD

42

Manchester Ave.

Firestone Blvd.

HUNTINGTON PARK

710

19

Los Angeles International Airport

Long Beach Blvd.

DOWNEY

42

Imperial Hwy.

EL SEGUNDO

1

405

Hawthorne Blvd.

Crenshaw Blvd.

Western Ave.

Harbor Fwy.

Rosecrans Ave.

5

San Gabriel River Fwy.

MANHATTAN BEACH

Alondra Blvd.

COMPTON

605

HERMOSA BEACH

91

TORRANCE

Lakewood Blvd.

San Gabriel Blvd.

LAKEWOOD

REDONDO BEACH

Sepulveda Blvd.

Long Beach Fwy.

PACIFIC OCEAN

Pacific Coast Hwy.

1

110

Willow St.

710

19

PALOS VERDES ESTATES

Pacific Coast Hwy.

Ocean Blvd.

1

RANCH PALOS VERDES

SAN PEDRO

LONG BEACH

N

0   5 miles

0   5 km

on notorious suicides and visits the scenes of various murders, scandals, and other crimes via a luxuriously renovated hearse. Tours are daily at noon for two hours; cost is $30 per person reserved, $25 standby.

Hollywood Fantasy Tours (6773 Hollywood Blvd., Hollywood 90028, tel. 213/469–8184) has one tour that takes you through Beverly Hills, down Rodeo Drive, around Bel Air, and up and down colorful Sunset Strip, then on to exclusive Holmby Hills, home of *Playboy* magazine's founder Hugh Hefner. If you're only interested in Hollywood, ask about a tour of that area, pointing out television and film studios as well as famous stores such as Frederick's of Hollywood.

Visitors who want something dramatically different should check with Marlene Gordon of **The Next Stage** (Box 35269, Los Angeles 90035, tel. 213/939–2688). This innovative tour company takes from four to 46 people, on buses or vans, in search of ethnic L.A., Victorian L.A., Underground L.A. (in which all the places visited are underground), and so on. The Insomniac Tour visits the flower market and other places in the wee hours of the morning. Gordon also plans some spectacular tours outside of Los Angeles: a bald eagle tour to Big Bear with a naturalist; a whale-watching and biplane adventure; and a glorious garlic train, which tours Monterey and Carmel, and takes in the Gilroy Garlic Fest.

LA Today Custom Tours (14964 Camarosa Dr., Pacific Palisades 90272, tel. 310/454–5730) also has a wide selection of offbeat tours, some of which tie in with seasonal and cultural events, such as theater, museum exhibits, and the Rose Bowl. Groups range from 8 to 50, and prices from $6 to $50. The least expensive is a two-hour walking tour of hotel lobbies in downtown Los Angeles that costs $6.

Guided and self-guided tours of the many architectural landmarks in Los Angeles are becoming increasingly popular. Buildings run the gamut from the Victorian Bradbury Building in the downtown core, to the many fine examples of Frank Lloyd Wright's works—the Ennis-Brown House, Hollyhock House, and Snowden House among them. On the last Sunday of April each year the **Los Angeles County Museum of Art** (tel. 213/857–6500) holds a fund-raising tour of a selection of special houses in the city.

Walking Tours   Walking is something that Angelenos don't do much of, except perhaps in Westwood and Beverly Hills and in parks throughout the city. But there is no better way to see things close up.

A very pleasant self-guided walking tour of **Palisades Park** is detailed in a brochure available at the park's Visitors Center (1430 Ocean Blvd.). Many television shows and movies have been filmed on this narrow strip of parkland on a bluff overlooking the Pacific. The 26-acre retreat is always bustling with walkers, skaters, Frisbee throwers, readers, and sunbathers.

The **Los Angeles Conservancy** (tel. 213/623–CITY) offers low-cost walking tours of the downtown area. Each Saturday at 10 AM one of six different tours leaves from the Olive Street entrance of the Biltmore Hotel; reservations are necessary. The Pershing Square Tour includes visits to buildings that span four decades of Los Angeles history, with such stops as the Biltmore Hotel, the Edison Building, and the Subway Terminal

Building. On the Palaces of Finance Tour the elegant architecture of the Wall Street of the West is explored. The Broadway Theaters Tour takes in splendid movie palaces—the largest concentration of pre–World War II movie houses in America. The Mecca for Merchants Tour explores the city's first shopping district. The Art Deco Tour explores great examples of this modernistic style at such places as the Oviatt Building, the green Sun Realty Building, and the turquoise Eastern Columbia Building. The Terra Cotta Tour takes a look at clay architectural ornamentation at the Palace Theater, the Wurlitzer Building, and other downtown locales.

Personal Guides **Elegant Tours for the Discriminating** (tel. 310/472–4090) is a personalized sightseeing and shopping service for the Beverly Hills area. Joan Mansfield offers her extensive knowledge of Rodeo Drive to one, two, or three people at a time. Lunch is included.

L.A. Nighthawks (Box 10224, Beverly Hills 90213, tel. 310/392–1500) will arrange your nightlife for you. For a rather hefty price, you'll get a limousine, a guide, and a gourmet dinner, as well as immediate entry into L.A.'s hottest night spots. For a group of eight, prices come down considerably because vans or tour buses are used. Nighthawks proprietor Charles Andrews is a music writer and 20-year entertainment-business veteran.

Credit Cards

The following credit card abbreviations are used in this guide: AE, American Express; D, Discover; DC, Diners Club; MC, MasterCard; V, Visa.

2 Portrait of Los Angeles

There Must Be a There Here Somewhere

By Jane E. Lasky

Hollywood is a town that has to be seen to be disbelieved.
—Walter Winchell

While hosting a British broadcaster-friend on his first trip to Los Angeles, I reluctantly took him to the corner of Hollywood and Vine. Driving toward the renowned street-corner, I explained (again) that this part of town isn't the "real" Hollywood. But he wasn't listening. He was on a pilgrimage, too filled with the anticipation of coming upon a sacred place to hear my warning. When we reached the intersection, his reaction was written all over his face: He was, as he later said, "gobsmacked."

As we pulled up to the light, a bedraggled hooker crossed Hollywood Boulevard. Worse, this looked like someplace where nothing noteworthy or memorable ever had, would, or could happen. The area has been called squalid, but that gives it too much credit for being interesting. All there was to see were a few small and struggling businesses, the hulk of a long-defunct department store, and a couple of unremarkable office buildings.

To rescue the moment from complete disaster, I went into my standard routine: I pointed out that the northwest corner is where the illustrious Brown Derby restaurant once stood. I hoped this would conjure a strong enough image of movie stars dining in a giant hat to blot out the sun-bleached desolation before our eyes. I then recounted historian Richard Alleman's theory about how this unprepossessing street-corner got so famous. Alleman, who wrote *The Movie Lover's Guide to Hollywood,* believes that, because the radio networks, which maintained studios in the vicinity during the 1930s and 1940s, began their broadcasts with the words "brought to you from the corner of Hollywood and Vine . . ." the intersection became glamorous by association—at least to radio listeners who'd never seen it.

Any first-time visitor to Tinseltown is bound for some initial disappointment because, like a matinee idol, the place looks somehow smaller in person. Between the world-famous landmarks and the stars' names embedded in the sidewalks are long stretches of tawdriness that have resisted more than a decade of cleanup and restoration, looking worse under the vivid glare of the Southern California sun. Even the best of Hollywood comes off as a little wan and sheepish in broad daylight, as if caught in the act of intruding upon a reality in which it does not belong.

Pressed to show my British friend the "real" Hollywood, I took him on a tour of the more outstanding architecture along Hollywood Boulevard. He was duly captivated by the lunatic exuberance of Hollywood's art-deco movie palaces, exemplified in the zigzaggy Moderne contours of the Pantages, and by the flamboyant absurdity of such thematically designed theaters as Mann's Chinese, the Egyptian, the baroque El Capitan, and other architectural treasures in and around Hollywood. No, they have nothing directly to do with movies, yet they are spiritual cousins. Among the more notable are the Tail O' the Pup hotdog stand; the Capitol Records building, looking—deliberately, mind you—like a 14-story stack of 45s; and an assortment of mock Mayan-, Mission-, Moorish-, Moderne-, and made-up-style structures housing video stores, fast-food franchises, and offices.

Yet despite the grand movie houses, the famous names underfoot, and the impressively zany architecture, my friend still felt he'd missed the enchantment, the excitement . . . the movies.

It's hard to fault the intrepid visitor for expecting a more dynamic, glitzier dream capital. Even seasoned locals, who understand that Hollywood is much more a state of mind than a geographical location, can only just manage to intellectualize the concept. They, too, still secretly hunger for evidence that all the magic and glamour come from an appropriately magical and glamorous place. But, except for the occasional gala premiere, you're not likely to see any movie stars in Hollywood. The workaday world of filmmaking and the off-duty hangouts of the movie crowd have largely moved elsewhere. There is only one movie studio—Paramount—still operating within Hollywood's city limits. Universal Studios and the Burbank Studios are both in the San Fernando Valley, across the hills to the north, as are most network-television studios. And, although firmly rooted in the spirit of Hollywood, Disneyland is a world away in Anaheim.

Even a cursory glance at Hollywood's history raises serious doubts that the town was ever as glamorous as we insist it no longer is. Pinning down exactly when its star-studded golden era was is a slippery business. Most people point to the 1930s and 1940s, and the images evoked by those days are irresistible: tan, handsome leading men posed, grinning, with one foot on the running board of a snazzy convertible; heartbreakingly beautiful actresses clad in slinky silk gowns and mink, stepping from long black limousines into the pop of photographers' flash bulbs. Hollywood was an industry—an entire city—whose purpose was to entertain and that further dazzled us with its glittering style of life. The view from ground zero, naturally, was a bit different: long hours; the tedium of the filmmaking process; the rarity of achieving and maintaining a successful career, much less stardom; and, for those who did achieve it, the precarious tightrope walk balancing publicity and privacy. Both sides of the equation are well known and much documented. Indeed, for a place so enamored of its own appeal, Hollywood has never been shy about depicting itself in an unflattering light. Some of the most memorable films ever are grim portrayals of the movie business: *A Star is Born, Sunset Boulevard,* and, most recently, *The Player.* That there is a very seamy side to the movie business is very old news and is as much a part of the legend as are fame and fortune. Scandal is a long-running subplot in Hollywood's epic history and has often proved as much a box-office draw as a liability.

The trick to seeing Hollywood is knowing *how* to look at it, as well as where to look for it. The magic of movies is that reality, at least on film, can be made to look any way the filmmakers want it to look. The problem with visiting Hollywood is that your own field of vision isn't as selective as a movie camera's lens, and you're working without a script. It may be helpful to think of Hollywood the town as something of a relic, a symbol of past grandeur (both real and imagined), an open-air museum of artifacts and monuments, but hardly the whole story. Tennessee Williams said, "Ravaged radiance is even better than earnest maintenance," and, as regards Hollywood, I couldn't agree more. It helps a bit to visit in the evening, when the neon, theater marquees, and orchestrated lighting show off the extravagant buildings' shapes to advantage.

It may be that in order to fully experience Hollywood, you have to go outside it.

Only after we'd driven through the canyons, Beverly Hills, and Bel Air and were rounding the last corner of Sunset that leads to the Pacific Coast Highway and out to Malibu did my British visitor feel truly satisfied. "Yes, well," he said finally, "this is really much more like it, then," and seemed almost physically relieved to have found someplace that matched his expectations of luxurious living. And these are physically lovely places, fitting backdrops for a Hollywood lifestyle, and, in fact, where successful movie people live.

The variety of fun and fanciful buildings you'll see throughout Los Angeles reveals, I think, the essence of Hollywood. How else to explain the incongruous jumble of architectural styles sitting side by side in almost any neighborhood? A '50s futuristic house next door to a Queen Anne Victorian, a Craftsman bungalow abutting a French château, a red-brick Georgian across the street from a tile-roof Spanish revival—all on the same block—can be viewed as an extrapolation of a movie-studio back lot, on which a New York street is steps from a Parisian sidewalk café, and both are just a stone's throw from an antebellum plantation house.

If it's celebrity sightings you want, you'll have to take your chances. Many Angelenos live long, happy, and productive lives without ever personally sighting a movie star, but, for the visitor, not seeing one can be a bigger letdown than a rainy week at the beach. Here are a few things you can do to greatly improve the odds of seeing somebody famous: Book a table (weeks in advance) at Spago, Wolfgang Puck's star-studded hot spot off Sunset; dine at Musso & Franks, Hollywood's oldest restaurant and a favorite celebrity hangout for more than 60 years; wander Rodeo Drive on a sunny afternoon, paying close attention to Fred Hayman of Beverly Hills and the Alaia Chez Gallery, known for their high-profile clientele; stroll Melrose Avenue between La Brea and Fairfax during the dinner hour; stop by Tower Records on Sunset, especially if some blockbuster CD has just been released.

Although it's almost become an amusement-park thrill ride, Universal Studios' tour does give a good in-person approximation of the excitement you get from the movies, and, in the bargain, offers a fun look behind the scenes of filmmaking. Universal Studios aside, the business of Hollywood is making movies and getting people into theaters, not drumming up tourism for the town where it all started. And, besides, there are limits to what even movie magicians can do, especially in broad daylight. Given that the original appeal of Hollywood to moviemakers was the perpetual sunshine that allowed them to shoot outdoors on virtually any day of the year (and thereby make more movies and, therefore, more money) and the ready access to dozens of different landscapes, it is no small irony that over the years the most compelling reason to shoot a movie in Hollywood has become the ready access to soundstages in which the world (this one and others) can be re-created and the weather made to perform on cue. Hollywood has never hesitated to substitute reality with a more convenient or photogenic stand-in. This is an industry whose stock-in-trade is sleight of hand. Along with romance, car chases, and happy endings.

Whatever Hollywood is or isn't, I like the place just the way it is: flawed, scarred, energetic, and full of mysteries and contradictions. Living nearby and seeing it often haven't harmed my love of movies or taken any of the enchantment from the experience of sitting in a darkened theater and giving myself over to the doings on screen. After all, that's where the real Hollywood lives.

3 Exploring Los Angeles

*By Ellen
Melinkoff*

*Updated and
revised by
Jane E. Lasky*

In a city where the residents think nothing of a 40-mile commute to work, visitors have their work cut out for them. To see the sites—from the Huntington Library in San Marino to the *Queen Mary* in Long Beach—requires a decidedly organized itinerary. Be prepared to put miles on the car. It's best to view Los Angeles as a collection of destinations, each to be explored separately, and not to jump willy-nilly from place to place. In this guide, we've divided up the major sightseeing areas of Los Angeles into eight major tours: Downtown; Hollywood; Wilshire Boulevard, a major boulevard that slices through a fascinating cross-section of the city; the posh and trendy Westside neighborhoods; the beachside towns of Santa Monica, Venice, Pacific Palisades, and Malibu; the often overlooked coastal towns of Palos Verdes, San Pedro, and Long Beach; the well-to-do northern inland suburbs of Highland Park, Pasadena, and San Marino; and the San Fernando Valley, a world unto itself. For sights in Orange County, *see* Chapter 10. For attractions appealing especially to children, *see* Chapter 13.

After the eight exploring tours, the rest of Los Angeles's most noteworthy attractions have been organized into four miscellaneous sections. Other Places of Interest includes sites outside the map areas but definitely worth visiting. Los Angeles for Free suggests some good low-cost activities. Off the Beaten Track highlights a few unusual, lesser-known sights. Sightseeing Checklists is a comprehensive alphabetical list of sites in various categories, including those covered in the exploring tours. For example, every noteworthy museum in Los Angeles is listed in the Museums checklist; the Huntington Museum is mentioned there, but cross-referenced to the Highland Park, Pasadena, and San Marino tour, where it is more fully described.

Highlights for First-Time Visitors

Farmer's Market, Wilshire Boulevard
Griffith Park Observatory (*see* Other Places of Interest)
Huntington Library, Art Gallery, and Botanical Gardens, Pasadena
J. Paul Getty Museum, Malibu
Mann's Chinese Theater, Hollywood
Melrose Avenue, Westside
Olvera Street, Downtown Los Angeles
Queen Mary, Long Beach
Santa Monica Pier, Santa Monica
Universal Studios, San Fernando Valley

Tour 1: Downtown Los Angeles

Numbers in the margin correspond to points of interest on the Tour 1: Downtown Los Angeles map.

All those jokes about Los Angeles being a city without a downtown are simply no longer true. They might have had some ring of truth to them a few decades ago when Angelinos ruthlessly turned their backs on the city center and hightailed it to the suburbs. There *had* been a downtown, once, when Los Angeles was very young, and now the city core is enjoying a resurgence

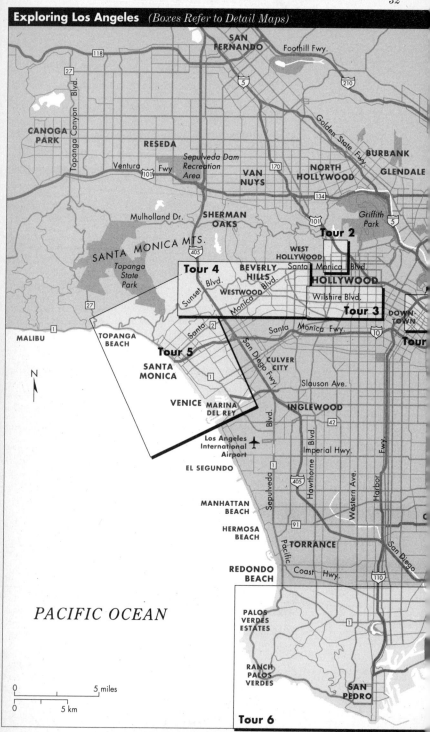

SAN FERNANDO

Foothill Fwy.

118

27

5

210

Golden State Fwy.

CANOGA PARK

RESEDA

BURBANK

GLENDALE

Ventura 101 Fwy

Sepulveda Dam Recreation Area

VAN NUYS

170

NORTH HOLLYWOOD

134

Mulholland Dr.

SHERMAN OAKS

101

Griffith Park

5

SANTA MONICA MTS.

405

WEST HOLLYWOOD

Tour 2

Topanga State Park

Tour 4

BEVERLY HILLS

Blvd.

Santa Monica Blvd.

HOLLYWOOD

27

Sunset

Blvd.

WESTWOOD

Monica Blvd.

Wilshire Blvd.

Tour 3

DOWN-TOWN

1

MALIBU

TOPANGA BEACH

Santa

2

Santa Monica Fwy.

10

Tour

N

Tour 5

SANTA MONICA

1

San Diego Fwy.

CULVER CITY

Slauson Ave.

VENICE

MARINA DEL REY

INGLEWOOD

42

Blvd.

Los Angeles International Airport

EL SEGUNDO

1

Sepulveda

405

Hawthorne Blvd.

Imperial Hwy.

Western Ave.

Harbor Fwy.

MANHATTAN BEACH

91

HERMOSA BEACH

Pacific

TORRANCE

San Diego

REDONDO BEACH

Coast Hwy.

110

PACIFIC OCEAN

PALOS VERDES ESTATES

1

0   5 miles

0   5 km

RANCH PALOS VERDES

SAN PEDRO

Tour 6

Hwy. 2

Angeles Crest SAN GABRIEL MOUNTAINS

LA CANADA
FLINTRIDGE

▲ Mt. Wilson

2

PASADENA

Foothill Fwy. 210

Tour 7

SAN
MARINO

39

2

Pasadena Fwy.

110

ALHAM-
BRA

SAN
GABRIEL

EL
MONTE

San Bernardino Fwy. 10

Dodger
Stadium

MONTEREY
PARK

ur 1

60

Pomona Fwy.

Santa Ana Fwy.

Rosemead Blvd.

Fwy.

WHITTIER

72

HUNTINGTON
PARK

710

River

19

DOWNEY

San Gabriel

42

39

5

COMPTON

Riverside Fwy.

91

Long Beach

Fwy.

710

605

LAKEWOOD

ANAHEIM

19

Pacific Coast

GARDEN
GROVE

Fwy.

LONG
BEACH

Hwy.

San Diego Fwy. 39

55

1

of attention from urban planners, real estate developers, and intrepid downtown office workers who have discovered the advantages of living close to the office.

Downtown Los Angeles can be explored on foot (or better yet, on DASH—more about that in a minute). The natives might disagree, but these are the same natives who haven't been downtown since they took out a marriage license at city hall 30 years ago; don't follow their lead. During the day, downtown is relatively safe and very interesting. Our tour of downtown cuts through more than a century of history and colorful ethnic neighborhoods.

Getting around to the major sites in downtown Los Angeles is actually quite simple, thanks to DASH (Downtown Area Short Hop). This minibus service travels in a loop past most of the attractions listed here, stopping every two blocks or so. Every ride costs 25¢, so if you hop on and off to see attractions, it'll cost you every time. But the cost is worth it, since you can travel quickly and be assured of finding your way. DASH (tel. 213/689–8822) runs weekdays and Saturday 6:30 AM–10 PM. To follow the tour outlined below, you can get on the DASH at ARCO Plaza (505 S. Flower St., between 5th and 6th Sts.).

Hidden directly under the twin ARCO towers, ARCO Plaza is a subterranean shopping mall that's jam-packed with office workers during the week, nearly deserted on weekends. The

① **Los Angeles Visitor and Convention Bureau** is nearby. It offers free information about attractions as well as advice on public transportation. *685 S. Figueroa St., between 7th St. and Wilshire Blvd., tel. 213/689–8822. Open weekdays 8–6, Sat. 8:30–5.*

② Just north of ARCO, the **Westin Bonaventure Hotel** (404 S. Figueroa St., tel. 213/624–1000) is unique in the L.A. skyline: five shimmering cylinders in the sky, without a 90 degree angle in sight. Designed by John Portman in 1974, the building looks like science-fiction fantasy. Nonguests can use only one elevator, which rises through the roof of the lobby to soar through the air outside to the revolving restaurant and bar on the 35th floor. The food here is expensive; a better bet is to come for a drink (still overpriced) and nurse it for an hour as Los Angeles makes a full circle around you.

In the 19th century, the downtown area called Bunker Hill was the site of many stately mansions. Thanks to bulldozers, there's not much of a hill left, but the area is being redeveloped. Two major sites here showcase visual arts (painting, sculpture, and environmental work) and media and performing arts.

③ The **Museum of Contemporary Art** houses a permanent collection of international scope, representing modern art from 1940 to the present. Included are works by Mark Rothko, Franz Kline, and Susan Rothenberg. The red sandstone building was designed by renowned Japanese architect Arata Isozaki, and opened in 1986. Pyramidal skylights add a striking geometry to the seven-level, 98,000-square-foot building. Don't miss the gift shop or the lively Milanese-style café. *250 S. Grand Ave., tel. 213/626–6222. Admission: $4 adults, children under 12 free; free to all after 5 PM Thur. Open Tues., Wed., Fri., Sat., and Sun. 11–5, Thur. 11–8. Closed Mon.*

④ Walk north to the **The Music Center,** which has become the cultural center for Los Angeles since it opened in 1969. For years,

Tour 1: Downtown Los Angeles

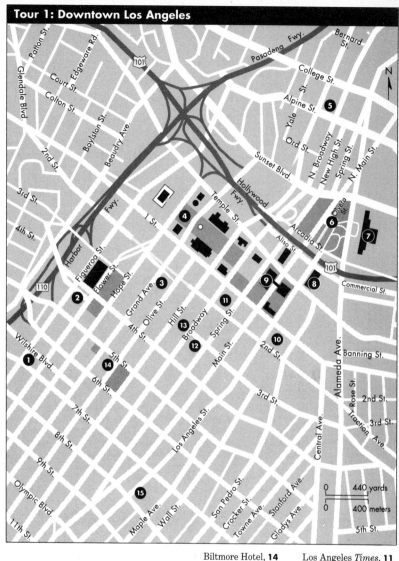

Biltmore Hotel, **14**

Bradbury Building, **12**

Chinatown, **5**

El Pueblo State Historic Park, **6**

Garment District, **15**

Grand Central Market, **13**

Little Tokyo, **10**

Los Angeles Children's Museum, **8**

Los Angeles City Hall, **9**

Los Angeles *Times*, **11**

Los Angeles Visitor and Convention Bureau, **1**

Museum of Contemporary Art, **3**

The Music Center, **4**

Union Station, **7**

Westin Bonaventure Hotel, **2**

it was the site of the Academy Awards each spring: The limousines arrived at the Hope Street drive-through and celebrities were whisked through the crowds to the Dorothy Chandler Pavilion, the largest and grandest of the three theaters. It was named after the widow of the publisher of the Los Angeles *Times*, who was instrumental in fundraising efforts to build the complex. The round building in the middle, the Mark Taper Forum, is a smaller theater. Most of its offerings are of an experimental nature, many of them on a pre-Broadway run. The Ahmanson, at the north end, is the venue for many musical comedies. The plaza has a fountain and sculpture by Jacques Lipchitz. *First St. and Grand Ave., tel. 213/972–7211. Free 70-min tours are offered Tues.–Sat. 10–1:30. Schedule subject to change; call for reservations.*

❺ L.A.'s **Chinatown** runs a pale second to San Francisco's Chinatown but still offers visitors an authentic slice of life, beyond the tourist hokum. The neighborhood is bordered by Yale, Bernard, and Ord streets, and Alameda Avenue. The main drag is North Broadway, where, every February, giant dragons snake down the center of the pavement during Chinese New Year celebrations. More than 15,000 Chinese and Southeast Asians (mostly Vietnamese) actually live in the Chinatown area, but many thousands more regularly frequent the markets (filled with exotic foods unfamiliar to most Western eyes) and restaurants (dim sum parlors are currently the most popular).

❻ **El Pueblo State Historic Park** preserves the "birthplace" of Los Angeles (no one knows exactly where the original 1781 settlement was), the oldest downtown buildings, and some of the only remaining pre-1900 buildings in the city. The state park covers 44 acres, bounded by Alameda, Arcadia, Spring, and Macy streets.

Olvera Street is the heart of the park and one of the most popular tourist sites in Los Angeles. With its cobblestone walkways, pinatas, mariachis, and authentic Mexican food, Olvera Street should not be dismissed as merely some gringo approximation of the real thing. Mexican-American families come here in droves, especially on weekends and Mexican holidays—to them it feels like the old country.

Begin your walk of the area at the **Plaza**, on Olvera Street between Main and Los Angeles streets, a wonderful Mexican-style park with shady trees, a central gazebo, and plenty of benches and walkways for strolling. On weekends there are often mariachis and folklorico dance groups here. You can have your photo taken in an oversize velvet sombrero, astride a stuffed donkey (a take-off of the zebra-striped donkeys that are a tradition on the streets of Tijuana). Two annual events are particularly worth seeing here: the Blessing of the Animals, at 2 PM on the Saturday before Easter, when residents bring their pets (not just dogs and cats but horses, pigs, cows, birds, hamsters, and more) to be blessed by a local priest; and Las Posadas, every night December 16–24, when merchants and visitors parade up and down the cobblestone street, led by children dressed as angels, to commemorate Mary and Joseph's search for shelter on Christmas Eve.

Head north up Olvera Street proper. Midblock is the park's **Visitors Center,** housed in Sepulveda House (622 N. Main St., tel. 213/628–1274; open weekdays 10–4, Sat. 10–4:30). The

Eastlake Victorian was built in 1887 as a hotel and boarding-house. **Pelanconi House** (17 Olvera St.), built in 1855, was the first brick building in Los Angeles and has been home to the La Golondrina restaurant for more than 50 years. During the 1930s, famed Mexican muralist David Alfaro Siquieros was commissioned to paint a mural on the south wall of the **Italian Hall** building (650 N. Main St.). The patrons were not prepared for—and certainly not pleased by—this anti-imperialist mural depicting the oppressed workers of Latin America held in check by a menacing American eagle. It was promptly white-washed into oblivion, and remains under the paint to this day. While preservationists from the Getty Conservation Trust work on ways of restoring the mural, copies can be seen at the Visitors Center.

Walk down the east side of Olvera Street to mid-block, passing the only remaining sign of Zanja Ditch (mother ditch), which supplied water to the area in the earliest years. **Avila Adobe** (E–10 Olvera St., open weekdays 10–4:30), built in 1818, is generally considered the oldest building still standing in Los Angeles. This graceful, simple adobe is designed with the traditional interior courtyard and is furnished in the style of the 1840s.

On weekends, the restaurants are packed, and there is usually music in the plaza and along the street. Two Mexican holidays, Cinco de Mayo (May 5) and Independence Day (September 16), also draw huge crowds—and long lines for the restaurants. To see Olvera Street at its quietest and perhaps loveliest, visit on a late weekday afternoon. The long shadows heighten the romantic feeling of the street and there are only a few strollers and diners milling about.

South of the plaza is an area that has undergone recent renovation but remains, for the most part, only an ambitious idea. Although these magnificent old buildings remain closed, awaiting some commercial plan (à la Ghirardelli Square in San Francisco) that never seems to come to fruition, docent-led tours explore the area in depth. Tours depart Tuesday–Saturday 10–1, on the hour, from the **Old Firehouse** (south side of plaza, tel. 213/628–1274), an 1884 building that contains early fire-fighting equipment and old photographs. Buildings seen on tours include the Merced Theater, Masonic Temple, Pico House, and the Garnier Block—all ornate examples of the late-19th-century style. Under the Merced and Masonic Temple are the catacombs, secret passageways and old opium dens used by Chinese immigrants.

Time Out   The dining choices on Olvera Street range from fast-food stands to comfortable, sit-down restaurants. The most authentic Mexican food is at **La Luz del Dia** (107 Paseo de la Plaza, tel. 213/628–7495). Here they serve traditional favorites like barbecued goat and pickled cactus, as well as handmade tortillas patted out in a practiced rhythm by the women behind the counter. **La Golondrina** (tel. 213/628–4349) and **El Paseo** (tel. 213/626–1361) restaurants, across from each other in mid-block, have delightful patios and extensive menus.

❼ **Union Station** (800 N. Alameda St.), directly east of Olvera Street across Alameda, is one of those quintessentially Californian buildings that seemed to define Los Angeles to movie-goers all over the country in the 1940s. Built in 1939, its Spanish Mission style is a subtle combination of Streamline Moderne and Moorish. The majestic scale of the waiting room alone is worth the walk over. The place is so evocative of its heyday that you'll half expect to see Carole Lombard or Groucho Marx or Barbara Stanwyck step onto the platform from a train and sashay through.

8 **Los Angeles Children's Museum** was the first of several strictly-for-kids museums now open in the city. All the exhibits here are hands-on, from Sticky City (where kids get to pillow-fight with abandon in a huge pillow-filled room) to a TV studio (where they can put on their own news shows). *310 N. Main St., tel. 213/687–8800. Admission: $5, children under 2 free. Open weekends 10–5.*

9 **Los Angeles City Hall** is another often-photographed building and well-known from its many appearances on "Dragnet," "Superman," and other television shows. Opened in 1928, the 27-story City Hall remained the only building to break the 13-story height limit (earthquakes, you know) until 1957. There is a 45-minute tour and ride to the top-floor observation deck, and, although some newer buildings (e.g., the Bonaventure) offer higher views, City Hall has a certain landmark panache. *200 N. Spring St., tel. 213/485–4423. Tours by reservation only, weekdays at 10 and 11.*

10 **Little Tokyo** is the original ethnic neighborhood for Los Angeles's Japanese community. Most have deserted the downtown center for suburban areas such as Gardena and West Los Angeles, but Little Tokyo remains a cultural focal point. Nisei (the name for second-generation Japanese) Week is celebrated here every August with traditional drums, obon dancing, a carnival, and huge parade. Bounded by First, San Pedro, Third, and Los Angeles streets, Little Toyko has dozens of sushi bars, tempura restaurants, trinket shops, and even a restaurant that serves nothing but eel. The Japanese American Cultural and Community Center presents such events as kabuki theater straight from Japan.

11 The **Los Angeles *Times*** complex is made up of several, supposedly architecturally harmonious, buildings, and combines several eras and styles, but looks pretty much like a hodge-podge. *202 W. 1st St., tel. 213/237–5000. Two public tours given weekdays: 35-min. tour of old plant and 45-min. tour of new plant. Tour times vary. Call for information. Reservations required.*

Broadway between First and Ninth is one of Los Angeles's busiest shopping streets. The shops and sidewalk vendors cater primarily to the Hispanic population with bridal shops, immigration lawyers, and cheap stereo equipment. First-floor rental space is said to be the most expensive in the city, even higher than in Beverly Hills. This can be an exhilarating slice-of-life walk, past the florid old movie theaters like the Orpheum (842 S. Broadway) and the Million Dollar (310 S. Broadway)

12 and the perennially classy **Bradbury Building** (304 S. Broadway, tel. 213/626–1893), a marvelous specimen of Victorian-era commercial architecture at the southeast corner of Third Street and Broadway. Once the site of turn-of-the-century sweatshops, it now houses somewhat more genteel law offices. The interior courtyard, with its glass skylight and open balconies and elevator, is picture perfect and, naturally, a popular movie locale. The building is only open weekdays 9–5, and its owners prefer that you not wander too far past the lobby.

⓭ **Grand Central Market** (317 S. Broadway, tel. 213/624–2378) is the most bustling market in the city and a testimony to the city's diversity. It's open Monday–Saturday 9–6, Sunday 10–5. This block-through marketplace of colorful and exotic produce, herbs, and meat draws a faithful clientele from the Hispanic community, senior citizens on a budget, along with Westside matrons for whom money is no object. Even if you don't plan to buy anything, Grand Central Market is a delightful place in which to browse: The butcher shops display everything from lamb heads and bulls' testicles, to pigs' tails; the produce stalls are piled high with the ripest, reddest tomatoes; and the herb stalls promise remedies for all your ills. Mixed among them are fast-food stands (one Chinese but most Mexican).

⓮ The **Biltmore Hotel** (515 S. Olive St.), built in 1923, rivals Union Station for sheer architectural majesty in the Spanish-Revival tradition. The public areas have recently been restored, with the magnificent hand-painted wood beams brought back to their former glory.

⓯ The **Garment District** (700–800 blocks of Los Angeles St.) is an enclave of jobbers and wholesalers that sell off the leftovers from Los Angeles's considerable garment industry production. The **Cooper Building** (860 S. Los Angeles St.) is the heart of the district and houses several of what local bargain-hunters consider to be the best pickings.

Tour 2: Hollywood

Numbers in the margin correspond to points of interest on the Tour 2: Hollywood map.

"Hollywood" once meant movie stars and glamour. The big film studios were here; starlets lived in sorority-like buildings in the center of town; and movies premiered beneath the glare of klieg lights at the Chinese and the Pantages theaters.

Those days are long gone. Paramount is the only major studio still physically located in Hollywood; and though some celebrities may live in the Hollywood Hills, there certainly aren't any in the "flats." In short, Hollywood is no longer "Hollywood." These days it is, even to its supporters, a seedy town that could use a good dose of urban renewal (some projects are, in fact, finally under way). So why visit? Because the legends of the golden age of the movies are heavy in the air. Because this is where the glamour of Hollywood originated, and where those who made it so worked and lived. Judy Garland lived here and so did Marilyn Monroe and Lana Turner. It is a tribute to Hollywood's powerful hold on the imagination that visitors are able to look past the junky shops and the lost souls who walk the streets to get a sense of the town's glittering past. Besides, no visit to Los Angeles is truly complete without a walk down Hollywood Boulevard.

❶ Begin your tour of Hollywood simply by looking to the **Hollywood sign** in the Hollywood Hills that line the northern border of the town. Even on the smoggiest days, the sign is visible for miles. It is on Mt. Lee, north of Beachwood Canyon, which is approximately 1 mile east of Hollywood and Vine. The 50-foot-

Tour 2: Hollywood

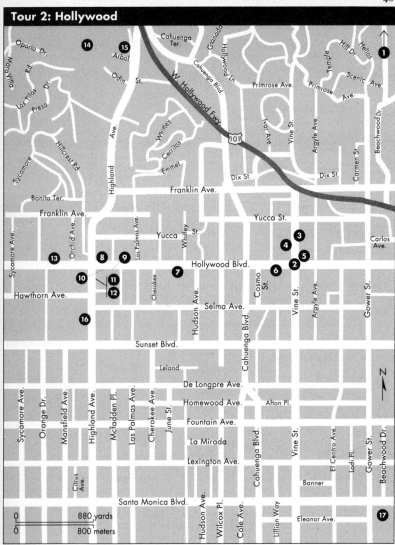

Capitol Records
Building, **3**

Frederick's of
Hollywood, **7**

Hollywood Bowl, **14**

Hollywood Guinness
World of Records, **9**

Hollywood High
School, **16**

Hollywood Memorial
Cemetery, **17**

Hollywood sign, **1**

Hollywood Studio
Museum, **15**

Hollywood and Vine, **2**

Hollywood Walk of
Fame, **6**

Hollywood Wax
Museum, **8**

Mann's Chinese
Theater, **13**

Max Factor
Museum, **11**

Museum of Hollywood
History, **12**

The Palace, **4**

The Pantages
Theater, **5**

Ripley's Believe It
or Not, **10**

tall letters, originally spelling out "Hollywoodland," were erected in 1923 as a promotional scheme for a real estate development. The "land" was taken down in 1949.

❷ Hollywood and Vine was once considered the heart of Hollywood. The mere mention of this intersection still inspires images of a street corner bustling with movie stars, starlets, and moguls passing by, on foot or in snazzy convertibles. But these days, Hollywood and Vine is far from the action, and pedestrian traffic is, well, pedestrian. No stars, no starlets, no moguls. The Brown Derby restaurant that once stood at the northwest corner is long gone, and the intersection these days is little more than a place for visitors to get their bearings.

❸ Capitol Records Building (1756 N. Vine St.) opened in 1956, the very picture of '50s chic. When Capitol decided to build its new headquarters here, two of the record company's big talents of the day (singer Nat King Cole and songwriter Johnny Mercer) suggested that it be done in the shape of a stack of records. It was, and compared to much of what's gone up in L.A. since then, this building doesn't seem so odd.

❹ The Palace (1735 N. Vine St., tel. 213/467–4571), just across the street from the Capitol Building, was opened in 1927 as the Hollywood Playhouse. It has played host to many shows over the years, from Ken Murray's *Blackouts* to Ralph Edwards's *This Is Your Life*. It is now the site of popular rock concerts and late-night weekend dancing.

❺ When the **Pantages Theater,** at 6233 Hollywood Boulevard, just east of Vine, opened in 1930, it was the very pinnacle of movie-theater opulence. From 1949 to 1959, it was the site of the Academy Awards, and today hosts large-scale Broadway musicals.

❻ The Hollywood Walk of Fame is at every turn along the sidewalks as you make your way through downtown Hollywood. The name of one or other Hollywood legend is embossed in brass, each at the center of a pink-colored star embedded in a dark gray terrazzo circle. The first eight stars were unveiled in 1960 at the northwest corner of Highland Avenue and Hollywood Boulevard: Olive Borden, Ronald Colman, Louise Fazenda, Preston Foster, Burt Lancaster, Edward Sedgwick, Ernest Torrence, and Joanne Woodward (some of these names have stood the test of time better than others!). In the 30 years since, 1,800 others have been added. But this kind of immortality doesn't come cheap—the personality in question (or more likely his or her movie studio or record company) must pay $3,500 for the honor. Walk a few blocks and you'll quickly find that not all the names are familiar. To aid in the identification, celebrities are classified by one of five logos: a motion picture camera, a radio microphone, a television set, a record, or theatrical masks. Here's a guide to a few of the more famous stars: Marlon Brando at 1765 Vine, Charlie Chaplin at 6751 Hollywood, W.C. Fields at 7004 Hollywood, Clark Gable at 1608 Vine, Marilyn Monroe at 6774 Hollywood, Rudolph Valentino at 6164 Hollywood, and John Wayne at 1541 Vine.

❼ After decades of sporting a gaudy lavender paint job, the exterior of **Frederick's of Hollywood** (6608 Hollywood Blvd., tel. 213/466–8506) has been restored to its original understated Art Deco look, gray with pink awnings. Fear not, however, that the place has suddenly gone tasteful; inside is all the risque and trashy lingerie that made this place famous. There is also a bra museum that features the undergarments of living and no longer living Hollywood legends. This is a popular tourist spot, if only for a good giggle.

8 **Hollywood Wax Museum** offers visitors sights that real life no longer can (Mary Pickford, Elvis Presley, and Clark Gable) and a few that even real life never did (Rambo and Conan). Recently added living legends on display include actors Kevin Costner and Patrick Swayze. A short film on Academy Award winners is shown daily. *6767 Hollywood Blvd., tel. 213/462–8860. Admission: $7.95 adults, $6.95 senior citizens, $5 children; under 6 free if with adult. Open Sun.–Thur. 10 AM–midnight, Fri.–Sat. 10 AM–2 AM.*

9 The **Hollywood Guinness World of Records,** across the street from the Hollywood Wax Museum, is a testament to just how far some people will go to achieve record-book immortality. Visitors can tap into a computer system that officially records who holds what record. Also on view are videos documenting various feats, as well as life-size replicas—like the one of Robert Wardlow, the world's tallest man, who, when standing, was 8 feet, 11¼ inches. *6764 Hollywood Blvd., tel. 213/463–6433. Admission: $7.95 adults, $6.95 senior citizens, $5 children under 12. Open Sun.–Thur. 10–midnight, Fri. and Sat. 10–2 AM.*

10 **Ripley's Believe It or Not** is for people who like to gawk at freaks of nature and strange illusions. This wacky museum, opened in 1992, contains more than 300 weird exhibits such as a two-headed baby skeleton from the turn of the century, a shrunken head from Ecuador, and a life-sized portrait of John Wayne made of dryer lint. *6870 Hollywood Blvd., tel. 213/466–6335. Admission: $7.95 adults, $6.95 senior citizens, $5 children; under 6 free if with adult. Open daily 10 AM–midnight.*

11 **The Max Factor Museum** (1666 N. Highland Ave., tel. 213/463–6668) lets civilians in on the beauty secrets of screen idols from flicks from as far back as the turn of the century. Set to open **12** in the same building in 1994 is the **Museum of Hollywood History,** displaying memorabilia of favorite films, television shows, and radio programs. *1666 N. Highland Ave. Admission free. Open Mon.–Sat. 10–4.*

13 Finally, most residents no longer call **Mann's Chinese Theater** (6925 Hollywood Blvd., tel. 213/464–8111) "Grauman's Chinese," and the new owners seem to have a firm hold on the place in the public's eye. The architecture is a fantasy of Chinese pagodas and temples as only Hollywood could turn out. Although you'll have to buy a movie ticket to appreciate the interior trappings, the courtyard is open for browsing, where you'll see the famous cement hand- and footprints. The tradition is said to have begun at the theater's opening in 1927, with the premiere of Cecil B. DeMille's *King of Kings,* when actress Norma Talmadge accidentally stepped into the wet cement. Now more than 160 celebrities have added their footprints or handprints, along with a few oddball prints like the one of Jimmy Durante's nose. Space has pretty much run out now.

14 Summer evening concerts at the **Hollywood Bowl** have been a tradition since 1922, although the bandshell has been replaced several times. The musical fare ranges from pop to jazz to classical; the L. A. Philharmonic has its summer season here. The 17,000-plus seating capacity ranges from boxes (where local society matrons put on incredibly fancy alfresco preconcert meals for their friends) to concrete bleachers in the rear. Some people actually prefer the back rows for their romantic appeal. *2301 N. Highland Ave., tel. 213/850–2000. Grounds open daily summer, 9–sunset. Call for program schedule.*

⓯ The **Hollywood Studio Museum** sits in the Hollywood Bowl parking lot, east of Highland Boulevard. The building, recently moved to this site, was once called the Lasky–DeMille Barn; in it Cecil B. DeMille produced the first feature-length film, *The Squaw Man.* In 1927, the barn became Paramount Pictures, with the original company of Jesse Lasky, Cecil B. DeMille, and Samuel Goldwyn. The museum contains a re-creation of De-Mille's office, original artifacts, and a screening room showing vintage film footage of Hollywood and its legends. A great gift shop sells such quality vintage memorabilia as autographs, photographs, and books. *2100 N. Highland Ave., tel. 213/874–2276. Admission: $4 adults, $3 children. Free parking. Open weekends 10–4.*

Such stars as Carol Burnett, Linda Evans, Rick Nelson, and
⓰ Lana Turner attended **Hollywood High School** (1521 N. Highland Ave.). Today the student body is as diverse as Los Angeles itself, with every ethnic group represented.

Many of Hollywood's stars, from the silent-screen era on, are
⓱ buried in **Hollywood Memorial Cemetery,** a few blocks from Paramount Studios. Walk from the entrance to the lake area and you'll find the crypt of Cecil B. DeMille and the graves of Nelson Eddy and Douglas Fairbanks, Sr. Inside the Cathedral Mausoleum is Rudolph Valentino's crypt (where fans, the press, and the famous Lady in Black turn up every August 23, the anniversary of his death). Other stars interred in this section are Peter Lorre and Eleanor Powell. In the Abbey of Palms Mausoleum, Norma Talmadge and Clifton Webb are buried. *6000 Santa Monica Blvd., tel. 213/469–1181. Open daily 8–5.*

Tour 3: Wilshire Boulevard

Numbers in the margin correspond to points of interest on the Tour 3: Wilshire Boulevard map.

Wilshire Boulevard begins in the heart of downtown Los Angeles and runs west, through Beverly Hills and Santa Monica, ending at the cliffs above the Pacific Ocean. In 16 miles it moves through fairly poor neighborhoods populated by recent immigrants, solidly middle-class enclaves, and through a corridor of the highest priced high-rise condos in the city. Along the way, and all within a few blocks of each other, are many of Los Angeles's top architectural sites, museums, and shops.

This linear tour can be started at any point along Wilshire Boulevard but to really savor the cross-section view of Los Angeles that this street provides, take the Bullocks-west-to-the-sea approach. If you have only limited time, it would be better to skip Koreatown and Larchmont and pare down the museum time than to do only one stretch. All these sites are on Wilshire or within a few blocks north or south.

"One" Wilshire, at the precise start of the boulevard in downtown Los Angeles, is just another anonymous office building.

Begin, instead, a few miles westward, past the Harbor Freeway. As Wilshire Boulevard moves from its downtown genesis, it quickly passes through neighborhoods now populated by recent immigrants from Central America. Around the turn of the century, however, this area was home to many of the city's wealthy citizens, as the faded Victorian houses on the side streets attest.

As the population crept westward, the distance to downtown shops began to seem insurmountable and the first suburban
❶ department branch store, **I. Magnin Bullocks Wilshire** (3050 Wilshire Blvd., tel. 213/382–6161), was opened in 1929. Although it closed for business in March 1993, it is protected as a historical landmark and will not be torn down—Cal Tech purchased it but has announced no plans yet for the building. The behind-the-store parking lot was quite an innovation in 1929 and the first accommodation a large Los Angeles store made to the automobile age. On the ceiling of the porte cochere, a mural depicts the history of transportation.

❷ **Koreatown** begins almost at I. Magnin Bullocks Wilshire's backdoor. Koreans are one of the latest and largest groups in this ethnically diverse city. Arriving from the old country with generally more money than most immigrant groups do, Koreans nevertheless face the trauma of adjusting to a new language, new alphabet, and new customs. Settling in the area south of Wilshire Boulevard, along Olympic Boulevard between Vermont and Western avenues, the Korean community has slowly grown into a cohesive neighborhood with active community groups and newspapers. The area is teeming with Asian restaurants (not just Korean but also Japanese and Chinese, because Koreans are fond of those cuisines). Many of the signs in this area are in Korean only. For a glimpse of the typical offerings of Korean shops, browse the large enclosed **Koreatown Plaza** mall, on the corner of Western and San Marino avenues.

At the southwest corner of Wilshire and Western Avenue sits
❸ **Wiltern Theater** (3780 Wilshire Blvd.), part of the magnificent Wiltern Center and one of the city's best examples of full-out Art Deco architecture. The 1930s zigzag design was recently restored to its splendid turquoise hue. Inside, the theater is full of opulent detail at every turn. Originally a movie theater, the Wiltern is now a multi-use arts complex.

Continuing west on Wilshire, the real estate values start to make a sharp climb. The mayor of Los Angeles has his official
❹ residence in **Getty House** (605 S. Irving Blvd.), one block north of Wilshire in the Hancock Park district. This is one of the city's most genteel neighborhoods, remaining in vogue since its development in the 1920s. Many of L.A.'s old-money families live here in English Tudor homes with East Coast landscaping schemes that defy the local climate and history. The white-brick, half-timber mayor's residence was donated to the city by the Getty family.

❺ Hancock Park has its own little shopping street: **Larchmont Boulevard.** Named after the New York suburb, Larchmont is a very un–Los Angeles shopping district, a bit of small-town America in the middle of the metropolitan sprawl. The tree-lined street has 45-degree-angle parking and a cozy, everybody-knows-everybody feeling. Many celebrities live in the

Tour 3: Wilshire Boulevard

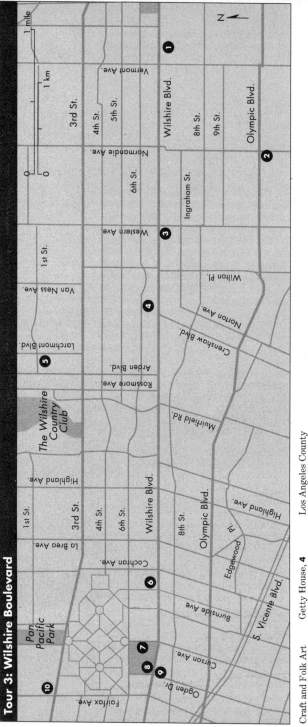

Craft and Folk Art Museum, **9**
Farmer's Market, **10**
George C. Page Museum of La Brea Discoveries, **7**
Getty House, **4**
I. Magnin Bullocks Wilshire, **1**
Koreatown, **2**
Larchmont Boulevard, **5**
Los Angeles County Museum of Art, **8**
Miracle Mile, **6**
Wiltern Theater, **3**

area and can be seen darting in and out of the boutiques, health food store, and the old-time five-and-dime. There are also several chic restaurants here.

Drop back down to Wilshire Boulevard again and continue
❻ westward. **Miracle Mile,** the strip of Wilshire Boulevard between La Brea and Fairfax avenues, was so dubbed in the 1930s as a promotional gimmick to attract shoppers to the new stores. The area went into something of a decline in the '50s and '60s, but is now enjoying a comeback, as Los Angeles's Art Deco architecture has come to be appreciated, preserved, and restored. Exemplary buildings like the **El Rey Theater** (5519 Wilshire) stand out as examples of period design (in spite of the fact that it now houses a restaurant). In **Callender's Restaurant** (corner of Wilshire and Curson), recent murals and old photographs effectively depict life on the Miracle Mile in its heyday.

Across Curson Avenue is **Hancock Park,** an actual park, not to be confused with Hancock Park, the residential neighborhood. This park is home to the city's world-famous fossil source, the **La Brea Tar Pits.** Despite the fact that *la brea* already means "tar" in Spanish and to say "La Brea Tar Pits" is redundant, the name remains firm in local minds. About 35,000 years ago, deposits of oil rose to the Earth's surface, collected in shallow pools, and coagulated into sticky asphalt. In the early 20th century, geologists discovered that the sticky goo contained the largest collection of Pleistocene fossils ever found at one location: more than 200 varieties of birds, mammals, plants, reptiles, and insects. More than 100 tons of fossil bones have been removed over 70 years of excavations. Statues of mammoths in the big pit near the corner of Wilshire and Curson depict how many of them were entombed: Edging down to a pond of water to drink, animals were caught in the tar and unable to extricate themselves. There are several pits scattered around Hancock Park; construction in the area has often had to accommodate these oozing pits, and in nearby streets and along sidewalks, little bits of tar occasionally ooze up, unstoppable.

❼ The **George C. Page Museum of La Brea Discoveries,** a satellite of the Los Angeles County Museum of Natural History, is situated at the tar pits and set, bunkerlike, half underground. A bas-relief around four sides depicts life in the Pleistocene era, and the museum has over one million Ice Age fossils. Exhibits include reconstructed, life-size skeletons of saber-tooth cats, mammoths, wolves, sloths, eagles, and condors. The glass-enclosed Paleontological Laboratory permits observation of the ongoing cleaning, identification, and cataloguing of fossils excavated from the nearby asphalt deposits. *The La Brea Story* and *Dinosaurs, the Terrible Lizards* are short documentary films shown every 15–30 minutes. A hologram magically puts flesh on "La Brea Woman," and a tar contraption shows visitors just how hard it would be to free oneself from the sticky mess. *5801 Wilshire Blvd., tel. 213/936–2230. Admission: $5 adults, $1 children; free 2nd Tues. of month. Open Tues.–Sun. 10–5.*

❽ The **Los Angeles County Museum of Art,** also in Hancock Park, is the largest museum complex in Los Angeles, comprised of five buildings surrounding a grand central court. The Times Mirror Central Court provides both a visual and symbolic focus for the museum complex. The Ahmanson Building, built around a central atrium, houses the museum's collection of paintings, sculpture, costumes and textiles, and decorative arts from a wide range of cultures and periods. Highlights include a unique assemblage of glass from Roman times to the 19th century; the renowned Gilbert collection of mosaics and monumental silver; one of the nation's largest holdings of costumes and textiles; and an Indian and Southeast Asian art collection considered to be one of the most comprehensive in the world.

The Hammer Building features major special loan exhibitions as well as galleries for prints, drawings, and photographs. The Anderson Building features 20th-century painting and sculpture as well as special exhibitions. The museum's collection of Japanese sculpture, paintings, ceramics, and lacquerware, including the internationally renowned Shin'enkan collection of Japanese paintings and a collection of extraordinary *netsuke*, is on view in the Pavillion for Japanese Art. The Contemporary Sculpture Garden comprises nine large-scale outdoor sculptures. The B. Gerald Cantor Sculpture Garden features bronzes by Auguste Rodin, Emile-Antoine Bourdelle, and George Kolbe. *5905 Wilshire Blvd., tel. 213/857–6111; ticket information, 213/857–6010. Admission: $5 adults, $3 children ($2 for special exhibits). Open Tues.– Thur. 10–5, Fri. 10–9, Sat.–Sun. 11–6.*

The County Museum, Page Museum, and indeed all of Hancock Park itself are brimming with visitors on warm weekends. Although crowded, it can be the most exciting time to visit the area. Mimes and itinerant musicians ply their trades. Street vendors sell fast-food treats and there are impromptu soccer games on the lawns. To really study the art, though, a quieter weekday visit is recommended.

❾ The **Craft and Folk Art Museum,** across Wilshire Boulevard from Hancock Park, offers consistently fascinating exhibits of both contemporary crafts and folk crafts from around the world. The museum's collections include Japanese, Mexican, American, and East Indian folk art, textiles, and masks. Six to eight major exhibitions are planned each year. The International Festival of Masks, one of the more popular, is held annually the last week in October across the street in Hancock Park. *5800 Wilshire Blvd; mailing address, 6067 Wilshire Blvd., Los Angeles, CA 90036; tel. 213/937–5544. Admission free. Open Tues.–Sat. 10–5, Sun. 11–5.*

Time Out Just a few doors down from the Craft and Folk Art Museum, and across from the County Museum, **The Greenhouse** is a casual midday hangout on the ground level of an office building (5900 Wilshire Blvd., tel. 213/933–8333).

Continue west on Wilshire a few blocks to the corner of Fairfax Avenue. On the northeast corner is the **May Co. department store,** another 1930s landmark with a distinctive curved corner.

❿ Head north on Fairfax a few blocks to the **Farmer's Market,** a favorite L.A. attraction since it opened in 1934. Along with the 120 shops, salons, stores, and produce stalls, there are 21 restaurants (some of which offer al fresco dining under umbrellas), serving an interesting variety of international and domestic fare. Although originally exactly what the name implies—a farmer's market—these days you will find not only food and produce, but gifts, clothing, beauty shops, and even a shoe repair. Because it is next door to the CBS Television Studios, you never know who you will run into, as TV celebrities shop and dine here often. *6333 W. 3rd St., tel. 213/933–9211. Open Mon.–Sat. 9–6:30, Sun. 10–5. Open later during summer.*

Time Out **Kokomo** (on Third St. side of market, tel. 213/933–0773) is not only the best eatery inside the Farmer's Market, it's got some of the best new-wave diner food anywhere in L.A. Lively, entertaining service is almost always included in the reasonable prices. For those in a hurry, Kokomo A Go Go, their takeout store, is adjacent.

North of the market, Fairfax is the center of Los Angeles's Jewish life. The shops and stands from Beverly Boulevard north are enlivened with friendly conversations between shopkeepers and regular customers. **Canter's Restaurant, Deli, and Bakery** (419 N. Fairfax, tel. 213/651–2030) is a traditional hangout.

Tour 4: The Westside

Numbers in the margin correspond to points of interest on the Tour 4: Westside map.

The Westside of Los Angeles—which to residents means from La Brea Avenue westward to the ocean—is where the rents are the most expensive, the real estate prices sky high, the restaurants (and the restaurateurs) the most famous, and the shops the most chic. It's the best of the good life, Southern California style, and to really savor (and understand) the Southland, spend a few leisurely days or half days exploring this area. Short on such traditional tourist attractions as amusement parks, historic sites, and museums, it more than makes up for those gaps with great shopping districts, exciting walking streets, outdoor cafés, and a lively nightlife.

The Westside can be best enjoyed in at least three separate outings, allowing plenty of time for browsing and dining. Attractions 1 through 4 are in the West Hollywood area; 5 through 8 in Beverly Hills; and 9 through 11 in Westwood. But the Westside is also small enough that you could pick four or five of these sites to visit in a single day, depending on your interests.

West Hollywood Once an almost forgotten parcel of county land surrounded by the city of L.A. and Beverly Hills, West Hollywood became an official city in 1984. The West Hollywood attitude—trendy, stylish, and with plenty of disposable income—spills over beyond the official city borders.

① **Melrose Avenue,** which isn't exactly in West Hollywood, nevertheless remains firmly fixed in residents' minds as *very* West Hollywood. If you're entertained by post-punk fashion plates, people in spiked hairdos, and just about the most outlandish ensembles imaginable, then Melrose is the place for you. It's where panache meets paparazzi, and Beverly Hills chic meets Hollywood hip. The busiest stretch of Melrose is between Fairfax and La Brea avenues. Here you'll find one-of-a-kind boutiques and small, chic restaurants for more than a dozen blocks. Park on a side street (and read the parking signs carefully: Parking regulations around here are vigorously enforced and a rich vein for the city's coffers) and begin walking. On the 7400 block are **Tempest** and **Notorious,** boutiques with the latest of

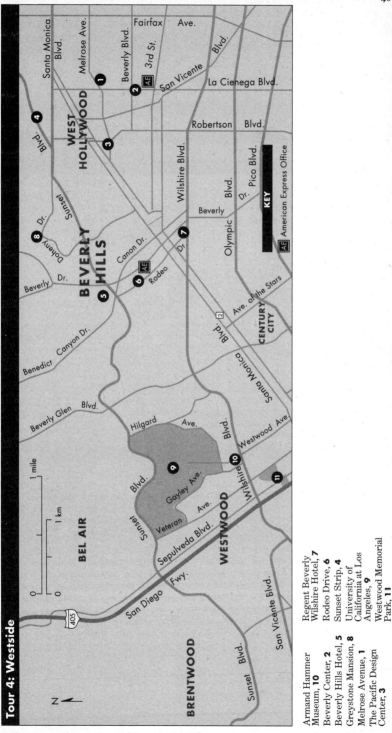

Tour 4: Westside

Armand Hammer Museum, **10**
Beverly Center, **2**
Beverly Hills Hotel, **5**
Greystone Mansion, **8**
Melrose Avenue, **1**
The Pacific Design Center, **3**

Regent Beverly Wilshire Hotel, **7**
Rodeo Drive, **6**
Sunset Strip, **4**
University of California at Los Angeles, **9**
Westwood Memorial Park, **11**

California's trend-setting designers' clothes for women, along with **Mondial,** for men, and **Mark Fox,** which supplies the sought-after Western look. On the next block over, **Cocobianca** (8443) and **Maxfield** (8825) provide excellent special occasion designs. In the other direction—in more ways than one—**A Star Is Worn** (7303) is a resale boutique for celebrity and designer clothing. A list at the entrance notes the celebrities whose clothes are on the racks. Creations for Cher and Liza Minnelli are usually found there. **Melrose Place Antique Market** (7002 Melrose) is a collection of small items, vintage in nature, high in appeal.

Time Out   Melrose has no shortage of great eateries. Part of any visit here is trying to pick one from the dozens of choices: Thai, Mexican, sausages, yogurt, Italian, and more. The ultimate Melrose "joint" is **Johnny Rocket's** (7507 Melrose Ave., tel. 213/651–3361), a very hip '50s-style diner near the corner of Gardner Street. It's just stools at a counter, the best of old-time rock and roll on tape, and great hamburgers, shakes, and fries—and almost always crowded, with people lined up behind the stools to slip in the moment they are vacated.

That hulking monolith dominating the corner of La Cienega and Beverly boulevards is none other than the **Beverly Center** (8500 Beverly Blvd., tel. 310/854–0070). Designed as an all-in-one stop for shopping, dining, and movies, it has been a boon to Westsiders—except for those who live so close as to suffer the consequences of the heavy traffic. Parking is on the second through fifth floors, shops on the sixth, seventh, and eighth, and movies and restaurants on the eighth floors. The street level features **Irvine Ranch Market,** a gourmet's grocery haven; **Conran's Habitat** for home furnishings; and **Hard Rock Cafe** (look for the vintage green Cadillac in the roof). In the center proper are two major department stores, **Bullocks** and **The Broadway,** as well as dozens of upscale clothing boutiques, 13 movie theaters, and a wide variety of restaurants (California Pizza Kitchen, Siam Orchid, La Rotisserie, plus Mrs. Field's Cookies and Haagen Daz ice cream outlets). **Sam Goody's,** whose 15,000 square feet make it the world's largest enclosed music store, features a glass-walled, and spectacular, view of Hollywood. A uniquely L.A. shop here is the **Warner Bros. Studio Store.** Popular with both adults and kids, it's crammed with movie and cartoon memorabilia and apparel.

West Hollywood is the center of Los Angeles's thriving interior decorating business. **The Pacific Design Center** (8687 Melrose Ave., tel. 310/657–0800) is known to residents as the "Blue Whale." The blue-glass building, designed by Cesar Pelli in 1975, houses to-the-trade-only showrooms filled with the most tempting furnishings, wall coverings, and accessories. In 1988 the center added a second building by Pelli, this one clad in green glass. The building is open to the public (Mon.–Fri. 9–5), who are allowed to browse in many of the more than 200 showrooms. Purchases, however, can be made only through design professionals. A referral system is available. The **Murray Feldman Gallery,** featuring various art, design, and cultural exhibitions, sits on the adjacent 2-acre landscaped public plaza (open Tues.–Sat. noon–6).

Along the "Robertson Boulevard," the area that surrounds the Blue Whale, are more to-the-trade showrooms. These are not confined to Robertson Boulevard and are well represented along Beverly Boulevard and Melrose Avenue. This area is exceptionally walkable, and residents often walk their dogs here in the evening (even driving them here to then do their walking) so they can browse the well-lit windows. A few of the showrooms will accommodate an occasional retail buyer, so if you see something to die for, it's worth an inquiry inside.

❹ Sunset Strip was famous in the '50s, as in "77 Sunset Strip," but it was popular as far back as the 1930s, when nightclubs like Ciro's and Mocambo were in their heyday, and movie stars frequented the Strip as an after-work gathering spot. This winding, hilly stretch is a visual delight, enjoyed both by car (a convertible would be perfect) or on foot. Drive it once to enjoy the hustle-bustle, the vanity boards (huge billboards touting new movies, new records, new stars), and the dazzling shops. Then pick a section and explore a few blocks on foot. The Sunset Plaza section is especially nice for walking. The stretch is a cluster of expensive shops, and outdoor cafés (Tutto Italia, Chin Chin) that are packed for lunch and on warm evenings. At Horn Street, **Tower Records** (a behemoth of a CD store with two satellite shops across the street), **Book Soup** (L.A.'s literary bookstore), and Wolfgang Puck's famous restaurant **Spago** (a half block up the hill on Horn) make satisfying browsing, especially in the evening.

Beverly Hills The glitz of Sunset Strip ends abruptly at Doheny Drive, where Sunset Boulevard enters the world-famous and glamorous city of Beverly Hills. Suddenly the sidewalk street life gives way to expansive, perfectly manicured lawns and palatial homes.

❺ West of the Strip a mile or so is the **Beverly Hills Hotel** (9641 Sunset Blvd.), whose Spanish Colonial Revival architecture and soft pastel exterior have earned it the name "the Pink Palace." The venerable hotel is closed for extensive renovations (through early 1995), but you can still look at the outside.

It is on this stretch of Sunset, especially during the daytime, that you'll see hawkers peddling maps to stars' homes. Are the maps reliable? Well, that's a matter of debate. Stars do move around, so it's difficult to keep any map up to date. But the fun is in looking at some of these magnificent homes, regardless of whether or not they're owned by a star at the moment.

Beverly Hills was incorporated as a city early in the century and has been thriving ever since. As a vibrant city within the larger city, it has retained and enhanced its reputation for wealth and luxury, an assessment with which you will surely agree as you drive along any of its main thoroughfares; Sunset or Wilshire boulevards, or Santa Monica Boulevard (which is actually two parallel streets at this point: "Big Santa Monica" is the northern one; "Little Santa Monica," the southern).

Within a few square blocks in the center of the Beverly Hills are some of the most exotic, to say nothing of high-priced, stores in southern California. Here you can find such items as a $200 pair of socks wrapped in gold leaf, and stores that take customers only by appointment. A fun way to spend an afternoon is to stroll famed **Rodeo Drive** between Santa Monica and Wilshire boulevards. Some of the Rodeo (pronounced ro-DAY-o) shops may be familiar to you since they supply clothing for major network television shows and their names often appear among the credits. Others, such as Gucci, have a worldwide reputation. Fortunately, browsing is free (and fun), no matter how expensive the store is. Several nearby restaurants have outside patios where you can sit and sip a drink while watching the fashionable shoppers stroll by.

7 The **Regent Beverly Wilshire Hotel** (9500 Wilshire Blvd., tel. 310/275–5200) anchors the south end of Rodeo Drive, at Wilshire. Opened in 1928, and vigorously expanded and renovated since, the hotel is often home to visiting royalty and celebrities; it's where the millionaire businessman played by Richard Gere ensconced himself with the hooker played by Julia Roberts in the movie *Pretty Woman.* The lobby is quite small for a hotel of this size and offers little opportunity to meander; you might stop for a drink or meal in one of the hotel's restaurants.

8 The **Greystone Mansion** was built by oilman Edward Doheny in 1927. This Tudor-style mansion, now owned by the city of Beverly Hills, sits on 18½ landscaped acres and has been used in such films as *The Witches of Eastwick* and *All of Me.* The gardens are open for self-guided tours and peeking (only) through the windows is permitted. Picnics are permitted in specified areas during hours of operation. *905 Loma Vista Dr., tel. 310/550–4796. Admission free. Open daily 10–5.*

Westwood Westward from Beverly Hills, Sunset continues to wind past
9 palatial estates and passes by the **University of California at Los Angeles.** Nestled in the Westwood section of the city and bound by LeConte Street, Sunset Boulevard, and Hilgard Avenue, the parklike UCLA campus is an inviting place for visitors to stroll. The most spectacular buildings are the original ones, Royce Hall and the library, both in Romanesque style. In the heart of the north campus is the Franklin Murphy Sculpture Garden, with works by Henry Moore and Gaston Lachaise dotting the landscaping. For a gardening buff, UCLA is a treasure of unusual and well-labeled plants. The Mildred Mathias Botanic Garden is located in the southeast section of campus and is accessible from Tiverton Avenue. Sports fans will enjoy the Morgan Center Hall of Fame (west of Campus book store), where memorabilia and trophies of the athletic departments are on display. Maps and information are available at drive-by kiosks at major entrances, even on weekends, and free 90-minute, guided walking tours of the campus are offered on weekdays. The campus has several indoor and outdoor cafés, plus bookstores that sell the very popular UCLA Bruins paraphernalia. *Tours (tel. 310/206–8147) weekdays at 10:30 AM and 1:30 PM. Call for reservations. Meet at 10945 LeConte St., room 1417, on the south edge of the campus, facing Westwood.*

Directly south of the campus is Westwood, once a quiet college town and now one of the busiest places in the city on weekend evenings—so busy that during the summer, many streets are closed to car traffic and visitors must park at the Federal Building (Wilshire and Veteran) and shuttle over. However you arrive, Westwood remains a delightful village filled with clever boutiques, trendy restaurants, movie theaters, and colorful street life.

10 **Armand Hammer Museum of Art and Cultural Center** is one of the city's newest museums. Although small compared to other museums in Los Angeles, the permanent collection here includes thousands of works by Honoré Daumier, and a rare portfolio of Leonardo Da Vinci's technical drawings. However, the Hammer regularly features special blockbuster displays that cannot be seen elsewhere such as the 1992 exhibit "Catherine the Great: Treasures of Imperial Russia." *10899 Wilshire Blvd., tel. 310/443–7000. Admission: $4.50 adults, $3 students and senior citizens, free to 17 and under. Open Tues.–Sun. 10–6 (extended hrs during special exhibitions).*

The Westwood stretch of Wilshire Boulevard is a corridor of cheek-by-jowl office buildings whose varying architectural styles can be jarring, to say the least. Tucked behind one of these behemoths is **Westwood Memorial Park** (1218 Glendon Ave.). In this very unlikely place for a cemetery is one of the most famous graves in the city. Marilyn Monroe is buried in a simply marked wall crypt. For 25 years after her death, her former husband Joe DiMaggio had six red roses placed on her crypt three times a week. Also buried here is Natalie Wood.

Tour 5: Santa Monica, Venice, Pacific Palisades, Malibu

Numbers in the margin correspond to points of interest on the Tour 5: Santa Monica and Venice map.

The towns that hug the coastline of Santa Monica Bay reflect the wide diversity of Los Angeles, from the rich-as-can-be Malibu to the cheek-by-jowl Yuppie/seedy mix of Venice. The emphasis is on being out in the sunshine, always within sight of the Pacific. You would do well to visit the area in two excursions: Santa Monica to Venice in one day and Pacific Palisades to Malibu in another.

Santa Monica   Santa Monica is a sensible place. It's a tidy little city, 2 miles square, whose ethnic population is largely British (there's an English music hall and several pubs here), attracted perhaps by the cool and foggy climate. The sense of order is reflected in the economic/geographic stratification: The most northern section has broad streets lined with superb, older homes. As you drive south, real estate prices drop $50,000 or so every block or two. The middle class lives in the middle and the working class, to the south, along the Venice border.

1 Begin exploring at **Santa Monica Pier,** located at the foot of Colorado Avenue and easily accessible for beach-goers as well as drive-around visitors. Cafés, gift shops, a psychic advisor, bumper cars, and arcades line the truncated pier, which was severely damaged in a storm a few years ago. The 46-horse carousel, built in 1922, has seen action in many movie and television shows, most notably the Paul Newman/Robert Redford film *The Sting. Tel. 310/394–7554. Rides: 50¢ adults, 25¢ children. Carousel open in summer, Tues.–Sun. 10–9; in winter, weekends 10–5.*

2 **Palisades Park** is a ribbon of green that runs along the top of the cliffs from Colorado Avenue to just north of San Vicente Boulevard. The flat walkways are usually filled with casual strollers as well as joggers who like to work out with a spec-

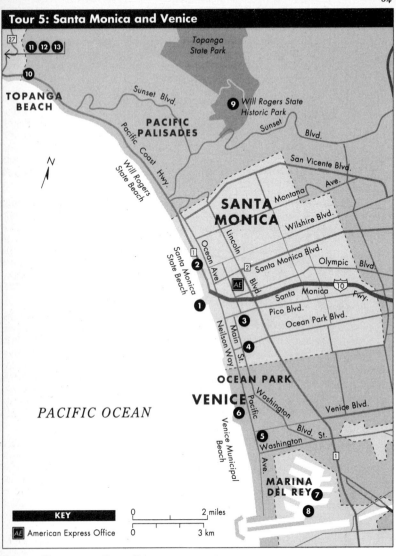

Tour 5: Santa Monica and Venice

Map labels:

Topanga State Park

TOPANGA BEACH

Sunset Blvd.

PACIFIC PALISADES

Pacific Coast Hwy.

Will Rogers State Beach

Will Rogers State Historic Park

Sunset Blvd.

San Vicente Blvd.

Montana Ave.

SANTA MONICA

Wilshire Blvd.

Lincoln

Ocean Ave.

Santa Monica Blvd.

Olympic Blvd.

Santa Monica State Beach

Santa Monica Fwy.

Pico Blvd.

Ocean Park Blvd.

Neilson Way

Main St.

OCEAN PARK

VENICE

Washington

Pacific

Venice Blvd.

Blvd. St.

Washington

PACIFIC OCEAN

Venice Municipal Beach

Ave.

MARINA DEL REY

KEY

AE American Express Office

0 — 2 miles
0 — 3 km

Adamson House, **11**

Burton Chase Park, **7**

Canals, **5**

Fisherman's Village, **8**

J. Paul Getty Museum, **10**

Malibu Lagoon State Park, **12**

Palisades Park, **2**

Pepperdine University, **13**

Santa Monica Heritage Museum, **4**

Santa Monica Museum of Art, **3**

Santa Monica Pier, **1**

Venice Boardwalk, **6**

Will Rogers State Historic Park, **9**

tacular view of the Pacific as company. It is especially enjoyable at sunset.

The **Santa Monica Visitor Information Center,** located in the park at Santa Monica Boulevard, offers bus schedules, directions, and information on Santa Monica–area attractions. *Tel. 310/393–7593. Open daily 10–4.*

❸ Santa Monica has grown into a major center for the L.A. art community, and the **Santa Monica Museum of Art** is poised to boost that reputation. Designed by local architect Frank Gehry, the museum presents the works of performance and video artists and exhibits works of lesser-known painters and sculptors. *2437 Main St., tel. 310/399–0433. Admission: $3 adults, $1 artists, students, and senior citizens. Open Wed. and Thur. 11–6, Fri.–Sat. 11–10, Sun. 11–6.*

❹ The **Santa Monica Heritage Museum,** housed in an 1894-vintage, late-Victorian home once owned by the founder of the city, was moved to its present site on trendy Main Street in the mid-1980s. Three rooms have been fully restored: the dining room in the style of 1890 to 1910; the living room, 1910–1920; and the kitchen, 1920–1930. The second-floor galleries feature photography and historical exhibits as well as shows by contemporary Santa Monica artists. *2612 Main St., tel. 310/392–8537. Admission: $2. Open Wed.–Sat. 11–4, Sun. noon–4.*

The museum faces a companion home, another Victorian delight moved to the site that is now **Monica's** restaurant. These two dowagers anchor the northwest corner of the funky **Main Street area** of Santa Monica. Several blocks of old brick buildings here have undergone a recent rejuvenation (and considerable rent increases) and now house galleries, bars, cafés, omelet parlors, and boutiques. With its proximity to the beach, parking can be tight on summer weekends. Best bets are the city pay lots behind the Main Street shops, between Main and Neilsen Way.

Venice Venice was a turn-of-the-century fantasy that never quite came true. Abbot Kinney, a wealthy Los Angeles businessman, envisioned this little piece of real estate, which then seemed so far from downtown, as a romantic replica of Venice, Italy. He developed an incredible 16 miles of canals, floated gondolas on them, and built scaled-down versions of the Saint Marks Palace and other Venetian landmarks. The name remains but the connection with the Old World Venice is as flimsy as ever. Kinney's project was plagued by ongoing engineering problems and dis-
❺ asters and drifted into disrepair. Three small **canals** and bridges remain and can be viewed from the southeast corner of Pacific Avenue and Venice Boulevard. But long-gone are the amusement park, swank seaside hotels, and the gondoliers. By the late 1960s, however, actors, artists, musicians, and hippies, and anyone who wanted to live near the beach but couldn't afford to, were attracted by the low rents in Venice, and the place quickly became SoHo-by-the-Sea. The trade-off was that the area was pretty run-down, and the remaining canals were stagnant and fairly smelly, but as the area's appeal grew, and a more upscale crowd started moving in, these drawbacks were rectified. Venice's locals today are a grudgingly thrown-together mix of aging hippies, Yuppies with the disposable income to spend on inflated rents, senior citizens who have lived here for decades, and the homeless.

6 Venice has the liveliest waterfront walkway in Los Angeles, known as both Ocean Front Walk and the **Venice Boardwalk.** It begins at Washington Street and runs north. Save this visit for a weekend. There is plenty of action year-round: bicyclists, bikini-clad rollerskaters gather crowds as they put on impromptu demonstrations, vying for attention with the unusual breeds of dogs that locals love to prance along the walkway. A local body-building club works out on the adjacent beach, and it's nearly impossible not to stop to ogle at the pecs as these strong men lift weights.

At the south end of the boardwalk, along Washington Street, near the Venice Pier, in-line skates, roller skates, and bicycles (some with baby seats) are available for rent.

Time Out The boardwalk is lined with fast-food stands, and food can then be brought a few feet away to be enjoyed as a beachy picnic. But for a somewhat more relaxing meal, stand in line for a table at **Sidewalk Cafe** (1401 Ocean Front Walk, tel. 310/399–5547). Wait for a patio table, where you can watch the free spirits on parade.

Marina del Rey Just south of Venice is a quick shift of the time frame. Forget about Venice—Italy or California—Marina del Rey is a modern and more successful, if less romantic, dream. It is the largest man-made boat harbor in the world, with a commercial area catering to the whims of boat owners and boat groupies. The stretch between Admiralty Way and Mindinao Way has some of the area's best restaurants. Expensive but worth it. Most of the better hotel chains, such as the Ritz-Carlton, also have properties here.

7 For boatless visitors, the best place from which to view the marina is **Burton Chase Park,** at the end of Mindinao Way. Situated at the tip of a jetty and surrounded on three sides by water and moored boats, this small, six-acre patch of green offers a cool and breezy spot from which to watch boats move in and out of the channel, and it's great for picnicking.

8 **Fisherman's Village** is a collection of cute Cape Cod clapboards housing shops and restaurants (open daily 8 AM–9 PM). It's not much of a draw unless you include a meal or a snack or take one of the 45-minute marina cruises offered by **Hornblower Dining Outs** that depart from the village dock. *13755 Fiji Way, tel. 310/301–6000. Tickets: $7 adults, $4 senior citizens and children. Cruises leave every hr, weekdays 12–3, weekends 11–5.*

Pacific Palisades From Santa Monica, head north on Pacific Coast Highway toward Malibu, a pleasant drive in daytime or evening. The narrow-but-expensive beachfront houses were home to movie stars in the 1930s.

9 Spend a few hours at **Will Rogers State Historic Park** in Pacific Palisades and you may understand what endeared America to this cowboy/humorist in the 1920s and 1930s. The two-story ranch house on Rogers's 187-acre estate is a folksy blend of Navajo rugs and Mission-style furniture. Rogers's only extravagance was raising the roof several feet (he waited till his wife was in Europe to do it) to accommodate his penchant for practicing his lasso technique indoors. The nearby museum features Rogers memorabilia. Short films show his roping technique and his homey words of wisdom. Rogers was a polo enthusiast, and in the 1930s, his front-yard polo field attracted such friends as Douglas Fairbanks for weekend games. The tradition continues, with free games scheduled when the weather's good. The park's broad lawns are excellent for picnicking, and there's hiking on miles of eucalyptus-lined trails. Those who make it to the top will be rewarded with a panoramic view of the mountains and ocean. Neighborhood riders house their horses at the stable up the hill and are usually agreeable to some friendly chatter (no rental horses, alas). *14253 Sunset Blvd., Pacific Palisades, tel. 310/454–8212. Admission free; parking $5. Call for polo schedule.*

Malibu You'll want to plan in advance to visit the **J. Paul Getty Museum,**
⑩ which contains one of the country's finest collections of Greek and Roman antiquities. The oil millionaire began collecting art in the 1930s, concentrating on three distinct areas: Greek and Roman antiquities, Baroque and Renaissance paintings, and 18th-century decorative arts. In 1946 he purchased a large Spanish-style home on 65 acres in a canyon just north of Santa Monica to house the collection. By the late 1960s, the museum could no longer accommodate the rapidly expanding collection and Getty decided to build this new building, which was completed in 1974. It's a re-creation of the Villa dei Papiri, a luxurious 1st-century Roman villa that stood on the slopes of Mount Vesuvius overlooking the Bay of Naples, prior to the volcano's eruption in AD 79. The villa is thought to have once belonged to Lucius Calpurnius Piso, the father-in-law of Julius Caesar. The two-level, 38-gallery building and its extensive gardens (which includes trees, flowers, shrubs, and herbs that might have grown 2,000 years ago at the villa) provide an appropriate and harmonious setting for Getty's classical antiquities.

The main level houses sculpture, mosaics, and vases. Of particular interest are the 4th-century Attic stelae (funerary monuments) and Greek and Roman portraits. The decorative arts collection on the upper level features furniture, carpets, tapestries, clocks, chandeliers, and small decorative items made for the French, German, and Italian nobility, with a wealth of royal French treasures (Louis XIV to Napoleon). Richly colored brocaded walls set off the paintings and furniture to great advantage. All major schools of Western art from the late 13th century to the late 19th century are represented in the painting collection, which emphasizes Renaissance and Baroque art and includes works by Rembrandt, Rubens, de la Tour, Van Dyck, Gainsborough, and Boucher. Recent acquisitions include Old Master drawings, and medieval and Renaissance illuminated manuscripts, works by Picasso, Van Gogh's *Irises,* and a select collection of Impressionist paintings including some by Claude Monet. The only catch in visiting this museum is that parking reservations are necessary—there's no way to visit it without using the parking lot unless you are dropped off or take a tour bus—and they should be made one week in advance by telephoning or writing to the museum's Reservations Office. *17985 Pacific Coast Hwy., tel. 310/458–2003. Admission free. Open Tues.–Sun. 10–5.*

⑪ **Adamson House** is the former home of the Rindge family, which owned much of the Malibu Rancho in the early part of the 20th century. Malibu was quite isolated then, with all visitors and supplies arriving by boat at the nearby Malibu Pier (and it can still be isolated these days when rock slides close the highway).

The Moorish-Spanish home, built in 1928, has been opened to the public and may be the only chance most visitors get to be inside a grand Malibu home. The Rindges led an enviable Malibu lifestyle, decades before it was trendy. The house is right on the beach (high chain-link fences keep out curious beach-goers). The family owned the famous Malibu Tile Company and their home is predictably encrusted with some of the most magnificent tilework in rich blues, greens, yellows, and oranges. Even an outside dog shower, near the servants' door, is a tiled delight. Docent-led tours help visitors to envision family life here as well as to learn about the history of Malibu and its real estate (you can't have one without the other). *23200 Pacific Coast Hwy., tel. 310/456–8432. Admission: $2 adults, $1 children. Open Wed.–Sun. 11–3.*

⑫ Adjacent to Adamson House is **Malibu Lagoon State Park** (23200 Pacific Coast Hwy.), a haven for native and migratory birds. Visitors must stay on the boardwalks so that the egrets, blue herons, avocets, and gulls can enjoy the marshy area. The signs that give opening and closing hours refer only to the parking lot; the lagoon itself is open 24 hours and is particularly enjoyable in the early morning and at sunset. Luckily, streetside parking is available then (but not midday).

⑬ **Pepperdine University** (24255 Pacific Coast Hwy.) looks exactly like a California school should. Designed by William Pereira, this picture-perfect campus is set on a bluff above the Pacific. The school's fine athletic facilities have been used for those televised "Battle of the Network Stars" workouts. On a loftier note: A new art center houses an authentic Japanese teahouse where students can learn the correct protocol of the ritual tea ceremony that is so important for those who do business in the Orient.

Tour 6: Palos Verdes, San Pedro, and Long Beach

Numbers in the margin correspond to points of interest on the Tour 6: Palos Verdes, San Pedro, and Long Beach map.

Few local residents take advantage of Long Beach's attractions. If they ever took a day to see the *Queen Mary* when their in-laws visited from back east, they were duly astounded to discover Long Beach's impressive skyline, the string of hotels along Ocean Boulevard, the revitalized downtown area, and the city's close proximity to the rest of L.A. and Orange County. How could this entire city, the fifth largest in the state, have been right here and they never really knew about it?

If it's still operating as a visitable attraction, allow a generous half day or more to explore the *Queen Mary.* Plump up the itinerary with a glorious drive through Palos Verdes and a few short stops at local historic sites and parks.

Palos Verdes Palos Verdes Peninsula is a hilly haven for horse lovers and other gentrified folks, many of them executive transplants from east of the Mississippi. The real estate in these small peninsula towns, ranging from expensive to very expensive, are zoned for stables and you'll often see riders along the streets (they have the right of way).

❶ South Coast Botanic Gardens began life ignominiously—as a garbage dump–cum–landfill. It's hard to believe that as recently as 1960, truckloads of waste (3.5 million tons) were being deposited here. With the intensive ministerings of the experts from the L.A. County Arboreta department, the dump soon boasted lush gardens with plants from every continent except Antarctica. The gardens are undergoing an ambitious five-year reorganization at the end of which all the plants will be organized into color groups. Self-guided walking tours take visitors past flower and herb gardens, rare cacti, and a lake with ducks. Picnicking is limited to a lawn area outside the gates. *26300 S. Crenshaw Blvd., Rancho Palos Verdes, tel. 310/544–6815. Admission: $3 adults, $1.50 children and senior citizens. Open daily 9–4:30.*

The drive on Palos Verdes Drive around the water's edge takes you high above the cliffs. An aerial shot of this area was used in the opening of television's "Knots Landing."

❷ Wayfarers Chapel (5755 Palos Verdes Dr. S, Rancho Palos Verdes, tel. 310/377–1650) was designed by architect Lloyd Wright, son of Frank Lloyd Wright, in 1949. He planned this modern glass church to blend in with an encircling redwood forest. The redwoods are gone (they couldn't stand the rigors of urban encroachment), but another forest has taken their place, and the breathtaking combination of ocean, trees, and structure remains. This "natural church" is a popular wedding site.

San Pedro San Pedro shares the peninsula with the Palos Verdes towns, but little else. Here, the cliffs give way to a hospitable harbor. The 1950s-vintage executive homes give way to tidy 1920s-era white clapboards, and horses give way to boats. San Pedro (locals steadfastly ignore the correct Spanish pronunciation—it's "San Peedro" to them) is an old seaport community with a strong Mediterranean and Eastern European flavor. There are enticing Greek and Yugoslavian markets and restaurants throughout the town.

❸ Cabrillo Marine Museum is a gem of a small museum dedicated to the marine life that flourishes off the Southern California coast. Recently installed in its new home in a modern Frank Gehry–designed building right on the beach, the museum is popular with school groups because its exhibits are especially instructive as well as fun. The 35 saltwater aquariums include a shark tank, and a see-through tidal tank gives visitors a chance to see the long view of a wave. On the back patio, docents supervise as visitors reach into a shallow tank to touch starfish and sea anemones. *3720 Stephen White Dr., tel. 310/548–7546. Parking $5.50. Admission free. Open Tues.–Fri. noon–5, weekends 10–5.*

If you're lucky enough to visit at low tide, take time to explore the tide pool on nearby Cabrillo Beach (museum staff can direct you).

❹ Ports O' Call Village is a commercial rendition of a New England shipping village, an older version of Fisherman's Village in Marina del Rey, with shops, restaurants, and fast-food windows. Two companies run 1- to 1½-hour harbor cruises ($10

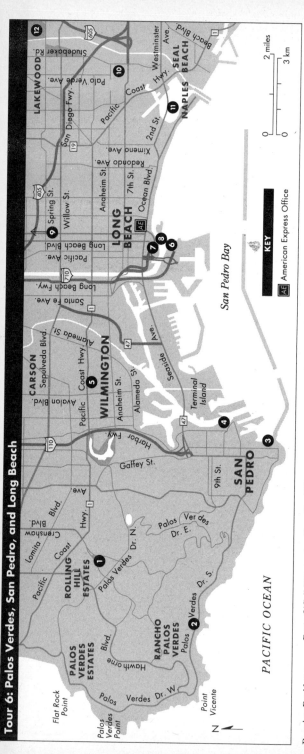

Tour 6: Palos Verdes, San Pedro, and Long Beach

60

PACIFIC OCEAN

Flat Rock Point

Point Vicente

Palos Verdes Point

PALOS VERDES ESTATES

ROLLING HILLS ESTATES

RANCHO PALOS VERDES

CARSON

WILMINGTON

SAN PEDRO

LAKEWOOD

LONG BEACH

SEAL BEACH

NAPLES

San Pedro Bay

Terminal Island

Banning Residence Museum and Park, **5**
Cabrillo Marine Museum, **3**
El Dorado Regional Park, **12**
Naples, **11**

Ports O'Call Village, **4**
Queen Mary, **6**
Rancho Los Alamitos, **10**
Rancho Los Cerritos, **9**
Shoreline Aquatic Park, **8**

Shoreline Village, **7**
South Coast Botanic Garden, **1**
Wayfarers Chapel, **2**

KEY

AE American Express Office

0   2 miles

0   3 km

adults, $5 children) and whale-watching cruises, January–April ($12–$15 adults, $5–$8 children). Cruises depart from the village dock; call 310/547–9977 for schedules.

Wilmington In order to preserve transportation and shipping interests for the city of Los Angeles, Wilmington was annexed in the late 19th century. A narrow strip of land, mostly less than a ½ mile wide, it follows the Harbor Freeway from downtown south to the port. **Banning Residence Museum and Park** is a pleasant, low-keyed stop here. General Phineas Banning, an early entrepreneur in Los Angeles, is credited with developing the harbor into a viable economic entity and naming the area Wilmington (he was from Delaware). Part of his estate has been preserved in a 20-acre park that offers excellent picnicking possibilities. A 100-year-old wisteria, near the arbor, blooms in the spring. The interior of the house can be seen on docent-led tours. *401 E. M St., Wilmington, tel. 310/548–7777. Admission to house: $2. House tours Tues.–Thur. 12:30–2:30, Sat. and Sun. 12:30–3:30, on ½ hr.*

Long Beach Long Beach began as a seaside resort in the 19th century and during the early part of the 20th century was a popular destination for Midwesterners and Dust Bowlers in search of a better life. They built street after street of modest wood homes.

6 The first glimpse of the *Queen Mary,* the largest passenger ship ever built, as she sits so smugly in Long Beach Harbor is disarming. What seemed like sure folly when Long Beach officials bought her in 1964 put the city on the proverbial map. She stands permanently moored at Pier J. The 50,000-ton *Queen Mary* was launched in 1934, a floating treasure of Art Deco splendor. It took a crew of 1,100 to minister to the needs of 1,900 demanding passengers. This most luxurious of luxury liners is completely intact, from the extensive wood paneling to the gleaming nickel- and silver-plated handrails and the hand-cut glass. Tours through the ship are available, and guests are invited to browse the 12 decks and witness close-up the bridge, staterooms, officers' quarters, and engine rooms. There are several restaurants and shops on board. *Pier J, tel. 310/435–3511. Admission free. Guided 45-min. tour ($5 adults, $3 children 3–11) daily 10–4.*

7 **Shoreline Village** is the most successful of the pseudo–New England harbors here. Its setting, between the downtown Long Beach and the *Queen Mary,* is reason enough to stroll here, day or evening (when visitors can enjoy the lights of the ship twinkling in the distance). In addition to gift shops and restaurants there's a 1906 carousel with bobbing giraffes, camels, and horses. *Corner of Shoreline Dr. and Pine Ave., tel. 310/590–8427. Rides: $1. The carousel is open daily 10–10 in summer, 10–9 the rest of the year.*

8 **Shoreline Aquatic Park** (205 Marina Dr.) is literally set in the middle of Long Beach Harbor and is a much-sought-after resting place for RVers. Kite-flyers also love it, because the winds are wonderful here. Casual passersby can enjoy a short walk, where the modern skyline, the quaint Shoreline Village, the *Queen Mary,* and the ocean all vie for attention. The park's lagoon is off-limits for swimming, but aquacycles and kayaks can be rented during the summer months. Contact **Long Beach Water Sports** (730 E. 4th St., tel. 310/432–0187) for information on sea kayaking lessons, rentals, and outings.

❾ **Rancho Los Cerritos** is a charming Monterey-style adobe built by the Don Juan Temple family in 1844. Monterey-style homes can be easily recognized by two features: They are always two-storied and have a narrow balcony across the front. Seen from the outside, it's easy to imagine Zorro, that swashbuckling fictional hero of the rancho era, jumping from the balcony onto a waiting horse and making his escape. The 10 rooms have been furnished in the style of the period and are open for viewing. But don't expect an Old California–style Southwest fantasy with primitive Mexican furniture, and cactus in the garden. The Temple family shared the prevalent taste of the period, in which the American East Coast and Europe still set the style, emphasizing fancy, dark woods and frou-frou Victorian bric-a-brac. The gardens here were designed in the 1930s by well-known landscape architect Ralph Cornell and have been recently restored. *4600 Virginia Rd., tel. 310/424–9423. Admission free. Open Wed.–Sun. 1–5. Self-guided tours on weekdays. Free 50-min guided tours on weekends hourly 1–4.*

❿ **Rancho Los Alamitos** is said to be the oldest one-story domestic building still standing in the county. It was built in 1806 when the Spanish flag still flew over California. There's a blacksmith shop in the barn. *6400 E. Bixby Hill Rd., tel. 310/431–3541. Admission free. Open Wed.–Sun. 1–5. 90–min. Free tours leave every ½ hr until 4.*

⓫ The **Naples** section of Long Beach is known for its pleasant and well-maintained canals. Canals in *Naples*, you ask? Yes, this is a misnomer. But better misnamed and successful than aptly named and a bust. The developer who came up with the Naples canal idea learned from the mistakes and bad luck that did in Venice, just up the coast, and built the canals to take full advantage of the tidal flow that would keep them clean. Naples is actually three small islands in man-made Alamitos Bay. It is best experienced on foot. Park near Bayshore Drive and Second Street and walk across the bridge, where you can begin meandering the quaint streets with very Italian names. This well-restored neighborhood boasts eclectic architecture—vintage Victorians, Craftsman bungalows, and Mission Revivals. You may spy a real gondola or two on the canals. You can hire them for a ride but not on the spur of the moment. **Gondola Getaway** offers one-hour rides, usually touted for romantic couples, although the gondolas can accommodate up to four people. *5437 E. Ocean Blvd., tel. 310/433–9595. Rides: $50 a couple, $10 for each additional person. Reservations essential, at least 1 to 2 wks. in advance. Open 11 AM–midnight.*

⓬ **El Dorado Regional Park** (7550 E. Spring St.) played host to the 1984 Olympic Games archery competition and remains popular with local archery enthusiasts. Most visitors, however, come to this huge, 800-acre park for the broad, shady lawns, walking trails, and the lakes. Several small lakes are picturesquely set among cottonwoods and pine trees. This is a wonderful picnicking spot. Fishing is permitted in all the lakes (stocked with catfish, carp, and trout), but the northernmost one is favored by local anglers. Pedal boats are available by the hour (one hour of pedaling is plenty for most people). The Nature Center is a bird and native plant sanctuary.

Tour 7: Highland Park, Pasadena, and San Marino

Numbers in the margin correspond to points of interest on the Tour 7: Highland Park, Pasadena, San Marino map.

The suburbs north of downtown Los Angeles have much of the richest architectural heritage in Southern California as well as several fine museums. To take advantage of the afternoon-only hours of several sites, the Highland part of this tour is best scheduled in the afternoon. Pasadena could take a full day; more if you want to savor the museums' collections.

To reach this area, drive north on the Pasadena Freeway (110), which follows the curves of the arroyo (creek bed) that leads north from downtown. It was the main road during the early days of Los Angeles where horses-and-buggies made their way through the chaparral-covered countryside to the small town of Pasadena. In 1942, the road became the Arroyo Seco Parkway, the first freeway in Los Angeles, later renamed the Pasadena Freeway. It remains a pleasant drive in nonrush-hour traffic, with the freeway lined with old sycamores and winding up the arroyo like a New York parkway.

Highland Park Midway between downtown Los Angeles and Pasadena, Highland Park was a genteel suburb in the late 1800s, where the Anglo population tried to keep an Eastern feeling alive in their architecture in spite of the decidedly Southwest landscape. The streets on both sides of the freeway are filled with faded beauties, classic old clapboards that have gone into decline in the past half century.

❶ Heritage Square is the ambitious attempt by the Los Angeles Cultural Heritage Board to save from the wrecking ball some of the city's architectural gems of the 1865–1914 period. During the past 20 years four residences, a depot, a church, and a carriage barn have been moved to this small park from all over the city. The most breathtaking building here is **Hale House,** built in 1885. The almost-garish colors of both the interior and exterior are not the whim of some aging hippie painter, but rather a faithful re-creation of the palette that was actually in fashion in the late 1800s. The **Palms Depot,** built in 1886, was moved to the site from the Westside of L.A. The night the building was moved, down city streets and up freeways, is documented in photomurals on the depot's walls. *3800 Homer St., off Ave. 43 exit, tel. 818/449–0193. Admission: $5 adults, $3 children 12–17 and senior citizens. Open Fri., Sat, Sun., most holidays noon–4 PM. Tours every 45 minutes or so.*

❷ El Alisal was the home of eccentric Easterner-turned-Westerner-with-a-vengeance Charles Lummis. This Harvard graduate was captivated by Indian culture (he founded the Southwest Museum), often living the lifestyle of the natives, much to the shock of the staid Angelenos of the time. His home, built from 1898 to 1910, is constructed of boulders from the arroyo itself, a romantic notion until recent earthquakes made the safety of such homes questionable. The Art Nouveau fireplace was designed by Gutzon Borglum, the sculptor of Mount

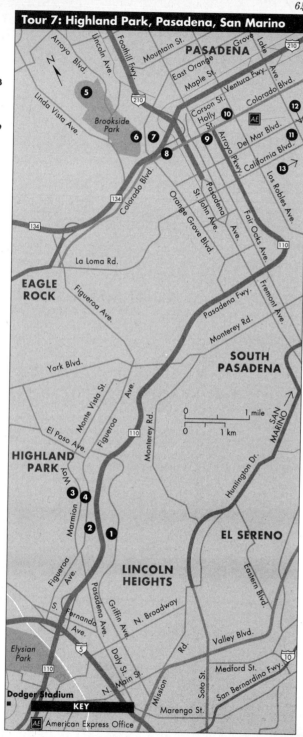

Tour 7: Highland Park, Pasadena, San Marino

PASADENA

Mountain St.

East Orange Grove

Maple St.

Foothill Fwy.

Lincoln Ave.

Arroyo Blvd.

Linda Vista Ave.

Brookside Park

Ventura Fwy.

Colorado Blvd.

Corson St.

Holly St.

Del Mar Blvd.

California Blvd.

Arroyo Pkwy.

Pasadena Ave.

St. John Ave.

Orange Grove Blvd.

Fair Oaks Ave.

Fremont Ave.

Los Robles Ave.

La Loma Rd.

EAGLE ROCK

Figueroa Ave.

Pasadena Fwy.

Monterey Rd.

SOUTH PASADENA

York Blvd.

Monte Vista St.

Figueroa Ave.

El Paso Ave.

HIGHLAND PARK

Marmion Way

SAN MARINO

Huntington Dr.

Monterey Rd.

0   1 mile

0   1 km

LINCOLN HEIGHTS

Figueroa Ave.

S. Fernando Ave.

Pasadena Ave.

Griffin Ave.

N. Broadway

Daly St.

N. Main St.

Mission Rd.

EL SERENO

Eastern Blvd.

Valley Blvd.

Medford St.

San Bernardino Fwy.

Soto St.

Marengo St.

Elysian Park

Dodger Stadium

KEY

AE American Express Office

Rushmore. *200 E. Ave. 43 (entrance on Carlota Blvd.) tel. 213/222–0546. Admission free. Open weekends 1–4.*

③ The Southwest Museum is the huge Mission Revival building that stands halfway up Mount Washington and can be seen from the freeway. It contains an extensive collection of Native American art and artifacts, with special emphasis on the people of the Plains, Northwest Coast, Southwest U.S., and Northern Mexico. The basket collection is outstanding. *234 Museum Dr., off Ave. 43 exit, tel. 213/221–2163. Admission: $5 adults, $3 senior citizens and students, $2 children 7–18, free to those 6 and under. Open Tues.–Sun. 11–5.*

④ Casa de Adobe, a satellite of the Southwest Museum, is located directly below it at the bottom of the hill. What appears to be the well-preserved, authentically furnished hacienda of an Old California don is actually a 1917 re-creation of a 19th-century rancho. The central courtyard plan is characteristic of the style. *4605 Figueroa St., tel. 213/221–2163. Admission free. Open Tues.–Sun. 11–5.*

Time Out   Just blocks down the street in either direction from the Southwest Museum you'll discover authentic Mexican food that is downright cheap. The first, **Senior Fish** (5111 Figueroa St., tel. 213/257–2498), looks like a taco stand—but don't pass it up. Its intriguing selections include octopus tostada, scallop burritos, and refreshing ceviche. A few minutes' walk in the other direction, you'll come across **La Abeja** (3700 Figueroa St., tel. 213/221–0474), a Mexican cafe that's been around for two dozen years. The word inexpensive takes on new meaning at this hangout, known for its salsas and steak picado.

Pasadena   Although now fully absorbed into the general Los Angeles sprawl, Pasadena was once a separate and distinctly defined, and refined, city. Its varied architecture, augmented by lush landscaping, is the most spectacular in Southern California. With only a few hours to spend, visitors should consider at least driving past the Gamble House, through Old Town, and then on to the grand old neighborhood of the Huntington Library, spending most of their time there.

⑤ The Rose Bowl (991 Rosemont Ave.) is set at the bottom of a wide area of the arroyo in an older wealthy neighborhood that must endure the periodic onslaught of thousands of cars and party-minded football fans. The stadium is closed except for games and special events such as the monthly Rose Bowl Swap Meet. Held the second Sunday of the month, it is considered the granddaddy of West Coast swap meets.

⑥ Gamble House, built by Charles and Henry Greene in 1908, is the most spectacular example of Craftsman-style bungalow architecture. The term "bungalow" can be misleading, since the Gamble House is a huge two-story home. To wealthy Easterners such as the Gambles, this type of vacation home seemed informal compared with their accustomed mansions. What makes visitors swoon here is the incredible amount of hand craftsmanship: the hand-shaped teak interiors, the Greene-designed furniture, the Louis Tiffany glass door. The dark exterior has broad eaves, with many sleeping porches on the second floor. It's on a private road, which is not well marked; take Orange Grove Boulevard to the 300 block to find Westmoreland Place. *4 Westmoreland Pl., tel. 818/793–3334. Admission: $4 adults, $2 students, $3 senior citizens, children 12 and under free. Open Thur.–Sun. noon–3. 1-hr. tours every 15–20 min.*

7 The **Pasadena Historical Society** is housed in Fenyes Mansion. The 1905 building still holds the original furniture and paintings on the main and second floors; in the basement, the focus is on Pasadena's history. There are also four acres of well-landscaped gardens. *470 W. Walnut St., tel. 818/577–1660. Admission: $4 adults, $3 students and senior citizens, children under 12 free. Open Tues., Thur., and first and last Sun. of the month, 1–4.*

8 **The Norton Simon Museum** will be familiar to television viewers of the Rose Parade: the sleek, modern building makes a stunning background for the passing floats. Like the more famous Getty Museum, the Norton Simon is a tribute to the art acumen of an extremely wealthy businessman. In 1974, Simon reorganized the failing Pasadena Museum of Modern Art and assembled one of the world's finest collections, richest in its Rembrandts, Goyas, Degas, and Picassos—and dotted with Rodin sculptures throughout. Rembrandt's development can be traced in three oils—"The Bearded Man in the Wide Brimmed Hat," "Self Portrait," and "Titus." The most dramatic Goyas are two oils—"St. Jerome" and the portrait of "Dona Francisca Vicenta Chollet y Caballero." Down the walnut and steel staircase is the Degas gallery. Picasso's renowned "Woman with Book" highlights a comprehensive collection of his paintings, drawings, and sculptures. The museum's collections of Impressionist (van Gogh, Matisse, Cézanne, Monet, Renoir, et al.) and Cubist (Braque, Gris) work is extensive. Older works range from Southeast Asian artworks from 100 BC, bronze, stone, and ivory sculptures from India, Cambodia, Thailand, and Nepal. The museum also has a wealth of Early Renaissance, Baroque, and Rococo artworks: church works by Raphael, Guariento, de Paolo, Filippino Lippi, and Lucas Cranach give way to robust Rubens maidens and Dutch landscapes, still lifes, and portraits by Frans Hals, Jacob van Ruisdael, and Jan Steen, and a magical Tiepolo ceiling highlights the Rococo period. The most recent addition to the collection are seven 19th-century Russian paintings. *411 W. Colorado Blvd., tel. 818/449–6840. Admission: $4 adults, $2 students and senior citizens. Open Thur.–Sun. noon–6.*

9 Half a mile east of the museum, **Old Town Pasadena** is an ambitious, ongoing restoration. Having fallen into seedy decay in the past 50 years, the area is being revitalized as a blend of restored brick buildings with a Yuppie overlay. Rejuvenated buildings include bistros, elegant restaurants, and boutiques. On Raymond Street, the Hotel Green, now the Castle Apartments, dominates the area. Once a posh resort hotel, the Green is now a faded Moorish fantasy of domes, turrets, and balconies reminiscent of the Alhambra but with, true to its name, a greenish tint. Holly Street, between Fair Oaks and Arroyo, is home to several shops offering an excellent selection of vintage '50s objects, jewelry, and clothes. This area is best explored on foot. Old Town is bisected by Colorado Boulevard, where on New Year's Day throngs of people line the street for the Rose Parade.

Time Out If browsing the Holly Street shops leaves you both nostalgic and hungry, walk down Fair Oaks Avenue to the **Rose City Diner** (45 S. Fair Oaks Ave., tel. 818/793–8282). Classic diner fare, from chicken-fried steak and eggs to macaroni and cheese, is served in an *American Graffiti* setting.

⓾ **The Pacific Asia Museum** is the gaudiest Chinese-style building in Los Angeles outside of Chinatown. Designed in the style of a Northern Chinese imperial palace with a central courtyard, it is devoted entirely to the arts and crafts of Asia and the Pacific Islands. Most of the objects are on loan from private collections and other museums, and there are usually changing special exhibits that focus on the objects of one country. *46 N. Los Robles Dr., tel. 818/449–2742. Admission: $3 adults, $1.50 students and senior citizens, children free. Open Wed.–Sun. noon–5.*

⓫ **Kidspace** is a children's museum housed in the gymnasium of an elementary school. Here kids can talk to a robot, direct a television or radio station, dress up in the real (and very heavy) uniforms of a fire fighter, an astronaut, a football player, and more. A special "Human Habitrail" challenges children by changing architectural environments, and "Illusions" teases one's ability to perceive what is real and what is illusion. *390 S. El Molino Ave., tel. 818/449–9144. Admission: $4 adults, $5 children 2 and over, $2.50 children 1–2, $3.50 senior citizens. Open during the school year, Wed. 2–5, weekends 12:30–5; school vacations Mon.–Fri. 1–5; summer Tues.–Fri. 1–5.*

⓬ **The Ritz-Carlton, Huntington Hotel** (1401 S. Oak Knoll Ave., tel. 818/568–3900) is situated in Pasadena's most genteel neighborhood, Oak Knoll, close to San Marino. The hotel, built in 1906, reopened in March of 1991, after five years of renovations necessary to bring it up to earthquake code standards, while still preserving its original design, including the Japanese and Horseshoe Gardens. Don't miss the historic Picture Bridge with its murals depicting scenes of California along its 20 gables. Features include the Japanese Garden and the Picture Bridge. You can still make reservations here, but only for the 106 newer rooms.

San Marino The **Huntington Library, Art Gallery, and Botanical Gardens** is
⓭ the area's most important site. If you only have time for a quick drive through the area and one stop, this should be it. Railroad tycoon Henry E. Huntington built his hilltop home in the early 1900s. It has established a reputation as one of the most extraordinary cultural complexes in the world, annually receiving more than a half million visitors. The library contains six million items, including such treasures as a Gutenberg Bible, the earliest known edition of Chaucer's *Canterbury Tales,* George Washington's genealogy in his own handwriting, and first editions by Ben Franklin and Shakespeare. In the library's hallway are five tall hexagonal towers displaying important books and manuscripts.

The art gallery, devoted to British art from the 18th and 19th centuries, contains the original "Blue Boy" by Gainsborough, "Pinkie," a companion piece by Lawrence, and the monumental "Sarah Siddons as the Tragic Muse" by Reynolds.

The Huntington's awesome 130-acre garden, formerly the grounds of the estate, now includes a 12-acre Desert Garden featuring the largest group of mature cacti and other succulents in the world, all arranged by continent. The Japanese Garden offers traditional Japanese plants, stone ornaments, a moon bridge, a Japanese house, a bonsai court, and a Zen rock garden. Besides these gardens, there are collections of azaleas and 1,500 varieties of camellias, the world's largest public collection. The 1,000-variety rose garden displays its collection historically so that the development leading to today's strains of roses can be observed. There are also herb, palm, and jungle gardens plus a Shakespeare garden, where plants mentioned in Shakespeare's works are grown.

A variety of orientation options is available for visitors to this vast property, including: a 12-minute slide show introducing the Huntington; a 1¼-hour guided tour of the gardens; a 45-minute audio tape about the art gallery (which can be rented for a nominal fee); a 15-minute introductory talk about the library; and inexpensive, self-guided tour leaflets.

The Huntington Pavilion, built in 1980, offers visitors unmatched views of the surrounding mountains and valleys and houses a bookstore, displays, and information kiosks as well. Both the east and west wings of the pavilion display paintings on public exhibition for the first time. The Ralph M. Parsons Botanical Center at the pavilion includes a botanical library, a herbarium, and a laboratory for research on plants. *1151 Oxford Rd., tel. 818/405–2100. Donation requested. Open Tues.–Fri. 1–4:30, weekends 10:30–4:30. Reservations required Sun.*

The San Fernando Valley

The San Fernando Valley is northwest of downtown Los Angeles, past Hollywood and accessible through the Cahuenga Pass (where the Hollywood Freeway now runs). Although there are other valleys in the Los Angeles area, this is the one that people refer to simply as "the Valley." Sometimes there is a note of derision in their tone, since the Valley is still struggling with its stepchild status. City people still see it as a mere collection of bedroom communities, not worth serious thought. But the Valley has come a long way since the early 20th century when it was mainly orange groves and small ranches.

The Valley is now home to over one million people (it even has its own monthly magazine). For many, this area is idyllic: Neat bungalows and ranch-style homes are situated on tidy parcels of land; and shopping centers are never too far away. It boasts fine restaurants and several major movie and television studios.

We are grouping the major attractions of the Valley into one Exploring section to give readers a sense of the place. Because the Valley is such a vast area, however, focus on one or two attractions and make them the destination for a half- or full-day trip. Try to avoid the rush-hour traffic jams on the San Diego and Hollywood freeways. They can be brutal.

Universal City If you drive into the area on the Hollywood Freeway, through the Cahuenga Pass, you'll come first to one of the most recently developed areas of the Valley: Universal City. It is a one-industry town and that industry is Universal Studios. Its history goes back decades as a major film and television studio, but in the past few years it has also become a major tourist attraction. Today this hilly area boasts the Universal Studios Tour, the Universal Amphitheater, a major movie complex, hotels, and restaurants.

Universal Studios Hollywood is the best place in Los Angeles for seeing behind the scenes of the movie industry. The five- to seven-hour Universal tour is an enlightening and amusing (if a bit sensational) day at the world's largest television and movie studio, complete with live shows based on "Miami Vice," *Conan the Barbarian,* and "Star Trek." The complex stretches across more than 420 acres, many of which are traversed during the course of the tour by trams featuring usually witty running commentary provided by enthusiastic guides. You can experience the parting of the Red Sea, an avalanche, and a flood, meet a 30-foot-tall version of the legendary King Kong, as well as Kit, the talking car from the NBC television series "Knightrider"; live through an encounter with a runaway train and an attack by the ravenous killer shark of *Jaws* fame and endure a confrontation by aliens armed with death rays—all without ever leaving the safety of the tram. And now, thanks to the magic of Hollywood, you can also experience the perils of The Big One—an all-too-real simulation of an 8.3 earthquake, complete with collapsing earth, deafening train wrecks, floods, and other life-threatening amusements. There is a New England village, an aged European town, and a replica of an archetypal New York street. The newest exhibits are *Back To the Future,* a show showing off state-of-the-art special effects, and *Lucy: A Tribute to Lucille Ball,* housed in a 2,200-square-foot heart-shaped museum containing a re-creation of the "I Love Lucy" set, plus television film clips, costumes, and bound scripts from the beloved redhead's television show, which aired from 1951 to 1957. The tour stops at the snack bar and picnic area before taking in the Entertainment Center, the longest and last stop of the day, where you stroll around to enjoy various shows. In one theater animals beguile you with their tricks. In another you can pose for a photo session with the Incredible Hulk. Visit Castle Dracula and confront a variety of terrifying monsters. At the Star Trek Theater, you can have yourself filmed as an extra and placed into a scene from a galactic adventure already released that is then re-edited to include you. *100 Universal Pl., tel. 818/508–9600. Box office open daily 8:30–4. Admission: $26 adults, $19 senior citizens and children 3–11.*

Burbank Warner Brothers and Columbia Studios share the lot of **Burbank Studios,** where a two-hour guided walking tour is available. Because the tours involve a lot of walking, you should dress comfortably and casually. This tour is somewhat technically oriented and centered more on the actual workings of filmmaking than the one at Universal. It also varies from day to day to take advantage of goings-on on the lot. Most tours see the backlot sets, prop construction department, and sound complex. *400 Warner Blvd., tel. 818/954–1008. Tours given weekdays at 10 and 2. Admission: $25. No children under 10 permitted. Reservations essential, 1 wk in advance.*

NBC Television Studios are also in Burbank, as any regular viewer of *The Tonight Show* can't help knowing. For those who wish to be part of a live studio audience, free tickets are still being made available for tapings of the various NBC shows. *3000 W. Alameda Ave., Burbank, tel. 818/840–3537.*

San Fernando San Fernando, in the northeast corner of the valley that bears its name, is one of the few separate cities in the Valley. It has only one important attraction: **Mission San Fernando Rey de España,** one of a chain of 21 missions established by 1823, which extend from San Diego to Sonoma along the coastal route known as ElCamino Real. Today U.S. 101 parallels the historic Mission Trail and is one of the state's most popular tourways.

San Fernando Mission was established in 1797 and named in honor of King Ferdinand III of Spain. Fifty-six Indians joined the mission to make it a self-supportive community. Soon wheat, corn, beans, and olives were grown and harvested there. In addition workshops produced metalwork, leather goods, cloth, soap, and candles. Herds of cattle, sheep, and hogs also began to prosper. By 1833, after Mexico extended its rule over California, a civil administrator was appointed for the mission and the priests were restricted to religious duties. The Indians began leaving and what had been flourishing one year before became unproductive. Thirteen years later the mission, along with its properties (those being the entire San Fernando Valley), was sold for $14,000. During the next 40 years, the mission buildings were neglected; settlers stripped roof tiles, and the adobe walls were ravaged by the weather.

Finally in 1923 a restoration program was initiated that resulted in a recovery of the rustic elegance and the feeling of history within the mission walls. Today, as you walk through the mission's arched corridors, you may experience déjà vu and you probably have, vicariously, through an episode of "Gunsmoke," "Dragnet," or dozens of movies. The church's interior is decorated with Indian designs and artifacts of Spanish craftsmanship depicting the mission's 18th-century culture. There is a small museum and gift shop. In 1991, the wacky Steve Martin comedy *L. A. Story* was filmed here. *15151 San Fernando Mission Rd., tel. 818/361–0186. Admission: $3 adults, $1.50 children. Open daily 9–4.*

Encino The main attraction at **Los Encinos State Historic Park** is the early California dwelling, which was built in 1849 by Don Vicente de la Osa and is furnished with historically accurate furniture, household goods and tools, and a two-story French-style home, dated 1870. The grounds are serene, especially on weekdays, when there are fewer people around, and you may have the duck pond and shade trees largely to yourself. *16756 Moorpark St., tel. 818/784–4849. Admission to house: $2 adults, $1 children 6–15, under 6 free. Tours available Wed.–Sun. 1–4.*

Calabasas Calabasas, in the southwest corner of the Valley, was once a stagecoach stop on the way from Ventura to Los Angeles. The name means "pumpkins" in Spanish. The little town has retained some of the flavor of its early days. The **Leonis Adobe** is one of the most charming adobes in the county, due in part to its fairly rural setting and barnyard animals, especially the Spanish red hens. With a little concentration, visitors can imagine life in the early years. The house was originally built as a one-story adobe, but in 1844 Miguel Leonis decided to remodel rather than move and added a second story with a balcony. *Voila!* A Monterey-style home. The furnishings are authentic to the period. Considering its distance, this stop is most highly recommended for history buffs. *23537 Calabasas Rd., tel. 818/712–0734. Admission free. Open Wed.–Sun. 1–4.*

Time Out **The Sagebrush Cantina** (23527 Calabasas Rd., tel. 818/222–6062), just next door to the Leonis Adobe, is a casual, outdoorsy place, and perfect for families. The specialty here, as the name suggests, is Mexican fare. There's a large bar for the singles set and outdoor tables for leisurely meals. It's busy—and best—on weekends.

Other Places of Interest

Scattered across Los Angeles County are attractions that don't fit neatly into any organized drive or walk. Some, such as Dodger Stadium, are major sites. Others, such as Watts Towers, are quirky places. If Los Angeles is anything, it's a something-for-everybody city.

Dodger Stadium has been home of the Los Angeles Dodgers since 1961, when Chavez Ravine was chosen as the site of the newly-arrived-from-Brooklyn team's home base. The stadium seats 56,000 and parking is fairly easy. *1000 Elysian Park Ave., tel. 213/224–1400, accessible from the Pasadena Freeway just north of downtown Los Angeles. Open only during games.*

El Mercado lies in East Los Angeles, the heart of the Mexican barrio. While Olvera Street draws both Mexican and gringo customers, this is the real thing: a huge, three-story marketplace that a close cousin to places like Libertadad in Guadalajara. There are trinkets (pinatas and soft-clay pottery) to buy here, but the real draw is the authentic foods and mariachi music. The mid-level food shops offer hot tortillas, Mexican herbs, sauces, and cheeses. Upstairs is where the action is, especially on weekends when several local mariachi bands stake out corners of the floor and entertain—all at the same time. You'll either love it or hate it. The food on the top floor is only so-so, but the feeling of Old Mexico is palpable. *3425 E. 1st St., Los Angeles, tel. 213/268–3451. Open weekdays 10–8, later on weekends.*

Exposition Park was the site of the 1932 Olympics and the impressive architecture still stands. Adjoining the University of Southern California, Exposition Park is the location of two major museums: the **California Museum of Science and Industry** and the **Natural History Museum** (*see* Museums, *below*). Also included in the 114-acre park is the **Los Angeles Swimming Stadium** (home of Los Angeles aquatic competitions), which is open to the public in summer, and **Memorial Coliseum,** the site of college football games. There are plenty of picnic areas on the grounds as well as a sunken rose garden. *Figueroa St. at Exposition Blvd., Los Angeles.*

Forest Lawn Memorial Park is more than just a cemetery: It covers 300 formally landscaped acres and features a major collection of marble statuary and art treasures, including a replica of Leonardo da Vinci's "The Last Supper" done entirely in stained glass. In the Hall of the Crucifixion–Resurrection is one of the world's largest oil paintings incorporating a religious theme, "The Crucifixion" by artist Jan Styka. The picturesque grounds are perfect for a leisurely walk. Forest Lawn was the model for the setting of Evelyn Waugh's novel *The Loved One.* Many celebrities are buried here, some more flamboyantly than others. Silent-screen cowboy star Tom Mix is said to be buried in his good-guy clothes: white coat, white pants, and a belt buckle with his name spelled out in diamonds. Markers for

Walt Disney and Errol Flynn are near the Freedom Mausoleum. Inside the mausoleum are the wall crypts of Nat King Cole, Clara Bow, Gracie Allen, and Alan Ladd. Clark Gable, Carole Lombard, Theda Bara, and Jean Harlow are among the luminaries buried in the Great Mausoleum. *1712 S. Glendale Ave., Glendale, tel. 213/254–3131. Open daily 8–5.*

Forest Lawn Memorial Park–Hollywood Hills is the 340-acre sister park to Forest Lawn Glendale, situated just west of Griffith Park on the north slope of the Hollywood Hills. Dedicated to the theme of American liberty, it features bronze and marble statuary including Thomas Ball's 60-foot Washington Memorial and a replica of the Liberty Bell. There are also reproductions of Boston's Old North Church and Longfellow's Church of the Hills. The film *The Many Voices of Freedom* is shown daily and Revolutionary War documents are on permanent display. Among the famous people buried here are Buster Keaton, Stan Laurel, Liberace, Charles Laughton, and Freddie Prinze. *6300 Forest Lawn Dr., Hollywood, tel. 213/254–7251. Open daily 8–5.*

Gene Autry Western Heritage Museum celebrates the American West, both the movie and real-life versions, with memorabilia, artifacts, and art in a structure that draws on Spanish Mission and early Western architecture. The collection includes Teddy Roosevelt's Colt revolver, Buffalo Bill Cody's saddle, and Annie Oakley's gold-plated Smith and Wesson guns, alongside video screens showing clips from old Westerns. *4700 W. Heritage Way, Los Angeles, tel. 213/667–2000. Admission $6 adults, $4.50 senior citizens, $2.50 children 2–12. Open Tues.–Sun. 10–5.*

Griffith Park Observatory and Planetarium, located on the south side of Mount Hollywood in the heart of Griffith Park, offers dazzling daily shows that duplicate the starry sky. A guide narrates the show and points out constellations. One of the largest telescopes in the world is open to the public for free viewing every clear night. Exhibits display models of the planets with photographs from satellites and spacecraft. A Laserium show is featured nightly, and other special astronomy shows are offered frequently. The Observatory sits high above Los Angeles and from the outside decks and walkways offers a spectacular view of the city, very popular on warm evenings. *Griffith Park, tel. 213/664–1191. Enter at the Los Feliz Blvd. and Vermont Ave. entrance. Hall of Science and telescope are free. Planetarium shows: $3.50 adults, $2 children. Laserium show: $6.50 adults, $5.50 children. Call for schedule. Open Tues.–Fri. 2–10, weekends 12:30–10.*

Hollyhock House was the first of several houses Frank Lloyd Wright designed in the Los Angeles area. Built in 1921 and commissioned by heiress Aline Barnsdall, it exemplifies the pre-Columbian style Wright was fond of at that time. As a unifying theme, he used a stylized hollyhock flower, which appears in a broad band around the exterior of the house and even on the dining room chairs. Now owned by the city, as is Barnsdall Park, where it is located, Hollyhock House has been restored and furnished with original furniture designed by Wright and reproductions. His furniture may not be the comfiest in the world, but it sure looks perfect in his homes. *4800 Hollywood Blvd., Hollywood, tel. 213/662–7272. Admission: $1.50 adults, $1 senior citizens, children free. Tours conducted Tues.–Sun., at noon, 1, 2, and 3.*

Mulholland Drive, one of the most famous thoroughfares in Los Angeles, makes its very winding way from the Hollywood Hills across the spine of the Santa Monica Mountains west almost to the Pacific Ocean. Driving its length is slow, but the reward is sensational views of the city, the San Fernando Valley, and the expensive homes along the way. For a quick shot, take Benedict Canyon north from Sunset Boulevard, just west of the Beverly Hills Hotel, all the way to the top and turn right at the crest, which is Mulholland. There's a turnout within a few feet of the intersection, and at night, the view of the valley side is incredible.

University of Southern California (USC, or simply "SC" to the locals) is the oldest major private university on the West Coast. The pleasant campus, which is home to nearly 30,000 students, is often used as a backdrop for television shows and movies. Two of the more notable of its 191 buildings are the Roman-esque **Doheny Memorial Library** and **Widney Hall,** the oldest building on campus, a two-story clapboard dated 1880. The **Mudd Memorial Hall of Philosophy** contains a collection of rare books from the 13th through 15th centuries. *Bounded by Figueroa, Jefferson, Exposition, and Vermont, and adjacent to Exposition Park, tel. 213/740–2300. Free 1-hr campus tours weekdays, on the hr 9–2.*

Watts Towers is the folk-art legacy of an Italian immigrant tile-setter, Simon Rodia, and one of the great folk-art structures in the world. From 1920 until 1945, without helpers, this eccentric and driven man erected three cement towers, using pipes, bed frames, and anything else he could find, and embellished them with bits of colored glass, broken pottery, sea shells, and as-sorted discards. The tallest tower is 107 feet. Plans are under way to stabilize and protect this unique monument, often com-pared to the 20th-century architectural wonders created by Barcelona's Antonio Gaudi. Well worth a pilgrimage for art and architecture buffs (or anyone else, for that matter). *1765 E. 107th St., Los Angeles.*

Los Angeles for Free

In Los Angeles, every day is a free event in terms of nature; the sun, sand, and ocean alone can fill a vacation. But there are plenty of other free activities, events, and cultural attractions to keep even those with limited budgets busy.

Cabrillo Marine Museum. *See* Palos Verdes, San Pedro, and Long Beach, *above.*

California Museum of Science and Industry. *See* Museums, *below.*

Casa de Adobe. *See* Highland Park, Pasadena, and San Marino, *above.*

Christmas Boat Parades at many local marinas celebrate Christmas in a special way. Boat owners decorate their boats with strings of lights and holiday displays and then cruise in a line for dockside visitors to see. Call for specific dates (Marina del Rey, tel. 310/821–0555; Port of Los Angeles, tel. 310/519–3508).

Craft and Folk Art Museum. *See* Wilshire Boulevard, *above.*

El Alisal. *See* Highland Park, Pasadena, and San Marino, *above.*

El Mercado. *See* Other Places of Interest, *above.*

El Pueblo State Historic Park. *See* Downtown Los Angeles, *above.*

Farmer's Market. *See* Wilshire Boulevard, *above.*

Forest Lawn Memorial Park. *See* Other Places of Interest, *below.*

Grand Central Market. *See* Downtown Los Angeles, *above.*

Greystone Mansion. *See* The Westside, *above.*

Hebrew Union College Skirball Museum. *See* Museums, *below.*

Hollywood Memorial Cemetery. *See* Hollywood, *above.*

Huntington Library, Art Gallery, and Botanical Gardens has a policy of admission by voluntary donation, which can be as little as you want. *See* Highland Park, Pasadena, and San Marino, *above.*

J. Paul Getty Museum. *See* Santa Monica, Venice, Pacific Palisades, and Malibu, *above.*

La Brea Tar Pits. *See* Wilshire Boulevard, *above.*

Laurel and Hardy's Piano Stairway. *See* Off the Beaten Track, *below.*

Leonis Adobe. *See* The San Fernando Valley, *above.*

Mulholland Drive. *See* Other Places of Interest, *above.*

Polo Games at Will Rogers State Historic Park. *See* Santa Monica, Venice, Pacific Palisades, and Malibu, *above.*

Rancho Los Alamitos. *See* Palos Verdes, San Pedro, and Long Beach, *above.*

Rancho Los Cerritos. *See* Palos Verdes, San Pedro, and Long Beach, *above.*

Rose Parade, seen from the streets (rather than the bleachers), is as free as it is on television. Arrive before dawn and dress warmly. Thousands of residents prefer to watch on television and then go out to East Pasadena a day or two later to view the floats, which are parked there for a few days for observation. *Corner of Sierra Madre Blvd. and Washington St., Pasadena. Call for viewing hrs, tel. 818/449-7673.*

Santa Anita Racetrack Workouts are held during the racing season (December 26–late April). The public is welcome to come out early in the morning to watch the workouts from the grandstands. There is an announcer who'll keep you advised of the horses' names and times. Breakfast is available in the restaurant. *Santa Anita Park, 285 W. Huntington Dr., Arcadia, tel. 818/574-7223. Enter Gate 8 off Baldwin Ave. or Gate 3 off Huntington Dr. Open 7:30 AM–9:30 AM.*

Santa Monica Mountains Nature Walks are led by rangers and docents of the many parks in the Santa Monica Mountains. There's an ambitious schedule of walks for all interests, ages, and levels of exertion. These include wildflower walks, moonlight hikes, tide-pool explorations, and much more. Several outings are held every day. For updated information, call the National Park Service (tel. 818/597-9192).

UCLA. *See* The Westside, *above.*

Watts Towers. *See* Other Places of Interest, *above.*

Westwood Memorial Park. *See* The Westside, *above.*

Off the Beaten Track

The Flower Market (just east of downtown, in the 700 block of Wall Street) is a block-long series of stores and stalls that open up in the middle of the night to sell wholesale flowers and house plants to the city's florists, who rush them to their shops to sell that day. Many of the stalls stay open until late morning to sell leftovers to the general public at the same bargain prices. And what glorious leftovers they are: Hawaiian ginger, Dutch tulips, Chilean freesia. The public is welcome after 9 AM and the stock is quickly depleted by 11 AM. Even if you don't buy, it's a heady experience to be surrounded by so much fragile beauty.

Laurel and Hardy's Piano Stairway (923–927 Vendome Street, in the Silverlake section of Los Angeles, a few miles northeast of downtown) was the setting for the famous scene in 1932 film *The Music Box* where Stan Laurel and Oliver Hardy try to get a piano up an outdoor stairway. The stairway remains today much as it was then.

Orcutt Ranch Horticultural Center (23600 Roscoe Blvd., Canoga Park, tel. 818/883–6641, admission free), once owned by William Orcutt, a well-known geologist who was one of the excavators of the La Brea Tar Pits, is a surprisingly lush and varied garden in the west San Fernando Valley. Orcutt is filled with interesting little areas to explore, such as the rose garden, herb garden, and stream banked with shady trees and ferns (a wonderful picnic site). The house, where the Orcutts lived, is open to the public every day, 8–5. Two weekends a year (late June or early July) the extensive orange and grapefruit groves are open for public picking. It's a chance to enjoy the Valley as it was in the years when groves like these covered the landscape for miles. You'll need an A-frame ladder or a special pole for dislodging the fruit up high. Bring along grocery sacks.

Pig Murals (on the corner of Bandini and Soto streets in Vernon) were probably the first public murals in Los Angeles. They were originally painted on the outside walls of the Farmer John Company by Leslie Grimes, who was killed in a fall from the scaffolding while painting. They depict bucolic scenes of farms and contented pigs, rather an odd juxtaposition to what goes on inside the packing plant. Vernon is the heart of Los Angeles's meat-packing industry and to be stuck in traffic on a hot summer afternoon in this part of town is an odorific experience not soon forgotten.

Sightseeing Checklists

Historical Buildings and Sites

When Los Angeles celebrated its bicentennial in 1981, it came as something of a shock to many Americans. Until then most people had assumed that Los Angeles came into being in the 1920s or thereabouts. The city's historical heritage has not always been carefully preserved. In fact, city officials and developers have been quite cavalier about saving many of the best examples of the city's architectural past. However, active restoration projects are taking place all the time and there is a great deal to be seen that predates the arrival of moving pictures.

Adamson House. *See* Santa Monica, Venice, Pacific Palisades, and Malibu, *above*.

Banning Residence Museum. *See* Palos Verdes, San Pedro, and Long Beach, *above*.

Bradbury Building. *See* Downtown Los Angeles, *above*.

Carroll Avenue (1300 block Carroll Ave., Angelino Heights, tel. 213/485–2433) has the highest concentration of Victorian homes in the city and has been designated a historical monument. It's in Angelino Heights, one of the oldest neighborhoods in Los Angeles, developed when the upper middle class of the 1880s sought out homes in this hilly section just northwest of downtown. The entire area has many fine examples of Victorian architecture, but this block is the best. Most of the homes have been renovated with a careful eye for historical accuracy. The Carroll Avenue Foundation sponsors several events during the year that include tours to the best restored homes. The **Sessions House,** at 1330 Carroll, is one of the finest.

El Alisal. *See* Highland Park, Pasadena, and San Marino, *above.*

El Pueblo State Historic Park. *See* Downtown Los Angeles, *above.*

Gamble House. *See* Highland Park, Pasadena, and San Marino, *above.*

Heritage Square. *See* Highland Park, Pasadena, and San Marino, *above.*

Hollyhock House. *See* Other Places of Interest, *below.*

Lasky–DeMille Barn. *See* Hollywood Studio Museum in Hollywood, *above.*

Leonis Adobe. *See* The San Fernando Valley, *above.*

I. Magnin Bullocks Wilshire. *See* Wilshire Boulevard, *above.*

Mission San Fernando Rey de Espana. *See* The San Fernando Valley, *above.*

Mission San Gabriel Archangel. Over 200 years ago Father Junipero Serra dedicated this mission to the great archangel and messenger from God, Saint Gabriel. As the founders approached the mission site, they were confronted with savage Indians. In the heat of battle, one of the padres produced the canvas painting "Our Lady of Sorrows," which so impressed the Indians that they laid down their bows and arrows. The miracle produced another painting, which is on display at the mission today. Within the next 50 years, the San Gabriel Archangel became the wealthiest of all California missions. In 1833 the Mexican government confiscated the mission and it began to decline; in 1855 the U.S. government returned the mission to the church, but by this time the Franciscans had departed. In 1908 the Claretian Fathers took charge and much care and respect has since been poured into the mission. Today Mission San Gabriel Archangel's adobe walls preserve an era of history, and the magnificent cemetery stands witness to the many people who lived here. The magnificent church and museum housing relics reflecting the history of the padres and early visitors to San Gabriel were closed for repairs after the October 1988 earthquake, but were due to reopen in late 1993. *537 W. Mission Dr., San Gabriel, tel. 818/282–5191. Open daily 9:30– 4:15.*

Rancho Los Alamitos. *See* Palos Verdes, San Pedro, and Long Beach, *above.*

Rancho Los Cerritos. *See* Palos Verdes, San Pedro, and Long Beach, *above.*

Santa Monica Heritage Museum. *See* Santa Monica, Venice, Pacific Palisades, and Malibu, *above.*

Virginia Robinson Gardens, the former estate of the heir to the Robinson Department Store chain, sits on 6.2 terraced acres in Beverly Hills. A guide will take you on an hour-long tour of the gardens and the exquisite exteriors of the main house, guest house, servants' quarters, swimming pool, and tennis court. A highlight of the tour is the collection of rare and exotic palms. Since the gardens' administration is trying to keep a low profile to avoid congestion in the cul-de-sac where the gardens are situated, visitors must call for reservations and be told the address and directions. *Tel. 310/276–5367. Admission: $5. Tours Tues.–Thur. 10 AM and 1 PM, Fri. 10 AM.*

Watts Towers. *See* Other Places of Interest, *above.*

William S. Hart County Park. *See* Parks and Gardens, *below.*

Will Rogers State Historic Park. *See* Santa Monica, Venice, Pacific Palisades, and Malibu, *above.*

Wiltern Theater. *See* Wilshire Boulevard, *above.*

Museums

Banning Residence Museum. *See* Palos Verdes, San Pedro, and Long Beach, *above.*

Cabrillo Marine Museum. *See* Palos Verdes, San Pedro, and Long Beach, *above.*

California Museum of Science and Industry is especially intriguing to children, with many exhibits they can operate by punching buttons, twisting knobs, or turning levers. The Aerospace Complex features a DC3, DC8, rockets, and satellites plus an IMAX motion picture theater. The Taper Hall of Economics and Finance has 62 3-D exhibits, most of them computer interactive for visitors. And a new miniature winery complements McDonald's Computer Chef exhibit of behind-the-scenes fast-food cooking (McDonald's is also open for business and quite a lure for children). The redesigned Hall of Health reveals the inner workings of the body and has a new Health for Life Arcade. There are exhibits on fiber optics, robotics, high technology, and also the ever-popular hatchery where 150 baby chicks hatch daily for all to see. *700 State Dr., Exposition Park, tel. 213/744–7400. Admission free, parking $3. Open daily 10–5.*

Children's Museum at La Habra. *See* Chapter 13.

Craft and Folk Art Museum. *See* Wilshire Boulevard, *above.*

George C. Page Museum of La Brea Discoveries. *See* Wilshire Boulevard, *above.*

Hebrew Union College Skirball Museum exhibits Judaic art, Palestinian archaeology, and anthropological material from the Negev Desert. Also in the collection are rare manuscripts, historical coins and medals, ceremonial art, ancient Israeli artifacts, and an extensive display of painting, graphics, and sculptures. The museum offers a unique opportunity to explore Judaism and its history and culture through aesthetic and material treasures of the Jewish people. The museum itself is of architectural note because of its series of arches representative of the Ten Commandments. *3077 University at 32nd and Hoover Sts., Los Angeles, tel. 213/749–3424. Admission free. Open Tues.–Fri. 11–4, Sun. 10–5. Public tours on Sun. at 1.*

Hollywood Guinness World of Records. *See* Hollywood, *above.*

Hollywood Studio Museum (Lasky–DeMille Barn). *See* Hollywood, *above.*

Hollywood Wax Museum. *See* Hollywood, *above.*

Huntington Library, Art Gallery, and Botanical Gardens. *See* Highland Park, Pasadena, and San Marino, *above.*

J. Paul Getty Museum. *See* Santa Monica, Venice, Pacific Palisades, and Malibu, *above.*

Lomita Railroad Museum, hidden away in a typical suburban neighborhood, is a replica of a turn-of-the-century Massachusetts train station. Beyond the gate, discover one of the largest collections of railroad memorabilia in the West. Climb aboard a real steam engine and take a look at the immaculate interior of the car itself. *2137 250th St., Lomita, tel. 310/326–6255. Admission: $1. Open Wed.–Sun. 10–5.*

Long Beach Children's Museum. *See* Chapter 13.

Los Angeles Children's Museum. *See* Tour 1.

Los Angeles County Museum of Art. *See* Wilshire Boulevard, *above.*

Max Factor Museum. *See* Hollywood, *above.*

Museum of Contemporary Art. *See* Downtown Los Angeles, *above.*

Museum of Hollywood History. *See* Hollywood, *above.*

Natural History Museum of Los Angeles County is the fourth-largest natural history museum in the United States, with more than 35 halls and galleries. The main building is an attraction in itself: Spanish Renaissance in structure, it has travertine columns, walls, and domes; an inlaid marble floor heightens the overall magnificence. Opened in 1913, the museum has a rich collection of prehistoric fossils, an extensive bird- and marine-life exhibit, and a vast display of insect life. A brilliant display of stones can be seen in the Hall of Gems and Minerals, and there's an elaborate taxidermy exhibit of North American and African mammals set in detailed replicas of their natural habitats. Exhibits typifying various cultural groups include pre-Columbian artifacts and a display of crafts from the South Pacific. The Hall of American History presents everything from the paraphernalia of prominent historical figures to old American cars. The museum's new Ralph M. Parsons Discovery Center is a barn-size room that is a cross between a natural history museum and a children's museum with many hands-on, science-oriented exhibits. *900 Exposition Blvd., Exposition Park, tel. 213/744–3466 or 213/744–3414. Admission: $5 adults, $3.50 senior citizens and students, $2 children; free the first Tues. of every month. Open Tues.–Sun. 10–5.*

Norton Simon Museum. *See* Highland Park, Pasadena, and San Marino, *above.*

Pacific Asia Museum. *See* Highland Park, Pasadena, and San Marino, *above.*

Ripley's Believe It or Not. *See* Hollywood, *above.*

Santa Monica Heritage Museum. *See* Santa Monica, Venice, Pacific Palisades, and Malibu, *above.*

Southwest Museum. *See* Highland Park, Pasadena, and San Marino, *above.*

Parks and Gardens

The extensive Los Angeles park system provides a welcome oasis after the myriad concrete freeways and urban sprawl. They range from small, grassy knolls for picnicking and relaxing to huge wilderness areas offering a wide spectrum of recreational facilities, including tennis courts, golf courses, and lakes.

The **Los Angeles Department of Parks and Recreation** (tel. 213/485–5555) provides helpful information on locating and identifying park facilities. Parks and Rec also sponsors various activities such as marathon races, interpark sports contests, poetry readings, art shows, and chess tournaments.

Banning Residence Museum and Park. *See* Palos Verdes, San Pedro, and Long Beach, *above.*

Burton Chase Park. *See* Santa Monica, Venice, Pacific Palisades, and Malibu, *above.*

Descanso Gardens, once part of the vast Spanish Rancho San Rafael that covered more than 30,000 acres, now encompasses 165 acres of native chaparral-covered slopes. A forest of California live oak trees furnishes a dramatic backdrop for thousands of camellias, azaleas, and a four-acre rose garden. Descanso's Tea House features pools, waterfalls, a Zen garden, and a gift shop as well as a relaxing spot to stop for refreshments. Flower shows (including chrysanthemum, daffodil, camellia, and bonsai demonstrations) are held at various times of the year. Guided tours are available; trams traverse the grounds. *1418 Descanso Dr., La Canada, tel. 818/952–4400. Admission: $3 adults, $1.50 senior citizens and students, 75¢ children; free 3rd Tues. of month. Open daily 9–4:30.*

Douglas Park is a postage-stamp-size park (four acres) that's-jam-packed every weekend with Westside families. It offers pleasant spots for blanket picnics close to the playgrounds so parents can monitor their children and read the Sunday *Times* at the same time. The playground area seldom has an empty swing. A former wading pool is now a dry track for tiny children and their three-wheelers. Well-kept and frequented by friendly people, this park deserves its favorable word-of-mouth among locals.*1155 Chelsea Ave., Wilshire Blvd. near 25th St., Santa Monica.*

Eaton Canyon Park and Nature Center celebrates native plants and animals in a big but low-keyed way. It may look a bit dry and scrubby, compared to parks planted with lush East Coast trees and bushes, but for those who take the time to study the variety of plants and how they adapt to the meager rainfall, it is well worth a trip. The Nature Center helps to orient visitors before they start down the trails. From September through June (the best times to visit), docents offer easy, guided walks. They leave from the flagpole beginning at 9 AM. *1750 N. Altadena Dr., Pasadena, tel. 818/398–5420.*

Echo Park manages to rise above the seedy, urban patina it can't escape. If you're a half-full kind of person, you'll find plenty to rave about here. There's a feeling of romance, of a bygone era, of history, stories untold. Set in one of the older, tougher neighborhoods in the city, Echo Park is mostly lake with a little edging all around. The lake itself is famous for its lotus pads, and visitors can rent boats and paddle right up to them. There are a few palm-filled islands near the north end, tropical-feeling and very inviting. Echo Park is at its best in the late afternoon, when the area takes on a warm glow as the sun sets. Weekdays are quiet; weekends filled with families. *1632 Bellevue Ave., Echo Park.*

El Dorado Park. *See* Palos Verdes, San Pedro, and Long Reach, *above.*

Elysian Park covers 575 hilly acres overlooking downtown Los Angeles. Despite its size, Elysian Park should be classified as an "urban" park, as it offers refuge to downtowners who live in cramped apartments. It can be a lively excursion for those who like seeing families enjoying some fresh air on weekends, and these crowded family areas are the safest parts of the park (despite the presence of the L.A. Police Academy in the park, solo wanderings should be taken with caution, and explorations after dark forgotten altogether). Much of the park is still wilderness and there is a 10-acre rare tree grove completely labeled for convenient identification. The recreation center has volleyball and basketball courts. Plentiful play areas for children, nature trails for hiking, plus nine picnic spots with tables round out the park's offerings. Perched on the southeast corner, high above the smog, is Dodger Stadium, home of the Los Angeles Dodgers professional baseball team. *929 Academy Rd., Los Angeles, tel. 213/225–2044.*

Franklin Canyon Ranch has been embraced with a vengeance by Westside nature-buff do-gooders, who keep it busy with special-interest hikes and other outdoor events. The big draw is the nature walks for preschoolers and their parents, but the schedule is also filled with aerobic walks and moonlit hikes (to the top of the ridge for a breathtaking view of the city). There is a nice broad lawn for games and good picnicking. *1936 N. Lake Dr., north of Beverly Hills, tel. 310/858–3834.*

Griffith Park is the largest city park in the United States. Donated to the city in 1896 by mining tycoon Griffith J. Griffith, it contains 4,000 acres. There are seemingly endless picnic areas, as well as hiking and horseback riding trails. Travel Town, with its miniature railroad, is a favorite with children. Pony rides and stagecoach rides are also available. The park is home to two 18-hole golf courses (Harding and Wilson) and one nine-hole executive course (Roosevelt), a pro shop, a driving range, and tennis courts. A swimming pool and soccer fields are nearby. The world-famous **Los Angeles Zoo** (*see below*) is on the park's north side. The Griffith Park Observatory and Planetarium is located on the park's south side, high atop the Hollywood Hills (*see* Other Places of Interest, *above*). Near the Western Avenue entrance is Fern Dell, a half mile of shade that includes paths winding their way amid waterfalls, pools, and thousands of ferns. *Entrances at north end of Vermont Ave., Los Feliz district, tel. 213/665–5188.*

Hannah Carter Japanese Garden, located in Bel Air just north of the UCLA campus, is owned by UCLA and may be visited by making phone reservations two weeks in advance. *Tel. 310/825–4574.*

Los Angeles Zoo, one of the major zoos in the United States, is noted for its breeding of endangered species. Koalas and white tigers are the latest additions. The 113-acre compound holds more than 2,000 mammals, birds, amphibians, and reptiles. Animals are grouped according to the geographical areas where they are naturally found—Africa, Australia, Eurasia, North America, and South America. A tram is available for stops at all areas. Seeing the zoo calls for a lot of walking, seemingly all uphill, so strollers or backpacks are recommended for families with young children. The zoo is beautifully landscaped and areas for picnicking are available. Not-to-be-missed features at the zoo include Adventure Island, a new children's zoo offering interactive exhibits and featuring animals of the American Southwest; a walk-through bird exhibit with more than 50 species from all over the world; and a koala area, where the furry creatures live amid eucalyptus trees in an environment resembling their native Australia. *Junction of Ventura and Golden State freeways, Griffith Park, tel. 213/666–4090. Admission: $6 adults, $5 senior citizens, $2.75 children under 12. Open daily 10–5.*

MacArthur Park was a popular hangout for the elite during the 1920s and 1930s—a favorite spot for a leisurely stroll, boating, or an afternoon concert. How times have changed! The surrounding neighborhood is now a rundown section of town, teeming with Mexican and Central American immigrants and more than its share of winos. The park has suffered, but it remains well-used by the local population. For people who enjoy street life and consider themselves urban explorers, MacArthur Park still has something to offer. Dress to blend in (no Yuppie duds here) and relax. It's best to visit on weekends when the crowds provide some safety as well as a wonderfully rich panoply of human life. The grassy areas surrounding the recently cleaned lake are the most picturesque. The rental pedal-boats allow visitors to observe the human condition from a safe distance. You can even get here on Los Angeles's new subway line from Union Station. *2230 W. Sixth St., Los Angeles.*

Malibu Creek State Park, nestled deep in the Santa Monica Mountains, crystallizes what the mountains are all about: an incredibly varied chaparral landscape and a get-away-from-it-all feeling. Century Lake, a small, man-made lake a mile from the road, is an excellent picnic site. *¼ mi south of intersection of Las Virgenes Rd. and Mulholland Hwy., Malibu.*

Malibu Lagoon State Park. *See* Santa Monica, Venice, Pacific Palisades, and Malibu, *above.*

Peter Strauss Ranch is named for its former owner, actor Peter Strauss, who lived in the splendidly cozy stone house, now park headquarters. What makes this park such a pleasant spot to visit is the sense of being at someone's country home, not a public park. It's like joining in a big family reunion. The broad front lawn beckons Frisbees and kites. The hiking trails are easy enough for the whole family. Throughout the year there is an ambitious schedule of weekend entertainments, from folk dance ensembles to puppet shows. *Mulholland Hwy. at Kanon, Agoura, tel. 818/889–3150.*

Placerita Canyon Nature Center is perfect for hiking, with 8 miles of trails through 350 acres of both flat and hilly terrain along a streambed and through oak trees. Warm days, winter and spring, are the best times to visit, because there is a chance of water (and tadpoles) in the stream then. The deeply shaded picnic area is an excellent meeting place for picnics. Because the park is a wildlife refuge, picnicking is limited to the designated area. The half-mile ecology trail focuses on the flora and fauna of the area. Gold was first discovered in California in 1842, in this park (not in the Mother Lode as most assume) at a site designated by the Oak of the Golden Dream. The Nature Center features dioramas, indigenous animals, and a small museum. *19152 W. Placerita Canyon Rd., Newhall, tel. 805/259–7721.*

Roxbury Park is centrally located and attracts a good crowd every weekend. Young families hover around the playground and picnic tables (fully booked in advance for preschoolers' birthday parties), couples toss blankets on the flat lawns to catch some sun, and senior citizens head for the lawn bowling area. The park also offers a softball diamond and tennis courts. It has recently undergone a major face-lift (typical Beverly Hills!). *471 S. Roxbury Dr., at Olympic Blvd., Beverly Hills, just east of Century City, tel. 310/550–4761.*

Shoreline Aquatic Park. *See* Palos Verdes, San Pedro, and Long Beach, *above.*

Vasquez Rocks offers one of Los Angeles County's best photo opportunities. Sure, it's a two-hour drive from downtown but that doesn't stop the dozens of film, television, and ad-agency crews who truck out here each year to use the rocks as the archetypal Western backdrop. These 45-degree angled rocks (our fault line in action) will seem very familiar. Bad guys jumped off them to hoodwink the good guys; Chevys and Fords have been paraded in front of them. The stark rock landscape is best visited during the cool months since there is very little shade here. The park is named for early California bandit Tiburcio Vasquez, who used the rocks as his between-robberies hideout. *10700 E. Escondido Rd., Aqua Dulce, off Antelope Valley Fwy.*

William S. Hart County Park was once owned by cowboy star William S. Hart, who took his movie money and bought a large tract of land in the Santa Clarita Valley—in those days, far in the country. Hart has long since died, civilization (in the guise of housing tracts and shopping malls) has surrounded the area, but 253 acres remain a bucolic and very Western preserve. The park has nice flat lawns for picnics and games. Up the hill, Hart's home has been kept just as it was when he lived here in the 1920s. Docents lead tours through the exquisite Spanish Revival–style rooms, filled with priceless Russells and Remingtons, Navajo rugs, and cowboy relics. *24151 N. San Fernando Rd., Newhall, tel. 805/259–0855. House open Wed.– Fri. 10–12:30 and weekends 11–3:30, with tours every ½ hr.*

Will Rogers State Historic Park. *See* Santa Monica, Venice, Pacific Palisades, and Malibu, *above.*

4 Shopping

By Jane E. Lasky

When asked where they want to shop, visitors to Los Angeles inevitably answer, "Rodeo Drive." But this famous thoroughfare is only one of many enticing shopping streets Los Angeles has to offer. And there's also mall shopping, which in Los Angeles is an experience unto itself—the mall is the modern-day Angelino's equivalent of a main street, town square, back fence, malt shop, and county fair, all rolled into one. Distances between shopping spots can be vast, however, so don't choose too many different stops in one day—if you do, you'll spend more time driving than shopping!

Most Los Angeles shops are open from 10 to 6 although many remain open until 9 or later, particularly at the shopping centers, on Melrose Avenue, and in Westwood Village during the summer. Melrose shops, on the whole, don't get moving until 11 AM but are often open Sunday, too. At most stores around town, credit cards are almost universally accepted and traveler's checks are also often allowed with proper identification. If you're looking for sales, check the *Los Angeles Times.*

Shopping Districts

Downtown Although downtown Los Angeles has many enclaves to explore, we suggest that the bargain hunter head straight for the **Cooper Building** (860 S. Los Angeles St., tel. 213/622–1139). Eight floors of small clothing and shoe shops (mostly for women) offer some of the most fantastic discounts in the city. Grab a free map in the lobby, and seek out as many of the 82 shops as you can handle. Nearby are myriad discount outlets selling everything from shoes to suits to linens.

Near the Hilton Hotel, **Seventh Street Marketplace** (735 S. Figueroa, tel. 213/955–7150) is an indoor/outdoor multilevel shopping center with an extensive courtyard that boasts many busy cafés and lively music. The stores surrounding this courtyard include **G.B. Harb** (tel. 213/624–4785), a fine menswear shop, and **Bullocks** (tel. 213/624–9494), a small version of the big department store, geared to the businessperson.

Melrose Avenue West Hollywood, especially Melrose Avenue, is where young shoppers should try their luck, as should those who appreciate vintage styles in clothing and furnishings. The 1½ miles of intriguing, one-of-a-kind shops and bistros on Melrose stretch from La Brea to a few blocks west of Crescent Heights; this is definitely one of Los Angeles's trendiest shopping areas. A sampling of the stores that operate there:

Betsey Johnson (7311 Melrose Ave., tel. 213/931–4490) offers the designer's vivid, hip women's fashions. Watch for twice-yearly sales.
Comme des Fous (7384 Melrose Ave., tel. 213/653–5330) is an avant-garde (and pricey) clothing shop packed with innovative European designs many women would consider daring to wear.
Cottura (7215 Melrose Ave., tel. 213/933–1928) offers brightly colored Italian ceramics.
Emphasis (7361 Melrose Ave., tel. 213/653–7174) offers a pristine collection of fashion-forward clothes for women, including hats, belts, accessories, and a selection of unique lingerie.
Fantasies Come True (8012 Melrose Ave., tel. 213/655–2636) greets you with "When You Wish upon a Star" playing from a tape deck. The store, needless to say, is packed with Walt Disney memorabilia.

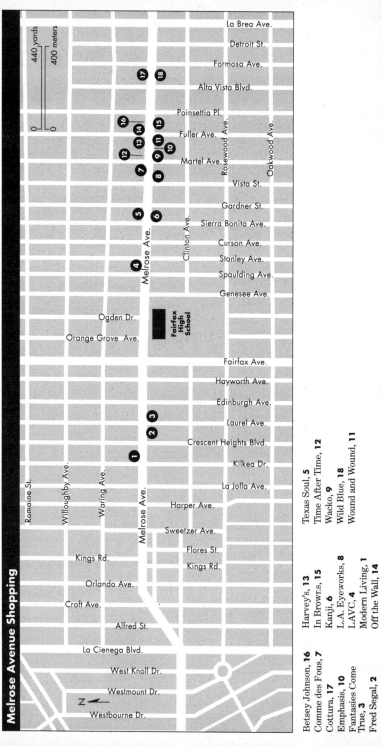

Melrose Avenue Shopping

Betsey Johnson, **16**
Comme des Fous, **7**
Cottura, **17**
Emphasis, **10**
Fantasies Come
  True, **3**
Fred Segal, **2**

Harvey's, **13**
In Brown, **15**
Kanji, **6**
L.A. Eyeworks, **8**
LAVC, **4**
Modern Living, **1**
Off the Wall, **14**

Texas Soul, **5**
Time After Time, **12**
Wacko, **9**
Wild Blue, **18**
Wound and Wound, **11**

Fred Segal (8118 Melrose Ave., tel. 213/651–1935) has a collection of shops providing stylish clothing for men and women. Among the designers and manufacturers they carry: Nancy Heller, New Man, Ralph Lauren, Calvin Klein. Children's clothing, accessories, and shoes—an impressive array—are also stocked at the Melrose store.

Harvey's (7367 Melrose Ave., tel. 213/852–1271) has everything from Victorian through 1950s-era designer pieces but specializes in the latter. Rattan is in one room, Art Deco furniture in the other.

In Browns (7353 Melrose Ave., tel. 213/653–7198) features clothes in lightweight fabrics for everyone (or almost everyone), since garments come in only one size (read: large). Check out the flowered hats, designed by a local artist.

Kanji (7320½ Melrose Ave., tel. 213/933–6364) carries an alluring mixture of conservative fashions and clothing with flair. You'll find European-style dresses, pants, and suits.

L.A. Eyeworks (7407 Melrose Ave., tel. 213/653–8255) is a hip boutique run by the world's most successful eye-fashion prognosticators; frame-wise, whatever's next in style around the globe will probably show up first in this leading-edge L.A. shop.

LAVC (Los Angeles Vintage Clothing) (7669 Melrose Ave., tel. 213/653–8834) sells recycled clothing such as broken-in Levi's, checked vests, and comfy pajamas. Purchases are very recession-proof—you can sell them back to the store when you no longer want them.

Modern Living (8125 Melrose Ave., tel. 213/655–3898) is a gallery of 20th-century design, representing renowned international furniture designers, including Philippe Starck, Ettore Sottsass, and Massino Isosaghini.

Off the Wall (7325 Melrose Ave., tel. 213/930–1185) specializes in "antiques and weird stuff."

Texas Soul (7515 Melrose Ave., tel. 213/658–5571) is the place for western footwear made in—you guessed it—the Lone Star State. Top-of-the-line boots such as Tony Lama's are big sellers, as are the tooled belts, leather jackets, and spurs that adorn this popular shop.

Time After Time (7425 Melrose Ave., tel. 213/653–8463), decorated to resemble a Victorian garden, has time-honored garments ranging from turn-of-the-century to the 1960s, especially antique wedding dresses.

Wacko (7416 Melrose Ave., tel. 213/651–3811) is a wild space crammed with all manner of blow-up toys, cards, and other semi-useless items that make good Los Angeles keepsakes.

Wild Blue (7220 Melrose Ave., tel. 213/939–8434) is a fine shop/gallery specializing in functional and wearable art created by exceptional contemporary artists, many of whom hail from the L.A. area.

Wound and Wound (7374 Melrose Ave., tel. 213/653–6703) has an impressive collection of wind-up toys and music boxes.

Larchmont One of L.A.'s most picturesque streets is Larchmont Boulevard, adjacent to the expensive residential neighborhood of Hancock Park. Stores that make Larchmont Village worth a detour include **Hollyhock** (214 N. Larchmont Blvd., tel. 213/931–3400), for exceptional new and antique furnishings; **Lavender & Lace** (656 N. Larchmont Blvd., tel. 213/856–4846), specializing in antique textiles, linens, and English pine furniture; **My Favorite Place** (204 N. Larchmont Blvd., tel. 461–5713), for comfortable women's clothing—silks and ethnic pieces in particular; and **Robert Grounds** (119 N. Larchmont Blvd., tel. 213/464–8304), for distinctive gifts and antiques.

Westwood Westwood Village, near the UCLA campus, is a young and lively area for shopping. The atmosphere is invigorating, especially during summer evenings when there's a movie line around every corner, all kinds of people strolling the streets (an unusual phenomenon in L.A., where few folks ever walk anywhere), and cars cruising along to take in the scene. Among the shops worth scouting out in this part of the city:

Aah's (1083 Broxton, tel. 310/824–1688) is good for stationery and fun gift items.

Chanin's (1030 Westwood Blvd., tel. 310/208–4500), with the best in casual wear, undoubtedly reflects the UCLA influence in the youthful and fun fashions sold here.

Copelands Sports (1001 Westwood Blvd., tel. 310/208–6444) offers a cornucopia of sportswear, beachwear, shoes, and shorts, along with a variety of skiing, camping, and other outdoor equipment.

Jazz'd (1069 Broxton, tel. 310/208–7950) sports work-out attire.

Morgan and Company (1131 Glendon, tel. 310/208–3377) is recommended for California jewelry.

Shanes Jewelers (1065 Broxton, tel. 310/208–8404) is a youth-oriented jewelry store specializing in earrings, engagement rings, chains, and watches. There is a good repair department.

Sisterhood Book Store (1351 Westwood Blvd., tel. 310/477–7300) stocks an incredible collection of women's books in all areas—history, health, and psychology among them.

The Wilger Company (10924 Weyburn, tel. 310/208–4321) offers fine men's clothing.

The Beverly Center The **Beverly Center** (tel. 310/854–0070), bound by Beverly **and Environs** Boulevard, La Cienega Boulevard, San Vicente Boulevard, and Third Street, covers more than seven acres and contains some 200 stores. Examples are **By Design** and **Habitat,** for home furnishings and furniture; **By Oliver,** for fashionable women's clothes; **Alexio,** for fashionable men's clothes; and two stores called **Traffic** for contemporary clothing for both genders.

The shopping center is anchored by the **Broadway** department store on one end, and **Bullocks** on the other. Inside, there are also some interesting restaurants (like the **Kisho-an,** a Japanese restaurant known for its fine sushi, and **The Hard Rock Cafe,** known for its bargain cuisine and fascinating decor, including a 1959 Caddy that dives into the roof of the building above the restaurant) and one of Los Angeles's finest cineplexes, with 14 individual movie theaters.

Directly across the street from the Beverly Center, on the east side of La Cienega between Beverly Boulevard and Third Street, is another mall, **The Beverly Connection** (tel. 213/651–3611), opened in 1990. Inside, you'll find **Book Star,** a giant warehouse-like store selling every conceivable sort of reading material at low prices; **Sports Chalet,** for all kinds of athletic equipment; **Cost Plus,** a bottom-of-the-line import emporium big on rattan furniture, gourmet food, ethnic jewelry, and simple clothing; and **Rexall Square Drug,** a.k.a. Drugstore of the Stars, where people like Dustin Hoffman and Goldie Hawn have been seen lurking in the amply stocked aisles.

In the immediate neighborhood you'll find some other interesting shops:

Andria's Hole in the Wall (8236 W. 3rd St., tel. 213/852–4955) is a special store where the talented namesake proprietor pulls together stylish outfits to instantly transform her customers into happening members of the L.A. scene.
Freehand (8413 W. 3rd St., tel. 213/655–2607) is a gallery shop featuring contemporary American crafts, clothing, and jewelry, mostly by California artists.
Trashy Lingerie (402 N. La Cienega, tel. 310/652–4543) is just what the name suggests. This is a place for the daring; models try on the sexy garments to help customers decide what to buy.

Century City　**Century City Shopping Center & Marketplace** (tel. 310/277–3898), set among gleaming, tall office buildings on what used to be Twentieth Century Fox Film Studios' back lot, is an open-air mall with an excellent roster of shops. Besides The Broadway and Bullocks, both department stores, you'll find **Sasha of London** for trendy shoes and bags; **Ann Taylor** for stylish but not outlandish clothing and Joan & David shoes; and **The Pottery Barn** for contemporary furnishings at comfortable prices. **Card Fever** is a whimsical boutique with fun and funky messages to send; **Brentano's** is one of the city's largest bookstores; and **Gelson's** is a gourmet food market.

Besides dozens of stores, there are five restaurants on the premises, among them **Houston's,** which gets down with its American fare of grilled fish and steak, and **Stage Deli,** the kind of New York–style deli that previously was hard to find in L.A. Also at Century City is the **AMC Century** 14-screen movie complex.

West Los Angeles　The **Westside Pavilion** (tel. 310/474–6255) is a pastel-colored postmodern mall on Pico and Overland boulevards. The three levels of shops and restaurants run the gamut from high-fashion boutiques for men and women to a store devoted solely to travelers' needs, large and small. Among them are **The Disney Store,** filled with novelties to make all your fantasies come true; **The May Company** and **Nordstrom,** two full-scale department stores; **Mr Gs for Kids,** a good place for children's gifts; **Chanin's,** filled with women's designer clothing; and **Victoria's Secret,** a scented lingerie boutique. Worth visiting even if you're not here to shop—and a welcome stop, if you are—is **Sisley Italian Kitchen,** which serves California-Italian dishes, pizzas, and terrific salads.

Santa Monica　Another worthwhile and multifaceted area, farther west and next to the ocean, offers both malls and street shopping.

Santa Monica Place Mall (315 Broadway, tel. 310/394–5451) is a three-story enclosed mall that's nothing special. Some of the stores inside are **Pacific Sunwear,** selling super bathing suits; **Jumping Dog,** for witty home furnishings; **Card Fever,** so you can write the folks back home; **Lechter's,** for stocking up on your favorite gourmet utensils; and **Wherehouse Records,** for the latest tunes. **Robinson's** and **The Broadway** are department stores in this complex.

Next door, **Third Street Promenade** (tel. 310/393–8355) is an open-air arena of shops, movie theaters, and restaurants, with pedestrian walkways and a landscaped island.

Along **Montana Avenue,** a stretch of a dozen or so blocks from Seventh to Seventeenth streets showcases boutique after boutique of quality goods. Among them:

A.B.S. Clothing (1533 Montana Ave., tel. 310/393–8770) sells contemporary sportswear designed in Los Angeles.

Brenda Cain (1617 Montana Ave., tel. 310/393–3298) is a place in which to step back in time with nostalgic clothes and antique jewelry. The hot ticket here is the amazing array of Hawaiian shirts for men and women.

Brenda Himmel (1126 Montana Ave., tel. 310/395–2437) is known for its fine stationery, but antiques, frames, photo albums and books also enhance this homey boutique.

Lisa Norman Lingerie (1134 Montana Ave., tel. 310/451–2026) sells high-quality lingerie from Europe and the United States—slips, camisoles, robes, silk stockings, and at-home clothes.

Weathervane II (1209 Montana, tel. 310/393–5344) is one of the street's larger shops, with a friendly staff who make browsing among the classic and offbeat fashions more fun.

The stretch of **Main Street** leading from Santa Monica to Venice (Pico Blvd. to Rose Ave.) makes for a pleasant walk, with a collection of quite good restaurants, unusual shops and galleries, and an ever-present ocean breeze.

San Fernando and San Gabriel Valleys This is mall country; among the many outlets are **Sherman Oaks Galleria** (tel. 818/783–7100), **The Promenade** in Woodland Hills (tel. 818/884–7090), **Glendale Galleria** (tel. 818/240–9481), and **Encino Town Center** and **Plaza de Oro** in Encino (tel. 818/788–6100).

Aside from shopping centers, some individual stores stand out along sections of Ventura Boulevard, which runs through Universal City, Sherman Oaks, Topanga, and Calabasas. Among the top shops:

The Cranberry House (12318 Ventura Blvd., Studio City, tel. 818/506–8945) is a huge shopping arena covering half a city block, packed with kiosks run by L.A.'s leading antiques dealers. Come here for vintage furniture, clothing, jewelry, and furnishings.

Jona (12532 Ventura Blvd., Sherman Oaks, tel. 818/762–5662) is a wardrobe/consultation service and store rolled into one. The store's buyer has impeccable taste in his choice of women's clothing.

Michael's Shoes (16600 Ventura Blvd., Encino, tel. 213/872–1568) is a discount shop packed with all manner of men's footwear, with an exceptional selection of Western boots made by Frye, Dan Post, and Acme. The store slogan claims that "every pair is on sale."

Sharper Image (14559 Ventura Blvd., Sherman Oaks, tel. 818/907–1557) has unique high-tech gift items.

Beverly Hills We've saved the most famous section of town for last. **Rodeo Drive** is often compared to such famous streets as Fifth Avenue in New York and the Via Condotti in Rome. Along the several blocks between Wilshire and Santa Monica boulevards, you'll find an abundance of big-name retailers—but don't shop Beverly Hills without shopping the streets that surround illustrious Rodeo Drive. There are plenty of treasures to be purchased on those other thoroughfares as well.

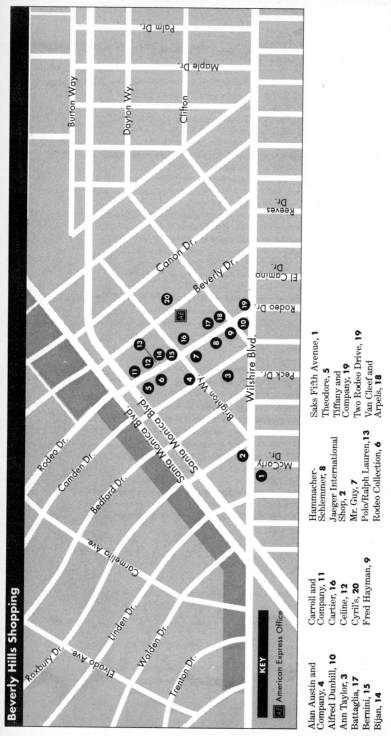

Beverly Hills Shopping

KEY

AE American Express Office

Alan Austin and
Company, **4**
Alfred Dunhill, **10**
Ann Taylor, **3**
Battaglia, **17**
Bernini, **15**
Bijan, **14**

Carroll and
Company, **11**
Cartier, **16**
Celine, **12**
Cyril's, **20**
Fred Hayman, **9**

Hammacher-
Schlemmer, **8**
Jaeger International
Shop, **2**
Mr. Guy, **7**
Polo/Ralph Lauren, **13**
Rodeo Collection, **6**

Saks Fifth Avenue, **1**
Theodore, **5**
Tiffany and
Company, **19**
Two Rodeo Drive, **19**
Van Cleef and
Arpels, **18**

Even Beverly Hills has a couple of shopping centers, although owners wouldn't dare call their collection of stores and cafés "malls." The **Rodeo Collection** (tel. 310/276–9600), at 421 North Rodeo Drive between Brighton Way and Santa Monica Boulevard, is nothing less than the epitome of opulence and high fashion. Many famous upscale European designers opened their doors in this piazzalike area of marble and brass. Among them: **Sonia Rykiel,** for country-club clothing for women; **Fila,** for the best in sports gear; **Mondi,** for high-style German fashions; and **Gianni Versace,** for trend-setting Italian designs.

A collection of glossy retail shops called **Two Rodeo Drive** (Rodeo Dr. and Wilshire Blvd.) is housed on a private cobblestone street that somewhat resembles a Hollywood backlot. Amid the Italianate piazza, outdoor cafés and sculpted fountains of Two Rodeo are some two dozen boutiques, including: **Christian Dior,** couture fashions known the world over; **Davidoff of Geneva,** for the finest tobacco and accessories; **Gian Franco Ferre,** for quality Italian designs; and **A. Sulka,** a noted men's haberdasher.

Some of the many other shops, boutiques, and department stores in Beverly Hills:

Fashions and Home Decor **Polo/Ralph Lauren** (444 N. Rodeo Dr., tel. 310/281–7200) serves up a complete presentation of Lauren's all-encompassing lifestyle philosophy. The men's area, reminiscent of a posh British men's club, offers roughwear and activewear. Some 200 antiques are used as a backdrop for the women's area. Upstairs resides the most extensive selection of Lauren's home-furnishing designs in the world.

Gifts **Hammacher-Schlemmer** (309 N. Rodeo Dr., tel. 310/859–7255) is a fabulous place to unearth those hard-to-find presents for adults who never grew up.

Jewelry **Cartier** (370 N. Rodeo Dr., tel. 310/275–4272) offers all manner of gifts and jewelry bearing the double-C logo.
Tiffany and Company (210 Rodeo Dr., tel. 310/273–8880), the famous name in fine jewelry, silver, and more, packages each purchase in a signature blue Tiffany box.
Van Cleef and Arpels (300 N. Rodeo Dr., tel. 310/276–1161) sells expensive baubles and fine jewelry.

Men's Fashions **Alfred Dunhill of London** (201 N. Rodeo Dr., tel. 310/274–5351) is an elegant shop selling British-made suits, shirts, sweaters, and slacks. Pipes, tobacco, and cigars, however, are this store's claim to fame.
Battaglia (306 N. Rodeo Dr., tel. 310/276–7184) features accessories, shoes, and men's apparel—the richest Italian fashions in luxurious silks, woolens, cottons, and cashmeres.
Bernini (362 N. Rodeo Dr., tel. 310/278–6287) specializes in contemporary Italian designer fashions. Look for fine leather accessories from Giorgio Armani.
Bijan (420 N. Rodeo Dr., tel. 310/273–6544) is a store where it helps to make an appointment. Bijan claims that many Arabian sheiks and other royalty shop here, along with some of the wealthiest men in the United States. Many designs are created especially by the owner.
Carroll and Co. (466 N. Rodeo Dr., tel. 310/273–9060) is a conservative man's shop that's been in business for nearly a dec-

ade. It's known for quality, service, and its professional and celebrity clientele.

Cyril's (370 N. Beverly Dr., tel. 310/278–1330) features fine clothing in the latest European styles and carries labels like Cerruti and Michel Axel.

Mr. Guy (301 N. Canon Dr., tel. 310/275–4143) answers all the needs of the well-dressed man.

Women's Fashions   **Alan Austin and Company** (9533 Brighton Way, tel. 310/275–1162) has traditional clothing in a wide selection of fabrics and colors. The store manufactures its own designs, so clothing can be made to order.

Ann Taylor (357 N. Camden Dr., tel. 310/858–7840) is the flagship shop of this chain of women's clothing stores, offering the epitome of the young executive look, and a good selection of casual clothing and Joan & David shoes as well.

Celine (460 N. Rodeo Dr., tel. 310/273–1243) is for luggage, shoes, and accessories as well as traditionally tailored clothing made of fine fabrics. Expect Old World craftsmanship and classic designs.

Fred Hayman (273 N. Rodeo Dr., tel. 310/271–3000) is an illustrious store where one does not merely shop for glitzy American and European clothing, accessories, and footwear; one also refreshes oneself at the stunning Oak Bar that separates the women's from the men's clothes.

Jaeger International Shop (9699 Wilshire Blvd., tel. 310/276–1062) is one of Britain's best-known clothiers, with a complete line of cashmere and woolen separates available in traditionally designed fashions.

Theodore (453 N. Rodeo Dr., tel. 310/276–9691) offers trendy items in fabulous fabrics for men and women from Kenzo, Sonia Rykiel, and Claude Montana. Everything is done with a real eye for color.

Department Stores

The Broadway (The Beverly Center, 8500 Beverly Blvd., tel. 310/854–7200) offers merchandise in the moderate price range, from cosmetics to housewares to linens to clothing for men and women. There are stores throughout Los Angeles.

Bullocks (The Beverly Center, 8500 Beverly Blvd., tel. 310/854–6655), which is more upscale than The Broadway, carries an extensive collection of clothing for men and women, as well as housewares and cosmetics. Stores are throughout Southern California.

I. Magnin (9634 Wilshire Blvd., tel. 213/382–6161) is a large store with many designer labels for men and women and a good handbag and luggage department. There are branches throughout Southern California; the flagship store on Wilshire Boulevard, now closed for shopping, is an Art Deco landmark (*see* Tour 3: Wilshire Boulevard in Chapter 3).

The May Company (620 Seventh St., downtown, tel. 213/683–1144) sells modestly priced clothing and furniture without glitz or glitter in stores throughout Southern California.

Nordstrom (Westside Pavilion at 10830 W. Pico Blvd., in West Los Angeles, tel. 310/470–6155) is a Seattle-based department store that has infiltrated Southern California within the past decade. It brings with it a wide selection of clothing for men and women as well as a reputation for fine customer service, a huge shoe department, and the entertainment of popular music played on the store's grand piano.

Robinson's (9900 Wilshire Blvd., Beverly Hills, tel. 310/275–5464) is a high-end department store that has many women's selections, a few men's selections, a good housewares department, and stores throughout Southern California.

Saks Fifth Avenue (9600 Wilshire Blvd., Beverly Hills, tel. 213/275–4211) in Los Angeles isn't as impressive as the one you'll find next to St. Patrick's in Manhattan. Still, the buyers have good taste.

Specialty Shops

Antiques La Cienega Boulevard, between Santa Monica Boulevard and Beverly Boulevard, is lined with antiques dealers selling everything from Chinese to French to Viennese collectibles.

Nearby lies L.A.'s poshest antiquarian niche: Melrose Place. **Rose Tarlow Antiques** (8454 Melrose Pl., 213/653–2122) and **Licorne** (8432 Melrose Ave., tel. 213/852–4765), operated by French émigrés, sell fine 17th-century furnishings. **City Antiques** (8424 Melrose Ave., tel. 213/658–6354) provides an eclectic assortment of French and English antiques. **J.F. Chen Antiques** (8414 Melrose Ave., tel. 213/655–6310) specializes in ancient Oriental pieces, among them bronzes and tapestries.

For more intrepid hunters, Western Avenue (between 1st and 2nd streets) offers some valuable finds in some very low-key shops, including: **French Kings Antiques** (135 S. Western Ave., tel. 213/383–4430) with furniture, bronzes, and clocks; and **Used Stuff** (151 S. Western Ave., tel. 213/487–5226), which resembles a jumble of estate and garage sales.

At **The Antique Guild** (8800 Venice Blvd., Los Angeles, tel. 310/838–3131), you'll find treasures from all over the world and a gigantic inventory in a warehouse-size space.

Books **The Bodhi Tree** (8585 Melrose, West Hollywood, tel. 310/659–1733) is the place to find books on metaphysical subjects.
Book Soup (8818 Sunset Blvd., West Hollywood, tel. 310/659–3110) stocks a wide variety of volumes, with particularly strong photography, film, new fiction, and international magazines sections, and is frequently the site of book-signings.
Paperback Trader (511 Wilshire Blvd., Santa Monica, tel. 310/394–8147) has an astounding assortment of paperbacks, especially the used kind—what the shop calls "recycled reading."

Clothing **Esprit** (8491 Santa Monica Blvd., tel. 310/659–9797) is a high-styled shop that was once a roller disco. Customers at this sports clothing outlet use grocery carts to push purchases through the store.
Maxfield (8825 Melrose Ave., tel. 310/274–8800) is among the most elite clothing stores in L.A. Designers carried here include Azzedine Alaia, Comme des Garçons, Maud Frizon, Issey Miyake, Giorgio Armani, Byblos, Missoni. The store also houses Yohiji Yamamoto's only L.A. boutique. Maxfield is the supplier of choice for sundry celebrities as well as the wardrobe people responsible for dressing the more fashionable shows on television.

Secondhand **American Rag** (150 S. La Brea Ave., tel. 213/935–3154) offers inexpensive, downtown-chic clothes for men and women. Much of the stock is "previously owned," though some items are on the racks for the first time.

Charlie's (115 N. LaBrea, tel. 213/931–2486) sells a cornucopia of '50s and '60s clothes, with a few choice furnishings as well. This place has vintage evening gowns in impeccable condition.

Gifts and Crafts **Del Mano Gallery** (11981 San Vicente Blvd., Brentwood, tel. 310/476–8508), owned by Jan Peters and Ray Leier, handles the work of contemporary artists. Del Mano stocks everything from handcrafted handbags to glass and ceramic treasures.

Tesoro (319 S. Robertson, tel. 310/273–9890) is a large boutique that stocks everything from trendy Swid-Powell dishware to Southwestern blankets, ceramics, and art furniture. The wide-ranging work by area artists is well worth browsing.

Home Furnishings **Pacific Design Center** (corner of Melrose Ave. and San Vicente Blvd., tel. 310/657–0800; *see* Exploring Los Angeles, Tour 4: The Westside) is where leading interior designers find the best in home furnishings and accessories for clients who aim to impress. Most of the PDC's exclusive showrooms sell only to the trade. If you would like to do more than look here, contact **LA Design Concepts,** an interior-design shopping service (8811 Alden Dr., tel. 310/276–2109). A design professional will guide you through the PDC for an hourly fee, offer advice, and order items for you at less than half the standard industry markup of 33%.

Leather **North Beach Leather** (8500 Sunset Blvd., West Hollywood, tel. 310/652–3224) offers a great selection of clothing made of leather and suede, for both men and women.

Musical Recordings **Aron's Record** (1150 N. Highland Ave., Los Angeles, tel. 213/469–4700) carries an extensive selection of old records, perhaps the largest on the West Coast, and has low prices on new albums.

Rockaway (2395 Glendale Blvd., Silverlake, tel. 213/664–3232), in an unlikely section of town, is one of L.A.'s best CD stores for hard-to-find and used discs. Nostalgic artifacts from the early days of rock 'n' roll are on display.

5 Sports and Fitness

Participant Sports

If you're looking for a good workout, you've come to the right city. Los Angeles is one of the major sports capitals of the United States. Whether your game is basketball, golf, billiards, or bowling, L.A. is a dream town for athletes of all kinds. Not only does the near-perfect climate allow sports enthusiasts to play outdoors almost year-round, but during some seasons it's not impossible to be surfing in the morning and snow skiing in the afternoon . . . all in the same county.

While there are almost as many sports in Los Angeles as there are people, the following list is a compilation of the more popular activities. For any additional information on facilities closer to where you're staying or on other sports not listed, two agencies will gladly assist you:

City of Los Angeles Department of Recreation and Parks (200 N. Main St., Suite 1380, City Hall East, LA 90012, tel. 213/485–5515); **Los Angeles County Parks and Recreation Department** (433 S. Vermont Ave., 4th floor, LA 90020, tel. 213/738–2961).

Bicycling

In the last few years, Los Angeles has made a concerted effort to upgrade existing bike paths and to designate new lanes along many major boulevards for cyclists' use.

Perhaps the most famous bike path in the city, and definitely the most beautiful, can be found on the **Pacific Ocean beach,** from Temescal Canyon down to Redondo Beach. **San Vicente Boulevard** in Santa Monica has a nice wide cycling lane next to the sidewalk that run for about 5 miles. **Balboa Park** in the San Fernando Valley is another haven for two-wheelers.

A map of bike trails throughout the county can be obtained from the **L.A. County Parks and Recreation Department** (*see above*). You can pick one up in person or call to have one sent to you.

Billiards

As old as Hollywood itself is **Hollywood Billiards,** located at the corner of Hollywood Boulevard and Western Avenue (5504 Hollywood Blvd., tel. 213/465–0115). This 24-hour multiactivity locale includes backgammon, darts, and football, as well as pool, snooker, chess, and video games. The hall has casual dining (hamburgers, hot dogs, snacks, Thai food) and valet parking.

About 2 miles west of Hollywood Billiards is the **Hollywood Athletic Club** (6525 W. Sunset Boulevard, tel. 213/962–6600). This venue boasts full-size vintage snooker tables circa 1923, and a tournament room.

Bowling

Bowling has seen a resurgence in popularity. While there are bowling alleys all over the city, a few are attracting the attention of the neo-bowler. **Sports Center Bowl** in the Valley (12655 Ventura Blvd., Studio City, tel. 818/769–7600) has open bowling hours from 9–5 Monday–Saturday, 8–5 Sunday and after 9 Friday–Sunday. **Hollywood Star Lanes** (5777 Santa Monica Blvd., in East Hollywood, tel. 213/665–4111), in an appropriately down-market neighborhood, has open bowling Wednesday-Sunday nights and is open 24 hours.

Fishing

The best lakes for **freshwater fishing** in the area are Big Bear and Arrowhead in the San Bernardino National Forest, east of Los Angeles. Rainbow trout, bass, carp, blue gill and catfish are the typical catch, and the scenery in these mountains will enhance your outing, whether you hook anything or not. Juniper Point on the north shore of Big Bear Lake is a favorite trout hangout. For fishing information in the area, call 909/866–5796.

If your fish stories are more abundant than the fish on your plate, a sure catch can be found at **Trout Dale** (in Agoura, 3 miles south of the Ventura Freeway on Kanan Rd., tel. 818/889–9993, open Wed.–Sun. 10–5). Three picturesque ponds are set up for picnicking or "force" fishing. A $2 entry fee includes your license and pole, but there's an extra charge for each trout you push up onto the banks. **L.A. Harbor Sportfishing** (tel. 310/547–9916) offers whale-watching off Berth 79 from late December through March at the San Pedro Harbor, as well as just plain fishing. Boat rentals are $20–$90 per hour.

Saltwater fishing in L.A. offers the gamesman a number of different ways to get hold of a fresh catch from the Pacific. Shore fishing and surf casting are excellent on many of the beaches (*see* Beaches, *below*). Pier fishing is another popular method of hooking your dinner. The Malibu, Santa Monica, and Redondo Beach piers each offer nearby bait-and-tackle shops, and you can generally pull in a healthy catch. If you want to break away from the piers, however, the **Malibu Pier Sport Fishing Company** (23000 Pacific Coast Hwy., tel. 310/456–8030) offers boat excursions for $20 per half day. The **Redondo Sport Fishing Company** (233 N. Harbor Dr., tel. 310/372–2111) have half-day and full-day charters. Half-day charters, 7:30 AM–12:30 PM or 1 PM–6 PM, run about $18 per person; a three-quarter day costs $27, and a full day goes for about $65. You can rent a pole for $7. Sea bass, halibut, bonita, yellowtail, and barracuda are the usual catch.

For something with a little more bite, there are a number of fishing charters out of Marina del Rey, like **Twenty Second Street Landing** (141 W. 22nd St., San Pedro, tel. 310/832–8304). Since you can't see the fish anyway, this overnight charter is perfect because at least it affords you a look at the stars while waiting for a bite. Complete with bunk beds and full galley, these boats leave at 10 PM and 10:30 PM and dock between 5 PM and 9 PM the next night. Per-person price is $60. Day charters are available as well, at $25–$40, with half-day excursions on weekends for $20.

The most popular and unquestionably the most unusual form of fishing in the L.A. area involves no hooks, bait, or poles. The great **grunion runs,** which take place March–August, are a spectacular natural phenomenon in which hundreds of thousands of small silver fish, called grunion, wash up on Southern California beaches to spawn and lay their eggs in the sand. The **Cabrillo Marine Museum** in San Pedro (tel. 310/548–7562, *see*

Tour 6: Palos Verdes, San Pedro, and Long Beach in Chapter 3) has entertaining and educational programs about grunion during most of the runs. In certain seasons, however, touching grunion is prohibited, so it's advisable to check with the Fish and Game Department (tel. 310/590–5132) before going to see them wash ashore.

Golf

The Department of Parks and Recreation lists seven public 18-hole courses in Los Angeles. **Rancho Park Golf Course** (10460 W. Pico Blvd., tel. 310/838–7373) is one of the most heavily played links in the entire country. It's a beautifully designed course but the towering pines will make those who slice or hook regret that they ever took up golf. There's a two-level driving range, a nine-hole pitch 'n' putt (tel. 310/839–4374), a snack bar, and a pro shop where you can rent clubs.

Several good public courses are located in the San Fernando Valley. The **Balboa and Encino Golf Courses** are located right next to each other at 16821 Burbank Boulevard in Encino, tel. 818/995–1170. The **Woodley Golf Course** (6331 Woodley Ave. in Van Nuys, tel. 818/780–6886) is flat as a board, and with no trees! During the summer months, the temperature in the Valley can get high enough to fry an egg on your putter, so be sure to bring lots of sunscreen and plenty of water. Down the road in Pacoima, you'll find little escape from the summer heat, but the **Hansen Dam Public Golf Course** (10400 Glen Oaks Blvd., tel. 818/899–2200) has a dining area that serves plenty of cold drinks, as well as a driving range where you can warm up.

Perhaps the most concentrated area of golf courses in the city can be found in **Griffith Park.** Here you'll find two splendid 18-hole courses along with a challenging nine-hole course. **Harding Golf Course** and **Wilson Golf Course** (both at 4730 Crystal Springs Dr., tel. 213/663–2555) are located about a mile and a half inside the Griffith Park entrance at Riverside Drive and Los Feliz Boulevard. Bridle paths surround the outer fairways, and the San Gabriel Mountains make up the rest of the gallery in a scenic background. The nine-hole **Roosevelt Course** (2650 N. Vermont Ave., tel. 213/665–2011) can be reached through the Hillhurst Street entrance to Griffith Park.

Yet another course in the Griffith Park vicinity, and one at which there's usually no waiting, is the nine-hole **Los Feliz Pitch 'n' Putt** (3207 Los Feliz Blvd., tel. 213/663–7758). Other pitch 'n' putt courses in Los Angeles include **Holmby Hills** (601 Club View Dr., West LA, tel. 310/276–1604) and **Penmar** (1233 Rose Ave., Venice, tel. 310/396–6228).

Miniature Golf For the super-amateur linkster, or just for the heck of it, you might want to try one of the spectacular miniature golf facilities in the L.A. area. **Malibu Castle Park** (4989 Sepulveda Blvd., Sepulveda, tel. 818/990–8100) is the San Fernando Valley's Cadillac of mini courses. **Arroyo Seco Miniature Golf Course** in South Pasadena (1055 Lohman La., tel. 818/255–1506) is a favorite place to putter around.

Health Clubs

Many movies, TV shows, and songs have depicted Angelinos as mythological creatures possessing the secret of the three

Ts: tanning, toning, and tightening. Well, that sort of definition doesn't just grow on you when you get off the plane at LAX . . . it takes hard work.

There are dozens of health-club chains in the city that offer monthly and yearly memberships. **Bally's Nautilus Aerobics Plus** and **Bally's Holiday Spa Health Clubs** are the most popular local chains. The Holiday Club located between Hollywood and Sunset boulevards (1628 El Centro, tel. 213/461–0227) is the flagship operation. This place has everything, including racquetball courts, indoor running tracks, pools, men's and women's weight and aerobics rooms, and a juice bar. To find the Holiday Spa nearest you, call 800/695–8111. **Sports Club L.A.** (1835 S. Sepulveda Blvd., West L.A., tel. 310/473–1447) is a hot spot, attracting a diverse group of celebrities such as James Woods and Princess Stephanie of Monaco. Not only does the gym have valet parking, it also contains the newest technology in fitness equipment. This is the place to go if you're looking to get fit or just looking.

Probably the most famous body-pumping facility of this nature in the city is **Gold's Gym** (360 Hampton Dr., Venice, tel. 310/392–6004). This is where all the incredible hulks turn themselves into modern art. For $15 a day or $50 a week, several tons of weights and Nautilus machines can be yours. **World Gym** (812 Main St., Venice, tel. 310/399–9888) is another famous iron-person's club. **Powerhouse Gym** (formerly Easton's, 8053 Beverly Blvd., West Hollywood, tel. 213/651–3636) is another place to seek out if you're looking to pump yourself up while in town.

Hotel Health Clubs A few hotels in the city also have health spas, and some are open to the public. The **Century Plaza Hotel** (Beverly Hills, tel. 310/277–2000) also has weights, aerobics, and saunas. The spa is open to hotel guests and the public at $15 per day. And if you're in town briefly on a layover, the **Marriott at LAX** (tel. 310/641–5700) has Universal weights, Lifecycles, Stairmasters, a spa, a sauna, and an Olympic-size pool—all free to guests. *See* Lodging for other details on these hotels.

Hiking

What makes Los Angeles a hiker's paradise is the multitude of different land- and seascapes to explore. **Arrowhead** and **Big Bear**, in the **San Bernardino National Forest,** and many parts of the **Angeles National Forest,** and the **Angeles Crest** area have spectacular mountain hiking trails. Much of the terrain here is rugged, and if you're not familiar with these regions, it's advisable to contact the National Forest Service (tel. 818/790–1151) for information before you go.

Closer to the city, **Will Rogers State Park,** off Sunset Boulevard near Pacific Palisades, has a splendid nature trail that climbs from the polo fields to the mountaintop where you can get a spectacular view of the ocean. Other parks in the L.A. area that also have hiking trails include **Brookside Park, Elysian Park,** and **Griffith Park.** For more information on the parks, *see* Chapter 3.

In the Malibu area, **Leo Carillo State Beach** and the top of **Corral Canyon** offer incredible rock formations and caves to be explored on foot. In the hills east of **Paradise Cove,** a horse trail winds back into the canyons along a stream for several miles, eventually winding up at a beautiful waterfall. *See* Beaches, *below.*

For further information on these or any other hiking locations in Los Angeles, contact the **Sierra Club** (3550 W. 6th St., Suite 321, tel. 213/387–4287).

Horseback Riding

Although horseback riding in Los Angeles is extremely popular, stables that rent horses are becoming an endangered species. Of the survivors, **Bar "S" Stables** (1850 Riverside Dr., in Glendale, tel. 818/242–8443) will rent you a horse for $13 an hour (plus a $10 deposit). Riders who come here can take advantage of over 50 miles of beautiful bridle trails in the Griffith Park area. **Sunset River Trails** (Rush St., at end of Peck Rd., El Monte, tel. 818/444–2128) offers riders the nearby banks of the San Gabriel River to explore at $15 an hour. **Los Angeles Equestrian Center** (480 Riverside Dr., Burbank, tel. 818/840–8401) rents pleasure horses—English and Western—for riding along bridle paths throughout the Griffith Park hills. Horses cost $13 per hour. **Sunset Stables** (3400 Beachwood Dr., Hollywood, tel. 213/469–5450) offers a "dinner cruise" at $30, not including cost of the dinner. Riders take a trail over the hill into Burbank at sunset where they tie up their horses and have a feast at a Mexican restaurant.

Ice Skating

Rinks are located all over the city. In the Valley, there's **Ice Capades Chalet Center** (6100 Laurel Canyon Blvd., North Hollywood, tel. 818/985–5555) and the **Pickwick Ice Arena** (1001 Riverside Dr., Burbank, tel. 818/846–0032). In Pasadena, try the **Ice Skating Center** (300 E. Green St., tel. 818/578–0800), and in Rolling Hills, try the **Culver City Ice Arena** (4545 Sepulveda Ave., tel. 310/398–5718).

Jogging

Most true joggers don't care where they run, but if you've got the time to drive to a choice location to commence your leg-pumping exercises, here are a few suggestions: First of all, just about every local high school and college in the city has a track. Most are public and welcome runners, and the private schools usually don't give a hoot who jogs on their tracks between 5 AM and 8 AM. A popular scenic course for students and downtown workers can be found at **Exposition Park.** Circling the Coliseum and Sports Arena is a jogging/workout trail with pull-up bars, and other simple equipment spread out every several hundred yards. **San Vicente Boulevard** in Santa Monica has a wide grassy median that splits the street for several picturesque miles. The **Hollywood Reservoir,** just east of Cahuenga Boulevard in the Hollywood Hills, is encircled by a 3.2-mile asphalt path and has a view of the Hollywood sign. Within hilly **Griffith Park** are thousands of acres worth of hilly paths and challenging terrain, although Crystal Springs Drive from the main entrance at Los Feliz to the zoo is a relatively flat 5 miles. Circle Drive, around the perimeter of **UCLA** in Westwood, provides a 2.5-mile run through academia, L.A.-style. Of course, the premium spot in Los Angeles for any kind of exercise can be found along any of the beaches.

Racquetball and Handball

As with tennis, there are dozens of high schools and colleges all over town that have three-walled courts open to the public. The only catch is you have to wait until after school's out, or the weekend.

For more serious players—or just for rainy days—there are several indoor racquetball facilities throughout the city: **The Racquet Center,** located in the San Fernando Valley (10933 Ventura Blvd., Studio City, tel. 818/760–2303), offers court time for $10–$14, depending on when you play. There's another Racquet Center in South Pasadena (920 Lohman La., tel. 213/258–4178). The **John Wooden Center** on the UCLA campus (405 Hilgard Ave., tel. 310/206–8307) has several spectacular glass-enclosed courts, but these facilities are open to the public only if you are sponsored by a student. Court time goes for $4 per hour. Advance reservations (one day for weekdays and two days for weekends) are required. **YMCAs** throughout the city also have courts available based on hourly rates.

Roller Skating

All of the areas mentioned in Bicycling (*see above*) are also excellent for roller skating, even though cyclists still have the right of way. Venice Beach is the skating capital of the city—maybe the world.

If you're looking to get off the streets, there are a number of skating rinks in L.A. **Moonlight Rollerway** (5110 San Fernando Rd., Glendale, tel. 818/241–3630) and **Skateland** (18140 Parthenia St., Northridge, tel. 818/885–1491) are two of the more popular rinks in the city.

Skiing

Cross-Country If you're into cross-country skiing, **Idyllwild,** above Palm Springs, offers excellent trails during most of the heavy-snow season. For information, call the Idyllwild Chamber of Commerce (tel. 909/659–3259).

Downhill A relatively short drive from downtown will bring you to some of the best snow skiing in the state. Just north of Pasadena, in the San Gabriel Mountains, are two ski areas: **Mt. Waterman** (tel. 909/440–1041) and **Kratka Ridge** (tel. 909/449–1749), both of which have a couple of lifts and a range of slopes for beginning and advanced skiers. Farther east is **Mt. Baldy** (tel. 909/981–3344), off I–10 at the top of Mountain Avenue.

Ski resorts with accommodations can be found within 90 minutes of Los Angeles proper. **Big Bear** (*see* Chapter 9) is one of the most popular ski retreats on the West Coast. A full range of accommodations, several new ski lifts, night skiing, and one of the largest snow-making operations in California make this a great weekend-getaway spot. For information about Big Bear ski conditions, hotels, and special events, contact the Tourist and Visitor's Bureau (tel. 909/866–4601) or the Big Bear Lake Visitor's Authority (tel. 909/866–7000).

Other ski areas in the vicinity of Big Bear include **Bear Mountain** (tel. 909/585–2517), **Snow Valley** (tel. 909/867–5151), **Mountain High** (tel. 909/874–7050), and **Snow Summit** (tel. 909/866–4621). All have snow-making capabilities, and many have lights for night skiing. Call for directions and information about ski conditions.

Tennis

And on the eighth day, God created the tennis court. At least, it can seem that way when you drive around most L.A. neighborhoods. If you want to play tennis, you'll have no problem finding a court in this town—although you might have to wait a while for it once you get there. Many public parks have courts that require an hourly fee. **Lincoln Park** (Lincoln and Wilshire Blvd., Santa Monica), **Griffith Park** (Riverside and Los Feliz), and **Barrington Park** (Barrington just south of Sunset in L.A.), all have well-maintained courts with lights.

For a shorter wait, and no fee at all, there are a number of local high schools and colleges that leave their court gates unlocked on the weekends. There are several nice courts on the campus of **USC** (off the Vermont St. entrance), a few on the campus of **Paul Revere Junior High School** (in Brentwood at Sunset and Mandeville Canyon Rd.), and a few more at **Palisades High School** (in Pacific Palisades on Temescal Canyon Rd.)—and that's only the tip of this iceberg.

For a complete list of the public tennis courts in Los Angeles, contact the L.A. Department of Recreation and Parks (tel. 213/485–5515) or the **Southern California Tennis Association** Los Angeles Tennis Center, UCLA Campus (420 Circle Dr., Los Angeles 90024, tel. 310/208–3838).

Hotel Tennis Courts If you're just in town for a few days and you don't have time to shop around for a court, you may already be staying at a hotel that has facilities. The **Ritz-Carlton Marina del Rey** (4375 Admiralty Way, tel. 310/823–1700) has three lighted courts. Per-person, hourly rates are $20 for hotel guests and $30 for the public. The **Sheraton Town House** (2961 Wilshire Blvd., tel. 213/382–7171) has four courts available at $10 an hour to guests only. *See* Lodging for other details on these hotels.

Water Sports

Whether the surf's up in L.A. or not, the Pacific coast is the preeminent amusement park for water sports. But the ocean isn't the only place in Southern Californian to get wet. Los Angeles is a mecca for aqua-sports enthusiasts of all kinds, with access to everything from crystal mountain-lake fishing to jet skiing in the Pacific.

Boating **Sailing** is one of the most popular activities in Southern California, and you don't have to own a boat to captain one. **Rent-A-Sail** (13719 Fiji Way, Marina del Rey, tel. 310/822–1868) will rent you everything from canoes to power boats or 14–25-foot sailboats for anywhere from $16 to $36 per hour plus a $20 deposit. No boating licenses are required, but if you've got your eye on one of the larger vessels, you must have prior sailing experience.

Paddle boats in Echo Park near downtown offer a more sedentary and less salty water experience. For information about rentals, call 213/250–3387.

Big Bear and **Lake Arrowhead** (*see* Chapter 9) open up a whole different world of freshwater adventure. Canoes, motor boats, and waterskiing equipment can be rented from a number of outfits in both towns. Big Bear even offers parasailing for those who'd rather be above it all. For information about both of these lakes and nearby rental facilities, contact the Big Bear Chamber of Commerce (tel. 714/866–4607).

Jet Skiing This is another booming sport in the southland. You'll find as many jet skiers on the lakes at Big Bear and Arrowhead as you will in Marina del Rey. Jet skis are expensive to rent. Two of the more popular places that carry them are **Del Rey Jet Ski,** (4144 Lincoln Blvd., Marina del Rey, tel. 310/821–4507), and in the summer, **Malibu Jet Ski** (22718 W. Pacific Coast Hwy., tel. 310/456–2424). A rubber raft takes you and the jet ski out to a floating dock for your launch.

Scuba Diving and Snorkeling Diving and snorkeling off Leo Carillo State Beach, Catalina, and the Channel Islands is considered some of the best on the Pacific coast. Dive shops, such as **New England Divers** (4148 Viking Way, Long Beach, tel. 310/421–8939) and **Dive & Surf** (504 N. Broadway, Redondo Beach, tel. 310/372–8423), will provide you with everything you need for your voyage beneath the waves. Snorkeling equipment runs $9–$14 per day, while full scuba gear for certified divers runs $50–$62.50 per day, with prices cut for subsequent days. Diving charters to Catalina and the Channel Islands as well as certification training can be arranged through these outfits.

Surfing The signature water sport in L.A. is surfing . . . and rightfully so. Southern California beaches offer a wide variety of surfing venues, along with a number of places to rent boards. For a complete listing of the best surfing areas, *see* Beaches, *below.*

Swimming Pools There are numerous public swimming pools in the L.A. area. The **Los Angeles Swim Stadium** (tel. 213/485–2844), next door to the L.A. Coliseum—not such a safe area, so beware—was built for the 1932 summer Olympic games. The huge grandstands can make this an ominous place for a casual afternoon dip. Another popular pool is **Pacific Park Pool** (tel. 818/240–4130), run by the Glendale YMCA, in Glendale on the corner of Riverdale Drive and Pacific Avenue. This is a much more woodsy setting than the Olympic pool, and there is a public park right next door. The **Griffith Park** pool (tel. 213/665–4372) at the intersection of Los Feliz Boulevard and Riverside Drive is another favorite splash point, so much so that it's often packed to the gills, as is the **North Hollywood Park** public pool (tel. 818/763–7651) off the Hollywood Freeway at Magnolia Avenue, in the San Fernando Valley. Most public pools are open in the summer only.

Water Parks **Raging Waters** off I–210 in San Dimas (tel. 909/592–6453) is a sort of aquatic Disneyland. Mammoth water slides, water swings, and inner-tube rapids designed to bump you, spin you, and throw you have made this "the" place to be on a hot day. Palm Springs has a similar water park called **Oasis** (tel. 619/325–7873). Both are closed in winter.

Windsurfing Hanging ten has traditionally involved a surfer, a board, a wave, and a few toes. Since a sail was added to this equipment, however, windsurfing has become one of the most popular water sports ever. Good windsurfing can be found all along the coast, and there are a number of places from which to rent equipment for certified windsurfers. **Action Water Sports** (4144 Lincoln Blvd., Marina del Rey, tel. 310/306–9539) rents rigs at $20 an hour during the summer. For novices, a three-hour lesson with an instructor runs $70. Farther north, contact **Natural Progression** (22935 Pacific Coast Hwy., Malibu, tel. 310/456–6302). Cost is $40 per day, 10–5.

Spectator Sports

If you enjoy watching professional sports, you'll never hunger for action in this town. Los Angeles is the home of some of the greatest franchises in pro basketball, football, and baseball. And while most cities would be content to simply have one team in each of those categories, L.A. fans can root for two.

Some of the major sports venues in the area are **Anaheim Stadium** (Anaheim, tel. 213/625–1123), **Great Western Forum** (3900 W. Manchester, Inglewood, tel. 310/673–1773), **L.A. Coliseum** (3911 S. Figueroa, downtown, tel. 213/747–7111), and **L.A. Sports Arena** (downtown, next to the Coliseum).

Baseball

The **Dodgers** will take on all of their National League rivals in another eventful season at the ever-popular Dodger Stadium (1000 Elysian Park Ave., exit off I–110, the Pasadena Fwy.). For ticket information, call 213/224–1400. Down the freeway a bit in Anaheim, the **California Angels** continue their quest for the pennant in the American League West. For Angel ticket information, contact Anaheim Stadium: tel. 213/625–1123.

Basketball

College The **University of Southern California** (for tickets, tel. 213/740–2311) plays at the L.A. Sports Arena, and the Bruins of the **University of California at Los Angeles** (for tickets, tel. 310/825–2101) play at Pauley Pavilion on the UCLA campus; these schools mix it up in Pac 10 competition each season. Another local team to watch is the Lions of **Loyola Marymount University** (for tickets, tel. 310/338–4532).

Pro While the great American pastime may be baseball, in the town where the perennial world champion **Los Angeles Lakers** display what they call "showtime," basketball is king. The Lakers' home court is the Forum; for ticket information, call 310/419–3182. L.A.'s "other" team, the **Clippers,** make their home at the L.A. Sports Arena; for ticket information, call 213/748–6131.

Boxing and Wrestling

Championship competitions take place in both of these sports year-round at the Forum.

Football

College The **USC Trojans's** (for tickets, tel. 213/740–2311) home turf is the Coliseum, and the **UCLA Bruins** (for tickets, tel. 310/825–2101) pack 'em in at the Rose Bowl in Pasadena. Each season, the two rivals face off in one of college football's oldest and most exciting rivalries.

Pro The **L.A. Raiders** play at the Coliseum, downtown; for tickets, call Ticket Master at 213/480–3232. The **Los Angeles Rams** play at Anaheim Stadium; for ticket information, call 213/625–1123; team information, call 713/937–6767.

Golf

The hot golf ticket in town each February is the **Los Angeles Open** (tel. 213/482–1311). The tournament attracts the best golfers in the world and is played in Pacific Palisades at the Riviera Country Club.

Hockey

The **L.A. Kings** put their show on ice at the Forum, November–April. Ticket information: tel. 310/419–3182.

Horse Racing

Santa Anita Race Track (Huntington Dr. and Colorado Pl., Arcadia, tel. 818/574–7223) is still the dominant site for exciting Thoroughbred racing. You can always expect the best racing in the world at this beautiful facility.

Hollywood Park is another favorite racing venue. Since the completion of the Cary Grant Pavilion, a sense of class and style has been restored to this once-great park. The track is next to the Forum in Inglewood, at Century Boulevard and Prairie, tel. 310/419–1500. It's open late April–mid-July.

For harness racing, **Los Alamitos** (4961 Katella Ave.) has both day and night racing. For track information, call 714/236–4400 or 310/431–1361.

Several grand-prix jumping competitions and western riding championships are held throughout the year at the **Los Angeles Equestrian Center** in Burbank (480 Riverside Dr., tel. 818/840–9063).

Polo

Will Rogers State Park (14253 Sunset Blvd., Pacific Palisades) offers lovely picnic grounds where you can feast while enjoying an afternoon chukker of polo. For polo season information, call 310/454–8212. If it doesn't rain during the week, games are played Saturdays at 2 PM and Sundays at 10 AM. Parking fee is $5 per car.

Tennis

The Volvo/Los Angeles Pro Tournament is held in August at UCLA. The competition usually attracts some of the top-seeded players on the pro tennis circuit. For information, call 310/208–3838.

Beaches

The beach scene is an integral part of the Southern California lifestyle. There is no public attraction more popular in L.A. than the white, sandy playgrounds that line the deep blue Pacific.

From downtown, the easiest way to hit the coast is by taking the Santa Monica Freeway (I–10) due west. Once you reach the end of the freeway, I–10 turns into the famous Highway 1, better known as the Pacific Coast Highway, or PCH, and continues up to Oregon. Other basic routes from the downtown area include Pico, Olympic, Santa Monica, Sunset, or Wilshire boulevards. The RTD bus line runs every 20 minutes to and from the beaches along each of these streets.

Los Angeles County beaches (and state beaches operated by the county) have lifeguards. Public parking (for a fee) is available at most. The following beaches are listed in north–south order. Some are excellent for swimming, some for surfing (check with lifeguards for current conditions for either activity), others better for exploring.

Leo Carillo State Beach. This beach along a rough and mountainous stretch of coastline is the most fun at low tide, when a spectacular array of tide pools blossom for all to see. Rock formations on the beach have created some great secret coves for picnickers looking for solitude. There are hiking trails, sea caves, and tunnels, and whales, dolphins, and sea lions are often seen swimming in the offshore kelp beds. The waters here are rocky and best for experienced surfers and scuba divers; fishing is good. Picturesque campgrounds are set back from the beach. Camping fee is $14 per night. *35000 block of PCH, Malibu, tel. 818/880–0350. Facilities: parking, lifeguard, rest rooms, showers, fire pits.*

Zuma Beach County Park. This is Malibu's largest and sandiest beach, and a favorite spot of surfers. It's also a haven for high school students who've discovered Nautilus Plus. *30050 PCH, Malibu, tel. 310/457–9891. Facilities: parking, lifeguard, rest rooms, showers, food, playground, volleyball.*

Westward Beach/Point Dume State Beach. Another favorite spot for surfing, this ½-mile-long sandy beach has tide pools and sandstone cliffs. *South end of Westward Beach Rd., Malibu, tel. 310/457–9891. Facilities: parking, lifeguard, rest rooms, food.*

Paradise Cove. With its pier and equipment rentals, this sandy beach is a mecca for sport-fishing boats. Though swimming is allowed, there are lifeguards during the summer only. *28128 PCH, Malibu, tel. 310/457–2511. Facilities: parking, rest rooms, showers, food (concessions open summer only).*

Surfrider Beach/Malibu Lagoon State Beach. The steady 3- to 5-foot waves make this beach, just north of Malibu Pier, a great long-board surfing beach. The International Surfing Contest is held here in September. Water runoff from Malibu Canyon forms a natural lagoon, which is a sanctuary for many birds. There are also nature trails perfect for romantic sunset strolls. *23200 block of PCH, Malibu, tel. 818/880–0350. Facilities: parking, lifeguard, rest rooms, picnicking, visitor center.*

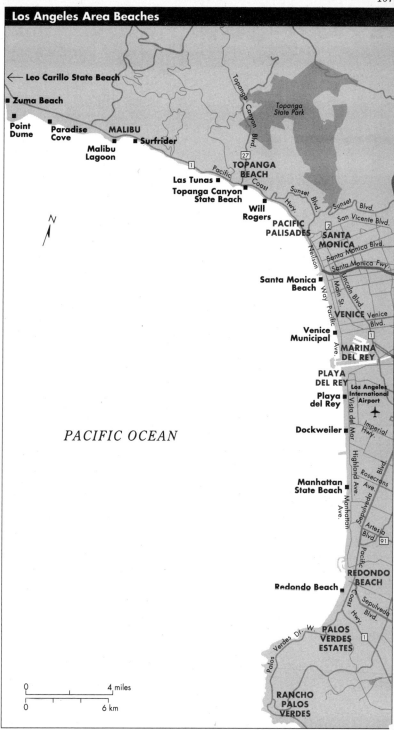

Los Angeles Area Beaches

← Leo Carillo State Beach

■ Zuma Beach

■ Point Dume

■ Paradise Cove

MALIBU ■

■ Surfrider

Malibu Lagoon

Topanga Canyon Blvd.

Topanga State Park

[1] Pacific Coast

[27]

TOPANGA BEACH ■

Las Tunas ■

Topanga Canyon State Beach ■

Will Rogers ■

Sunset Blvd.

Sunset Blvd.

San Vicente Blvd.

PACIFIC PALISADES

[2]

SANTA MONICA

Santa Monica Blvd.

Santa Monica Fwy.

Santa Monica ■ Beach

Neilson

Main St.

Lincoln Blvd.

Way Pacific

VENICE Venice Blvd.

Venice ■ Municipal

[1]

Abbot Kinney Ave.

MARINA DEL REY

PLAYA DEL REY

Playa ■ del Rey

Los Angeles International Airport ✈

Vista del Mar

Imperial Hwy.

Dockweiler ■

Highland Ave.

Sepulveda Blvd.

Rosecrans Ave.

Manhattan ■ State Beach

Manhattan Ave.

Artesia Blvd. [91]

PACIFIC OCEAN

REDONDO BEACH

Redondo Beach ■

Pacific Coast Hwy.

Sepulveda Blvd.

W. Palos Verdes Dr.

PALOS VERDES ESTATES

[1]

Palos Verdes Dr.

RANCHO PALOS VERDES

N

0   4 miles

0   6 km

Las Tunas State Beach. Las Tunas is small (1,300 feet long, covering a total of only two acres), narrow, and sandy, with some rocky areas, and set beneath a bluff. Surf fishing is the biggest attraction here. There is no lifeguard, and swimming is not encouraged because of steel groins set offshore to prevent erosion. *19400 block of PCH, Malibu, tel. 310/457–9891. Facilities: parking, rest rooms.*

Topanga Canyon State Beach. This rocky beach stretches from the mouth of the Topanga Canyon down to Coastline Drive. Catamarans dance in these waves and skid onto the sands of this popular beach, where dolphins sometimes come close enough to shore to startle sunbathers. The area near the canyon is a great surfing spot. *18700 block of PCH, Malibu, tel. 310/394–3266. Facilities: parking, lifeguard, rest rooms, food.*

Will Rogers State Beach. This wide, sandy beach is several miles long and has even surf. Parking in the lot here is limited, but there is plenty of beach, volleyball, and body surfing. *15800 PCH, Pacific Palisades, tel. 310/394–3266. Facilities: parking, lifeguard, rest rooms.*

Santa Monica Beach. This is one of L.A.'s most popular beaches. In addition to a pier and a promenade, a man-made breakwater just offshore has caused the sand to collect and form the widest stretch of beach on the entire Pacific coast. And wider beaches mean more bodies. If you're up for some sightseeing on land, this is one of the more popular gathering places for L.A.'s young, toned, and bronzed. All in all, the 2-mile-long beach is well equipped with bike paths, facilities for the disabled, playgrounds, and volleyball. In summer, free rock and jazz concerts are held at the pier on Thursday nights. *West of PCH, Santa Monica, tel. 310/394–3266. Facilities: parking, lifeguard, rest rooms, showers.*

Venice Municipal Beach. While the surf and sands of Venice are fine, the main attraction here is the boardwalk scene. Venice combines the beefcake of some of L.A.'s most serious bodybuilders with the productions of lively crafts merchants and street musicians. There are roller skaters and break dancers to entertain you, and cafés to feed you. You can rent bikes at Venice Pier Bike Shop (21 Washington St.) and skates at Skatey's (102 Washington St.). *1531 Ocean Front Walk, Venice, tel. 310/394–3266. Facilities: parking, rest rooms, showers, food, picnicking.*

Playa del Rey. South of Marina del Rey lies one of the more underrated beaches in Southern California. Its sprawling white sands stretch from the southern tip of Marina del Rey almost two miles down to Dockweiler Beach. The majority of the crowds that frequent these sands are young. One of the more attractive features of this beach is an area called Del Rey Lagoon, a grassy oasis in the heart of Playa del Rey. A lovely pond is inhabited by dozens of ducks, and barbecue pits and tables are available to picnickers. *6660 Esplanade, Playa del Rey. Facilities: parking, lifeguard, rest rooms, food.*

Dockweiler State Beach. There are consistent waves for surfing here, and it is not crowded, due to an unsightly power plant with towering smokestacks parked right on the beach. While the plant presents no danger to swimmers in the area, its mere presence, combined with the jumbo jets taking off overhead from L.A.'s International Airport, makes this beach a better place for surfing or working out than for lying out. There is firewood for sale for barbecues on the beach; beach fires are legal in this area as long as they are contained within the special pits that are already set up along the beach. *Harbor Channel to Vista del Mar and Grand Ave., Playa del Rey, tel. 310/322–5008. Facilities: parking, lifeguard, rest rooms, showers.*

Manhattan State Beach. Here are 44 acres of sandy beach for swimming, diving, surfing, and fishing. Polliwog Park is a charming, grassy landscape a few yards back from the beach that parents with young children may appreciate. Ducks waddle around a small pond, picnickers enjoy a full range of facilities including grills and rest rooms. *West of Strand, Manhattan Beach, tel. 310/372–2166. Facilities: volleyball, parking, lifeguard, rest rooms, showers, food.*

Redondo State Beach. The beach is wide, sandy, and usually packed in summer, and parking is limited. The Redondo Pier marks the starting point of the beach area, which continues south for more than 2 miles along a heavily developed shoreline community. Storms have damaged some of the restaurants and shops along the pier, but plenty of others are still functioning. Excursion boats, boat launching ramps, and fishing are other attractions. There is a series of rock and jazz concerts held at the pier during the summer. *Foot of Torrance Blvd., Redondo Beach, tel. 310/372–2166. Facilities: volleyball, parking, lifeguard, rest rooms, showers, food.*

6 Dining

By Bruce David Colen

Since 1974, Bruce David Colen has been the restaurant and food critic for Los Angeles magazine. He has also written on food and travel for Town & Country, Architectural Digest, Bon Appetit, Travel and Leisure, *and* Endless Vacations.

The high-living '80s saw Los Angeles emerge as a top gastronomic capital of the world. It was an amazing and delicious transformation. Where once the city was known only for its chopped Cobb salad, Green Goddess dressing, drive-in hamburger stands, and outdoor barbecues, today it is home to many of the best French and Italian restaurants in the United States, and so many places featuring international cuisines that listing them would be like roll call at the United Nations. There are so many new—and good—dining establishments opening every week that, currently, there are more chairs, booths, and banquettes than there are bodies to fill them. The result is a fierce competition among upscale restaurateurs that has made L.A. one of the least expensive big cities—here or abroad—in which to eat well.

Locals tend to dine early, between 7:30 and 9 PM, in part a holdover from when this was a "studio" town, and the film-making day started at 6 AM, but these days more to allow for early morning jogging and gym time. Advance reservations are essential at the best restaurants, and at almost all restaurants on weekend evenings.

Highly recommended restaurants are indicated by a star ★.

Category	Cost*
Very Expensive	over $50
Expensive	$30–$50
Moderate	$20–$30
Inexpensive	under $20

*per person, excluding 8.25% tax, service, and drinks

American

Beverly Hills
★ **The Grill.** This is the closest Los Angeles comes in looks and atmosphere to one of San Francisco's venerable bar and grills, with their dark-wood paneling and brass trim. The food is basic American, cleanly and simply prepared, and includes fine steaks and chops, grilled fresh salmon, corned beef hash, braised beef ribs, and a creamy version of the Cobb salad. *9560 Dayton Way, tel. 310/276–0615. Reservations required. Dress: casual. AE, DC, MC, V. Closed Sun. Valet parking in evening. Moderate.*

Ed Debevic's. This is a good place to take the kids, or a good place to go yourself if you're feeling nostalgic. Old Coca-Cola signs, a blaring juke box, gum-chewing waitresses in bobby sox, and meat loaf and mashed potatoes will take you back to the diners of the '50s. *134 N. La Cienega, tel. 310/659–1952. No weekend reservations; weekday reservations advised. Dress: casual. No credit cards. Valet parking. Inexpensive.*

RJ'S the Rib Joint. There is a large barrel of free peanuts at the door, sawdust on the floor, and atmosphere to match. The outstanding salad bar has dozens of fresh choices and return privileges, and there are big portions of everything—from ribs, chili, and barbecued chicken, to mile-high layer cakes—all at very reasonable prices. *252 N. Beverly Dr., tel. 310/274–RIBS. Reservations advised. Dress: casual. AE, DC, MC, V. Valet parking in evening. Inexpensive.*

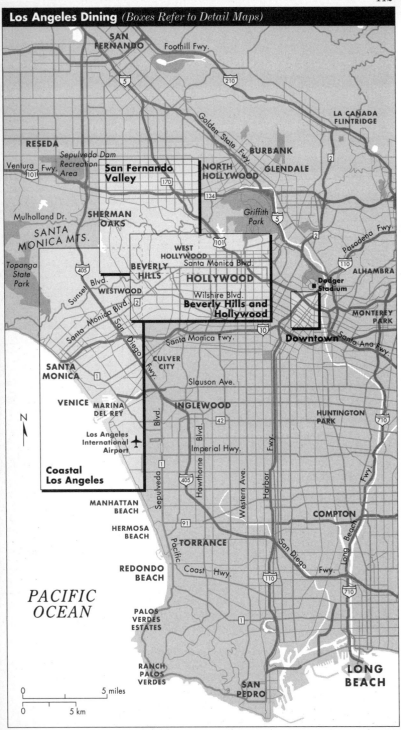

Los Angeles Dining *(Boxes Refer to Detail Maps)*

Downtown Los Angeles Dining

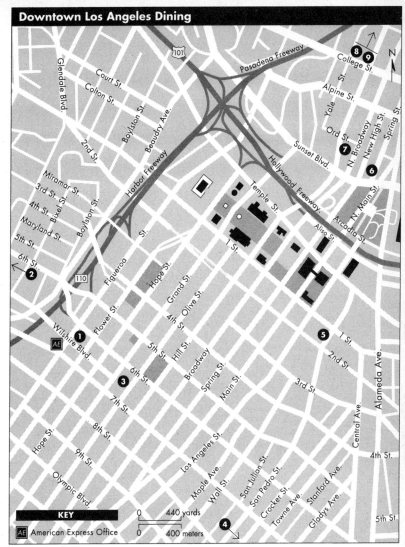

The Chronicle, **8**

Engine Co. #28, **1**

Mon Kee Seafood Restaurant, **6**

Ocean Seafood, **7**

Pacific Dining Car, **2**

Restaurant Horikawa, **5**

Rex Il Ristorante, **3**

Vickman's, **4**

Yujean's, **9**

Beverly Hills and Hollywood Dining

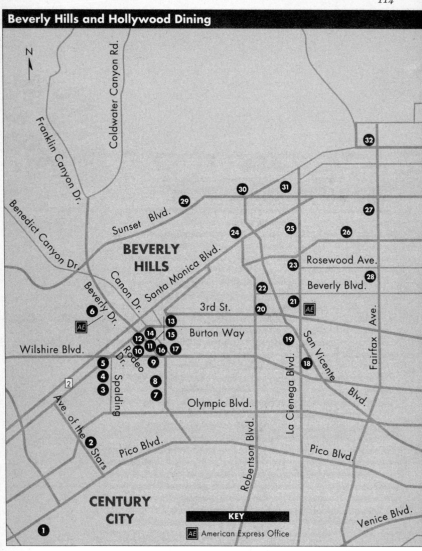

Antonio's
Restaurant, **36**
Arnie Morton's of
Chicago, **19**
The Bistro, **16**
The Bistro Garden, **17**
Ca' Brea, **33**
California Pizza
Kitchen, **8**
Canter's, **28**
Carnegie Deli, **14**
Cha Cha Cha, **41**
Chan Dara, **38**
Chasen's, **22**

Chopstix, **35**
Citrus, **37**
Columbia Bar and
Grill, **39**
The Dining Room, **9**
Ed Debevic's, **18**
El Cholo, **40**
Greenblatt's, **32**
The Grill, **10**
Hard Rock Cafe, **21**
Harry's Bar &
American Grill, **2**
Il Fornaio Cucina
Italiana, **13**

Jimmy's, **3**
Joss, **29**
La Veranda, **7**
Le Chardonnay, **26**
Le Dome, **31**
L'Escoffier, **4**
Locanda Veneta, **20**
L'Orangerie, **25**
The Mandarin, **12**
Morton's, **23**
Nate 'n Al's, **15**
The Palm, **24**
Prego, **6**

Primi, **1**
RJ's the Rib Joint, **11**
Restaurant Katsu, **42**
Spago, **30**
Tommy Tang's, **34**
Trader Vic's, **5**
Tuttobene, **27**

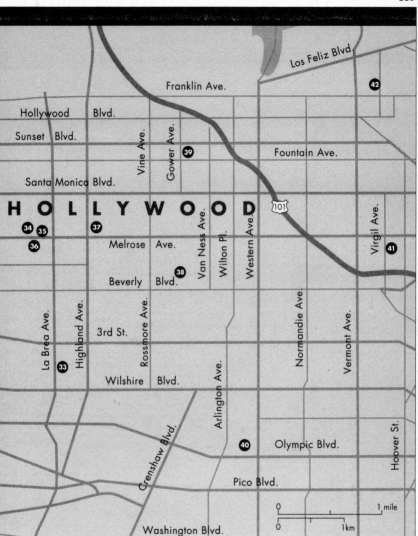

Beaurivage, **2**
Border Grill, **7**
Broadway Deli, **6**
Chinois on Main, **9**
Dynasty Room, **15**
Edie's Diner, **12**
Gilliland's, **8**
Gladstone's 4 Fish, **4**
The Good Earth, **14**
Granita, **1**
The Hotel Bel Air, **16**
Orleans, **10**
Tra di Noi, **3**
Valentino, **13**
Warszawa, **5**
West Beach Cafe, **11**

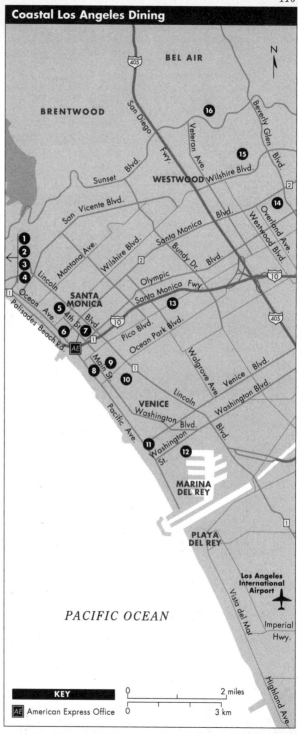

Coastal Los Angeles Dining

BEL AIR

BRENTWOOD

WESTWOOD

SANTA MONICA

VENICE

MARINA DEL REY

PLAYA DEL REY

Los Angeles International Airport

PACIFIC OCEAN

KEY

AE American Express Office

0   2 miles
0   3 km

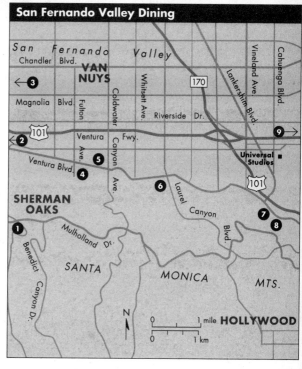

San Fernando Valley Dining

Downtown   **Pacific Dining Car.** This is one of L.A.'s oldest restaurants, located in a 1920s railroad car and expanded over the years. Best known for well-aged steaks, rack of lamb, and an extensive California wine list at fair prices, it's a favorite haunt of politicians and lawyers around City Hall and of sports fans after Dodger games. *1310 W. 6th St., tel. 213/483–6000. Reservations advised. Dress: casual. MC, V. Valet parking. Moderate–Expensive.*

Engine Co. #28. The ground floor of this National Historic Site building was refurbished and refitted to become a very polished, "uptown" downtown bar and grill, and it's been crowded from day one. The reason? All-American food carefully prepared and served with obvious pride. Don't miss the corn chowder, "Firehouse" chili, grilled pork chop, smoked rare tenderloin, and grilled ahi tuna. And there's a great lemon meringue pie. *Corner of Figueroa St. and Wilshire Blvd., tel. 213/624–6966. Reservations required. Dress: jacket and tie advised at lunch; casual at dinner. AE, MC, V. No weekend lunch. Valet parking. Moderate.*

Vickman's. Located next to the L.A. Produce Market, this bustling cafeteria opens at 3 AM to accommodate fleets of truck drivers, restaurant and hotel buyers, stall owners, curious night-people, and customers of the nearby flower mart. The dishes are simple, hearty, and bountiful: ham and eggs, grits, stuffed pork chops, giant sandwiches, and a famous fresh strawberry pie. It's a fun place to go to if you can't sleep. *1228 E. 8th St., tel. 213/622–3852. No reservations. Dress: casual. No credit cards. No dinner. Inexpensive.*

Eastside **The Chronicle.** You'll think you're in San Francisco's Sam's or
(Downtown the Tadich Grill, both very good places to be. The Chronicle's
Los Angeles steaks, chops, prime rib, oysters and other shellfish are excel-
Dining map) lent, and it has one of the best California wine lists south of the
Napa Valley. *897 Granite Dr., tel. 818/792–1179. Reservations
advised. Jacket and tie required. AE, D, DC, MC, V. Valet park-
ing. Moderate.*

Hollywood **Columbia Bar & Grill.** Located front and center in the heart of
Tinsel Town, this comfortably contemporary restaurant, with
Jasper Johns and David Hockneys on the walls, is the daytime
mecca for people from the surrounding television and film studios. The food is definitely above par. Don't pass up the crab
cakes; Caesar salad; or the fish, fowl, and meats grilled over a
variety of flavor-filled woods. *1448 N. Gower St., tel. 213/461–
8800. Reservations required. Dress: casual. AE, DC, MC, V.
Closed Sun. Valet parking. Moderate–Expensive.*

San Fernando **Paty's.** Located near NBC, Warner Brothers, and the Disney
Valley Studio, Paty's is a good place for stargazing without having to
mortgage your home to pay for the meal. This is an all-American–style upgraded coffee shop with a comfortable, eclectic
decor. Breakfasts are charming; the omelets are plump, and
the biscuits are homemade and served with high-quality jam.
Lunches and dinners include Swiss steak and a hearty beef
stew that is served in a hollowed-out loaf of home-baked bread.
Roast turkey is served with dressing and a moist, sweet loaf of
home-baked nut or raisin bread. All desserts are worth saving
room for: New Orleans bread pudding with a hot brandy sauce
is popular, and the Danishes are gigantic. *10001 Riverside Dr.,
Toluca Lake, tel. 818/760–9164. No reservations. Dress: casual.
No credit cards. Inexpensive.*

West Hollywood **Arnie Morton's of Chicago.** The West Coast addition to this
★ ever-expanding national chain brought joy and cholesterol to
the hearts of Los Angeles meat lovers, many of whom claim that
Morton's serves the best steaks in town. In addition to an 18-
ounce porterhouse, a New York strip, and a double-cut filet
mignon, there are giant veal and lamb chops, thick cuts of
prime rib, and Maine lobsters starting at $38 for a 2½ pounder.
Although the prices are steep, the produce is prime, as is the
service and private clublike atmosphere. You can save a few
dollars by going elsewhere, but you won't be as happy. *435 S.
La Cienega Blvd., tel. 310/246–1501. Reservations advised.
Jacket required. AE, D, DC, MC, V. No lunch. Expensive–Very
Expensive.*

Chasen's. It may no longer be Hollywood's "in" spot (and it
hasn't been for a very long time), but the clublike rooms are
full of nostalgia and have a quaintly formal charm, two qualities
that are making a come-back in the low-profile '90s. The dishes
that Alfred Hitchcock, Gary Cooper, and Henry Fonda loved—
and George Burns still does—are as good as ever: hobo steak,
double-rib lamb chops, boiled beef with matzo dumplings, and
the late Dave Chasen's famous chili. For the finales, try the
sensational banana shortcake or frozen éclair. This is a place
for special celebrations and great old-time service. *9039 Beverly Blvd., tel. 310/271–2168. Weekend reservations advised.
Jacket and tie required. AE, MC, V. Closed Mon. No weekend
lunch. Valet parking. Expensive.*

Morton's. When the brother-and-sister owners of this trendy
restaurant decided to open an upscale clubhouse for the music

and entertainment industry, it was only natural that choice steaks should be the cornerstone of the menu—their father is *the* Arnie Morton of Chicago (*see above*). Good broiled fish and chicken have since been added. Don't be intimidated by the celebrity-fawning waiters, all hoping for an acting job. *8764 Melrose Ave., tel. 310/276–5205. Reservations required. Jacket required. AE, MC, V. Closed Sun. Valet parking. Expensive.*

The Palm. If you don't mind the roar of the jocks, or having the New York–style waiters rush you through your Bronx cheese-cake, this is where you'll find the biggest and best steamed Maine lobster, good steaks and chops, great french-fried onion rings, and paper-thin potato slices. Have the roast beef hash for lunch, and you can skip dinner. A three-person-deep bar adds to the noise. *9001 Santa Monica Blvd., tel. 310/550–8811. Reservations advised. Dress: casual. AE, DC, MC, V. No weekend lunch. Valet parking. Expensive.*

Hard Rock Cafe. Big burgers, rich milkshakes, banana splits, BLTs, and other pre-nouvelle food delights, along with loud music, and rock 'n' roll memorabilia, have made this '50s-era barn of a cafe the favorite of local teenagers. There is a large and busy bar for curious adults, many of whom are parents watching the kids. The place drew national attention—and spawned other Hard Rocks—for its fish-tail Cadillac jutting out of the roof, Fonzie's leather jacket on the wall, and Elvis's motorcycle. *8600 Beverly Blvd., tel. 310/276–7605. No reservations. Dress: casual. AE, DC, MC, V. Valet parking. Moderate.*

Westside
(Coastal
Los Angeles
Dining map)
★

West Beach Cafe. It seems that Bruce Madder can do no wrong. More than 10 years ago, he opened this upscale restaurant within a Frisbee toss of the action on the Venice Beach strand. Next came Rebecca's, just across the street, where Mexican food is treated as semi-haute cuisine and idolized by the upscale. Then came his most recent hit, the Broadway Deli in Santa Monica (*see below*). Best bets at the West Beach are: Caesar salad, filet mignon taco, braised lamb shank, ravioli with port and radicchio, fisherman's soup, and what many consider the best hamburger and fries in all of Los Angeles. There's also a fabulous selection of French wines and liqueurs. *60 N. Venice Blvd., tel. 310/823–5396. Reservations advised. Dress: casual. AE, DC, MC, V. Valet parking. Moderate–Expensive.*

Gilliland's. Gerri Gilliland was teaching cooking in her native Ireland, took a vacation in Southern California, and never went back. Instead, she stayed and created this charming restaurant, which offers the best of both culinary worlds and showcases her fascination with Mediterranean dishes. The soda bread, Irish stew, and corned beef and cabbage are wonderful; and marvelous is the only word for her bitter lemon tart. The place is warm and friendly, just like its owner. *2424 Main St., Santa Monica, tel. 310/392–3901. Reservations advised. Dress: casual. AE, MC, V. Moderate.*

Broadway Deli. The name is misleading, so don't come here expecting hot corned beef and pastrami sandwiches. This joint venture of Michel Richard (Citrus) and Bruce Madder is a cross between a European brasserie and an upscale diner. Whatever you feel like eating, you will probably find it on the menu, from a platter of assorted smoked fish or Caesar salad to chicken pot pie, carpaccio, steak, and broiled salmon with cream spinach. There are also excellent desserts and freshly baked breads. The retail counter is the place to fill a picnic basket with the best European and domestic delicacies. *1457*

3rd St. Promenade, Santa Monica, tel. 310/451–0616. Reservations accepted. Dress: casual. AE, MC, V. Valet parking. Inexpensive–Moderate.

Gladstone's 4 Fish. This is undoubtedly the most popular restaurant along the Southern California coast, serving well over a million beachgoers a year. Perhaps the food is not the greatest in the world, but familiar seashore fare is prepared adequately and in large portions, and the prices are certainly right. Best bets: crab chowder, steamed clams, three-egg omelets, hamburgers, barbecued ribs, and chili. And then there's the wonderful view, especially from the beach-side terrace—ideal for whale-, porpoise-, and people-watching. *17300 Pacific Coast Hwy. (at Sunset Blvd.), Pacific Palisades, tel. 310/ GL4–FISH. Reservations advised. Dress: casual. AE, DC, MC, V. Valet parking. Inexpensive.*

Cajun

Westside
(Coastal Los Angeles Dining map)

Orleans. The jambalaya and gumbo dishes are hot—in more ways than one—at this spacious eatery, where the cuisine was created with the help of New Orleans celebrity-chef Paul Prudhomme. The blackened redfish is probably the best catch on the menu. *11705 National Blvd., W. Los Angeles, tel. 310/479–4187. Reservations advised. Dress: casual. AE, DC, MC, V. Moderate–Expensive.*

California Cuisine

Beverly Hills

The Bistro Garden. The flower-banked outdoor dining terrace makes this the quintessential Southern California luncheon experience. It's chic and lively without being pretentious or too "Hollywood." There's excellent smoked salmon, fresh cracked crab, steak tartare, calves' liver with bacon, and a unique apple pancake. *176 N. Canon Dr., tel. 310/550–3900. Reservations required. Jacket and tie required at dinner. AE, DC, MC, V. Closed Sun. Valet parking. Expensive.*

★ **The Dining Room.** Located in the remodeled Regent Beverly Wilshire, this elegant, European-looking salon is the best thing to happen to L.A. hotel dining in decades. Wonderful California cuisine, plus splendid service at surprisingly non-posh prices. Adjoining is an equally attractive, sophisticated cocktail lounge, with romantic lighting and a pianist playing show tunes. *9500 Wilshire Blvd., tel. 310/275–5200. Reservations advised. Jacket and tie required. AE, DC, MC, V. Valet parking. Expensive.*

La Veranda. David Slay had a very popular restaurant of the same name in St. Louis, then came West. He has succeeded in making his fortune in hyper-critical Beverly Hills, serving, of all things, middle-American cooking with Italian overtones. His small, intimate place is loaded with celebrities and just plain folk back for more of Slay's sautéed calves liver, peppered sirloin steak with horseradish sauce, and the grilled veal chop and roasted garlic. Best side dish: fried spinach with Parmesan cheese. *225 S. Beverly Dr., tel. 310/274–7246. Reservations advised. Jacket advised. AE, DC, MC, V. No weekend lunch. Moderate.*

California Pizza Kitchen. It's *the* place to go if you hanker for a good pizza at a fair price but don't feel like the usual pizza-parlor surroundings. There's an immaculate, pleasingly modern dining room, plus counter service by the open kitchen, and a wide, rather esoteric choice of pizza toppings. The pastas are equally interesting and carefully prepared. The few sidewalk tables are in great demand. *207 S. Beverly Dr., tel. 310/272–7878. No reservations. Dress: casual. AE, MC, V. Inexpensive.*

West Hollywood **L'Escoffier.** Opened in 1955 to celebrate the completion of Conrad Hilton's flagship hotel, this elegant penthouse restaurant introduced L.A. to the high-calorie delights of haute cuisine. With the Beverly Hilton now owned by Merv Griffin, the room and the menu have been updated for the '90s. Chef Michel Blanchet, a brilliant exponent of light French/California cuisine, produces the sort of dishes you can't say no to: smoked salmon and dill pancakes, mussel-saffron soup, lobster ravioli, boar stewed in cabernet, and, for dessert, apple tart and cinnamon ice cream. *9876 Wilshire Blvd., tel. 310/274–7777. Reservations required. Jacket and tie advised. AE, D, DC, MC, V. No lunch. Valet parking. Expensive–Very Expensive.*

★ **Citrus.** Tired of being known only as one of the country's greatest pastry chefs, Michel Richard opened this contemporary restaurant to display the breadth of his talent. He creates superb dishes by blending French and American cuisines. You can't miss with the delectable tuna burger, the thinnest-possible angel-hair pasta, or the deep-fried potatoes, sautéed foie gras, rare duck, or sweetbread salads. Get your doctor's permission before even looking at Richard's irresistible desserts. *6703 Melrose Ave., tel. 310/857–0034. Reservations advised. Jacket required. AE, MC, V. Closed Sun. Valet parking. Moderate–Expensive.*

★ **Spago.** This is the restaurant that propelled owner/chef Wolfgang Puck into the national and international culinary spotlights. He deserves every one of his accolades for raising California cuisine to an imaginative and joyous gastronomic level, using only the finest West Coast produce. The proof is in the tasting: grilled baby Sonoma lamb, pizza with Santa Barbara shrimp, thumbnail-size Washington oysters topped with golden caviar, grilled free-range chickens, and, from the North Pacific, baby salmon. As for Puck's incredible desserts, he's on Weight Watchers' Most Wanted List. This is the place to see *People* magazine live, but you'll have to put up with the noise in exchange. Be safe: Make reservations at least two weeks in advance. *1114 Horn Ave., tel. 310/652–4025. Reservations required. Jacket required. AE, DC, MC, V. No lunch. Valet parking. Moderate–Expensive.*

Westside **Hotel Bel-Air.** Even if the food were terrible, you wouldn't care,
(Coastal since the romantic, country-garden setting is, by itself, so sat-
Los Angeles isfying. But the California-Continental cooking is very good
Dining map) indeed, be it breakfast, lunch, or dinner. A meal at the Bel-Air is a not-to-be-missed experience. *701 Stone Canyon Rd., Bel Air, tel. 310/472–1211. Reservations advised. Jacket and tie advised at dinner. AE, DC, MC, V. Valet parking. Expensive.*

Granita. Wolfgang Puck's latest triumph, Granita has such stunning interior details as handmade tiles embedded with seashells, blown-glass lighting fixtures, and etched-glass panels with wavy edges. It's as close as you'll come to the beach without getting sand in your shoes. Even the blasé Malibu film colony is impressed. While Puck's menu here favors seafood items such as grilled John Dory with a Thai curry sauce, Mediterranean fish soup with half a lobster, and seared Nantucket scallops on black pepper fettuccini, the menu also features some of his standard favorites: spicy shrimp pizza, ginger duck stir-fry in a scallion pancake, grilled quail on pumpkin ravioli, and wild mushroom risotto. *23725 W. Malibu Rd., Malibu, tel. 310/456–0488. Reservations required 1 wk ahead, especially for weekend. Dress: casual but neat. AE, DC, MC, V. No lunch Mon. and Tues. Moderate–Expensive.*

Caribbean

Hollywood **Cha Cha Cha.** When the Cajun food craze cooled off among L.A. foodies, Caribbean cooking became the trend, and this small shack of a place was, for a while, the hottest spot in town. There's cornmeal chicken, spicy swordfish, fried banana chips, and assorted flans. This is a hangout for celebrities gone slumming. A "Valley" branch (17499 Ventura Blvd., Encino, tel. 818/789–3600) has recently opened, in much more stylish quarters. *656 N. Virgil Ave., tel. 310/664–7723. Reservations required, but expect wait. Dress: casual. AE, DC, MC, V. Valet parking. Moderate.*

Chinese

Beverly Hills **Joss.** This very elegant, attractively modern restaurant, popular with the natives of Beverly Hills and the Hollywood Hills, offers beautifully presented, aristocratic versions of Mandarin cuisine. Try the varied dim sum and the Peking duck served as two courses. Many claim Joss has the best cooking west of Downtown Chinatown. Service can be haughty. The sidewalk tables are a popular rendezvous for lunch. *9255 Sunset Blvd., tel. 310/276–1886. Reservations advised. Jacket required. AE, D, DC, MC, V. No weekend lunch. Moderate–Expensive.*

★ **The Mandarin.** Who said you only find great Chinese food in hole-in-the-wall places with oilcloth tabletops? Here is a good-looking restaurant with the best crystal and linens, serving an equally bright mixture of Szechuan and Chinese country-cooking dishes. Minced squab in lettuce-leaf tacos, Peking duck, a superb beggars chicken, scallion pancakes, and any of the noodle dishes are recommended. The no-frills, under-$10 luncheon is a great deal. *430 N. Camden Dr., tel. 310/272–0267. Reservations required. Jacket required. AE, DC, MC, V. No weekend lunch. Valet parking. Inexpensive–Moderate.*

Downtown **Ocean Seafood Restaurant.** A newcomer that is challenging Mon Kee (*see above*) for the garlic crab and catfish crown, it has what the vast majority, including the Chinese community, consider the greatest dim sum menu in town. This noisy, vast Great Banquet Hall of a place becomes far more intimate when the staff drops by your table with dozens of tasty little Cantonese treats. The perfect place for a Sunday breakfast or lunch. *747 N. Broadway, tel. 213/687–3088. Reservations accepted. Dress: casual. MC, V. Moderate.*

★ **Mon Kee Seafood Restaurant.** The name pretty much spells it out—except how good the cooking is and how morning-fresh the fish are. The delicious garlic crab is addictive; the steamed catfish is a masterpiece of gentle flavors. In fact, almost everything on the menu is excellent. This is a crowded, messy place; be prepared to wait for a table. *679 N. Spring St., tel. 213/628–6717. No reservations. Dress: casual. MC, V. Pay parking lot. Inexpensive–Moderate.*

Pasadena
★ **Yujean Kang's Gourmet Chinese Cuisine.** Despite its length, this name doesn't say it all. Mr. Kang, formerly of San Francisco, is well on his way to becoming the finest nouvelle-Chinese chef in the nation. Forget any and all preconceived notions of what Chinese food should look and taste like. Start with the tender slices of veal on a bed of enoki and black mushrooms, topped with a tangle of quick-fried shoestring yams, or the catfish with kumquats and a passion fruit sauce, and finish with poached plums, or watermelon ice under a mantle of white chocolate, and you will appreciate that this is no chop suey joint. *69 N. Raymond Ave., tel. 818/585–0855. AE, MC, V. Reservations advised. Dress: casual. Closed Tues. No lunch Thur.–Sun. Moderate–Expensive.*

West Hollywood
Chopstix. Never underestimate the ability of Californians to adopt—and adapt—an ethnic-food vogue. In this case, dim sum, subtly doctored for non-Oriental tastes. The result is nouvelle Chinese junk-food served in a mod setting, at high-stool tables or at a diner-like counter. The dishes are interesting, but don't expect a native Chinese to agree. Nonetheless, branches are appearing around the Southland, faster than you can say "I'd like one of those . . ." *7229 Melrose Ave., tel. 310/935–2944; 22917 Pacific Coast Hwy., Malibu, tel. 310/456–7774. No reservations. Dress: casual. AE, DC, MC, V. Inexpensive.*

Continental

Beverly Hills
The Bistro. The kitchen is not quite as good as Jimmy's (*see below*), but nobody has ever questioned that this replica of a Parisian boîte is one of the most stylish dining rooms west of Europe. The original owner, director Billy Wilder, was responsible for the interior design: mirrored walls, etched-glass partitions, giant bouquets of fresh flowers, and soft lighting. The food is more American bistro than French. There is a delicious, juicy chopped steak, good veal medallions, Eastern lobster on tagliatelli, and, most likely, the greatest chocolate soufflé you've ever tasted. *246 N. Canon Dr., tel. 310/273–5633. Reservations required. Jacket and tie required. AE, DC, MC, V. Closed Sun. No Sat. lunch. Valet parking. Expensive–Very Expensive.*

Century City
(Beverly Hills and Hollywood Dining map)
Jimmy's. When Beverly Hills C.E.O.s are not dining at home they head here or to the Bistro (*see above*). Owner Jimmy Murphy provides the warmth in this expensive, decorator-elegant restaurant. The best dishes on the broad menu include smoked Scottish salmon, prawns with herbs and garlic, saddle of lamb, Chateaubriand, and pheasant breast with wild blueberry sauce. There's a fine steak tartare at lunch. *201 Moreno Dr., tel. 310/879–2394. Reservations required. Jacket and tie required. AE, DC, MC, V. Valet parking. Expensive–Very Expensive.*

San Fernando Valley
Victoria Station. Located atop the Universal Studios hill, this restaurant has been built to resemble (sort of) a British railway station. The service is cheerful and efficient. Recommended are the quality top sirloin and good teriyaki steak; gooey, cheesy baked potato skins provide a perfect appetizer. The ribs here are a bit greasy, but they have a nice smoky flavor. Dinners come with soup of the day or a pleasant salad bar and whole-grain bread. There's also a great children's menu at reasonable prices. No matter what age you are, don't leave without trying the peanut-butter pie: It's a nutty peanut-butter filling frozen into a graham-cracker crust with whipped cream on top and

chocolate hot fudge sauce on the side. You'll find good value here. *3850 Lankershim Blvd., Universal City, tel. 818/760–0714. Reservations accepted. Dress: casual. AE, MC, V. Expensive.*

Europa. The menu here roams the world: great goulash, terrific teriyaki—even matzoh ball soup. The dining room is tiny and casual; reservations are a must, as this is a community favorite. *14929 Magnolia Blvd., Sherman Oaks, tel. 818/501–9175. Reservations advised. Dress: casual. MC, V. Closed Mon. No lunch. Inexpensive–Moderate.*

L'Express. At this cheerful brasserie, people from Hollywood's soundstages meet, mingle, and relax. Contemporary art and lots of neon add color, too. It's a great place for late-night snacks, croque monsieur, pizzas of all types, and very rich desserts. There is a full bar (and quite a bar scene). *14190 Ventura Blvd., Sherman Oaks, tel. 818/990–8683; 3573 Cahuenga Blvd., Universal City, tel. 818/876–3778. No reservations. Dress: casual. AE, MC, V. Inexpensive–Moderate.*

Santa Monica **Warszawa.** At this Polish restaurant, the food is hearty and heartwarming. Crisp roast duck stuffed with apples is a house favorite, as are the potato pancakes sprinkled with cinnamon and garnished with dried plums, sour cream, and apples. And, of course, there are all sorts of variations on goulash and dumplings. On a diet? Stick with the fresh rainbow trout, steamed with leeks and dill. *1414 Lincoln Blvd., tel. 310/393–8831. Reservations advised. Dress: casual. AE, D, DC, MC, V. No lunch. Moderate.*

Westwood **Dynasty Room.** This peaceful, elegant room in the Westwood *(Coastal* Marquis Hotel has a European flair and tables set far enough *Los Angeles* apart for privacy. Besides well-handled Continental fare, there *Dining map)* is a *cuisine minceur* menu for calorie counters. Best of all, an especially lavish, excellent Sunday brunch. *930 Hilgard Ave., tel. 310/208–8765. Reservations required. Jacket and tie required. AE, DC, MC, V. No lunch. Valet parking. Expensive.*

Deli

Beverly Hills **Carnegie Deli.** Oil millionaire Marvin Davis got tired of jetting cheesecake, pastrami, and lox back from the parent Carnegie in New York City, so he financed a Beverly Hills taste-alike to challenge Nate 'n Al's preeminence. His big guns are corned beef and pastrami sandwiches that are 4½ inches high, cheese blintzes under a snowcap of sour cream, and wonderfully creamy cole slaw. *300 N. Beverly Dr., tel. 310/275–3354. No reservations. Dress: casual. AE, MC, V. Inexpensive.*

Nate 'n Al's. A famous gathering place for Hollywood comedians, gag writers, and their agents, Nate 'n Al's serves first-rate matzo-ball soup, lox and scrambled eggs, cheese blintzes, potato pancakes, and the best deli sandwiches west of Manhattan. *414 N. Beverly Dr., tel. 310/274–0101. No reservations. Dress: casual. AE, V. Free parking. Inexpensive.*

San Fernando **Art's Delicatessen.** One of the best Jewish-style delicatessens **Valley** in the city serves breakfast, lunch, and dinner daily. The sand-★ wiches are mammoth and are made from some of the best corned beef, pastrami, and other cold cuts around. Matzo-ball soup and sweet-and-sour cabbage soup are specialties, and there is good chopped chicken liver. *12224 Ventura Blvd., Studio City, tel. 818/762–1221. No reservations. Dress: casual. D, DC, MC, V. Inexpensive.*

West Hollywood **Canter's.** Ex–New Yorkers claim that this grandaddy of delicatessens (it opened in 1928) is the closest thing in atmosphere,
smell, and menu to a Big Apple corned-beef and pastrami hangout. The elderly waitresses even speak with a New York accent.
It's open 24 hours a day and has an in-house bakery. *419 N.
Fairfax Ave., tel. 213/651–2030. Reservations accepted. Dress:
casual. MC, V. Valet parking. Inexpensive.*

Greenblatt's. Who ever heard of a deli famous for its extensive
wine list? This one also serves wood-smoked ribs, rotisserie
chicken, and 20 different salads, along with the usual sandwiches. *8017 Sunset Blvd., tel. 213/656–0606. No reservations.
Dress: casual. AE, MC, V. Parking lot. Inexpensive.*

French

San Fernando **Pinot.** The only culinary area that Los Angeles has been slow
Valley in developing is genuine bistro cooking. All that changed when
★ Joachim Spliechel, owner-chef of top-rated Patina, opened this
perfectly designed synthesis of remembered Parisian bistros.
One can almost smell the fumes of Gauloises and the scent of
pastis, and the dishes are equally authentic: smoked eel and
trout, five kinds of fresh oysters, country pâtés, bouillabaisse,
braised tongue and spinach, pot au feu, and steak with pommes
frites. Patina's pastry chef, who specializes in chocolate desserts, also orchestrates Pinot's scandalous finales. *12969 Ventura Blvd., tel. 818/990–0500. Reservations advised. Jacket
required. AE, MC, V. Valet parking. Moderate–Expensive.*

West Hollywood **L'Orangerie.** For sheer elegance and classic good taste, it would
★ be hard to find a lovelier restaurant in this country. And the
cuisine, albeit nouvelle-light, is as French as the l'orangerie at
Versailles. Specialties include coddled eggs served in the shell
and topped with caviar, squab with foie gras, pot-au-feu, rack
of lamb for two, and an unbeatable apple tart served with a jug
of double cream. *903 N. La Cienega Blvd., tel. 213/652–9770. Reservations required. Jacket and tie required. AE, DC, MC, V. No
weekend lunch. Valet parking. Expensive–Very Expensive.*

Le Dome. For some reason, local food critics have never given
this brasserie the attention it deserves. Perhaps they are intimidated by the hordes of show- and music-biz celebrities that
keep the place humming. By and large the food is wonderful,
honest, down-to-earth French: cockles in white wine and shal-
lots, veal ragout, marvelous veal sausage with red cabbage, and
a genuine, stick-to-the-ribs cassoulet. *8720 Sunset Blvd., tel.
213/659–6919. Reservations required. Dress: casual. AE, DC,
MC, V. Closed Sun. Valet parking. Expensive.*

Le Chardonnay. The interiors are Art Deco in this unabashed
copy of a famous Left Bank bistro, circa 1920. Despite the high
noise level, it's a most romantic rendezvous, with comfortable,
cozy booths. Specialties include warm sweetbread salad, goat
cheese ravioli, roast venison, grilled fish, Peking duck with a
ginger and honey sauce, and lots of lush desserts. *8284 Melrose
Ave., tel. 213/655–8880. Reservations required. Jacket required.
AE, MC, V. Closed Sun. No Sat. lunch. Valet parking. Moderate.*

Westside **Beaurivage.** A charming, romantic restaurant designed in the
(Coastal fashion of an auberge on the Cote d'Azur, this is one of the few
Los Angeles Malibu dining places with a view of the beach and ocean. The
Dining map) menu complements the Provençal atmosphere: roast duckling
Mirabelle, pasta with shellfish, mussel soup, filet mignon with
a three-mustard sauce and, in season, wild game specials. It's

a satisfying getaway. *26025 Pacific Coast Hwy., tel. 310/456–5733. Reservations required. Dress: casual. Sun. brunch 11–4. No lunch. Parking lot. Moderate–Expensive.*

★ **Chinois on Main.** The second of the Wolfgang Puck pack of restaurants, this one is designed in tongue-in-cheek kitsch by his wife, Barbara Lazaroff. Both the look of the place and Puck's merging of Chinese and French cuisines are great good fun. A few of the least resistible dishes on an irresistible menu include Mongolian lamb with eggplant, poach-curried oysters, whole catfish garnished with ginger and green onions, and rare duck with a wondrous plum sauce. The best desserts are three differently flavored crèmes brûlées. This is one of L.A.'s most crowded spots—and one of the noisiest. *2709 Main St., Santa Monica, tel. 310/392–9025. Dinner reservations required. Dress: casual. AE, DC, MC, V. No lunch Sat.–Tues. Valet parking in evening. Moderate–Expensive.*

Greek

San Fernando Valley **Great Greek.** This joint jumps with Greek music and everyone joins in for Old World dancing. The food is a delight: loukaniki, Greek sausages; butter-fried calamari; and two kinds of shish-kebab. *13362 Ventura Blvd., Sherman Oaks, tel. 818/905–5250. Reservations advised. Dress: casual. AE, DC, MC, V. Valet parking. Moderate.*

Health Food

Westside **The Good Earth.** The menus of this health-oriented chain feature whole-grain breads, desserts baked with honey, and entrées heavy on fruit and vegetables rather than on meat. Even the decor, with earth-tone walls and furnishings and macramé and wicker baskets on the walls, is earthy. Breakfast items include turkey sausages, 10-grain sourdough pancakes, and a choice of omelets. Vegetarian burgers, curried chicken, and Zhivago's beef Stroganoff are superior lunch and dinner specialties. *10700 W. Pico, tel. 310/475–7557. Reservations accepted. Dress: casual. MC, V. Inexpensive–Moderate.*

Italian

Beverly Hills **Primi.** Valentino's younger, less expensive brother has a menu that features a wide variety of Northern Italian treats, including pasta and salad selections. This is a cheerful, contemporary setting, with a pleasant outside terrace. *10543 W. Pico Blvd., tel. 310/475–9235. Reservations advised. Jacket required. AE, DC, MC, V. Closed Sun. Valet parking. Moderate–Expensive.*

★ **Il Fornaio Cucina Italiana.** What was once a bakery-café has been expanded and remodeled into one of the best-looking contemporary trattorias in all of California, and the food is more than worthy of the setting. From the huge brass-and-stainless-steel rotisserie come crispy roasted duck, herb-basted chickens, and juicy rabbit. Nearby, cooks paddle a tasty variety of pizzas and calzones in and out of the oakwood-burning oven. Also emerging from the latter is a *bomba*, a plate-size, dome-shape foccacia shell draped with strips of smoked prosciutto. The thick Porterhouse steak alla Florentina at $16 is clearly the best beef buy around. The wines come from vineyards Il Fornaio owns in Italy. *301 N. Beverly Dr., tel. 310/550–8330. Re-*

servations accepted. *Dress: casual. AE, DC, MC, V. Valet parking. Inexpensive–Moderate.*

Prego. The baby lamb chops, large broiled veal chop, and Florentine rib steak here are more than satisfying, considering the low prices and attentive service. The baked-in-house bread sticks are great. *362 N. Camden Dr., tel. 310/277–7346. Reservations advised. Dress: casual. AE, DC, MC, V. No Sun. lunch. Valet parking in evening. Inexpensive–Moderate.*

Century City
(Beverly Hills and Hollywood Dining map)

Harry's Bar & American Grill. A more posh, private, and uptown version of Prego, it's run by the same management. The decor and selection of dishes are acknowledged copies of Harry's Bar in Florence. But you'll find that for first-rate food—paper-thin carpaccio, excellent pastas, grilled fish and steaks, along with a fine hamburger—the check will be far lower than it would be in Italy. *2020 Ave. of the Stars, tel. 310/277–2333. Reservations advised. Jacket required. AE, DC, MC, V. No weekend lunch. Valet parking. Moderate–Expensive.*

Downtown
★

Rex Il Ristorante. Owner Mauro Vincenti may know more about Italian cuisine than any other restaurateur in this country. The Rex is the ideal showcase for his talents: Two ground floors of a historic Art Deco building were remodeled to resemble the main dining salon of the circa-1930 Italian luxury liner *Rex*. The cuisine, the lightest of *nuova cucina*, is equally special. Be prepared for small and costly portions. *617 S. Olive St., tel. 213/627–2300. Reservations required. Jacket and tie required. AE, DC, MC, V. Closed Sun. No lunch Sat.–Wed. Valet parking. Very Expensive.*

San Fernando Valley

Adriano's Ristorante. A five-minute drive north of Sunset Boulevard is this countrified retreat, near the top of the Santa Monica Mountains. There's nothing backwoods about the food, though. Specialties include lobster with linguini, a T-bone veal chop, polenta risotto, roasted quail, and a delicious cheese soufflé. *2930 Beverly Glen Circle, tel. 310/475–9807. Reservations required. Jacket required. AE, DC, MC, V. No weekend lunch. Closed Mon. Free parking. Moderate–Expensive.*

Posto. Thanks to Piero Selvaggio, Valley residents no longer have to drive to the Westside for good modern Italian cuisine. His chef makes a tissue-thin pizza topped with flavorful ingredients, and the chicken, duck, and veal sausages are made each morning, as are the different herb breads, fried polenta, and wonderful risotto with porchini mushrooms. And, if you are not too stuffed yourself after that, the desserts are delicious. *14928 Ventura Blvd., Sherman Oaks, tel. 818/784–4400. Dress: casual. AE, DC, MC, V. No weekend lunch. Moderate.*

West Hollywood
★

Ca'Brea. Signoris de Mori and Tomassi were so successful with Locanda Veneta (*see below*) that they took a gamble and opened a much larger and lower price place only 20 blocks away. Ca'Brea has turned into the Italian-restaurant smash hit of the penny-pinching '90s, and there isn't a pizza on the menu. You won't care, either, what with the osso buco, the linguini and baby clams, baby back ribs, shrimp and crab cakes, risotto with spinach and wild nettle, Italian beans and sage, and homemade mozzarella salads. *348 S. La Brea Ave., tel. 310/938–2863. Reservations advised. Dress: casual. Closed Sun. No weekend lunch. AE, DC, M, V. Moderate.*

★ **Locanda Veneta.** The food may be more finely wrought at one or two other spots, but the combination of a splendid Venetian chef, Antonio Tomassi, and a simpatico co-owner, Jean Louis de Mori, have re-created the atmospheric equivalent of a genuine Italian trattoria, at reasonable prices. Specialties include fried white-bait, risotto with porcini mushrooms, veal chop, ricotta and potato dumplings, linguini with clams, lobster ravioli with saffron sauce, and pear tart. *8638 W. 3rd St., tel. 310/274–1893. Reservations required. Jacket required. AE, DC, MC, V. Closed Sun. No Sat. lunch. Valet parking. Moderate.*

Tuttobene. Silvio de Mori, Jean Louis's older brother, is a genuinely gracious, caring host who also happens to provide some of the most delectable trattoria dishes west of Tuscany. There are different, freshly baked breads every day, superb down-to-earth pastas and gnocci, luscious risotto with wild mushrooms, picked-that-morning arugula salad—all at very fair prices. *945 N. Fairfax Ave., tel. 213/655–7051. Reservations required. Dress: casual. AE, MC, V. Valet parking. Moderate.*

Westside
(Coastal Los Angeles Dining map)
★

Valentino. Rated among the best Italian restaurants in the nation, Valentino is generally considered to have the best wine list outside Italy. Owner Piero Selvaggio is the man who introduced Los Angeles to the best and lightest of modern-day Italian cuisine. There's superb prosciutto, bresola, fried calamari, lobster cannelloni, fresh broiled porcini mushrooms, and osso buco. *3115 Pico Blvd., Santa Monica, tel. 213/829–4313. Reservations required. Jacket required. AE, DC, MC, V. Closed Sun. No lunch Sat.–Thur. Valet parking. Expensive–Very Expensive.*

Tra di Noi. The name means "between us," and Malibu natives are trying to keep this charming, simple *ristorante* just that—a local secret. It's run by a mama (who does the cooking), son, and daughter- in-law. Regular customers, film celebrities and non–show-biz folk alike, love the unpretentious atmosphere and bring their kids. Nothing fancy or *nuovo* on the menu, just great lasagna, freshly made pasta, mushroom and veal dishes, and crisp fresh salads. *3835 Cross Creek Rd., tel. 310/456–0169. Reservations advised. Dress: casual. Inexpensive–Moderate.*

Japanese

Downtown

Restaurant Horikawa. A department store of Japanese cuisines includes sushi, teppan steak tables, tempura, sashimi, shabu- shabu, teriyaki, and a $50-per-person kaiseki dinner. All are good or excellent, but the sushi bar is the best. The decor is traditional Japanese, with private sit-on-the-floor dining rooms for 2 to 24. *111 S. San Pedro St., tel. 213/680–9355. Reservations advised. Jacket and tie required. AE, DC, MC, V. No weekend lunch. Valet parking. Moderate–Expensive.*

Los Feliz
(Beverly Hills and Hollywood Dining map)
★

Restaurant Katsu. A stark, simple, perfectly designed sushi bar with a small table area serves some of the most exquisite and delicious delicacies east of Japan. This is a treat for eye and palate. *1972 N. Hillhurst Ave., tel. 213/665–1891. No lunch reservations; dinner reservations advised. Dress: casual. AE, MC, V. No Sat. lunch. Valet parking. Expensive.*

Mexican

Hollywood

El Cholo. The progenitor of this upscale chain, this place has been packing them in since the '20s. It serves good bathtub-size margaritas, a zesty assortment of tacos, make-your-own tortillas, and, from June through September, green-corn tamales. It's friendly and fun, with large portions for only a few pesos.

1121 S. Western Ave., tel. 213/734–2773. Reservations advised. Dress: casual. AE, MC, V. Parking lot. Inexpensive.

Santa Monica **Border Grill.** This very trendy, very loud eating hall is owned by two talented female chefs with the most eclectic tastes in town. The menu ranges from crab tacos to vinegar-and-pepper-grilled turkey to pickled pork sirloin. It's worth dropping by for the fun of it, if you don't mind the noise. *1445 4th St., tel. 310/451–1655. Reservations advised. Dress: casual. AE, MC, V. Inexpensive–Moderate.*

West Hollywood **Antonio's Restaurant.** Don't let the strolling mariachis keep you from hearing the daily specials: authentic Mexico City dishes that put this unpretentious favorite several cuts above the ubiquitous taco-enchilada cantinas. Be adventurous and try the chayote (squash) stuffed with ground beef; ricotta in a spicy tomato sauce; pork ribs in a sauce of pickled chipotle peppers; veal shank with garlic, cumin, and red pepper; or and chicken stuffed with apples, bananas, and raisins. Have the flan for dessert. *7472 Melrose Ave., tel. 310/655–0480. Dinner reservations advised. Dress: casual. AE, MC, V. Valet parking. Inexpensive–Moderate.*

Polynesian

Beverly Hills **Trader Vic's.** Sure, it's corny, but this is the most restrained and elegant of the late Victor Bergeron's South Sea extravaganzas. Besides, who says corn can't be fun—and tasty, too. The crab Rangoon, grilled cheese wafers, skewered shrimp, grilled pork ribs, and the steaks, chops, and peanut-butter–coated lamb cooked in the huge clay ovens, are just fine. As for the array of exotic rum drinks, watch your sips. *9876 Wilshire Blvd., tel. 310/274–7777. Reservations required. Jacket and tie required. AE, DC, MC, V. No lunch. Valet parking. Moderate–Expensive.*

Thai

Hollywood **Chan Dara.** Here you'll find excellent Thai food in a bright and shiny Swiss chalet! Try any of the noodle dishes, especially those with crab and shrimp. *310 N. Larchmont Blvd., tel. 213/467–1052. Reservations advised for parties of more than 4. Dress: casual. AE, MC, V. Inexpensive–Moderate.*

West Hollywood **Tommy Tang's.** At this very "in" grazing ground for yuppies and celebs alike, so much people-watching goes on, nobody seems to notice the small portions on their plates. The kitchen features crisp duck marinated in ginger and plum sauce, blackened sea scallops, and a spinach salad tossed with marinated beef. There is also a sushi bar. *7473 Melrose Ave., tel. 213/651–1810. Reservations advised. Dress: casual. AE, DC, MC, V. No lunch. Valet parking. Moderate.*

7 Lodging

By Jane E. Lasky

Because Los Angeles is so spread out—it's actually a series of suburbs connected by freeways—it's a good idea to select a hotel room not only for its ambience, amenities, and price but also for a location that is convenient to where you plan to spend most of your time.

West Hollywood and Beverly Hills are at the heart of the city, equidistant from the beaches and downtown. These are also the primary shopping districts of Los Angeles, with Rodeo Drive the central axis of Beverly Hills, and Melrose Avenue the playground for trendier purchases. The more recently developed Century City, located between Westwood and Beverly Hills, offers top-notch hotels, a terrific mall, movie and legitimate theaters—and quick access to Rodeo Drive shopping. It's also an important Los Angeles business center. Hollywood, unfortunately, has lost much of its legendary glamor, so don't book a room there expecting to be in the lap of luxury—parts of Hollywood are downright seedy.

Downtown is attractive if you are interested in Los Angeles's cultural offerings, since this is where the Music Center and the Museum of Contemporary Art are located. It is also the heartland for Los Angeles's conventions.

For closest proximity to Pacific Ocean beaches, check-in in Santa Monica, Marina del Rey, or Malibu. The San Fernando Valley is a good place to stay if you're looking for a suburban setting and quarters close to the movie and television studios on that side of the hills.

It's best to plan ahead and reserve a room; many hotels offer special prices for weekend visits and offer tickets to amusement parks or plays. A travel agent can help in making your arrangements.

Highly recommended accommodations are indicated by a star ★. Hotels listed below are organized according to their geographic location, then by price category, following this scale.

Category	Cost*
Very Expensive	over $160
Expensive	$100–$160
Moderate	$65–$100
Inexpensive	under $65

All prices are for a double room.

Downtown

Very Expensive   **Biltmore Hotel.** Since its 1923 opening, the Biltmore has hosted such notables as Mary Pickford, J. Paul Getty, Eleanor Roosevelt, Princess Margaret, and several U.S. presidents. Now a historic landmark, it was renovated in 1986 for $35 million, with modern, updated guest rooms decorated in pastels. The lobby ceiling was painted by Italian artist Giovanni Smeraldi; imported Italian marble and plum-color velvet grace the Grand Avenue Bar, which features excellent jazz nightly. Bernard's is an acclaimed Continental restaurant. The private, swank health club has a Roman bath motif. Banquet and meet-

Los Angeles Lodging (Boxes Refer to Detail Maps)

SAN FERNANDO

Foothill Fwy.

5

210

LA CANADA
FLINTRIDGE

Golden State Fwy.

BURBANK

GLENDALE

RESEDA

170

**San Fernando
Valley**

Ventura Fwy.

101

Sepulveda Dam
Recreation
Area

134

2

Pasadena Fwy.

Mulholland Dr.

SHERMAN
OAKS

101

Griffith
Park

5

SANTA
MONICA MTS.

405

**WEST
HOLLYWOOD**

ALHAMBRA

110

Dodger
Stadium

Topanga
State
Park

Sunset Blvd.

WESTWOOD

BEVERLY
HILLS

Santa Monica Blvd.

HOLLYWOOD

Wilshire Blvd.

**Beverly Hills
and Hollywood**

MONTEREY
PARK

Santa Monica Blvd.

2

Downtown

Santa Ana Fwy.

Santa Monica Fwy.

10

SANTA
MONICA

**Coastal
Los Angeles**

1

San Diego Fwy.

CULVER CITY

Slauson Ave.

VENICE

MARINA
DEL REY

INGLEWOOD

42

HUNTINGTON
PARK

710

Los Angeles
International
Airport

Sepulveda Blvd.

1

Imperial Hwy.

N

EL
SEGUNDO

405

Blvd.

Western Ave.

Harbor Fwy.

MANHATTAN
BEACH

91

Hawthorne Blvd.

COMPTON

San Diego Fwy.

Long Beach Fwy.

710

HERMOSA
BEACH

TORRANCE

Pacific

REDONDO
BEACH

Coast Hwy.

110

*PACIFIC
OCEAN*

PALOS
VERDES
ESTATES

1

RANCH
PALOS
VERDES

SAN
PEDRO

**LONG
BEACH**

0   5 miles

0   5 km

Downtown Los Angeles Lodging

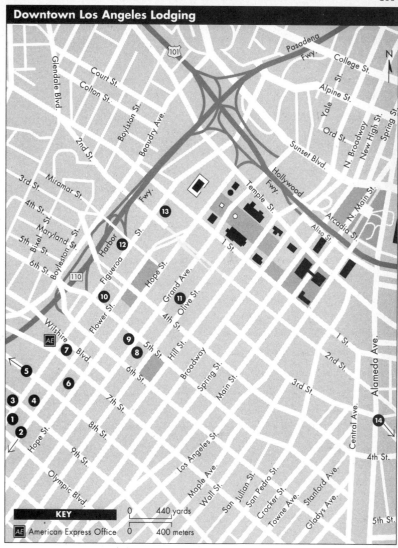

KEY

AE American Express Office

0 ——— 440 yards
0 ——— 400 meters

Best Western Inntowne, **1**

The Biltmore Hotel, **8**

Checkers Hotel Kempinski, **9**

Comfort Inn, **14**

Figueroa Hotel, **3**

Holiday Inn L.A. Downtown, **5**

Hotel Inter-Continental Los Angeles, **11**

Hyatt Regency Los Angeles, **6**

Los Angeles Hilton Hotel and Towers, **7**

The New Otani Hotel and Garden, **13**

Orchid Hotel, **4**

Sheraton Grande Hotel, **12**

University Hilton Los Angeles, **2**

The Westin Bonaventure, **10**

Beverly Hills and Hollywood Lodging

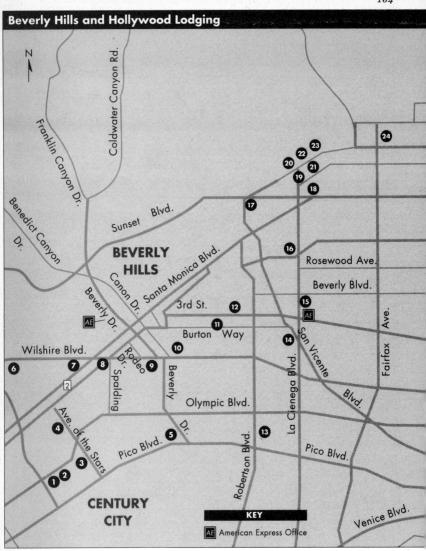

HOLLYWOOD

Los Feliz Blvd.

Franklin Ave.

Hollywood (25) Blvd.

Sunset Blvd.

Vine Ave.

Gower Ave.

Fountain Ave.

Santa Monica Blvd.

(26)

Melrose Ave.

Van Ness Ave.

Wilton Pl.

Western Ave.

[101]

Hollywood Fwy.

Virgil Ave.

Beverly Blvd.

La Brea Ave.

Highland Ave.

Rossmore Ave.

3rd St.

Normandie Ave.

Vermont Ave.

Wilshire Blvd.

Arlington Ave.

(27)

Hoover St.

Crenshaw Blvd.

Olympic Blvd.

Pico Blvd.

0 ___ 1 mile
0 ___ 1km

Washington Blvd.

Airport Marina
Hotel, **19**

Airport Park View
Hotel, **25**

Barnaby's Hotel, **27**

Best Western Royal
Palace Hotel, **13**

Carmel Hotel, **1**

Century Wilshire, **14**

Doubletree Marina
del Rey L.A., **11**

Holiday Inn Crowne
Plaza, **26**

Holiday Inn-LAX, **22**

Holiday Inn Santa
Monica Beach , **6**

The Hotel Bel Air, **16**

Hyatt Hotel-LAX, **20**

Loews Santa Monica
Beach Hotel, **3**

The Los Angeles
Airport Marriott, **23**

Marina del Rey
Hotel, **10**

Marina del Rey
Marriott Inn, **12**

Marina International
Hotel, **8**

Marina Pacific Hotel &
Suites, **7**

Miramar Sheraton, **2**

Pacific Shore, **4**

Palm Motel, **5**

Radisson Bel-Air, **15**

Red Lion Inn, **18**

The Ritz-Carlton,
Marina del Rey, **9**

Sheraton Los Angeles
Airport Hotel, **21**

Westin Hotel LAX, **24**

Westwood Marquis
Hotel and Gardens, **17**

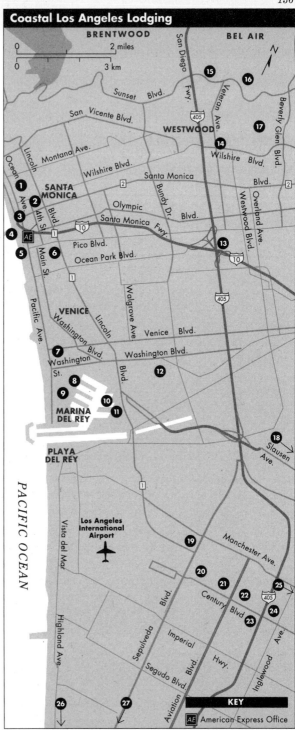

Coastal Los Angeles Lodging

KEY

AE American Express Office

ing rooms serve up to 1,200; the special club floor boa
noon tea, Continental breakfast, board games, a fax machine,
and wide-screen TV. *506 S. Grand Ave., 90071, tel. 213/624–1011
or 800/245–8673, fax 213/612–1545. 704 rooms. Facilities: 3 restaurants, lounge, entertainment, health club. AE, DC, MC, V.*

Checkers Hotel Kempinski. With its excellent pedigree and
smaller scale, Checkers is a sophisticated, welcome addition to
the downtown hotel scene. Set in one of this neighborhood's
few remaining historic buildings, this property opened as the
Mayflower Hotel in 1927. Rooms are furnished with oversize
beds, upholstered easy chairs, writing tables, and minibars. A
library is available for small meetings or tea. *535 S. Grand Ave.,
90071, tel. 213/624–0000 or 800/426–3135. 190 rooms. Facilities:
restaurant, rooftop spa and lap pool, exercise studio. AE, DC,
MC, V.*

Hotel Inter-Continental Los Angeles. This imposing 17-story
structure was introduced to the downtown skyline at the end
of 1992, the first hotel to be built in this section of town in the
past decade. Part of California Plaza (where the Museum of
Contemporary Art is) and within walking distance of the Music
Center, the sleek Inter-Continental boasts floor-to-ceiling
views. Guest rooms are decorated in contemporary style, with
glass-topped tables and desks, in color schemes of either ivory
and peach or celadon and brown. The sculpture *Yellow Fin*, by
Richard Serra, dominates the large lobby, and other artworks
are on view throughout, on loan from the Museum of Contemporary Art. The Angel's Flight restaurant and lounge serves
California cuisine against the backdrop of an urban garden,
replete with water fountains synchronized to soothing music.
Coffee-shop fare is available at The Cafe. *251 S. Olive St., 90012,
tel. 213/617–3300 or 800/442–5251, fax 213/617–3399. 439 rooms.
Faciliites: 2 restaurants, lounge, business center, club floors,
health club, outdoor lap pool. AE, D, DC, MC, V.*

Hyatt Regency Los Angeles. The Hyatt is located in the heart
of the "new" downtown financial district, minutes away from
the Convention Center, Dodger Stadium, and the Music Center. Each room has a wall of windows with city views. The Regency Club has a private lounge. The hotel is part of the
Broadway Plaza, comprising 35 shops. Nearby tennis and
health club facilities are available at an extra cost. *711 S. Hope
St., 90017, tel. 213/683–1234 or 800/233–1234. 485 rooms. Facilities: restaurant, coffee shop, lounge, entertainment. AE, DC,
MC, V.*

Los Angeles Hilton Hotel and Towers. Located right on Wilshire Boulevard, the Hilton contains a fine Italian restaurant,
Cardini, as well as a Japanese eatery and City Grill Restaurant.
The rooms are conservatively decorated in beige and green.
The hotel is convenient to Dodger Stadium, museums, Chinatown, and the Music Center. Parking is expensive. *930 Wilshire
Blvd., 90017, tel. 213/629–4321. 901 rooms. Facilities: 3 restaurants, lounge, coffee shop, pool, gym with Nautilus equipment,
business center, large banquet and meeting facilities, parking
(fee). AE, DC, MC, V.*

★ **Sheraton Grande Hotel.** Opened in 1983, this 14-story, mirrored
hotel is near Dodger Stadium, the Music Center, and downtown's Bunker Hill District. Rooms have dark-wood furniture,
sofas, minibars; colors are aqua or copper; baths are marble.
There's butler service on each floor. Stay in the penthouse suite
if you can afford it. A limousine is available for Beverly Hills

shopping, and there are privileges at a local health club. *333 S. Figueroa St., 90071, tel. 213/617–1133 or 800/325–3535, fax 213/613–0291. 469 rooms. Facilities: 3 restaurants, bar, outdoor pool, 4 movie theaters. AE, DC, MC, V.*

Westin Bonaventure. This is architect John Portman's striking masterpiece: a 35-story, circular-towered, mirrored-glass high rise in the center of downtown. Rooms have a wall of glass, streamlined pale furnishings, and comfortable appointments. The outside elevators provide stunning city views; there are also 5 acres of ponds and waterfalls in the lobby. At the top of the hotel are the Bona Vista revolving lounge and Top of Five restaurant. A popular Sunday brunch is served in the atrium lobby. Parking is expensive. *404 S. Figueroa St., 90071, tel. 213/624–1000 or 800/228–3000. 1,468 rooms. Facilities: restaurant, lounge, entertainment, pool, executive floor, 5-level shopping arcade. AE, DC, MC, V.*

Expensive– Very Expensive ★
New Otani Hotel and Garden. East meets west in L.A., and the exotic epicenter downtown is this 21-story, ultramodern hotel surrounded by Japanese gardens and waterfalls. The decor combines a serene blend of Westernized luxury and Japanese simplicity. Each room has a refrigerator, an alarm clock, color TV, and phone in the bathroom, and most provide a yukata (robe). For the ultimate Little Tokyo experience, book a Japanese suite, where guests sleep on futons on mats on the floor. Concrete walls give great noise control. A Thousand Cranes offers classic Japanese cuisine; the Azalea Restaurant serves Continental cuisine. The Genji Bar features live entertainment. *120 S. Los Angeles St., 90012, tel. 213/629–1200 or 800/421–8795; in CA, 800/273-2294. 440 rooms. Facilities: 2 restaurants, nightclubs, sauna and massage (fee), parking (fee). AE, DC, MC, V.*

University Hilton Los Angeles. If you're doing business at USC, the Coliseum, or the Sports Arena, this is the best hotel in the area. All the modern-style rooms have a view of the pool area, the lush gardens, or the nearby USC campus. It's well-equipped to handle banquets and conventions. *3540 S. Figueroa St., 90007, tel. 213/748–4141 or 800/872–ll04; in CA, 800/244–7331. 243 rooms. Facilities: restaurant, coffee shop, lounge, pool, parking (fee). AE, DC, MC, V.*

Moderate
Best Western Inntowne. This three-story hotel has large beige-and-white rooms. It's 1½ blocks from the Convention Center and just down the street from the famous 24-hour Pantry restaurant. The swimming pool is surrounded by palm trees and a small garden. *925 S. Figueroa St., 90015, tel. 213/628–2222 or 800/528–1234, fax 213/687–0566. 169 rooms. Facilities: restaurant, lounge, pool, free parking. AE, DC, MC, V.*

Figueroa Hotel. This hotel has managed to keep its charming Spanish style intact as it enters its second half-century. There's a poolside bar. With hand-painted furniture and, often, ceiling fans, the guest rooms carry out the Spanish look. The hotel is on the Gray Line sightseeing tour route and there is airport service every hour to LAX. *939 S. Figueroa St., 90015, tel. 213/627–8971, 800/421–9092, fax 213/689–0305. 285 rooms. Facilities: 3 restaurants, coffee shop, lounge, pool, free parking. AE, DC, MC, V.*

Holiday Inn L.A. Downtown. This chain hotel, renovated in 1992, offers Holiday Inn's usual professional staff and services, and standard room decor. Pets are allowed, and there is plenty of free parking. It's also close to the Museum of Contemporary

Art and Dodger Stadium. *750 Garland Ave., 90017, tel. 213/628–5242 or 800/628–5240. 204 rooms. Facilities: restaurant, lounge, pool, free parking. AE, DC, MC, V.*

Inexpensive **Comfort Inn.** With its central location between downtown and Hollywood, near the Wilshire commercial district, this hotel is convenient for businesspeople. The modern rooms offer color TVs and VCRs. *3400 3rd St., 90020, tel. 213/385–0061. 120 rooms. Facilities: coffee shop, pool. AE, DC, MC, V.*

Orchid Hotel. One of the smaller downtown hotels, this is very reasonably priced. There are no frills, but the standard rooms are clean, with modern decor in pastel tones. Note that there is no parking at the hotel, but public lots are close by. *819 S. Flower St., 90017, tel. 213/624–5855, fax 213/624–5855. 64 rooms. Facilities: coin-operated laundry. AE, DC, MC, V.*

Mid-Wilshire

Expensive– **Radisson Plaza Hotel and Garden.** One of Wilshire Boulevard's
Very Expensive largest hotels, this 12-story building's interior was renovated in 1992, with green-and-ivory-stripe awnings. The rooms have views of either Hollywood or downtown and have contemporary decor in light beige or gray. Corporate clients often use the large banquet and meeting rooms that hold up to 400 people. *3515 Wilshire Blvd., 90010, tel. 213/381–7411 or 800/333–3333, fax 213/386–7379. 396 rooms. Facilities: 2 restaurants, lounge, exercise room, parking (fee). AE, DC, MC, V.*

Hollywood and West Hollywood

Very Expensive **Le Bel Age Hotel.** This all-suite, European-style hotel has a
★ distinctive restaurant, which features fine Russian meals with an elegant French flair. There are many extravagant touches, like three telephones with five lines in each suite, original art, private terraces, and daily newspaper. Suites that face south have terrific views looking out over the L.A. skyline as far as the Pacific. The decor is French-country style. *1020 N. San Vicente Blvd., West Hollywood 90069, tel. 310/854–1111 or 800/424–4443. 190 suites. Facilities: 2 restaurants, lounge, pool. AE, DC, MC, V.*

Le Dufy Hotel. This luxury hotel features all suites, decorated in a modern style in shades of blue, pink, and salmon. All have private balconies. It's great for business travelers, near "Restaurant Row," and not as expensive as other hotels in this price category. *1000 Westmont Dr., West Hollywood 90069, tel. 310/657–7400. 103 suites. Facilities: restaurant, bar, pool, whirlpool, spa, sauna, sun deck, exercise room. AE, DC, MC, V.*

Le Mondrian Hotel. This giant structure is a monument to the Dutch artist from whom the hotel takes its name. The outside of the 12-story hotel is actually a giant surrealistic mural; inside there's fine artwork. Accommodations are spacious, with pale-wood furniture and curved sofas in the seating area. Ask for south-corner suites; they tend to be quieter than the rest. A chauffeured limo is placed at each guest's disposal for a fee. Nouvelle cuisine is served at Cafe Mondrian. The hotel is convenient to major recording, film, and TV studios. *8440 Sunset Blvd., West Hollywood 90069, tel. 213/650–8999 or 800/525–8029. 220 suites. Facilities: restaurant, pool, health club, parking (fee). AE, DC, MC, V.*

Saint James's Club/Los Angeles. Located on the Sunset Strip, this is one of the prestigious group of St. James's Clubs, and the first in the United States. The building has been around since the 1930s; today all the furnishings are exact replicas of Art Deco masterpieces, the originals of which are in New York's Metropolitan Museum of Art. Ask for a city or mountain view. Both are great (although a bit on the small side by Los Angeles standards), but the cityside accommodations are more expensive. The hotel also features a 1930s-style supper club (California cuisine) with piano entertainment, a club bar, and a lounge. *8358 Sunset Blvd., West Hollywood 90069, tel. 213/654–7100 or 800/225–2637. 63 rooms. Facilities: restaurant, health center, sauna, pool, secretarial services, small meeting facilities. AE, DC, MC, V.*

Sunset Marquis Hotel and Villas. Lovely landscaping highlights this three-story property near La Cienega and Sunset boulevards, most recently renovated in 1993. The hotel is decorated in Mediterranean style; most guests stay in either suites or individual villas. Fashion-magazine photographs are often shot in the hotel's lush gardens. The intimate gourmet restaurant on the premises is called Notes. *1200 N. Alta Loma Rd., West Hollywood 90069, tel. 3l0/657–1333 or 800/858–9758, fax 310/652–5300. 118 rooms. Facilities: dining room, 2 pools, sauna, whirlpool, exercise room, in-room refrigerators, free parking. AE, DC, MC, V.*

Expensive **Chateau Marmont Hotel.** Although planted on the Sunset Strip amid giant billboards and much sun-bleached Hollywood glitz, this castle of Old World charm and French Normandy design still promises its guests a secluded hideaway close to Hollywood's hot spots. A haunt for many show-biz personalities and discriminating world travelers since it opened in 1929, this is the ultimate in privacy. All kinds of accommodations are available, including fully equipped cottages, bungalows, and a penthouse. Small pets are allowed. *8221 Sunset Blvd., Hollywood 90046, tel. 213/656–1010 or 800/CHATEAU. 63 rooms. Facilities: dining room, pool, fitness room. AE, MC, V.*

Hyatt on Sunset. In the heart of the Sunset Strip, this Hyatt is a favorite of music-biz execs and rock stars who appreciate the two-line phones and voice mail available here. There are penthouse suites, some rooms with private patios, and a rooftop pool. The rooms are decorated in peach colors and modern furniture; some have aquariums. The Silver Screen sports bar is a fun spot. *8401 W. Sunset Blvd., West Hollywood 90069, tel. 213/656–4101 or 800/233–1234. 262 rooms. Facilities: restaurant, lounge, entertainment, pool, parking (fee). AE, DC, MC, V.*

Radisson Hollywood Roosevelt. This hotel across from Mann's Chinese Theater was considered state-of-the-art Hollywood glamour and luxury before it gradually fell into disrepair. But in true Hollywood fashion, this site of the first Academy Awards ceremony made a comeback in 1985, thoroughly restored right down to the ornate Art Deco lobby and elegant courtyard. Highlights are the Olympic-size pool decorated by artist David Hockney and the Tropicana Bar in the courtyard. Most rooms have a light gray decor with pine furniture, but for fun, try one of the 40 Hollywood-theme suites, such as the Gable/Lombard Suite or the Shirley Temple Suite. *7000 Hollywood Blvd., Hollywood 90028, tel. 213/466–7000 or 800/333–3333, fax 213/462–8056. 320 rooms, 90 poolside cabanas. Facilities: 3 restaurants, lounge, rental cars, valet parking. AE, DC, MC, V.*

American Express offers Travelers Cheques built for two.

American Express® Cheques *for Two*. The first Travelers Cheques that allow either of you to use them because both of you have signed them. And only one of you needs to be present to purchase them.

Cheques *for Two* are accepted anywhere regular American Express Travelers Cheques are, which is just about everywhere. So stop by your bank, AAA* or any American Express Travel Service Office and ask for Cheques *for Two*.

AMERICAN EXPRESS **Travelers Cheques** ®

Moderate **Hollywood Holiday Inn.** You can't miss this hotel, one of the tallest buildings in Hollywood. It's 23 stories high, topped by Windows, a revolving restaurant-lounge (the Sunday brunch served here is a local favorite). The rooms are decorated in light gray and rose in standard-issue Holiday Inn fashion. There is a safekeeping box in each room. The hotel is only minutes from the Hollywood Bowl, Universal Studios, and Mann's Chinese Theater, and it's a Gray Line Tour Stop. *1755 N. Highland Ave., Hollywood 90028, tel. 213/462–7181 or 800/465–4329. 470 rooms. Facilities: restaurant, coffee shop, pool, coin-operated laundry, parking (fee). AE, DC, MC, V.*

Inexpensive **Banana Bungalow Hotel and International Hostel.** You'll get the most for your money at this friendly Hollywood miniresort in the Hollywood Hills, about ½ mile from the Hollywood Bowl. Opened in 1992, it offers mostly hostel- style rooms, with three to six beds in each; you'll be sharing a room with people you don't know, unless you book one of the 12 double-occupancy rooms—be sure to specify what you want when booking. The decor is white and gray, with light wood furniture and plants. There's no curfew and no mandatory time to vacate your room. *2775 Cahuenga Blvd., West Hollywood 90068, tel. 213/851–1129 or 800/4–HOSTEL. 56 rooms. Facilities: complimentary Continental breakfast, laundry room, movie theater, pool, weight room, pool room, games arcade, free parking, free shuttle to attractions, airports, and train and bus terminals. MC, V.*

Beverly Hills

Very Expensive **Beverly Hilton.** This large hotel complex has a wide selection of restaurants and shops. Most rooms have balconies overlooking Beverly Hills or downtown. Trader Vic's and L'Escoffier are two of the city's better restaurants. There is free limo service within a 3- mile radius of the hotel. *9876 Wilshire Blvd., 90210, tel. 310/274–7777 or 800/445–8667, fax 310/285–1313. 581 rooms. Facilities: 3 restaurants, pool, wading pool, exercise room, refrigerators, parking (fee). AE, DC, MC, V.*

★ **Four Seasons Los Angeles.** This hotel combines the best in East and West Coast luxury. Formal European decorative details are complemented by outpourings of flora from the porte cochere to the pool deck on the second-story rooftop. There is an outstanding restaurant on the premises and great shopping only five minutes away on Rodeo Drive and Melrose Avenue. All suites have French doors and a balcony. *300 S. Doheny Dr., Los Angeles 90048, tel. 310/273–2222 or 800/332–3442. 285 rooms. Facilities: restaurant, pool, exercise equipment. AE, DC, MC, V.*

Hotel Nikko. Distinctive Japanese accents distinguish this contemporary hotel located near Restaurant Row. Guest rooms cater to the business traveler with oversize desks, and work areas with computer and fax hook-up capabilities. Traditional Japanese soaking tubs dominate luxurious bathrooms, and a bedside remote-control conveniently operates in-room lighting, temperature, TV, and stereo. Matrixx, the hotel restaurant, features California cuisine. *465 S. La Cienega Blvd., Los Angeles 90035, tel. 310/247–0400, 800/NIKKO–US, or 800/NIKKO–BH, fax 310/247–0315. 304 rooms. Facilities: restaurant, lounge, pool, Japanese garden, fitness center, business center. AE, DC, MC, V.*

Hotel Sofitel Ma Maison. This fine hotel offers first-class service and an intimacy usually reserved for small European-style hotels. The country-French guest rooms are done in terra-cotta and blues, with small prints. The hotel is next to some of L.A.'s best shopping, restaurants, and boutiques. It also faces a large brick wall; insist on a northern view. *8555 Beverly Blvd., Los Angeles 90048, tel. 310/278–5444 or 800/521–7772. 311 rooms. Facilities: 2 restaurants, pool, sauna, fitness center, parking. AE, DC, MC, V.*

Le Parc Hotel. An intimate European-style hotel housed in a modern low-rise building, it's located in a lovely residential area. Suites are decorated in earth tones and shades of wine and rust with balconies, fireplaces, VCRs, and kitchenettes. It's near Farmers' Market, CBS Television City, and the L.A. County Museum of Art. Cafe Le Parc is a private dining room for hotel guests only. *733 N.W. Knoll, West Hollywood 90069, tel. 310/855–8888 or 800/424–4442; in CA, 800/424–4443. 152 rooms. Facilities: lighted tennis courts, heated pool, whirlpool, spa, sauna, exercise room, free parking, chauffeured limo to Holly-wood and Beverly Hills. AE, DC, MC, V.*

★ **L'Ermitage Hotel.** L'Ermitage features Old World charm with modern conveniences. The property is near Beverly Hills' ele-gant shopping, and convenient to Twentieth Century Fox. The suites have balconies and sunken living rooms with fireplaces. The best is the Grande Class suite with whirlpool and steam/sauna shower. The fine The Club restaurant is reserved for hotel guests. Chauffeured limo service can take you around Beverly Hills. *9291 Burton Way, 90210, tel. 310/278–3344 or 800/800–2113. 112 rooms. Facilities: restaurant, rooftop pool, whirlpool, parking (fee). AE, DC, MC, V.*

The Peninsula Beverly Hills. Located in the heart of Beverly Hills, this luxury hotel was the first new property to open in this prestigious Los Angeles enclave in more than two decades when it made its debut in 1991. Surrounded by flowered hedges, poplar trees, and elephant ears, a circular motorcourt greets guests in rare style. The hotel's appearance is classic, done in French Renaissance architecture with contemporary overtones. Rooms are decorated like luxury homes, with an-tiques, rich fabrics, and marble floors. Minibars and refrigera-tors can be found behind French doors in all rooms, and all suites are equipped with compact disc players, fax machines, and individual security systems. *9882 Santa Monica Blvd., 90212, tel. 310/273–4888 or 800/462–7899, fax 310/858–6663. 200 rooms. Facilities: restaurant, bar, business center, lap pool, health club, poolside cabanas, 24-hr valet parking, 24-hr conci-erge, voice mail. AE, DC, MC, V.*

Regent Beverly Wilshire. This famous hotel facing Rodeo Drive and the Hollywood Hills is fittingly stylish, with personal ser-vice and extras to match. (*See* Tour 4 in Chapter 3). There are great restaurants on the premises, limo service to the airport, and a multilingual staff. *9500 Wilshire Blvd., 90212, tel. 310/275–5200 or 800/427–4354, fax 310/274–2851. 301 rooms. Facilities: 3 restaurants, pool, health spas, business center, parking (fee). AE, DC, MC, V.*

Expensive **Beverly Hills Ritz Hotel.** Because this is a low-rise hotel (only three floors), guests need not walk through long corridors to reach their rooms. All the suites are situated off the pool. Fur-nishings are smart and contemporary; all feature kitchen/liv-ing room, one bedroom, and bath. *10300 Wilshire Blvd., 90024, tel. 310/275–5575 or 800/800–1234. 116 rooms. Facilities: restau-rant, pool, small gym, Jacuzzi, garage. AE, DC, MC, V.*

Beverly Pavilion Hotel. Located near movie theaters and fashionable shopping, this hotel is popular with commercial travelers, and features the well-known restaurant Colette, with French cuisine and cocktail lounge. The rooms and executive suites have balconies and are decorated in contemporary styles, mostly in beige, blue, and mauve. *9360 Wilshire Blvd., 90212, tel. 310/273–1400 or 800/421–0545; in CA, 800/441–5050. 110 rooms. Facilities: restaurant, lounge, pool, valet. AE, DC, MC, V.*

Beverly Prescott Hotel. This 12-story small luxury hotel perched on a hill overlooking Beverly Hills, Century City, and the mighty Pacific, opened in May 1993. The open-air architecture is enhanced by soothing rooms decorated in warm tones of salmon and caramel. Furnishings are stylish, and the rooms are spacious, with private balconies. *1224 S. Beverwil Dr., 90035, tel. 310/277–2800 or 800/421–3212, fax 310/203–9537. 140 rooms. Facilities: business suites with computers and fax machines. AE, DC, MC, V.*

Carlyle Inn. Service is the byword of this intimate, small hostelry in the city's design district, opened in 1991. The four-story, contemporary-styled property offers guests several extras: a buffet breakfast of fruit, pastries, eggs, and meats; high tea in the afternoons; and wine by the glass in the evenings. Rooms are decorated in peach with light pine furniture and black accents. *1119 S. Robertson Blvd., 90035, tel. 310/275–4445 or 800/3–CARLYLE, fax 310/859–0496. 32 rooms. Facilities: restaurant, free parking, Jacuzzi, in-room computer hookups, free shuttle service within 5-mi radius.*

Century City

Very Expensive **Century Plaza Hotel and Tower.** This 20-story hotel (on 10 acres
★ of tropical plants and reflecting pools) features a 30-story tower, which is lavishly decorated with signature art and antiques, and is furnished like a mansion, with a mix of classic and contemporary appointments. Each room has a refrigerator and balcony with ocean or city view. There are three excellent restaurants here: the award-winning La Chaumiere for California/French cuisine, the Terrace for Mediterranean-Italian, and the Cafe Plaza, a French-style café serving American fare. *2025 Ave. of the Stars, 90067, tel. 310/277–2000 or 800/228–3000. 1,072 rooms. Facilities: 3 restaurants, 2 pools, whirlpools, poolside fitness centers, parking. AE, DC, MC, V.*

★ **J. W. Marriott Hotel at Century City.** This hotel is the West Coast flagship for the multifaceted Marriott chain. Its elegant, modern rooms are decorated in soft pastels and equipped with minibars, lavish marble baths, and facilities for the handicapped. Ask for accommodations that overlook Twentieth Century Fox's back lot. The hotel offers complimentary limo service to Beverly Hills and provides excellent service. *2151 Ave. of the Stars, 90067, tel. 310/277–2777 or 800/228–9290. 368 rooms. Facilities: restaurant, indoor and outdoor pools, whirlpools, fitness center. AE, DC, MC, V.*

Expensive **Century City Courtyard by Marriott.** This more-than-comfortable hotel near the Century City business complex mixes California architecture with English fabrics and furnishings, epitomized in the red welcome carpet and the London phone booth at the entrance. *10320 W. Olympic Blvd., Los Angeles 90067, tel. 310/556–2777 or 800/947–8521. 133 rooms. Facilities:*

*restaurant, exercise salon, whirlpool, London taxi service to
surrounding area. AE, DC, MC, V.*

Moderate **Century City Inn.** This hotel is small but designed for comfort.
Rooms have a refrigerator, microwave oven, remote control TV,
and VCR, as well as a 10-cup coffee unit with fresh gourmet-
blend coffee and tea. Baths have whirlpool tubs and a phone.
Complimentary Continental breakfast is also served. *10330 W.
Olympic Blvd., Los Angeles 90064, tel. 310/553–1000 or 800/553–
1005. 46 rooms. Facilities: video library, parking (fee). AE, DC,
MC, V.*

Bel Air, Westwood, and West Los Angeles

Very Expensive **Hotel Bel-Air.** This is a charming, secluded hotel (and celebrity
mecca) with lovely gardens and a creek complete with swans.
The rooms and suites are decorated individually in peach and
earth tones. All are villa/bungalow style with Mediterranean
decor. For their quietest accommodation, ask for a room near
the former stable area. The Bel-Air has a five-star rating from
the Mobil Guide, and five diamonds from AAA. *701 Stone Canyon Rd., Bel Air 90077, tel. 310/472–1211 or 800/648–4097. 52
rooms, 39 suites. Facilities: restaurant, lounge, pool, parking
(fee). AE, DC, MC, V.*

Westwood Marquis Hotel and Gardens. This hotel near UCLA
is a favorite of corporate and entertainment types. Each indi-
vidualized suite in its 15 stories has a view of Bel Air, the Pacific
Ocean, or Century City. South-facing suites overlooking the
pool also offer expansive views of the city and sea. Breakfast
and lunch are served in the Garden Terrace, which also serves
a popular Sunday brunch. The award-winning Dynasty Room
restaurant features Continental cuisine. European teas are
served in the afternoon in the Westwood Lounge. *930 Hilgard
Ave., Los Angeles 90024, tel. 310/208–8765 or 800/421–2317, fax
310/824–0355. 258 suites. Facilities: 2 restaurants, lounge, 2
pools, sauna, phones in bathrooms, concierge, exercise room,
parking (fee). AE, DC, MC, V.*

Expensive **Radisson Bel-Air.** This "bit of the Bahamas in Bel Air" (near
Brentwood) is furnished Italian style, with sleek, modern
shapes, and the fixtures in the rooms are Art Deco style. *11461
Sunset Blvd., Los Angeles 90049, tel. 310/476–6571 or 800/333-
3333. 161 rooms. Facilities: restaurant, lounge, pool, tennis
courts, parking (fee). AE, DC, MC, V.*

Moderate– **Century Wilshire.** Most units in this European-style hotel are
Expensive suites featuring kitchenettes. There are tiled baths and homey
English-style pastel decor. Within walking distance of UCLA
and Westwood Village, this simple hotel has views of Wilshire
and the courtyard. The clientele here is mostly European.
*10776 Wilshire Blvd., West Los Angeles 90024, tel. 310/474–4506
or 800/421–7223. 100 rooms. Facilities: complimentary Continental breakfast, pool, free parking. AE, DC, MC, V.*

Inexpensive **Best Western Royal Palace Hotel.** This small hotel located just
off I–405 (San Diego Freeway) is decorated with modern
touches, lots of wood and mirrors. In-room morning coffee and
tea are complimentary, as is parking to hotel guests. Suites
have kitchenettes. *2528 S. Sepulveda Blvd., West Los Angeles
90064, tel. 310/477–9066 or 800/528–1234. 23 rooms, 32 suites. Facilities: complimentary Continental breakfast, pool, Jacuzzi,*

exercise room and billiard room, laundry facilities, free parking. AE, DC, MC, V.

Santa Monica

Very Expensive **Loews Santa Monica Beach Hotel.** Set on the most precious of L.A. real estate—beachfront—this hotel is just south of the Santa Monica Pier. Most of the contemporary rooms have ocean views and private balconies, and all guests have direct access to the beach. Its restaurant, Riva, serves Northern Italian cuisine with an emphasis on seafood. *1700 Ocean Ave., 90401, tel. 310/458–6700 or 800/223–0888. 319 rooms, 31 suites. Facilities: restaurant, café, fitness center, indoor-outdoor pool, valet parking. AE, DC, MC, V.*

Miramar Sheraton. This hotel, "where Wilshire meets the sea," is close to all area beaches, across the street from Pacific Palisades Park, and near deluxe shopping areas and many quaint eateries. The landscaping incorporates the area's second-largest rubber tree. Many rooms have balconies overlooking the ocean. The hotel was renovated in 1992; the decor in some rooms is up-to-the-minute contemporary, with bleached wood, marble, granite, glass, and brick. *101 Wilshire Blvd., 90403, tel. 310/576–7777 or 800/325–3535. 303 rooms. Facilities: 2 restaurants, lounge, heated pool. AE, DC, MC, V.*

Moderate **Holiday Inn Santa Monica Beach.** Close to many restaurants, major shopping centers, the beach, and Santa Monica Pier, this inn features standard Holiday Inn rooms and amenities. *120 Colorado Ave., 90401, tel. 310/451–0676 or 800/947–9175. 132 rooms. Facilities: restaurant, lounge, pool, laundry facilities, free parking. AE, DC, MC, V.*

Pacific Shore. This modern hotel building is one block from the beach and many restaurants. The attractive rooms are decorated with contemporary fabrics and modern furniture; some have ocean views. *1819 Ocean Ave., 90401, tel. 310/451–8711 or 800/622–8711. 168 rooms. Facilities: restaurant, lounge, complimentary Continental breakfast, pool, sauna, Jacuzzi, laundry facilities, Avis Rent-a-Car, free parking. AE, DC, MC, V.*

Inexpensive **Carmel Hotel.** This charming hotel from the 1920s is one block from the beach and Santa Monica Place, as well as from movie theaters and many fine restaurants. Electric ceiling fans add to the room decor. *201 Broadway, 90401, tel. 310/451–2469, fax 310/393–4180. 102 rooms, 8 suites. Facilities: restaurant, parking (fee). AE, DC, MC, V.*

Palm Motel. This quiet, unceremonious motel has old-fashioned rooms, in which the decorative highlight is the color TV. But the motel does offer complimentary coffee, tea, and cookies at breakfast, and it's only a short drive away from several good restaurants. *2020 14th St., 90405, tel. 310/452–3822. 26 rooms. Facilities: self-service laundry, free parking. MC, V.*

Marina del Rey

Very Expensive **Doubletree Marina del Rey L.A.** This luxurious nine-story high-
★ rise hotel has high-tech design softened by a pastel-toned decor accented in brass and marble. Ask for upper-floor rooms that face the marina. There are lovely touches, such as a gazebo in the patio and rooms with water views. The restaurant Stones is known for its fresh seafood. The hotel offers 24-hour free transportation to and from LAX. All of the rooms are deco-

rated in pastels and have a safe for valuables. *4100 Admiralty Way, 90292, tel. 310/301–3000 or 800/528–0444. 386 rooms. Facilities: restaurant, lounges, pool, parking (fee). AE, DC, MC, V.*

Marina del Rey Hotel. Completely surrounded by water, this deluxe waterfront hotel is on the marina's main channel, making cruises and charters easily accessible. Guest rooms (contemporary with a nautical touch) offer balconies, patios, and harbor views. For splendid views, book a room that faces the water. The hotel is within walking distance of shopping and only a bike ride away from Fisherman's Village. There are meeting rooms and a beautiful gazebo area for parties. *13534 Bali Way, 90292, tel. 310/301–1000 or 800/882–4000; in CA, 800/8–MARINA. 158 rooms. Facilities: 2 restaurants, lounge, pool, putting green, airport transportation, free parking. AE, DC, MC, V.*

Expensive– Very Expensive **Marina del Rey Marriott Inn.** Located in a lively area—a shopping center near Fox Hills Mall and across the street from a movie theater—the hotel was built in 1977. The Old World–style rooms are decorated in light blue, rust, or light green. Tropical trees and foliage enhance the pool area; Sunday brunch is served by the water and a goldfish pond. *13480 Maxella Ave., 90292, tel. 310/822–8555 or 800/228–9290, fax 310/823–2996. 283 rooms. Facilities: restaurant, lounge, pool. AE, DC, MC, V.*

Marina International Hotel. Across from a sandy beach within the marina, this hotel is unique for its village-style decor. The rooms are done in earth tones with California-style furniture. Each of the very private rooms offers a balcony or patio that faces the garden or the courtyard. Ask for a bungalow—they're huge. The Crystal Fountain restaurant has Continental cuisine. Boat charters are available for up to 200 people. *4200 Admiralty Way, 90292, tel. 310/301–2000, 800/8–MARINA, or 800/882–4000. 110 rooms, 25 bungalows. Facilities: restaurant, lounge, pool, airport transportation, free parking. AE, DC, MC, V.*

The Ritz-Carlton, Marina del Rey. This sumptuous property sits on some prime real estate at the northern end of a basin, offering a panoramic view of the Pacific. The attractive rooms have marble baths, honor bars, and plenty of amenities—from maid service twice a day to plush terry robes. *4375 Admiralty Way, 90292, tel. 310/823–3656, fax 310/823–7318. 306 rooms. Facilities: 3 restaurants, pool, fitness center, tennis courts, complimentary transportation to LAX. AE, DC, MC, V.*

Moderate **Marina Pacific Hotel & Suites.** This hotel faces the Pacific and one of the world's most vibrant boardwalks; it's nestled among Venice's art galleries, shops, and elegant, offbeat restaurants. The marina is just a stroll away. Comfortable accommodations include suites, conference facilities, full-service amenities, and a delightful sidewalk café. For the active traveler, there are ocean swimming, roller skating along the strand, racquetball, and tennis nearby. *1697 Pacific Ave., Venice 90291, tel. 310/399–7770 or 800/421–8151, fax 310/452–5479. 57 rooms, 35 suites; 1-bedroom apartments available. Facilities: restaurant, laundry. AE, DC, MC, V.*

South Bay Beach Cities

Expensive– Very Expensive **Holiday Inn Crowne Plaza.** Located across the street from the Redondo Beach Pier, this swank five-story hotel overlooks the

Pacific. There are plenty of amenities, including indoor and outdoor dining and a nightclub. The rooms are decorated in a seaside theme of light woods and soft colors. *300 N. Harbor Dr., Redondo Beach 90277, tel. 310/318–8888 or 800/368–9760. 339 rooms. Facilities: restaurant, lounge, entertainment, pool, exercise room, game room, sauna, whirlpool, tennis, parking (fee). AE, DC, MC, V.*

Moderate **Barnaby's Hotel.** Modeled after a 19th-century English inn,
★ with four-poster beds, lace curtains, and antique decorations, Barnaby's also has an enclosed greenhouse pool. The London Pub resembles a cozy English hang-out, with live entertainment; Barnaby's Restaurant features Continental cuisine and curtained private booths. Complimentary English buffet breakfast is served. *3501 Sepulveda Blvd. (at Rosecrans), Manhattan Beach 90266, tel. 310/545–8466 or 800/552–5285. 126 rooms. Facilities: 2 restaurants, lounge, pool. AE, DC, MC, V.*

Airport

Expensive– **Sheraton Los Angeles Airport Hotel.** A luxurious 15-story hotel,
Very Expensive this is in a perfect setting for business and leisure travelers alike. The contemporary rooms are decorated in muted shades of mauve, brown, green, and purple. One hundred meeting rooms, with in-house audio-visual equipment, can accommodate groups up to 1,000. There are two restaurants: Plaza Brasserie, a coffee shop, and Landry's for California cuisine. Forty-eight of the rooms are especially designed for the disabled. *6101 W. Century Blvd., Los Angeles 90045, tel. 310/642–1111. 807 rooms. Facilities: 2 restaurants, lounges, exercise room, voice mail, complimentary in-room coffee, multilingual concierge, currency exchange. AE, DC, MC, V.*

Expensive **Hyatt Hotel–LAX.** Rich brown marble in the lobby entrance and dark wood columns delineate the neoclassical decor of this contemporary 12-story building. Close to LAX, Hollywood Park, the Forum, and Marina del Rey, the Hyatt keeps business travelers in mind, and offers large meeting rooms with ample banquet space. The hotel's staff is multilingual, and a concierge is on duty 24 hours a day. Try T.J. Peppercorn's for California cuisine, and Mrs. Candy's, a '50s-style soda fountain. *6225 W. Century Blvd., Los Angeles 90045, tel. 310/670–9000 or 800/233–1234. 596 rooms. Facilities: restaurant, lounge, coffee shop, no-smoking floors, in-room fax, computer hookups, voice mail, entertainment, pool, sauna, exercise room, parking (fee). AE, DC, MC, V.*

The Los Angeles Airport Marriott. One of the first luxury hotels to be built in the airport area, this 18-story Marriott is a fully equipped convention center, convenient to the beach, Marina del Rey, Fisherman's Village, the Forum, and the Coliseum. Complimentary airport bus service gets you to LAX in just four minutes. Seven restaurants and lounges offer gourmet elegance, family-style dining, and lavish California-style buffets. Champions is a sports bar with several television screens for easy viewing. All guest rooms are designed for maximum space and comfort in relaxing earth tones, some with sitting areas and balcony. *5855 W. Century Blvd., Los Angeles 90045, tel. 310/641–5700 or 800/228–9290. 1,012 rooms. Facilities: 4 restaurants, 2 lounges, entertainment, pool, health club, laundry facilities, parking (fee). AE, DC, MC, V.*

★ **Westin Hotel LAX.** This is a good place to stay if you're looking to be pampered but also need to be at the airport. Rooms and suites are decorated in muted earth tones to complement the contemporary decor; many suites have private outdoor spas. The expansive, luxurious lobby is decorated in marble and brass. The Trattoria Grande restaurant features pasta and seafood specialties. *5400 W. Century Blvd., Los Angeles 90045, tel. 310/216–5858 or 800/468–3571. 750 rooms. Facilities: 2 restaurants, lounge, entertainment, pool, sauna, fitness center, parking (fee). AE, DC, MC, V.*

Moderate **Airport Marina Hotel.** Located in a quiet, residential area, perfect for jogging, tennis, and golf, the hotel consists of four separate wings. The Marina Cafe has an international menu, and there's always plenty of celebration in the Jubilation Cocktail Lounge. The hotel also has a shuttle service to Los Angeles International Airport, Marina del Rey, and Fox Hills Mall. *8601 Lincoln Blvd., Los Angeles 90045, tel. 310/670–8111 or 800/225–8126. 780 rooms. Facilities: restaurant, airport transportation. AE, DC, MC, V.*

Inexpensive **Airport Park View Hotel.** Although nothing to write home about, this contemporary three-story hotel located across from Hollywood Park, near the Forum, and close by the 405 freeway, is a decent place to stay. Rooms, renovated in 1992, feel fresh if nondescript. *3900 Century Blvd., Inglewood 90303, tel. 310/677–8899 or 800/793–PARK, fax 310/677–6900. 178 rooms. Facilities: coffee shop, pool, free cable movies, meeting and banquet facilities. AE, D, DC, MC, V.*

Holiday Inn–LAX. This recently decorated, international-style hotel is ideal for families and business types. The hotel features standard Holiday Inn rooms in such colors as beige, burgundy, orange, or green. Other amenities include a California-cuisine restaurant and cocktail lounge; multilingual telephone operators; and tour information. *9901 La Cienega Blvd., Los Angeles 90045, tel. 310/649–5151 or 800/238–8000. 403 rooms. Facilities: restaurant, pool, free parking. AE, DC, MC, V.*

Red Lion Inn. Just 3 miles north of LAX and a few minutes from Marina del Rey, this deluxe hotel is convenient for business types. There is both elegant and casual dining. The Culver's Club Lounge has lively entertainment and dancing. The oversized guest rooms have art deco–style decor. Extra special is the California Suite, with beautiful decorations and its own Jacuzzi. *6161 Centinela Ave., Culver City 90230, tel. 310/649–1776 or 800/547–8010, fax 310/649–4411. 368 rooms. Facilities: restaurant, lounge, entertainment, pool, sauna, health club, free parking. AE, DC, MC, V.*

San Fernando Valley

Very Expensive **Sheraton Universal.** You're apt to see movie and TV stars in this large, 23-story hotel on the grounds of Universal Studios, near the Universal Amphitheater and Universal Studios Tour. The hotel overlooks Hollywood. After a major renovation in 1992, the rooms are now decorated in beige and mauve. *333 Universal Terrace Pkwy., Universal City 91608, tel. 818/980–1212. 444 rooms. Facilities: restaurant, sports bar, pool, whirlpool spa, gym. AE, DC, MC, V.*

Universal City Hilton and Towers. This 24-story glass tower blends contemporary luxury with the charm of an Old World

The Beverly Garland
Hotel, **4**

Burbank Airport
Hilton, **7**

Radisson Valley
Center, **3**

Ritz-Carlton
Huntington Hotel, **9**

St. George Motor
Inn, **2**

Safari Inn, **8**

Sheraton Universal, **6**

Sportsman's Lodge
Hotel, **1**

Universal City
Hilton, **5**

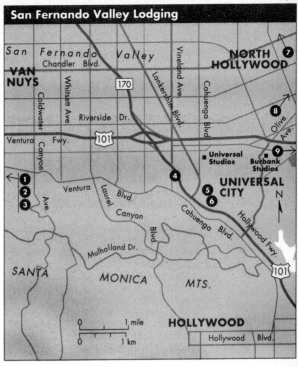

San Fernando Valley Lodging

European hotel. The pleasant rooms are decorated in warm
tones of burgundy and hunter green, and the bathrooms have
wall-to-wall marble. Breathtaking views of the San Fernando
Valley and hills can be enjoyed through floor-to-ceiling windows. Inside the 40-foot-high pavilions next to the guest tower
are two restaurants and two lounges. There is a nearby tennis
center and equestrian center, and golf courses are a short drive
away. A popular place for TV location filming, the hotel is also
close to the Universal Amphitheater, Universal Studios Tour,
and the Hollywood Bowl. *555 Universal Terrace Pkwy., Universal City 91608, tel. 818/506–2500. 456 rooms. Facilities: 2 restaurants, 2 lounges, pool, health spa. AE, DC, MC, V.*

Expensive– **Ritz-Carlton Huntingdon Hotel.** This landmark hotel, built in
Very Expensive 1906, was closed in 1986 for five years and virtually rebuilt to
conform to earthquake-code standards. Reopened in 1991, it
justifies the enormous effort. The main building, a Mediterranean-style structure in warm-colored stucco, fits perfectly
with the lavish houses of the surrounding Oak Knoll neighborhood, Pasadena's best. Walk through the intimate lobby into
the central courtyard, dotted with tiny ponds and lush plant-
ings, to the wood-paneled grand lounge, where you can have
afternoon tea while enjoying a sweeping view of Los Angeles
in the distance. Guest rooms are traditionally furnished and
handsome, although a bit small for the price; the large marble-
fitted bathrooms also look old-fashioned. The landscaped
grounds are lovely, with their Japanese and Horseshoe gardens and the historic Picture Bridge, which has murals depicting scenes of California along its 20 gables. The food is excellent
and the service attentive. *1401 S. Oak Knoll Ave., Pasadena*

91106, tel. 818/568–3900. 388 rooms. Facilities: 2 restaurants, tennis courts, gym, pool. AE, D, DC, MC, V.

Expensive **Burbank Airport Hilton.** This Hilton is located across the street from the Hollywood-Burbank Airport and close to Universal Studios. There are rooms here for anyone's taste, though all are done in standard-issue hotel decor, so don't expect anything snazzy. *2500 Hollywood Way, Burbank 91505, tel. 818/843–6000, fax 818/842–9720. 500 rooms. Facilities: restaurant, pool, whirlpool spa, in-room color TV and VCR, parking (fee). AE, DC, MC, V.*

Moderate **Beverly Garland Hotel.** There's a country-club atmosphere to this seven-story lodge-like hotel, which is popular with business and entertainment folk and offers private balconies and patios. Rooms carry out the early California look with distressed furniture and muted color schemes. It's convenient to Universal Studios. *4222 Vineland Ave., North Hollywood 91602, tel. 818/980–8000, fax 818/766–5230. 258 rooms. Facilities: restaurant, lounge, pool, children's pool, tennis courts, conference center, free parking. AE, DC, MC, V.*

Radisson Valley Center. In addition to excellent service and comfort, this former Hilton hotel boasts a convenient location (at the intersection of I–405 and Highway 101), fairly near to Universal Studios and other Southland attractions. It's well equipped for conventioneers, and there are plush executive suites. *15433 Ventura Blvd., Sherman Oaks 91403, tel. 818/981–5400. 217 rooms. Facilities: restaurant, lounge, fitness room, pool, parking (fee). AE, DC, MC, V.*

Sportsman's Lodge Hotel. An English country–style building with a resort atmosphere, this hotel features beautiful grounds with waterfalls. Guest rooms are large, with country decor in such colors as mauve and blue. Studio suites with private patios are available, and there's an Olympic-size swimming pool and a restaurant with American and Continental cuisines. The hotel is close to the Universal Studios Tour and Universal Amphitheater. *12825 Ventura Blvd., Studio City 91604, tel. 818/769–4700. 200 rooms. Facilities: restaurant, coffee shop, pool, free parking. AE, DC, MC, V.*

Inexpensive **Safari Inn.** Often used for location filming, this hotel, encompassing two buildings, has a homey, neighborhood feel. The rooms have recently been redone with a more modern flair. Some feature blond wood, some have rattan furniture. Suites with bars are available. There's a fine Italian restaurant called Jane's Cucina on the premises. *1911 W. Olive, Burbank 91506, tel. 818/845–8586. 110 rooms. Facilities: restaurant, lounge, pool, Jacuzzi, refrigerators, free parking. AE, DC, MC, V.*

St. George Motor Inn. This English Tudor–style hotel, near Warner Center, business hub of the west San Fernando Valley, features crisp, contemporary decor, redone in 1992. Though it has no restaurant, it's conveniently near such restaurants as Victoria Station and Charlie Brown's. *19454 Ventura Blvd., Tarzana 91356, tel. 818/345–6911 or 800/445–6911, fax 818/344–1217. 57 rooms. Facilities: pool, Jacuzzi, kitchenettes, free parking. AE, DC, MC, V.*

8 The Arts and Nightlife

For the most complete listing of weekly events, get the current issue of *Los Angeles* magazine. The Calendar section of the *Los Angeles Times* also offers a wide survey of Los Angeles arts events, as do the more irreverent free publications the *L.A. Weekly* and the *L.A. Reader.* For a telephone report on current music, theater, dance, film, and special events, call tel. 213/688–ARTS.

Most tickets can be purchased by phone (with a credit card) from **Ticketmaster** (tel. 213/480–3232), **TeleCharge** (tel. 800/762–7666), **Good Time Tickets** (tel. 213/464–7383), or **Murray's Tickets** (tel. 213/234–0123).

The Arts

Theater

If Los Angeles isn't quite the "Broadway of the West" as some have claimed—the scope of theater here really doesn't compare to that in New York—there are offerings worth any visitor's time in this entertainment-oriented city.

The theater scene's growth has been astounding. In 1978 only about 370 professional productions were brought to stages in Los Angeles; in 1993 more than 1,100 were scheduled. Small theaters are blossoming all over town, and the larger houses, despite price hikes to $35 for a single ticket, are usually full.

Even small productions might boast big names from "the Business" (the Los Angeles entertainment empire). Many film and television actors love to work on the stage between "big" projects or while on hiatus from a TV series as a way to refresh their talents or regenerate their creativity in this demanding medium. Doing theater is also an excellent way to be seen by those who matter in the glitzier end of show biz. Hence there is a need for both large houses—which usually mount productions that are road-company imports of Broadway hits or, on occasion, where Broadway-bound material gets a tryout—and a host of small, intimate theaters to showcase the talent that abounds in this city.

Major Theaters   **The Music Center** (135 N. Grand Ave., tel. 213/972–7211). This big downtown complex includes three theaters: the 3,200-seat **Dorothy Chandler Pavilion,** which offers a smattering of plays in between performances of the L.A. Philharmonic, L.A. Master Chorale, and L.A. Opera; the 2,071-seat **Ahmanson Theater,** presenting both classics and new plays (closed for renovation until mid-1995); and the 760-seat **Mark Taper Forum,** under the direction of Gordon Davidson, which presents new works that often go on to Broadway, such as *Children of a Lesser God* and *Jelly's Last Jam.*

James A. Doolittle Theater (1615 N. Vine St., Hollywood, tel. 213/462–6666; charge line, 213/851–9750). Located in the heart of Hollywood, this house offers an intimate feeling despite its 1,038-seat capacity. New plays, dramas, comedies, and musicals are presented here year-round.

John Anson Ford Theater (2580 Cahuenga Blvd., Hollywood, tel. 213/972–7353). This 1,300-seat outdoor house in the Hollywood hills is best known for its Shakespeare and free summer jazz, dance, and cabaret concerts.

Pantages (6233 Hollywood Blvd., Hollywood, tel. 213/480–3232). Once the home of the Academy Awards telecast and Hollywood premieres, this house is massive (2,600 seats) and a splendid example of high-style Hollywood Art Deco, although the acoustics could use some updating. Large-scale musicals from Broadway are usually presented here.

Westwood Playhouse (10886 Le Conte Ave., Westwood, tel. 310/208–6500 or 310/208–5454). An acoustically superior theater with great sightlines, the 498-seat playhouse showcases new plays in the summer, primarily musicals and comedies. Many of the productions here are on their way to or from Broadway. This is also where Jason Robards and Nick Nolte got their starts.

Wilshire Theater (8440 Wilshire Blvd., Beverly Hills, tel. 213/480–3232). The interior of this 1,900-seat house is Art Deco-style; musicals from Broadway are the usual fare.

Smaller Theaters **Cast Theater** (804 N. El Centro, tel. 213/462–0265). Musicals, revivals, and avant-garde improv pieces are done here.

The Coast Playhouse (8325 Santa Monica Blvd., West Hollywood, tel. 213/650–8507). This 99-seat house specializes in excellent original musicals and new dramas.

Fountain Theater (5060 Fountain Ave., tel. 213/663–1525). Seating 80, this theater presents original American dramas and stages Flamenco dance concerts. Marian Mercer and Rob Reiner got their starts here.

Japan America Theater (244 S. San Pedro, tel. 213/680–3700). This community-oriented 880-seat theater at the Japan Cultural Arts Center is home to local theater, dance troupes, and the L.A. Chamber Orchestra, plus numerous children's theater groups.

Santa Monica Playhouse (1211 4th St., Santa Monica, tel. 310/394–9779). This 99-seat house is worth visiting for its cozy, librarylike atmosphere; the good comedies and dramas presented here are further incentive.

Skylight Theater (1816½ N. Vermont Ave., Los Feliz, tel. 213/666–2202). With 99 seats, this theater has hosted many highly inventive productions.

Theatre/Theater (1713 Cahuenga Blvd., Hollywood, tel. 213/871–0210). Angelinos crowd into this 99-seat house to view original works by local authors.

Concerts

Los Angeles is not only the focus of America's pop/rock music recording scene, but now, after years of being denigrated as a cultural invalid, is also a center for classical music and opera.

Major Concert Halls **The Ambassador Auditorium** (300 W. Green St., Pasadena, tel. 818/304–6161). World-renowned soloists and ensembles perform in this elegant and acoustically impressive hall from September through June.

Dorothy Chandler Pavilion (135 N. Grand Ave., tel. 213/972–7211). Part of the Los Angeles Music Center and—with the Hollywood Bowl—the center of L.A.'s classical music scene, the 3,200-seat Pavilion is the home of the Los Angeles Philharmonic. The L.A. Opera presents classics from September through June.

The Greek Theater (2700 N. Vermont Ave., tel. 213/665–1927). This open-air auditorium near Griffith Park offers some classical performances in its mainly pop/rock/jazz schedule from June through October. Its Doric columns evoke the amphitheaters of ancient Greece.

The Hollywood Bowl (2301 Highland Ave., tel. 213/850–2000). Open since 1920, the Bowl is one of the world's largest outdoor amphitheaters, and located in a park surrounded by mountains, trees, and gardens. The Bowl's season runs early July–mid-September; the L.A. Philharmonic spends its summer season here. Performances are on Tuesday, Thursday, and weekends; the program ranges from jazz to pop to classical. Concert goers usually arrive early, bringing or buying picnic suppers. There are plenty of picnic tables, and box-seat subscribers can reserve a table right in their own box. Restaurant dining is available on the grounds (reservations recommended, tel. 213/851–3588). The seats are wood, so you might bring or rent a cushion—and bring a sweater; it gets chilly here in the evening. A convenient way to enjoy the Hollywood Bowl experience without the hassle of parking is to take one of the Park-and-Ride buses, which leave from various locations around town; call the Bowl for information.

Royce Hall (405 N. Hilgard, tel. 310/825–9261). Internationally acclaimed performers are featured in this 1,800-seat auditorium at UCLA. The university's **Schoenberg Hall,** smaller but with wonderful acoustics, also hosts a variety of concerts.

The Shrine Auditorium (665 W. Jefferson Blvd., tel. 213/749–5123). Built in 1926 by the Al Malaikah Temple, the auditorium's decor could be called Baghdad and Beyond. Touring companies from all over the world, along with assorted gospel and choral groups, appear in this one-of-a-kind, 6,200-seat theater.

The Wilshire Ebell Theater (4401 W. Eighth St., tel. 213/939–1128). The Los Angeles Opera Theatre comes to this Spanish-style building, erected in 1924, as do a broad spectrum of other musical performers.

Wiltern Theater (Wilshire Blvd. and Western Ave., tel. 213/380–5005 or 213/388–1400). Reopened in 1985 as a venue for the Los Angeles Opera Theater, the building was constructed in 1930, is listed in the National Register of Historic Places, and is a magnificent example of Art Deco in its green terra-cotta glory.

Dance

Due to lack of Music Center funding, Los Angeles lost the Joffrey Ballet in 1991, and Angelinos have since turned to local dance companies. You can find talented companies dancing around town at various performance spaces. Check the *L.A. Weekly* free newspaper under "dance" to see who is dancing where, or call **The Dance Resource Center** (tel. 213/227–9162).

L.A. still has one resident company, the **Bella Lewistsky Dance Co.** (tel. 213/627–5555), which performs around town.

Visiting companies such as Martha Graham, Paul Taylor, and Hubbard Street Dance Company perform in UCLA Dance Company's home space at **UCLA Center for the Arts** (405 N. Hilgard, tel. 310/825–9261).

Larger companies such as the Kirov, the Bolshoi, and the American Ballet Theater (ABT) perform at various times during the year at the **Shrine Auditorium** (665 W. Jefferson Blvd. tel. 213/749–5123).

Also, two prominent dance events occur annually: The Dance Fair in March and Dance Kaleidoscope in July. Both events take place at **Cal State L.A.'s Dance Department** (5151 State University Dr., tel. 213/343–5124).

Film

Spending two hours at a movie while visiting Los Angeles needn't be taking time out from sightseeing. Some of the country's most historic and beautiful theaters are found here, hosting both first-run and revival films.

Movie listings are advertised daily in the *Los Angeles Times* Calendar section. The price of admission to first-run movies is, as of this writing, $6.50–$7. Bargain prices as low as $3.50 are common for the first showing of the day.

Movie Palaces   **Mann's Chinese Theater** (6925 Hollywood Blvd., tel. 213/464–8111). Formerly owned by Sid Grauman, this Chinese pagoda-style structure is perhaps the world's best-known movie theater. It still carries on one of the oldest of Hollywood traditions: its famous hand- and footprinting ceremony, which was inspired by the mason who supervised the construction of the theater's forecourt. Grauman came upon Jean W. Klossner, a French immigrant, as he put his handprint in wet cement near the marquee after he finished laying the entrance to the theater. A descendant of generations of French masons, Klossner explained that his father, grandfather, and great-grandfather had placed their handprints and signatures at the curbstone of Notre Dame in Paris to mark their contributions to civilization. Grauman offered the Frenchman a 34-year contract to place the imprints of Hollywood's greatest stars in the secret cement mixture that Klossner had devised to stand the test of time. Mary Pickford and Douglas Fairbanks, Sr., were the first to leave their marks at the entrance to the theater during the opening ceremony on May 18, 1927. Today the Chinese houses three movie screens, and it still hosts many gala premieres.

Pacific Cinerama Dome (6360 Sunset Blvd., tel. 213/466–3401). This futuristic, geodesic structure was the first theater designed specifically for Cinerama in the United States. The gigantic screen and multitrack sound system create an unparalleled cinematic experience.

Pacific's El Capitan (6838 Hollywood Blvd., tel. 213/467–7674). Restored to its original Art Deco splendor, this classic movie palace reopened across the street from Mann's Chinese in 1991. First-run movies are on the bill. The Academy Award-winning Disney movie *The Little Mermaid* made its debut here in 1991.

Vista Theater (4473 Sunset Dr., tel. 213/660–6639). At the intersection of Hollywood and Sunset boulevards, this 70-year-old cinema was once Bard's Hollywood Theater, where both moving pictures and vaudeville played. A Spanish-style facade leads to an ornate Egyptian interior. D. W. Griffith's silent classic *Intolerance* was filmed on this site.

Neighborhood Theaters   **Aero** (Montana and 14th St., Santa Monica, tel. 310/395–4990). This movie theater has a cozy, hometown atmosphere; the glowing neon clock near the screen is an unusual touch.

AMC Century Fourteen Theaters (10250 Santa Monica Blvd., Century City, tel. 310/553–8900). This complex is located amid the restaurants and shops of the Century City Shopping Center.

Eagle Theater (4484 Eagle Rock Blvd., Eagle Rock, tel. 213/256–3996). Although a bit off the beaten track, this movie house may well be the cheapest theater in L.A.: the usual admission cost is $3, which often pays for a double bill, and on Thursday a mere $1 gets you through the turnstile.

Rialto Theater (1023 S. Fair Oaks Blvd., South Pasadena, tel. 818/799–9567). A richly decorated, spacious house, the Rialto was recently immortalized in Robert Altman's film *The Player.* It hasn't been converted—yet—into a multiscreen theater, as have most large, older theaters in town.

Royal Theatre (11523 Santa Monica Blvd., Santa Monica, tel. 310/478–1041). New films by independent filmmakers and foreign films are the usual fare at this art house.

Art Houses The **Laemmle Theater** chain hosts the best of the latest foreign releases. See their *Los Angeles Times* Calendar ad for listings. **Cineplex** (8522 Beverly Blvd., 8th fl. of Beverly Center, tel. 310/652–7760). This 14-screen cinema offers foreign films and first-run features.

Los Feliz Theater (1822 N. Vermont Ave., tel. 213/664–2169). It's a little run-down, but has a neighborhoody feel.

Melnitz Hall (405 Hilgard Ave., tel. 310/825–2345). UCLA's main film theater runs a mixture of the old, the avant-garde, and the neglected.

New Beverly Cinema (7165 Beverly Blvd., tel. 213/938–4038). Film festivals, Hollywood classics, documentaries, and notable foreign films are the fare at this theater. There is always a double bill.

Nuart (11272 Santa Monica, tel. 310/478–6379). The best-kept of L.A.'s revival houses, this place has an excellent screen, good double bills, and special midnight shows.

Silent Movie (611 North Fairfax Ave., tel. 213/653–2389). This theater revives classics like Charlie Chaplin's *The Gold Rush* and the portfolio of Buster Keaton films. Open Wednesday, Friday, and Saturday evenings, this is the only known silent movie house in the world, complete with a vintage organ.

Television

Audiences Unlimited (100 Universal City Plaza, Building 153, Universal City 91608, tel. 8l8/506–0043) is a nifty organization that helps fill seats for television programs (and sometimes theater events, as well). There's no charge, but the tickets are on a first-come, first-served basis. Shows to see include "Roseanne," "Designing Women," "Blossom," "Family Matters," "Love Connection," "Golden Palace," "Coach," "Empty Nest," and "Married . . .with Children," and tickets can be picked up at Fox Television Center (5746 Sunset Blvd., Van Ness Ave. entrance, weekdays 8:30–6, weekends 11–6) or at the Glendale Galleria Information Desk between 10 and 9 daily. Note: You must be 16 or older to attend a television taping. For a schedule, send a self-addressed envelope a couple of weeks prior to your visit to the address above.

Nightlife

Despite the high energy level of the nightlife crowd, Los Angeles nightclubs aren't known for keeping their doors open until the wee hours. This is still an early-to-bed city, and it's safe to say that by 2 AM, most jazz, rock, and disco clubs have closed for the night. Perhaps it's the temperate climate and the daytime sports orientation of the city: Most Angelenos want to be on the tennis court or out jogging first thing in the AM, making a late-night social life out of the question.

The accent in this city is on trendy rock clubs, smooth country-and-western establishments, intimate jazz spots, and comedy clubs. Consult *Los Angeles* magazine for current listings. The Sunday *Los Angeles Times* Calendar section and the free *L.A. Weekly* and *L.A. Reader* also provide listings.

The Sunset Strip, which runs from West Hollywood to Beverly Hills, offers a wide assortment of nighttime diversions. Comedy stores, restaurants with piano bars, cocktail lounges, and hard-rock clubs proliferate. Westwood, home of UCLA, is a college town, and this section of Los Angeles comes alive at night with rock and new-wave clubs playing canned and live music. It's one of the few areas in the city with a true neighborhood spirit. For years, downtown Los Angeles hasn't offered much in the way of nighttime entertainment (with the exception of the Music Center for concerts and theater), but that has gradually changed over the last year, with the openings of more theaters and trendy clubs. Some of Los Angeles's best jazz clubs, discos, and comedy clubs are scattered throughout the San Fernando and San Gabriel valleys.

Dress codes vary depending on the place you visit. Jackets are expected at cabarets and hotels. Discos are generally casual, although some will turn away the denim-clad. The rule of thumb is to phone ahead and check the dress code, but on the whole, Los Angeles is oriented toward casual wear.

Jazz

The Baked Potato (3787 Cahuenga Blvd. W, North Hollywood, tel. 818/980–1615). In this tiny club they pack you in like sardines to hear a powerhouse of jazz. The featured item on the menu is, of course, baked potatoes; they're jumbo and stuffed with everything from steak to vegetables.

Birdland West (105 W. Broadway, Long Beach, tel. 310/436–9341). This is the place to come for contemporary jazz, Art Deco decor, and great happy hours.

Catalina Bar and Grill (1640 N. Cahuenga Blvd., Hollywood, tel. 213/466–2210). Big name acts and innovators like Latin-influenced saxophonist Paquito D. Rivera light up this top Hollywood jazz spot. Continental cuisine is served.

Jax (339 N. Brand Blvd., Glendale, tel. 818/500–1604). This intimate club serves a wide variety of food, from sandwiches to steak and seafood; live music is an added draw.

The Jazz Bakery (3221 Hutchison, Culver City, tel. 310/271–9039). Jim Britt opens his photography studio, adjacent to the Helms Bakery Building, on the weekend to serve coffee, desserts, and a nice selection of world-class jazz, enhanced by great acoustics. The $15 admission (no credit cards) includes refreshments.

Le Cafe (14633 Ventura Blvd., Sherman Oaks, tel. 818/986–2662). The Room Upstairs has high-tech decor and features mellow jazz. Downstairs is a dynamic restaurant-café offering everything from onion soup to some of the best duck pâté in town.

The Lighthouse (30 Pier Ave., Hermosa Beach, tel. 310/372–6911 or 213/376–9833). Once one of Los Angeles's finest jazz venues, this club now offers a broad spectrum of music, from reggae to big band—though not much jazz anymore. The decor is wood, brass, and brick, with a lot of plants. Dine on appetizers or steaks while listening to the sounds.

Marla's Memory Lane (2323 W. Martin Luther King, Jr., Blvd., Los Angeles, tel. 213/294–8430). Owned by comedy star Marla Gibbs of "The Jeffersons" and "227," the room pops with blues, jazz, and easy listening. Kenny Burrell and Ernie Andrews play here from time to time. The Continental menu boasts prime rib.

Nucleus Nuance (7267 Melrose Ave., West Hollywood, tel. 213/939–8666). This Art Deco restaurant features vintage jazz every night.

Vine Street Bar and Grill (1610 N. Vine St., Hollywood, tel. 213/463–4375). This elegant club in the heart of Hollywood (across the street from the James Doolittle Theater) features two shows nightly. Past performers have included Eartha Kitt, Cab Calloway, and Carmen McRae. Italian food is served.

Folk, Pop, and Rock

Anti-Club (4658 Melrose Ave., Hollywood, tel. 213/661–3913). If you're looking for the underground (in rock bands, that is), look to this dimly lit, smoke-filled hangout.

At My Place (1026 Wilshire Blvd., Santa Monica, tel. 310/451–8596). This enterprise features a provocative blend of jazz/fusion, pop, and rhythm-and-blues music acts. Comedy performers open the weekend shows. Culinary specialties include quiche and designer pizza.

Blue Saloon (4657 Lankershim Blvd., North Hollywood, tel. 818/766–4644). For rock 'n' roll, this is the place to go. (You'll also catch a smattering of country and blues at times.) If your seat gets tired while listening to the music, rustle up a game of billiards or darts. This is the friendliest club around.

The Central (8852 Sunset Blvd., West Hollywood, tel. 310/652–5937). At this musicians' hangout, road crews, pop-act managers, and famous guitarists alike come to hear live music in the pop, soul, and jazz/fusion genres. Many celebrity musicians attend the Sunday-night jam sessions.

Club Lingerie (6507 Sunset Blvd., Hollywood, tel. 213/466–8557). One local describes this place as "clean enough for the timid, yet seasoned quite nicely for the tenured scenester." Best of all is its mix of really hot bands.

Kingston 12 (814 Broadway, Santa Monica, tel. 310/451–4423). This Santa Monica club features Daddy Freddie, the world's fastest rapper. Reggae music is also on the boards, as is a menu of fine Jamaican food.

McCabe's Guitar Shop (3101 Pico Blvd., Santa Monica, tel. 310/828–4497; concert information, 310/828–4403). Folk, acoustic-rock, bluegrass, and soul concerts are featured in this guitar store on weekend nights. Coffee, herbal tea, apple juice, and homemade sweets are served during intermission. Make reservations well in advance—McCabe's almost always sells out. Dan Hicks, Michelle Shocked, John Wesley Harding, and blues great John Hammond have headlined here.

The Music Machine (12220 W. Pico Blvd., West Los Angeles, tel. 310/820–5150). This rockin' club blasts reggae and the funkiest hip hop Tuesday through Saturday nights.

The Palace (1735 N. Vine St., Hollywood, tel. 213/462–3000). The "in" spot for the upwardly mobile, this plush Art Deco palace boasts live entertainment, a fabulous sound system, full bar, and dining upstairs. The patrons here dress to kill.

The Palladium (6215 W. Sunset Blvd., Hollywood, tel. 213/962–7600). This club is known for hosting fundraising concerts and events, such as the Magic Johnson AIDS benefit in 1992. The rest of the time, live bands appear here on Saturday, and draw in a funky, hip, younger crowd.

Pier 52 (52 Pier Ave., Hermosa Beach, tel. 310/376–1629). From Wednesday through Sunday there are live dance bands here playing pure rock and roll.

Raji's Club (6160 Hollywood Blvd., Hollywood, tel. 213/469–4552). Consider this the house of rock. Fun food—pizza, hot dogs, nachos—is served at Ba Ba's Bistro, on the premises.

The Roxy (9009 Sunset Blvd., West Hollywood, tel. 310/276–2222). The premier Los Angeles rock club, classy and comfortable, offers performance art as well as theatrical productions. Many famous Los Angeles groups got their start here as opening acts.

The Strand (1700 S. Pacific Coast Hwy., Redondo Beach, tel. 310/316–1700). This major concert venue covers a lot of ground, hosting hot new acts or such old favorites as Asleep at the Wheel, bluesman Albert King, rock vet Robin Trower, and Billy Vera, all in the same week. Who says you can't have it all?

The Troubador (9081 Santa Monica Blvd., West Hollywood, tel. 310/276–6168). In the early '70s this was one of the hottest clubs in town for major talent. Then business entered a shaky phase while the music industry changed its focus, but now it's rolling again, this time with up-and-coming talent. The adjoining bar is a great place in which to see and be seen.

Whiskey A Go Go (8901 Sunset Blvd., West Hollywood, tel. 310/652–4202). This, the most famous rock 'n' roll club on the Sunset Strip, has hosted everyone from Otis Redding to AC/DC and now presents up-and-coming heavy metal and very hard rock bands.

Cabaret

Blak and Bloo (7574 Sunset Blvd., Hollywood, tel. 213/876–1120). This place is a load of fun. Stop by to listen to live rock bands—the best in the city—or for a session of dancing every night. The adjoining restaurant specializes in Continental/Italian cuisine.

L.A. Cabaret (17271 Ventura Blvd., Encino, tel. 818/501–3737). The club features a variety of comedy acts nightly. Famous entertainers often make surprise appearances.

Rose Tatoo (665 Robertson Blvd., West Hollywood, tel. 310/854–4455). This New York–style cabaret features up-and-coming artists as well as household names. A lot of show-biz types come here. If you're hungry, seek out the upstairs restaurant.

The Queen Mary (12449 Ventura Blvd., Sherman Oaks, tel. 818/506–5619). Female impersonators vamp it up as Diana Ross, Barbra Streisand, and Bette Midler in this small club where every seat is a good one. Drinks are the only refreshment served, so eat first. Plenty of cross-dressers parade among the colorful clientele, which is never boring. Open Wednesday–Sunday.

Studio One Backlot (652 N. La Peer, West Hollywood, tel. 310/659–0472). This eclectic night spot features excellent musical acts, singers, comedians, and drag shows.

Discos and Dancing

Bar One (9229 Sunset Blvd., Beverly Hills, tel. 310/271–8355). Celebrities such as Warren Beatty and Charlie Sheen frequent this restaurant and bar. A hot, hip place for dancing, this is L.A.'s club of the moment. There's also a pool table and comfortable lounging areas.

Circus Disco and Arena (6655 Santa Monica Blvd., Hollywood, tel. 213/462–1291). A gay and mixed club, it features funk and rock; Thursday nights are exclusively new-wave music.

Coconut Teaszer (8177 Sunset Blvd., Los Angeles, tel. 213/654–4773). Dancing to live music, a great barbecue menu, and killer drinks make for lively fun.

Crush Bar Continental Club (1743 Cahuenga Ave., Hollywood, tel. 213/461–9017). If the 1960s is a decade that appeals to you, stop by this happening dance club, open Thursday–Saturday. After all, there's nothing like some golden Motown to get you moving.

Florentine Gardens (5951 Hollywood Blvd., Hollywood, tel. 213/464–0706). One of Los Angeles's largest dance areas, with spectacular lighting to match, it's open Friday and Saturday.

Glam Slam (333 S. Boylston, Los Angeles, tel. 213/747–4849). A New York–style club, this hot spot has a restricted entrance policy—there's a large celebrity clientele, and everybody's dressed to kill. The premises offers a large dance floor, live bands, balcony bar, and restaurant. It's open Friday and Saturday until 4 AM, which is unusually late for this city. This club is in a terrible neighborhood, so be prepared to shell out for valet parking.

Moonlight Tango Cafe (13730 Ventura Blvd., Sherman Oaks, tel. 818/788–2000). This high-energy club-restaurant, big on the swing era, really gets moving in the wee hours, when a conga line inevitably takes shape on the dance floor. Keep an eye on your waiter—he may just burst into song, as all staffers are hired to entertain as well as serve food.

Nucleus Nuance (7267 Melrose Ave., Los Angeles, tel. 213/939–8666). Casual, cool, and swinging, this club has dancing until 2 AM.

Oar House (2941 Main St., Santa Monica, tel. 310/396–4725). Perhaps because there's no cover charge, or maybe just because this is a relaxing place to hang out, this club is frequented by Westsiders who like pop music. Monday is oldies night.

Peanuts (7969 Santa Monica Blvd., West Hollywood, tel. 213/654–0280). A fun bar, Peanuts caters to a gay clientele, with live music and drag shows. There's a large dance floor and a super sound system.

Tatou (233 N. Beverly Dr., Beverly Hills, tel. 310/274–9955). This club has been called a 1990's version of Rick's Place (remember *Casablanca*?). The downstairs club/restaurant attracts a world-weary older crowd who often wander upstairs to mingle with the younger set on the spacious dance floor. Don't expect to hear "As Time Goes By," though—this place is strictly dedicated to contemporary sounds.

Country

In Cahoots (223 N. Glendale Ave., Glendale, tel. 818/800–1665). At this raucous dance hall, a la Nashville, on Tuesday nights you can learn how to two-step if you don't already know how. All week long there's live music by local country artists like Rosie Flores.

The Palomino (6907 Lankershim Blvd., North Hollywood, tel. 818/764–4010). There's occasionally a wild crowd at this premier country showcase, where good old boys and urban cowboys meet and everybody has a good time.

Hotel Lounges and Piano Bars

Alberto's Ristorante (8826 Melrose Ave., Los Angeles, tel. 310/278–2770). This piano bar draws a neighborhood crowd, mostly over 40 and well-to-do. Alberto's also serves excellent Italian food.

Century Plaza Hotel and Tower (2025 Ave. of the Stars, Century City, tel. 310/277–2000). The Lobby Court features piano music nightly.

Hollywood Roosevelt (700 Hollywood Blvd., Hollywood, tel. 213/466–7000). The grand lobby, done in shades of rose and taupe, is an elegant setting for cocktails.

Hotel Bel-Air (701 Stone Canyon Rd., Bel Air, tel. 310/472–1211). There's entertainment every night, alternating between a pianist and a vocalist, in one of Los Angeles's most famous hotels.

Hyatt Regency (711 S. Hope St., Los Angeles, tel. 213/683–1234). There's a good piano lounge in this spectacularly designed hotel. The lounge is open Tuesday–Saturday.

The New Otani Hotel and Garden (120 S. Los Angeles St., Los Angeles, tel. 213/629–1200). The Rendezvous Lounge of this Japanese-style hotel offers a sentimental pianist.

Radisson Bel-Air (11461 Sunset Blvd., Bel Air, tel. 310/476–6571). The Oasis Bar here features a singer-pianist who performs music from the '40s as well as more contemporary tunes.

Regent Beverly Wilshire (9500 Wilshire Blvd., Beverly Hills, tel. 310/275–5200). Plush sofas and high tables set the atmosphere for this elegant piano bar, in one of L.A.'s premier and most historical hotels.

Smoke House (4420 Lakeside Dr., Burbank, tel. 818/845–3731). There's a lounge room with assorted entertainment separate from the restaurant. Many musical acts of the 1950s are featured.

Sportsmen's Lodge Restaurant (12833 Ventura Blvd., Studio City, tel. 818/984–0202). The lounge connected to the main hotel features a pianist, and the setting, with brooks and swan-filled ponds, is very attractive.

Westin Bonaventure Hotel (5th and Figueroa Sts., L.A., tel. 213/624–1000). In the Lobby Court there is music nightly, consisting of popular favorites at the piano bar, or more jazz-oriented musical entertainers.

Westwood Marquis (930 Hilgard Ave., Westwood, tel. 310/208–8765). The Westwood Lounge of this chic hotel offers cozy settees, soft lights, and a piano or harp player. Vocalists are featured occasionally.

Wilshire Plaza (3515 Wilshire Blvd., Los Angeles, tel. 213/381–7411). Entertainment is featured in the Tulips Lounge.

Comedy and Magic

Comedy Act Theater (3339 W. 43rd St., near Crenshaw, tel. 310/677–4101). This club features comedy by and for the black community, Thursday through Saturday nights. Recent performers have been *Hollywood Shuffle*'s Robert Townsend and "Night Court's" Marcia Warfield.

Comedy and Magic Club (1018 Hermosa Ave., Hermosa Beach, tel. 310/372–1193). This beachfront club features many magicians and comedians seen on TV and in Las Vegas. The Unknown Comic, Elayne Boosler, Pat Paulsen, Jay Leno, and Harry Anderson have all played here.

Comedy Store (8433 Sunset Blvd., Hollywood, tel. 213/656–6225). Los Angeles's premier comedy showcase has been going strong for over a decade. Many famous comedians, including Robin Williams and Steve Martin, occasionally make unannounced appearances here.

Groundlings Theater (7307 Melrose Ave., Hollywood, tel. 213/934–9700). The entertainment here consists of original skits, music, and improv, with each player contributing his/her own flavor to the usually hilarious performance.

The Ice House Comedy Showroom (24 N. Mentor Ave., Pasadena, tel. 818/577–1894). Three-act shows here feature comedians, celebrity impressionists, and magicians from Las Vegas, as well as from television shows.

Igby's Comedy Cabaret (11637 Pico Blvd., Los Angeles, tel. 310/477–3553). You'll see familiar television faces as well as up-and-coming comedians Tuesday through Saturday. Cabaret fare includes cocktails and dining in a friendly ambience. Reservations are necessary.

The Improvisation (8162 Melrose Ave., West Hollywood, tel. 213/651–2583 and 321 Santa Monica Blvd., Santa Monica, tel. 310/394–8664). The Improv is a transplanted New York establishment showcasing comedians and some vocalists. This place was the proving ground for Liza Minnelli and Richard Pryor, among others. Reservations are recommended.

The Laugh Factory (8001 Sunset Blvd., Hollywood, tel. 213/656–8860). A variety of comedy acts and improvisation are performed here seven days a week.

Upfront Comedy Showcase (1452 3rd St., Santa Monica, tel. 310/319–3477). Located in the Third Street Promenade, this dinner club is a home for many local improvisation groups, including the Second City Alumni Players. Stand-up acts from all over also come to perform here.

Casinos

In the late 1930s the famed gambling ship *Rex*, anchored just outside the three-mile limit, catered to Angelenos looking for the occasional fling with Lady Luck. Each night tuxedoed men and gowned ladies took a motor launch out to the ship for an evening of gaming—blackjack, roulette, craps, or poker. Readers of Raymond Chandler's *Farewell My Lovely* will recognize the scene.

Today the *Rex* is only a memory. Anyone who lusts for the thrill of "bones" dancing across green felt has to hop a jet to Las Vegas; it's just an hour away.

Poker players, though, don't have to make that trek. Just 15 miles south of the Los Angeles Civic Center is the community of **Gardena,** home of six combination card rooms, restaurants, and cocktail lounges. These are not full gaming casinos, and there are no attached hotels. Although California law prohibits gambling, Gardena enacted an ordinance years ago allowing operators to run draw-poker, low-ball, and pan card games.

The six card rooms are fairly standardized, even though the decor varies, and limits on maximum bets differ. A card room, for example, can have no more than 35 tables. Typically a poker table has eight seats and a designated limit on bets. The minimum bet is $1 before the draw and $2 after the draw, with no limits on the number of raises. Some tables have a "house" dealer; the card room collects a fee, ranging from $1 up to $24 an hour in the $100–$200 games, from the players every half hour.

Gardena card rooms are open 24 hours a day, and you can play as long as your cash and stamina hold out. Card rooms also have surprisingly good food in their restaurants at reasonable prices. Law requires that the bar be separate and outside the building. You can't have a drink brought to your table like you can in Vegas.

The Eldorado Club (15411 S. Vermont Ave., Gardena, tel. 310/323–2800). This is the high rollers' club, and the only card room with a $100–$200-limit game going nonstop. That means that your first bet can be up to $100, and after the draw (cards from the dealer), the maximum bet is $200. With eight players and no limits on the number of times players can raise, pots easily can double or triple. The food, at bargain prices, is superb. One-third of the tables have house dealers. Establish credit and you can cash checks easily, but no credit cards are accepted for chips.

Normandie Casino (1045 W. Rosecrans, Gardena, tel. 310/515–1466). Most of the table games at this European-style card room are $40–$80 stakes, but some are lower. Pai Gow poker is offered, and there's Las Vegas–style entertainment with headliners like Juice Newton. Free instruction is offered by staffers. Coffee shop on premises.

Bars

Despite its well-publicized penchant for hedonism, Los Angeles, unlike New York, Chicago, and San Francisco, is not a saloon town. The practiced art of pub-crawling has never flourished here, mainly because the city has few real neighborhoods and plenty of freeways. Traditionally, unlike New Yorkers, Angelenos rarely pledge loyalty to any libational hangout; they're too nomadic. But there are hundreds of great cozy bars, lively pubs, and festive watering holes to quench your thirst for conversation and fine spirits.

South Bay bars and any place near the water have younger, hipper, and livelier crowds. Rugby shirts and cutoffs are commonplace, and the talk is largely about volleyball, beach parties, real estate syndications, and sports cars. **Westside** is typically more trendy; casual chic is the watchword. In **West Hollywood** and **Hollywood** environs, the attire is even more relaxed: young directors in jogging suits, out-of-work actors in jeans. Here bars buzz with the intoxicating talk of "deals," as in "three-picture deals," "development deals," "album deals." Autograph hounding of celebrities is discouraged by owner-managers, who are thrilled whenever stars frequent their places. **Pasadena** pubs, once fiercely conservative, have loosened and livened up. But the attire is still traditional: button-down shirts, rep ties, blue blazer—decidedly preppy. **Downtown** bars are generally a bastion for bankers, brokers, and other business folk. Two- and three-piece suits are de rigueur.

Monitor your intake of spirits if you're driving. California has enacted some very tough laws to rid its roads of intoxicated motorists. A first-time offender who has more than a .08% blood-alcohol reading gets 20 hours in jail and a stiff fine. So beware—or, better yet, find yourself a designated driver if you want to imbibe while you're out on the town.

Otherwise, welcome to Los Angeles—and bottoms up.

Airport and South Bay
Orville and Wilbur's (401 W. Rosecrans, tel. 310/545–6639). The clientele is an eclectic mix of surfers, business folks, and rugby-shirted beach rats. With its spectacular view of the Pacific, this is a real sundown place.

Tequila Willy's (3290 Sepulveda Blvd., Manhattan Beach, tel. 310/545–4569). This lively spot, featuring pool, backgammon, and even karaoke, is attached to the tacky El Torito Restaurant, should you hanker for some budget-price Mexican fare.

Beverly Hills
Ten years ago you'd never have found a corner saloon in Beverly Hills—too déclassé. But as the world citizenry flocked to this enclave of wealth, they brought with them some of the more easygoing customs of the leisurely rich, and now this small city is riddled with libational refuges from the rat race.

Carroll O'Connor's Place (369 N. Bedford Dr., tel. 310/273–7585). Formerly The Ginger Man, and now named for its long-time owner, this place is decorated with tile floors and green-shaded tables, and is, as ever, the stand-up-and-schmooze haunt of the many young execs. Lots of celebs, including Archie Bunker himself, are often in attendance.

La Scala (410 N. Canon, tel. 310/275–0579). A quaint bar with an immense wine cellar, La Scala is honeycombed with celebrities nightly.

R.J.'s (252 N. Beverly Dr., tel. 310/274–3474 or 310/274–7427). Behind the oak bar and brass rail are 800 bottles stacked to the ceiling. You can either listen to the piano player pound out his favorite ditty or bend your elbow at the bar with a brace of new buddies.

Stringfellows (206 Via Rodeo, tel. 310/285–9909). Sister club to the London hot spot, Stringfellows attracts a large crowd of yuppies who like to tell people where they've been and whom they've seen.

Century City Once the backlot of Twentieth Century Fox, this sprawling complex of towering office buildings and luxury condominiums is not without fine bars and saloons. Two of the best:

Harper's Bar and Grill (2040 Ave. of the Stars, tel. 310/553–1855). A central place to meet friends for cocktails before or after a show at the Shubert Theater, it offers warm decor and generous drinks.

Harry's Bar and American Grill (ABC Entertainment Center, 2020 Ave. of the Stars, tel. 310/277–2333). A reasonably authentic version of the famed Florentine bar and grill that Hemingway and other Lost Generation scribblers frequented, Harry's is unrivaled in L.A. for its potent cappuccino.

Downtown Downtown Los Angeles, once a ghost town after dusk, has been enjoying a renaissance as a dining, drinking, and socializing center for nighttime Angelenos. But go with someone who knows the territory; downtown isn't the safest place for a novice to go exploring.

Al's Bar (305 S. Hewitt, tel. 213/687–3558). Downtown's greatest dive, this is a dimly lit, SoHo-like haven for artist-types and the adventurous.

Casey's Bar (613 S. Grand, tel. 213/629–2353). The downtown location makes this probably the area's most popular pub, and usually crowded with corporate comers after work.

Engine Co. #28. (644 S. Figueroa, tel. 213/624–6996). This cozy bar (and restaurant), with dark mahogany accents and high-backed booths, attracts a lot of stockbrokers and lawyers.

Grand Avenue Bar (506 S. Grand, tel. 213/612–1595). This sleek bar in the Biltmore Hotel serves until 2 AM. There's also excellent jazz. Bring money.

Little Joe's (900 N. Broadway, tel. 213/489–4900). A must for sports buffs. The prices are low and the big-screen TV is always tuned to the hottest game. W.C. Fields frequented the bar in the '30s.

Pacific Dining Car (1310 W. 6th St., tel. 213/483–6000). This Los Angeles landmark has a large bar open 24 hours that also serves gourmet hors d'oeuvres nightly at no charge.

Redwood Second Street Saloon (316 W. Second St., tel. 213/617–2867). Reporters from the *Los Angeles Times* and United Press International pack this gaudy, gabby place after 5 PM to trade postmortems of the day's stories or to drink their lunch if they're working nightside.

Rex (617 S. Olive, tel. 213/627–2300). This piano bar on the ground floor of the historic Oviatt Building radiates the Art Deco ambience of a 1930s cruise liner. Sip slowly and enjoy.

Stepps (Wells Fargo Court, 350 S. Hope St., tel. 213/626–0900). In warmer months, TGIF celebrants gather at the portable outdoor bars of this major business-crowd hangout.

Hollywood The bar and saloon scene in the world's film capital is no longer the raucous, gin-soaked setting that Zelda and Scott Fitzgerald, Errol Flynn, Robert Benchley, or even Sinatra and Burton adored. The great Sunset Strip nightclubs—the Mocambo, Ciro's, Trocadero, Interlude—are long gone. The bar-hopping ritual of the 1940s, crawling down Sunset in a top-down '47 convertible in search of the next Cuba Libre, has been replaced by cruisers who clog that boulevard and others the moment the sun sets. But to briefly relive the halcyon days of yesteryear, there are some oases that should be visited.

Cobalt Cantina (4326 Sunset Blvd., tel. 213/953–9991). The bar, next door to a Tex-Mex restaurant, is decorated Santa Fe style. The clientele is a mix of business and "biz" folk who take advantage of its proximity to ABC's Prospect Studios, and PBS. The signature drink here is a cobalt blue margarita made with blue Caracao.

The Columbia Bar & Grill (1448 N. Gower, tel. 213/461–8800). Its proximity to several television studios helps this casually elegant spot draw quite a show-business crowd.

The Dresden (1760 N. Vermont, tel. 213/665–4294). Everything old is new again in L.A., as evidenced in this unassuming '40s-style bar that has been rediscovered by a happening '90s crowd.

El Coyote (7312 Beverly Blvd., tel. 213/939–7766). For a pick-me-up margarita, stop by this kitchy restaurant/bar and get a glass of the best—and cheapest—in town.

Magic Castle (7001 Franklin Ave., tel. 213/851–3313). As the guest of a member (the only way you'll get in), you still pay the $7.50 admission at the door and are required to buy dinner. Once you utter the magic words "open sesame" to a blinking owl, a bookcase slides back to reveal a secret panel and a three-level celebration of the magical arts. The Magic Castle maintains a strict dress code, so if you're male, don't forget your coat and tie.

Martoni's (1523 Cahuenga Blvd., tel. 213/466–3441). A venerable Italian restaurant launched decades ago by Frank Sinatra's former valet, this cozy bar is packed nightly with agents, studio musicians, and stars on the ascent.

Musso and Franks (6667 Hollywood Blvd., tel. 213/467–5123). Film-studio moguls and $2-a-day extras alike flock to this long-running hit, where the Rob Roys are just as smooth and the clientele just as eclectic as ever. No-nonsense bartenders will give you an oral history of the boulevard; just ask.

Nickodell (5511 Melrose Ave., tel. 213/469–2181). Because it's located next to Paramount Studios, you're likely to spy a few familiar TV personalities, nestled into the cozy booths, despite the dim lighting.

Nucleus Nuance (7267 Melrose Ave., tel. 213/939–8666). A variety of mixed imbibements can be enjoyed while you take in music of the '30s and '40s performed live at night in an adjacent room.

Smalls (5574 Melrose Ave., tel. 213/469–8258). A bar designed for social moguls—upscale business types who kick back and dress down in designer jeans.

Vine St. Bar & Grill (1610 N. Vine St., tel. 213/463–4375). The Art Deco–style bar re-creates the glamour of Duke Ellington's swingtime 1940s.

Yamashiro's (1999 N. Sycamore Ave., tel. 213/466–5125). A lovely tradition is to meet at this Japanese restaurant/bar at sunset for cocktails on the terrace.

Marina del Rey/ Venice

Black Whale (3016 Washington Blvd., tel. 310/823–9898). For swashbuckling saloon-goers, there are plenty of mates ready to swig rum with you.

Brennan's (4089 Lincon Blvd., tel. 310/821–6622). This Irish pub's big open bar is a pleasant backdrop for easy conversation. Turtle racing, a parking-lot grand prix, is a fixture here.

Casablanca (220 Lincoln, tel. 310/392–5751). At this Mexican bar and grill you can watch the cook pounding on and cooking tortillas.

Crystal Fountain Lounge (Marina International Hotel, 4200 Admiralty Way, tel. 310/301–2000). Even locals often overlook this dark and cozy spot. The pianist at the bar alternates with a guitarist.

Typhoon (3221 Donald Douglas Loop S., tel. 310/390–6565). This fun-filled bar right off the Santa Monica Airport's runway is known for a Typhoon Punch (triple sec, rums, and fruit juices) so potent that the umbrella sticking out of the glass is broken and blown inside-out.

The Warehouse (4499 Admiralty Way, tel. 310/823–5451). Ex-cinematographer Burt Hixon collected tropical drink recipes on his South Seas forays and whips up one of the most sinfully rich piña coladas this side of Samoa. The bar is popular, so get there early.

West Beach Cafe (60 N. Venice Blvd., tel. 310/823–5396). A popular night spot, the bar is often crowded with Westside Yuppies, and it has a changing contemporary art show.

Mid-Wilshire Wilshire Boulevard is lined with good—and some great—bars.

HMS Bounty (3357 Wilshire Blvd., tel. 213/385–7275). This is a businessperson's après-work watering hole; very clubby, very gabby.

Lowenbrau Keller (3211 Beverly Blvd., tel. 213/382–5732). A little bit of Bavaria gone Hollywood, this is where locals go to gobble up a plate of bratwurst and knock back a few steins. A grand piano accompanies swaying punters belting out the requisite German drinking songs.

Molly Malone's (575 S. Fairfax, tel. 213/935–1577). A small, cozy Irish pub, it features Gaelic music on weekends, Harp beer all the time, and a hamburger that is a feast in itself.

Tom Bergin's (840 S. Fairfax, tel. 213/936–7151). One of L.A.'s best Irish pubs, it's plastered with Day-Glo shamrocks perpetuating the names of the thousands of patrons who have passed through its door.

Pasadena Famed for the Rose Bowl game and the New Year's Day Rose Parade, Pasadena also boasts some of the friendliest bars and pubs in Southern California.

Beckham Place (77 W. Walnut, tel. 818/796–3399). A rather fancy "Olde English" pub, it's known for its huge drinks, free roast beef sandwiches, and wingback chairs placed near a roaring fire. It's often packed with engineers and science buffs; the conversation is heady, the serving wenches friendly.

Chronicle (897 Granite Dr., tel. 818/792–1179). This restaurant/bar with the feel of a turn-of-the-century mansion features friendly bartenders and generous drinks.

The Crossbow (1400 Huntington Dr., S. Pasadena, tel. 818/799–0758). A dark, clubby atmosphere pervades this entertaining club, attracting an older, Pasadena-esque group of people.

Crown City Brewery (300 S. Raymond Ave., tel. 818/577–5548). Beer brewed on the premises is the main attraction, and for good reason.

Islands (3533 Foothill Blvd., tel. 818/351–6543). At this Polynesian-style bar, surf videos blare in the background. Order up some tacos, burgers, or chicken sandwiches, and turn drink time into feast time.

John Bull (958 S. Fair Oaks, tel. 818/441–4353). This British pub looks as if it came straight here from London.

Lobby Bar (150 S. Los Robles, tel. 818/577–1000). You won't find any little old ladies from Pasadena in this turn-of-the-century Victorian bar, on the lower level of the Pasadena Hilton; this is action central.

Maldonado's (1202 E. Green, tel. 818/796–1126). A tiny European-style bar is attached to one of Pasadena's finest restaurants. Sit on a bar stool, order a glass of French wine, and enjoy live opera and Broadway show tunes.

Market City Cafe (33 South Fair Oaks, tel. 818/568–0203). This light and airy bar in Pasadena's Old Town is popular at lunch or in the early evening.

San Fernando Valley Commuters traverse the Ventura Freeway east to west and often stop to dine and drink at a potpourri of French, Italian, Asian, and trendy American bistros.

Sagebrush Cantina (23527 Calabassas Rd., tel. 818/222–6062). An indoor-outdoor saloon next to a Mexican restaurant, this spot is the Valley's version of the Via Veneto café scene. Motorcycle hippies mix comfortably with computer moguls and showbiz folk, including a platoon of stunt people. There's country-pop entertainment on weekends.

Santa Monica and the Beaches Santa Monica may be the most cosmopolitan city in Southern California. The British, for example, love its cool weather and its proximity to the ocean. Not surprisingly, among the bars here, are some authentic British pubs.

Chez Jay (1657 Ocean, tel. 310/395–1741). This shack of a saloon near Santa Monica Pier has endured for 30 years and seen the likes of Warren Beatty, Julie Christie, and former California governor Jerry Brown come through its door.

Galley Steak House (2442 Main, tel. 310/452–1934). This tiny restaurant-bar, thick with nautical mementos, is recommended for nostalgics who want to recapture Santa Monica circa 1940. The menu specialises in steamed clams.

The Oar House (2941 Main, tel. 310/396–4725). Something old has been glued or nailed to every square inch of this place, from motorcycles to carriages. Drinks are downright cheap.

Ye Olde King's Head (116 Santa Monica Blvd., tel. 310/451–1402). Reeking of ale, this is a gathering place for Brits eager to hear or dispense news from home.

West Hollywood **Barefoot** (8722 W. 3rd St., tel. 310/276–6223). Rich oak, Art Nouveau mirrors, brass tables, and a plush sofa along the wall make this place as inviting as one of the enormous martinis served here.

Dan Tana's (9071 Santa Monica Blvd., tel. 310/275–9444). Although it's mainly a restaurant, the busy bar is a favorite late-night haunt.

Le Dome (8720 W. Sunset, tel. 310/659–6919). The circular bar here draws the likes of Rod Stewart and Richard Gere. The best time to visit is after 11 PM, when it really starts to jump.

Morton's (8800 Melrose Ave., tel. 310/276–1253). Although it's a small bar, Morton's has a big-name, mostly show business, clientele.

The Royal (7321 Santa Monica Blvd., tel. 213/850–7471). Facing the old Goldwyn Studios, this combination bar-restaurant offers jazz standards to drink to.

Spago (1114 Horn Ave. at Sunset, tel. 310/652–4025). Celebrity watching is a polished art here. The tiny bar tucked away inside this ultrachic bistro is immensely popular; consider yourself fortunate if you can stake out a bar stool.

Westwood/Westside Westwood is the front door to UCLA and a popular hangout for kids of all ages. Both it and the area around it have some outstanding bars.

Acapulco (1109 Glendon, tel. 310/208–3884). Once an Irish pub, this Mexican restaurant/bar still has an air of conviviality. It also stocks a good assortment of Mexican beers.

Alice's (1043 Westwood Blvd., Westwood, tel. 310/208–3171). In the heart of Westwood Village, this restaurant/bar has plenty of tables as well as a long, marble bar. Two television monitors are bound to be tuned to the latest sporting event.

Hamburger Hamlet (11648 San Vicente, tel. 310/826–3558). This is one of the Westside's hottest singles bars, so don't walk in here looking for solitude.

Q's (11835 Wilshire Blvd., West Los Angeles, tel. 310/477–7550). This upscale pool hall and bar serves a Yuppified clientele.

San Francisco Saloon (11501 W. Pico Blvd., tel. 310/478–0152). The ambience is straight from a thrift store, and the place was once renowned for backgammon and chess games going on amid the din. Although you may still see a game or two, this is now a lively neighborhood hangout with friendly bartenders and a relaxed atmosphere.

9 Excursions from Los Angeles

By Aaron Sugarman

Updated by Mary Jane Horton

Even if Los Angeles is the center of your vacation plans, you are probably planning trips out of the city. Disneyland (*see* Chapter 10) is less than an hour's drive away; Santa Barbara (*see* Chapter 12) and Palm Springs (*see* Chapter 11) can be reached in a couple of hours. This chapter explores some excursions a little farther off the beaten track.

Antelope Valley

Antelope Valley, which makes up the western corner of the Mojave Desert, holds several unexpected pleasures. A sudden turn along a desert road reveals a riot of flaming orange poppies on acres of rolling hills nestled between barren rises and desolate flatlands. In the late summer and fall, after the flowers have faded, you can pick your own cherries, peaches, and pears at nearby orchards incongruously set in the desert. Head east and you can hike to the top of Saddleback Butte for a spectacular view of where the desert ends and the San Gabriel Mountains begin, their snow-capped peaks a beautiful contrast to the arid valley.

Another surprise is the valley's wildlife. No, don't look for the hoary antlers of the antelope that lent their name to the area. Once practically overrunning the region, the antelope went into decline with the arrival of the railroad in 1876. They apparently refused to cross the tracks that blocked the route to their traditional grazing grounds and many starved to death.

What you can see in Antelope Valley today are the increasingly rare desert tortoises, California's official state reptiles. Thanks to preservationists, a safe haven has been created for them here, and visiting the tortoise in its natural habitat is a great opportunity for budding photographers—not noted for their speed, the tortoises make willing subjects. If birds are more your fancy, there is also a 40-acre wildlife sanctuary in the valley noted for its winged inhabitants.

Man, of course, has also made his mark in Antelope Valley. You'll find gold mines and historic railroad towns that evoke the spirit of the Old West. Some $40 million in gold and silver was taken out of the hills between Rosemond and Mojave after a Mr. Hamilton hit pay dirt on what is now called Tropico Hill in the 1890s. The Burton Mining Company believes there is still some gold to be found in Tropico and is today excavating the same hill Hamilton made his fortune on.

Arriving and Departing

By Car Heading north from Los Angeles, I 5 will lead you to Highway 14, which runs north through Palmdale, Lancaster, Rosemond, and Mojave. It should take about 90 minutes to reach Palmdale and another hour between Palmdale and Mojave.

Exploring

To reach the **Antelope Valley California Poppy Reserve,** take the Avenue I exit in Lancaster off Highway 14 and head west about 10 miles. You can't miss the reserve—its orange glow with dots of purple lupine and yellow goldfields and fiddleneck can be seen long before you reach the reserve itself. The peak flower time is between March and May. There are four short

Excursions from Los Angeles

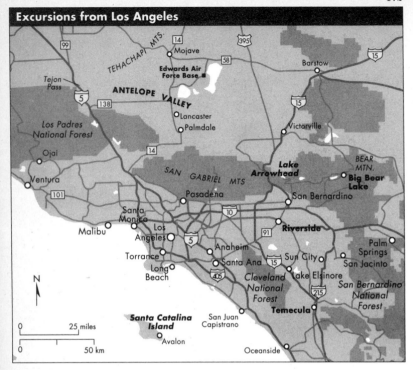

(between a mile and 2 miles) walking trails leading through the fields, some reaching wonderful viewpoints. While there is a perfectly serviceable picnic area by the parking lot, a snack on the bench atop Kitanemuk Vista (an easy five-minute stroll up a well-marked trail) offers much finer scenery. Take a few minutes to walk through the visitor center. The uniquely designed building is burrowed into a hill to keep the building cooler during the summer and warmer during the winter. You can pick up trail maps and other useful information. *Visitor Center open Mar.–May, daily 9–3. State Park day-use fee: $5 per car. For more information and schedules of guided tours, call the California Dept. of Parks and Recreation, tel. 805/942–0662 or 619/724–1180 during flower season for information on where to find best blooms.*

Antelope Valley Indian Museum contains an interesting collection of pottery and baskets made by Acoma, Papago, Pima, Apache, and Hopi tribes. There's a kachina collection, artifacts from coastal cultures. *15701 E. Ave. M, Lancaster, tel. 805/942–0662. Admission $2 adults, $1 children. Open weekends Oct.–June.*

The **Desert Tortoise Natural Area,** northeast of Mojave at California City, is a good place in which to commune with nature. Take Highway 14 about 4 miles past Mojave and then turn east on California City Boulevard through California City; turn left on Randsburg-Mojave Road and follow signs about 5 miles to the preserve.Cars must be left behind as you stroll along the preserve's interpretive nature trails. The best time of the year for viewing the tortoises is generally March through June, when naturalist-guided tours are available. Avoid the midafternoon, however, when it can get quite hot out here. The tortoises sensibly stay cool during the heat of the day by retiring to their shallow burrows. Two warnings about the natural area: The road into the area is wide and flat, but not paved, so your car is bound to get dusty; also, there is no drinking or other water available at the preserve. The preserve is open land, there is no admission charge, and you may feel free to roam about.

Take Avenue J (Rte. N5) east from Lancaster for about 19 miles to get to **Saddleback Butte State Park** (admission: $5 per car), a favorite among hikers and campers. A 2½-mile trail leads to the 3,651-foot summit of the butte the park is named for, which offers some grand views. Throughout the park there is plenty of typical high-desert plant and animal life—stands of Joshua trees, desert tortoises, golden eagles, and many other species of reptiles, mammals, and birds. Near the park headquarters is a picnic area with tables, stoves, and rest rooms.

You will find the area's fruit orchards east of Palmdale along State Highway 138, in the communities of **Littlerock** and **Pearblossom,** and in **Leonia,** southwest of Lancaster along Highway N2. Harvesting starts in June. The Lancaster Chamber of Commerce and Visitors Center (44335 Lowtree, Lancaster 93534, tel. 805/948–4518) has a map showing where to find peaches, apricots, plums, and pears.

Farther south is another popular spot for hikers—**Devils Punchbowl Natural Area Park.** Take Highway 138 southwest from Palmdale; just past Pearblossom turn south on Route N6 (Longview Rd.) and go about 8 miles. At the bottom of an ocean millions of years ago, and currently nestled between the active San Andreas and San Jacinto faults, the park offers a network of well-planned trails. The nearby **Hamilton Preserve** consists of 40 acres of pinyon-juniper woodland sheltering numerous bird species.

Antelope Valley is also home to **Edwards Air Force Base** and the **NASA Ames-Dryden Flight Research Facility** (off State Hwy. 14, northeast of Lancaster). Tours of the facility are available, with a film describing the history of flight test programs, a walk through a hangar, and a look at experimental aircraft. This is where Chuck Yeager and other fighter-jocks with the right stuff chased down the sound barrier in the late 1940s. This is also the place to see the space shuttle land. *Free tours weekdays 10:15 AM and 1:15 PM. Call ahead (tel. 805/258–3446), as the base is occasionally closed for security reasons.*

On Highway 138, you can continue southeast along the San Gabriel Mountains, pick up I–15 south through Cajon Pass, and return to Los Angeles via I–10 heading west.

Dining

Antelope Valley is not known for its fine dining. There are several fast-food and very average roadside restaurants in Lancaster, Palmdale, and Mojave. You might be better off packing a gourmet picnic basket before you leave Los Angeles.

Big Bear/Lake Arrowhead

Local legend has it that in 1845, Don Benito Wilson—General George Patton's grandfather—and his men charged up along the San Bernardino River in pursuit of a troublesome band of Indians. As Wilson entered a clearing, he discovered a meadow teeming with bear. The rest, of course, is history: Wilson later became mayor of Los Angeles, and the area he'd stumbled into was developed into a delightful mountain playground, centered around the man-made lakes of Arrowhead and Big Bear.

Today Angelinos seeking escape from urban life and other vacationers are far more plentiful in these mountain resort areas than bears ever were. Visitors come for downhill and cross-country skiing in the winter, a wide variety of water sports when the weather is warmer, and breathtaking vistas and romantic retreats at rustic cottages and inns year-round.

Along the edge of the San Bernardino Mountains, connecting Lake Arrowhead and Big Bear Lake, is a truly great scenic drive, the aptly named Rim of the World Drive. The alpine equivalent of the Pacific Coast Highway, it reaches elevations of 8,000 feet, offering views of sprawling San Bernardino, the San Gabriel range, and the Mojave Desert to the north.

Arriving and Departing

By Car Take Interstate 10 east from Los Angeles to Highway 330, which connects with Highway 18—the Rim of the World Drive. The trip should take about 90 minutes to Lake Arrowhead, two hours to Big Bear. Highway 38, the back way into Big Bear, is actually a longer route, but it can be faster when the traffic on the more direct route is heavy.

Exploring

Numbers in the margin correspond to points of interest on the Big Bear Lake map.

As you wind your way along Rim of the World Drive, there are several places to park, sip cool water from spring-fed fountains, and enjoy the view. At the village of Crestline, a brief diversion
1 off Highway 18 leads you to **Lake Gregory.** The newest of the high mountain lakes, Lake Gregory was formed by a dam constructed in 1938. Because the water temperature in summer is seldom extremely cold—as it can be in the other lakes at this altitude—this is the best swimming lake in the mountains. Rowboats can be rented at Lake Gregory Village.

2 Continuing east on Highway 18, you will pass the **Baylis Park Picnic Ground,** where you can have a barbecue in a wooded setting. A little farther along, just past the town of Rim Forest,
3 is the **Strawberry Peak** fire lookout tower. Visitors braving the steep stairway to the tower are treated to a magnificent view and a lesson on fire-spotting by the lookout staff.

4 Heading north on Highway 173 will lead you to **Lake Arrowhead Village** and the lake itself. Arrowhead Village draws mixed reviews: For some it is a quaint alpine village with shops

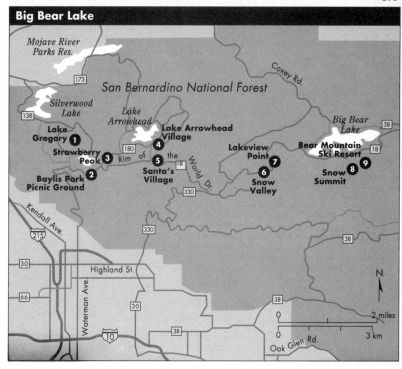

Big Bear Lake

and eateries; others feel it has all the ambience of a rustic-theme shopping mall. The lake, on the other hand, is decidedly a gem, although it can get crowded with speedboats and water-skiers in the summer. The *Arrowhead Queen* provides 45-minute cruises around the lake, leaving from the waterfront marina. Boat rentals are available on nearby public docks. These cruise boats, operated by LeRoy's Sports (tel. 714/336–6992), leave at noon from the south shore for a one-hour cruise. Call the Arrowhead Chamber of Commerce (tel. 714/337–3715) for information on events, camping, and lodging.

5 If you are traveling with children, you may want to consider a stop at nearby **Santa's Village.** The petting zoo, rides, riding stables, and a bakery filled with goodies make this place a fa-vorite of kids. *Located on Hwy. 18, Box 638, Skyforest 92385, tel. 714/337–2484. Admission: $9.50, children under 2 free. Hours change from season to season, so call ahead for information.*

6 Farther along the Rim Drive is **Snow Valley** (tel. 714/867–5151 or 714/867–2751), one of the major ski areas in the San Ber-nardinos, with a dozen lifts and snowmaking capabilities.

7 Beyond Snow Valley, the road climbs to **Lakeview Point,** where a spectacular view of the deep Bear Creek Canyon unfolds, and Big Bear Lake is usually visible in the distance. A 15.5-mile drive will take you completely around the lake. **Big Bear Lake Village** is located on the lake's south shore. The town is a pleas-ant combination of alpine and western mountain style, with the occasional chaletlike building. Equipment for whatever sport you fancy—from fishing to skiing to sailboarding—is available, and there are some surprisingly good restaurants. For general information, contact the Big Bear Tourist and Visitor Bureau (Box 3050G, Big Bear Lake 92315, tel. 714/866–5878).

8 9 **Snow Summit** and **Bear Mountain Ski Resort** are both just to the southeast of the Village. Snow Summit is probably the best of the area's ski resorts and has challenging runs. On busy winter weekends and holidays, your best bet is to reserve your tickets before you head for the mountain. *Snow Summit: general information, tel. 714/866–5766; lift ticket reservations, tel. 714/866–5841; snow report, tel. 310/306–0800, 818/888–2233, or 714/972–0601. Bear Mountain: information and snow report, tel. 714/585–2519.*

Dining

Big Bear **Blue Ox Bar and Grill.** A rustic and casual restaurant, complete with peanut shells on the floor, it serves oversize steaks, ribs, burgers, and chicken, cooked simply but well. *441 W. Big Bear Blvd., Big Bear City, tel. 714/585–7886. AE, MC, V. Moderate ($15–$25).*

George and Sigi's Knusperhauschen. Don't let the campy gingerbread-house look fool you; this restaurant offers wonderful Eastern European fare in a warm, charming atmosphere. The schnitzels and sauerbraten are a delight. *829 W. Big Bear Blvd., Big Bear City, tel. 714/585–8640. Reservations are a good idea. MC, V. Closed Mon.–Wed. Open holidays. Moderate ($15–$25).*

The Iron Squirrel. Hearty French cooking is presented in a country French setting. The veal Normande comes highly recommended, and other traditional dishes like rack of lamb with garlic are nicely prepared. *646 Pineknot Blvd., Big Bear Lake, tel. 714/866–9121. AE, MC, V. Moderate ($15–$25).*

Lake Arrowhead **Cliffhanger.** Go with traditional dishes—moussaka and lamb—and, despite the name, the cliffside locale is part of the charm. *25187 Hwy. 118, Lake Arrowhead, tel. 714/338–3806. MC, V. Moderate ($15–$25).*

Lodging

Big Bear Central Reservations (tel. 714/866–5877) can answer any questions you have and make arrangements for you.

Big Bear **Big Bear Inn.** This is a quasi-mountain chateau in the European tradition. The rooms are furnished with brass beds and antiques. Developer Paul Rizos's family has three luxury hotels on the Greek island of Corfu, and the inn shows its lineage—right down to the giant Greek statues in front of the property. *Box 1814, Big Bear Lake 92315, tel. 714/866–3471 or 800/BEAR–INN. 80 rooms. Facilities: restaurants, lounge, pool, Jacuzzi. AE, MC, V. Very Expensive (over $100).*

Gold Mountain Manor. A restored shingled mansion dating from the Roaring '20s now serves as a historic bed-and-breakfast inn. It earned its fame when Clark Gable and Carole Lombard honeymooned in what is now the Clark Gable Room. The rooms are furnished with quilts and antiques. Rates include breakfast. *Box 2027, Big Bear City 92314, tel. 714/585–6997. 7 rooms. MC, V. No smoking. Expensive–Very Expensive ($75–over $100).*

Knickerbocker Mansion. This is another historic bed-and-breakfast (built of logs), complete with brass kerosene lanterns, breakfast served on the veranda, and afternoon tea. The rooms have a country decor. *Box 3661, Big Bear Lake 92315, tel. 714/866–8221. 6 rooms with bath, 4 more share 2 baths. MC, V. Smoking limited. Expensive–Very Expensive ($75–over $100).*

Robinhood Inn and Lodge. This inn is well located, with reasonably priced rooms (with or without kitchen) and condos near Snow Summit. Each room (some with fireplaces) is individually decorated with modern furniture and bright colors. *Box 3706, Big Bear Lake 92315, tel. 714/866–4643. 20 rooms. Facilities: restaurant, spa. AE, MC, V. Expensive–Very Expensive ($75–over $100).*

Lake Arrowhead **Arrowhead Hilton Lodge.** The design and Old World graciousness of the lodge are reminiscent of the Alps. In addition to the lakeside luxury, guests receive membership privileges at the Village Bay Club and Spa. *Box 1699, Lake Arrowhead 92352, tel. 714/336–1511. 261 rooms. Facilities: restaurant, coffee shop, lounge, beach, pool, whirlpools, health club, tennis (fee). AE, MC, V. Very Expensive (over $100).*

Storybook Inn. The inn offers nine antiques-furnished rooms and suites and one cabin in an elegant estate, with a view over the valley. Breakfast is included, and can be served in your room or in the main dining area. *Box 362, Sky Forest 92385, tel. 714/336–1483. 10 rooms. Facilities: whirlpool. MC, V. Expensive–Very Expensive ($75–over $100).*

Catalina Island

When you approach Catalina Island through the typical early morning ocean fog, it's easy to wonder if perhaps there has been some mistake. What is a Mediterranean island doing 22 miles off the coast of California? Don't worry, you haven't left the Pacific—you've arrived at one of the Los Angeles area's most popular resorts.

Though lacking the sophistication of some European pleasure islands, Catalina does offer virtually unspoiled mountains, canyons, coves, and beaches. It is Southern California without the freeways, a place to relax and play golf or tennis, go boating, hiking, diving, or fishing, or just lie on the beach. The island's only "city" is Avalon, a charming, old-fashioned beach town, in some ways resembling an overgrown marina. Yachts are tied up in neat rows in the crescent-shape bay, palm trees rim the main street, and there are plenty of restaurants and shops.

Of course, life was not always this leisurely on Catalina. Discovered by Juan Rodriguez Cabrillo in 1542, the island has sheltered many dubious characters, from sun-worshiping Indians, Russian fur trappers (seeking sea-otter skins), slave traders, pirates, and gold miners, to bootleggers, filmmakers, and movie stars. In 1919, William Wrigley, Jr., the chewing-gum magnate, purchased controlling interest in the company developing the island. Wrigley had the island's most famous landmark, the Casino, built in 1929, and he made Catalina the site of spring training for his Chicago Cubs baseball team. The Santa Catalina Island Conservancy, a nonprofit foundation, acquired about 86% of the island in 1974 to help preserve Catalina's natural resources.

A wide variety of tours offers samples of those resources, either by boat along the island's coast or by bus or van into Catalina's rugged interior country. Depending on which route you take, you can expect to see roving bands of buffalo, deer, goats, and boar, or unusual species of sea life, including such oddities as electric perch, saltwater goldfish, and flying fish. The buffalo were brought to the island in 1924 for the filming of *The Vanishing American.*

Although Catalina can certainly be seen in a day, there are several inviting romantic hotels that make it worth extending your stay for one or more nights. Between Memorial Day and Labor Day, be sure to make reservations *before* heading out to the island. After Labor Day, rooms are much easier to find on shorter notice, and rates drop dramatically.

Arriving and Departing

By Boat Boats to Catalina run from San Pedro and Long Beach. **Catalina Express** (tel. 310/519–1212) makes the hour-long run from Long Beach or San Pedro to Avalon; round-trip fare from Long Beach is $35.50 for adults, $26.50 for children 2–11; from San Pedro, $34.50 for adults and $25.50 for children. **Catalina Cruises** (tel. 800/888–5939), also leaving from Long Beach, is a bit slower, taking two hours, but cheaper, charging $28.50 for adults, $24.50 for seniors, $18.50 for children 2–11, $2 for children under 2. Service is also available from Newport Beach through **Catalina Passenger Service** (tel. 714/673–5245), which leaves from Balboa Pavilion at 9 AM, takes 75 minutes to reach the island, and costs $32.50 round-trip for adults, $16.50 for children 12 and under. The return boat leaves Catalina at 4:30 PM. Advance reservations for all lines are advised.

By Plane **Island Express** (tel. 310/491–5550) flies from San Pedro and Long Beach. The trip takes about 15 minutes and costs $60 one-way, $100 round-trip.

Guided Tours

The major tour operators on the island are the **Santa Catalina Island Co.** (tel. 310/510–2000 or 800/428–2566). Tours include: coastal cruise to Seal Rocks (summer only), the Flying Fish boat trip (evenings, summer only), inland motor tour, Skyline Drive, casino tour, Avalon scenic tour, and the glass-bottom boat tour. Advance reservations are highly recommended for the inland tours; the others are offered several times daily. Costs range from $6.75 to $23 (adults); discounts are available for children under 12 years and senior citizens over 55. Catalina Adventure Tours also offers parasailing, fishing, and diving.

The Catalina Conservancy (tel. 310/510–1421) offers walks led by knowledgeable docents.

Exploring

Catalina Island is one of the few places in the L.A. environs where walking is considered quite acceptable; it is, in fact, virtually unavoidable. You cannot bring a car onto the island or rent one once you get there. If you are determined to have a set of wheels, rent a bicycle or golf cart along Crescent Avenue as you walk in from the docks. To hike into the interior of the island you will need a permit, available free from the L.A. County Department of Parks and Recreation (Island Plaza, Avalon, tel. 310/510–0688).

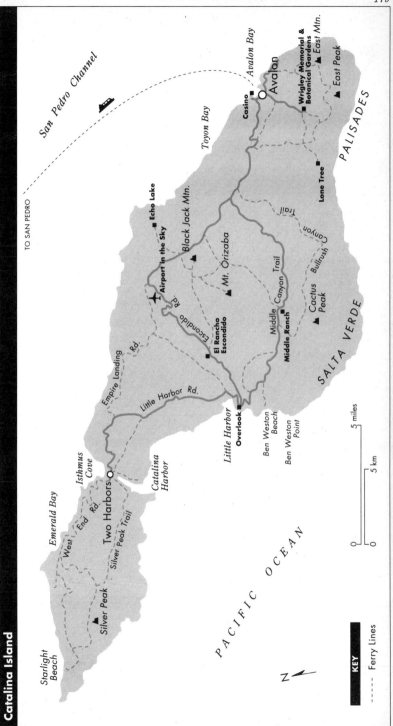

Catalina Island

TO SAN PEDRO

San Pedro Channel

Avalon Bay

Avalon

Casino

Toyon Bay

Wrigley Memorial & Botanical Gardens

East Mtn.

East Peak

PALISADES

Lone Tree

Echo Lake

Airport in the Sky

Black Jack Mtn.

Mt. Orizaba

Bullrush Canyon Trail

Middle Canyon Trail

Cactus Peak

SALTA VERDE

Escondido Rd.

El Rancho Escondido

Middle Ranch

Empire Landing Rd.

Little Harbor Rd.

Little Harbor Overlook

Ben Weston Beach

Ben Weston Point

Isthmus Cove

Emerald Bay

West End Rd.

Two Harbors

Silver Peak Trail

Catalina Harbor

Silver Peak

Starlight Beach

PACIFIC OCEAN

N

0   5 miles

0   5 km

KEY

- - - - - Ferry Lines

The **Chamber of Commerce Visitors Bureau** is a good place to get your bearings, check into special events, and plan your itinerary. The Visitors Center (tel. 310/510–1520) is located on the corner of Crescent Avenue and Catalina Avenue, across from the Green Pier; the Chamber's Visitors Bureau is on the pier.

Housed on the northwest point of Crescent Bay is the **Casino.** The round structure is an odd mixture of Spanish, Moorish, and Art Deco modern style, with Art Deco murals on the porch as you enter. "Casino" is the Italian word for "gathering place," and has nothing to do with gambling. At least not here. Inside the Casino are an art gallery, museum, movie theater (tel. 310/510–0179), and ballroom. Guided tours are available.

The Wrigley Memorial and Botanical Garden is 2 miles south of Avalon via Avalon Canyon Road. The Wrigley family commissioned this monument, replete with grand staircase and Spanish mausoleum with Art Deco touches. Despite the fact that the mausoleum was never used by the Wrigleys, who are instead buried in Los Angeles, the structure is worth a look, and the view from the mausoleum is all the more so. The garden is small but exceptionally well planted. Tram service between the memorial and Avalon is available daily between 8 AM and 5 PM. There is a nominal entry fee of $1.

If modern architecture interests you, be sure to stop by the **Wolfe House** (124 Chimes Rd.). Built in Avalon in 1928 by noted architect Rudolph Schindler, its terraced frame is carefully set into a steep site, affording extraordinary views. The house is a private residence, rarely open for public tours, but you can get a good view of it from the path below it and from the street.

El Rancho Escondido is a ranch in Catalina's interior, home to some of the country's finest Arabian horses. The ranch can be visited on the Inland motor tour *(see* Guided Tours, *above).*

Dining

American **The Sand Trap.** Omelets are the specialty at this local favorite located on the way to Wrigley Botanical Garden. *Falls Canyon, tel. 310/510–1349. Closed for dinner. No credit cards. Inexpensive (under $15).*

Italian **Cafe Prego.** This restaurant features an intimate setting on the waterfront, several good pasta dishes, and a hearty minestrone. *603 Crescent Ave., tel. 310/510–1218. AE, D, DC, MC, V. Closed for lunch. Moderate–Expensive ($15–$35).*
Antonio's Pizzeria. You'll find spirited atmosphere, decent pizza, and appropriately messy Italian sandwiches. *2 locations: 230 Crescent Ave., tel. 310/510–0008, and 114 Sumner Ave., tel. 310/510–0060. MC, V. Inexpensive–Moderate (under $15–$25).*

Seafood **Pirrone's.** This restaurant has a bird's-eye view of the bay and serves fresh seafood. *417 Crescent Ave., tel. 310/510–0333. MC, V. Closed for lunch, and Sun. dinner in winter. Moderate–Expensive ($15–$35).*

Lodging

Glenmore Plaza Hotel. This striking Victorian hotel dating from 1891 has hosted the likes of Clark Gable, Teddy Roosevelt, and Amelia Earhart. Located near the beach, the hotel offers complimentary breakfast and suites with whirlpool or Jacuzzi.

120 Sumner Ave., Avalon 90704, tel. 310/510–0017. 45 rooms. AE, D, DC, MC, V. Very Expensive (over $100).

Inn on Mt. Ada. The former Wrigley Mansion is now the island's most exclusive hotel. The views are spectacular, and the grounds superbly planted. All meals and the use of a golf cart are complimentary. *Box 2560, Avalon 90704, tel. 310/510–2030. 6 rooms. MC, V. Very Expensive (over $100).*

Hotel Catalina. A renovated Victorian, half a block from the beach, the Catalina offers a choice of rooms and cottages. Extra touches include an attractive sun deck with Jacuzzi and free movies every afternoon. *129 Whittley Ave., Avalon 90704, tel. 310/510–0027. 32 rooms, 4 cottages. AE, D, MC, V. Expensive–Very Expensive ($75–over $100).*

Zane Grey Pueblo Hotel. The former home of the famous American novelist, this hotel offers a stunning harbor view from its hilltop perch. Built in 1926 in Hopi Indian pueblo style, the Zane Grey offers such amenities as eccentric decor, a swimming pool, and a courtesy bus. No phones or TVs in rooms. *199 Chimes Tower Rd., Avalon 90704, tel. 310/510–0966. 18 rooms. AE, MC, V. Expensive–Very Expensive ($75–over $100).*

Riverside

Where Los Angeles tends to focus on the newest and latest—it's a city where '50s furniture is considered antique—Riverside wears its history on its sleeve. A delightful array of historic buildings rise up on almost every street corner in downtown Riverside. The range of styles is striking and eclectic, from Mission Revival and Beaux Arts to Renaissance Revival and Victorian. The centerpiece is the 100-year-old Mission Inn, a national historic landmark that's decidedly romantic, sprouting turrets, towers, and balconies above the arched courtyard area's fountains, and sculptures.

Riverside is a good place for a leisurely morning or afternoon stroll. There are several museums, a pleasant pedestrian mall lined with ornamental citrus trees, intriguing small shops, and even an opportunity to see the tree that launched the billion-dollar citrus industry in the western United States.

Arriving and Departing

By Car Take I–10 east out of Los Angeles to I–15E heading south. The trip should take about 90 minutes.

By Bus **Greyhound-Trailways** (tel. 213/620–1200) offers over a dozen daily departures to Riverside. The ride costs $8.50 one-way, $16.50 round-trip, and takes about 1½ hours. The station within walking distance from all downtown attractions.

Exploring

To get the proper historical perspective, make a quick stop at the **Parent Tree** (intersection of Market St. and Arlington Ave.). Planted in 1875 and still bearing fruit, this navel orange tree is the sole survivor of two trees brought to Riverside from Brazil. Cuttings from this tree have grown into today's citrus groves. Much of the money behind Riverside's architectural wealth did in fact grow on trees, so don't be surprised when you discover downtown streets named Orange, Lemon, and Lime.

Across the street from the famous Mission Inn (which has still not reopened after extensive renovations), is the **Municipal Museum.** A Renaissance Revival building constructed in 1912, the museum contains exhibits on early days of the citrus industry, local history, Native American culture, and natural history. *3720 Orange St., tel. 909/782–5273. Donations accepted. Closed Mon.*

Continuing down Seventh Street, you'll pass the **First Congregational Church,** a good example of the Mission Revival style, built in 1914, and clearly inspired by the California missions' spare, earthy look. Note the differences between it and the **Municipal Auditorium** across the street. Built in 1929 in Hispanic Revival style, the auditorium has distinctive blue, yellow, and white tile domes and is topped by an all-American eagle.

At Seventh and Lime streets is the **Riverside Art Museum,** designed in 1929 by Julia Morgan, the chief architect of Hearst Castle. Several galleries display the work of Southern California artists. *3425 7th St., tel. 909/684–7111. Admission: $1.*

Time Out | **A Moveable Feast** (tel. 909/369–9478), open weekdays, in the courtyard of the art museum, is a charming eatery in a delightful location. There are only a dozen small tables, and the moderately priced menu of soups, sandwiches, and homemade desserts changes regularly.

Riverside's other main strip is **Main Street,** a pedestrian mall running from 5th Street to 11th Street, where there are several shops and cafés to look into. The **California Museum of Photography** (3824 Main St., tel. 909/787–4787, admission $2, open Wed.–Sat. 11–5, Sun. noon–5) is located in the historic Kress Variety Store building. When you reach the **Riverside County Courthouse,** built in 1903, be prepared for a bit of a shock. Not even remotely like any typical California architectural style, this Beaux Arts beauty was modeled after the Grand Palace of Fine Arts in Paris.

A short drive south of downtown Riverside is the **Heritage House,** a Victorian building dating from 1891. The house, built for the family of a successful citrus grower, features period furniture, gas lamps, and tile fireplaces in every room. *8193 Magnolia Ave., between Adams and Jefferson, tel. 909/689–1333. Open Tues. and Thur. noon–2:30, Sun. noon–3:30.*

Castle Park is a family-oriented amusement park spread over 27 pleasantly landscaped acres. A state-of-the-art video arcade, miniature golf course, and collection of rides—including a restored carousel dating from 1909—are sure to keep the kids entertained. *3500 Polk St., tel. 909/785–4140. Admission: $4.75 adults, $3.75 children 11 and under for golf; 50¢ per ride in the ride park (discount books available). Golf and arcade open Sun.–Thur. 10–10, Fri.–Sat. 10–midnight; ride park open Fri. 6–11, Sat. noon–11, Sun. noon–8.*

The **Riverside Botanic Gardens,** on the campus of the University of California, covers 37 acres of hilly terrain. Spring, when many of the 2,000 plant species bloom, is the best time to visit. *Univ. of California–Riverside, tel. 909/787–4650. Admission free. Open daily 8–5.*

Temecula

Temecula, Southern California's only developed wine region, is a popular day or overnight excursion from Los Angeles, Orange County, or San Diego. More than 10 premium wineries can be found along Rancho California Road, as it snakes through the hills.

Arriving and Departing

By Car From Los Angeles or Orange County take Hwy. 91 or Hwy. 60 east to the intersection with I–15 or I–15E; then go south to Rancho California Road. From San Diego take I–15 north to Rancho California Road. The wineries are located east of I–15.

Exploring

The wineries are strung out along Rancho California Road in an agricultural preserve east of the town of Temecula. **Culbertson** (32575 Rancho California Rd., tel. 909/699–0099) produces several varieties of sparkling wine, offers tours and tastings, and also features the outstanding Champagne Restaurant. **Callaway Vineyard & Winery** (32720 Rancho California Rd., tel. 909/676–4001) has a staffed visitor center for tastings, a gift shop, and picnic area, and offers special themed dinners and luncheons. **Maurice Car'rie Vineyard & Winery** (34225 Rancho California Rd., tel. 909/676–1711) has a tasting room, gift shop, and picnic area, and is often the site of barn dances, and art, flower, and car shows.

Old Town Temecula was once a hangout for local cowboys, and still looks the part. It now has a number of antiques shops specializing in local and Old West memorabilia.

Lodging

Temecula Creek Inn. Minutes away from wine country proper, this upscale resort offers wine-country packages. *44501 Rainbow Canyon Rd., Temecula, tel. 909/676–5631. 80 rooms. Facilities: 27-hole golf course, tennis courts, restaurant, pool, whirlpool. AE, D, DC, MC, V. Very Expensive (over $100).*
Loma Vista Bed and Breakfast. A brand new Mission-style bed-and-breakfast, this is currently the only overnight accommodation right in the Temecula wine country. It has tranquil vineyard views and its own gardens. *3350 La Serena Way, Temecula, tel. 909/676–7047. 6 rooms. D, MC, V. Expensive–Very Expensive ($75–over $100)*

10 Orange County

Orange County is one of the top tourist destinations in California, and once you've arrived here it doesn't take long to see why. The county has made tourism its number one industry, attracting nearly 40 million visitors annually. Two theme parks, Disneyland and Knott's Berry Farm, attract millions. Orange County is the home of the California Angels baseball team and Los Angeles Rams football team. The enormous Anaheim Convention Center hosts an average of one meeting per day. Accommodations for visitors are plentiful and generally high quality.

People actually live in Orange County, too, many of them in high-priced pink, Mediterranean-style suburbs that are strung along the 24-mile-long coastline. Orange County residents actually shop in the classy malls that lure visitors as well. Like visitors, locals can be found at the beach sunning themselves or waiting for the big wave. Locals even dine and stay at the luxurious oceanfront resorts that perch on the edge of the Pacific.

Indeed, Orange County people believe that they've discovered the perfect place to live. They're anxious to share the pleasures of life in the Big Orange with visitors.

Served by convenient airports and only an hour's drive from Los Angeles, Orange County is both a destination on its own and a very popular excursion from Los Angeles.

Essential Information

Important Addresses and Numbers

Tourist Information   The main source of tourist information is the **Anaheim Area Convention and Visitors Bureau,** located at the Anaheim Convention Center (800 W. Katella Ave., 92802, tel. 714/999–8999). The **Visitor Information Hot Line** (tel. 714/635–8900) offers recorded information on entertainment, special events, attractions, and amusement parks; information about special events may be outdated.

Other area chambers of commerce and visitors bureaus are generally open weekdays 9–5 and will help with information. These include:

Buena Park Visitors Bureau, 6280 Manchester Blvd., 90261, tel. 714/994–1511.
Dana Point Chamber of Commerce, Box 12, 92629, tel. 714/496–1555.
Huntington Beach Conference and Visitors Bureau, 2100 Main St., Suite 190, 92648, tel. 800/729–62326.
Laguna Beach Chamber of Commerce, 357 Glenneyre, 92651, tel. 714/494–1018.
Newport Beach Conference and Visitors Bureau, 366 San Miguel Dr., Suite 200, 92660, tel. 800/942–6278.
San Clemente Tourism Bureau, 1100 N. El Camino Real, 92672, tel. 714/492–1131.
San Juan Capistrano Chamber of Commerce and Visitors Center, 31682 El Camino Real, 92675, tel. 714/493–4700.

Emergencies   Dial 911 for police and ambulance in an emergency.

Doctors Orange County is so spread out and comprises so many different communities that it is best to ask at your hotel for the closest emergency room. Here are a few: **Anaheim Memorial Hospital** (1111 W. La Palma, tel. 714/774–1450), **Western Medical Center** (1025 S. Anaheim Blvd., Anaheim, tel. 714/533–6220), **Hoag Memorial Hospital** (301 Newport Blvd., Newport Beach, tel. 714/645–8600), **South Coast Medical Center** (31872 Coast Hwy., South Laguna, tel. 714/499–1311).

Arriving and Departing

By Plane Several airports are accessible to Orange County. **John Wayne Orange County Airport** (tel. 714/252–5252), in Santa Ana, is centrally located, and the county's main facility. It is serviced by **Alaska Airlines** (tel. 800/426–0333), **America West Airlines** (tel. 800/247–5692), **American/American Eagle** (tel. 800/433–7300), **Continental** (tel. 800/525–0280), **Delta** (tel. 800/221–1212), **Morris** (tel. 800/444–5660), **Northwest** (tel. 800/225–2525), **TWA** (tel. 800/221–2000), **United/United Express** (tel. 800/251–6522), and **USAir** (tel. 800/428–4322).

Los Angeles International Airport is only 35 miles west of Anaheim; **Ontario Airport,** just northwest of Riverside, is 30 miles north of Anaheim; and **Long Beach Airport** is about 20 minutes by bus from Anaheim. (*See* Chapter 1 for details on all three airports.)

Between the **Airport Coach** (tel. 800/772–5299), a shuttle service, carries
Airports and Hotels passengers from LAX to Anaheim, Buena Park, and Pasadena. Fare from the airport to Anaheim is $8.

Prime Time Airport Shuttle (tel. 800/262–7433) offers door-to-door service to LAX and John Wayne airports, hotels near John Wayne, and the San Pedro cruise terminal. The fare is $12 from Anaheim hotels to LAX. Children under 2 ride free.

SuperShuttle (tel. 714/973–1100 or 800/554–6458) provides 24-hour door-to-door service from all the airports to all points in Orange County. Fare to the Disneyland area is $10 a person from John Wayne, $36 from Ontario, $13 from LAX. Phone for other fares and reservations.

By Car Two major freeways, I–405 (San Diego Freeway) and I–5 (Santa Ana Freeway), run north and south through Orange County. South of Laguna they merge into I–5. Avoid these during rush hours (6–9 AM and 3:30–6 PM), when they can slow to a crawl and back up for miles.

By Train **Amtrak** (tel. 800/872–7245) makes several stops in Orange County: Fullerton, Anaheim, Santa Ana, San Juan Capistrano, and San Clemente. There are 11 departures daily, nine on weekends.

By Bus The **Los Angeles RTD** has limited service to Orange County. You can get the No. 460 to Anaheim; it goes to Knott's Berry Farm and Disneyland. **Greyhound/Trailways** (tel. 714/635–5060) has scheduled bus service to Orange County.

Getting Around

By Car Highways 22, 55, and 91 go west to the ocean and east to the mountains: Take Highway 91 or Highway 22 to inland points (Buena Park, Anaheim) and take Highway 55 to Newport

Beach. Caution: Orange County freeways are undergoing major construction; expect delays at unexpected times.

Pacific Coast Highway (Highway 1) allows easy access to beach communities, and is the most scenic route. It follows the entire Orange County coast, from Huntington Beach to San Clemente.

By Bus The **Orange County Transit District** (tel. 714/636–7433) will take you virtually anywhere in the county, but it will take time; OCTD buses go from Knott's Berry Farm and Disneyland to Huntington and Newport beaches. The No. 1 bus travels along the coast.

Scenic Drives Winding along the seaside edge of Orange County on the **Pacific Coast Highway** is an eye-opening experience. Here, surely, are the contradictions of Southern California revealed—the powerful, healing ocean vistas and the scars of commercial exploitation; the appealingly laid-back, simple beach life and the tacky bric-a-brac of the tourist trail. Oil rigs line the road from Long Beach south to Huntington Beach, and then suddenly give way to pristine stretches of water and dramatic hillsides. Prototypical beach towns like Laguna Beach, Dana Point, and Corona del Mar serve as casual stopping points along the route.

For a scenic mountain drive, try **Santiago Canyon Road,** which winds through the Cleveland National Forest in the Santa Ana Mountains. Tucked away in these mountains are Modjeska Canyon, Irvine Lake, and Silverado Canyon, of silver mining lore.

Guided Tours

General-Interest Tours **Pacific Coast Sightseeing Tours** (tel. 714/978–8855) provides guided tours from Orange County hotels to Disneyland, Knott's Berry Farm, Universal, and the San Diego Zoo.

Boat Tours At the Cannery in **Newport Beach,** you can take a weekend brunch cruise around the harbor. Cruises last two hours and depart at 10 AM and 1:30 PM. Champagne brunches cost $30 per person. For more information call 714/675–5777.

Catalina Passenger Service (tel. 714/673–5245) at the Balboa Pavilion offers a full selection of sightseeing tours and fishing excursions to Catalina and around Newport Harbor. The 45-minute narrated tour of Newport Harbor, at $6, is the least expensive. Whale-watching cruises (Dec.–Mar.) are especially enjoyable.

Hornblower Yachts (tel. 714/631–2467) offers a number of special sightseeing brunch cruises. Whale-watching brunches (Jan.–Apr.) are scheduled each Saturday and Sunday.

Walking Tours For a respite from suburban sprawl and urban smog, the **Tucker Wildlife Preserve** (tel. 714/649–2760) in Modjeska Canyon, 17 miles southeast of the city of Orange via Chapman Avenue, is worth the effort. The preserve is a haven for more than 140 bird species, including seven varieties of hummingbird, and a variety of mammals and reptiles.

Free walking tours of **Mission San Juan Capistrano** are offered every Sunday at 1, whether the swallows are in town or not. The tours take in the ruins of the Great Stone Church, de stroyed by an earthquake in 1812, the Serra Chapel, the Mission's courtyards and fountains, and other historical sights.

Exploring Orange County

In planning your trip to Orange County, first select a basic destination, based on the main purpose of your trip. If Disneyland is the highlight, you'll probably want to organize your activities around the tourist attractions that fill the central county and take excursions to selected coastal spots. The reverse is true, of course, if you're planning to hang out on the beach. In that case, select a coastal headquarters and make forays to the Magic Kingdom.

If you're traveling with children, you could easily devote several full days to the theme parks: a day or two for Disneyland, a day for Knott's Berry Farm, and perhaps a day driving between some of the area's lesser-known attractions. To rent a sailboard or other water-sports paraphernalia, you'll have to head to the beach towns. Beach days can be a mix of sunning, studying surf culture, and browsing the small shops native to the beach communities.

Highlights for First-Time Visitors

Balboa Pavilion, Balboa Peninsula
Bolca Chica Ecological Reserve
Disneyland, Anaheim
Huntington Beach
Knott's Berry Farm, Buena Park
Mission San Juan Capistrano
Newport Harbor
South Coast Plaza, Costa Mesa

Inland Orange County

Numbers in the margin correspond to points of interest on the Orange County map.

With Disneyland as its centerpiece, Anaheim is indisputably the West's capital of family entertainment. Now at the center of a vast tourism complex that also includes the Anaheim Convention Center, Anaheim Stadium, and the Pond in Anaheim, Disneyland still dominates the city. The Anaheim Convention Center lures almost as many conventioneers as Disneyland attracts children, and for many visitors, a trip to the Magic Kingdom may be a bonus extra of an Anaheim meeting.

❶ Perhaps more than any other place in the world, **Disneyland,** the first Disney theme park, and the enduring physical evidence of Walt Disney's dream, is a symbol of the eternal child in all of us, a place of wonder and enchantment—also an exceptionally clean and imaginatively developed wonder.

When Disney carved the park out of the orange groves in 1955, it consisted of four lands and fewer than 20 major attractions radiating from his idealized American Main Street. Much has changed in the intervening years, including the massive expansion of the park to include four more lands and some 40 more attractions. But Main Street retains its turn-of-the-century charm, and in ever sharper contrast with the world just outside the gates of the park. Disney's vision of the Magic Kingdom was one of a never-ending fantasy. Thus designers and engineers continue to come up with new ways to tantalize and treat guests.

Disneyland is big, and, during the busy summer season, crowded. Planning a strategy for your visit, as the locals do, will help you get the most out of it. If you can, pick a rainy midweek day; surprisingly most Disney attractions are indoors. Arrive early; the box office opens a half hour before the park's scheduled opening time. Go immediately to the most popular attractions: Space Mountain, Star Tours, Pirates of the Caribbean, Haunted Mansion, It's a Small World, and Splash Mountain. Mickey's Toontown tends to be most crowded in the mornings. Lines for rides will also be shorter during the evening Fantasmic! show, parades, and the evening fireworks display (usually around 9:30), as well as near opening or closing times. Just the same, even on a slow day expect to wait in line for 15 minutes or so. As with the rides, strategize your eating as well. Restaurants are less crowded toward the beginning and end of meal periods. Also, fast-food spots abound, and you can now get healthy fare such as fruit, pasta, and frozen yogurt at various locations throughout the park. Whatever you wind up eating, food prices are higher than on the outside. When shopping, remember that there are lockers just off Main Street in which you can store purchases, and thereby avoid lugging bundles around all day or shopping just before the park's closing time when stores are crowded. If your feet get tired, you can move from one area of the park to another on the train or monorail, or even in a horse-drawn carriage.

Each of Disney's lands has its own themed rides. Stepping through the doors of Sleeping Beauty's castle into **Fantasyland** can be a dream come true for children. Mickey Mouse may even be there to greet them. Once inside they can join Peter Pan on his magic flight; take a Wild Ride with Mr. Toad; follow Alice and the White Rabbit down the hole; spin around in giant cups at the Mad Tea Party; swoosh through the Matterhorn; or visit It's a Small World where figures of children from 100 countries worldwide sing of unity and peace.

In **Frontierland** you can take a cruise on the steamboat Mark Twain or sailing ship Columbia and experience the sight and sound of spectacular Rivers of America. Kids of every age enjoy rafting to Tom Sawyer's Island for an hour or so of tracking and exploring.

Some visitors to **Adventureland** have taken the Jungle Cruise so many times that they know the patter offered up by the operators by heart. Other attractions here include shops with African and South Seas wares.

Time Out | **Blue Bayou,** featuring Creole food, is a great place to eat. It is located in the entrance to the Pirates of the Caribbean, so you can hear the antics in the background.

The twisting streets of **New Orleans Square** offer interesting browsing and shopping, strolling Dixieland musicians, and the ever-popular Pirates of the Caribbean ride. The **Haunted Man-**

Orange County

PACIFIC OCEAN

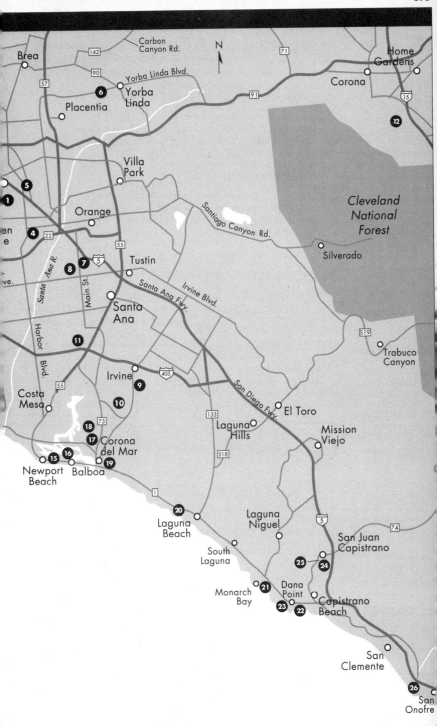

sion, populated by 999 holographic ghosts, is nearby. Theme shops purvey hats, perfume, Mardi Gras merchandise, gourmet items. The **Disney Gallery** here has now-trendy (and expensive) original Disney art.

The animated bears in **Critter Country** may charm kids of all ages, but it's **Splash Mountain,** the steepest, wettest Disney adventure, that keeps them coming back for more.

Disney's vision of the future in **Tomorrowland** has undergone the most changes over the years, reflecting advances in technology. You can still take a Submarine Voyage or ride the Monorail, but you can also be hurled into outer space on **Space Mountain,** take **Star Tours,** or watch Michael Jackson perform in the 3-D movie *Captain EO.*

Mickey's Toontown, a new "land" opened in 1993, is a child-sized interactive community where Mickey and other cartoon characters actually "live." The tykes can talk to manholes, sample Minnie's perfume, and bounce off the walls at Goofy's house.

A stroll along **Main Street** reveals a bit of treasured nostalgia, that of a small-town America, circa 1900, that never existed except in the popular imagination and fiction and films. Interconnected shops and restaurants line both sides of the street. **The Emporium** is the largest and most comprehensive of the shops offering a full line of Disney products. But you'll also find magic tricks, crystal, hobby and sports memorabilia, clothing, and photo supplies here. *1313 Harbor Blvd., Anaheim, tel. 714/999–4565. Admission: $28.75 adults, $23 children 3–11; allows entrance to all rides and attractions. Guided tours available. Open summer, Sun.–Fri. 9 AM–midnight, Sat. 9 AM–1 AM; fall, winter, and spring, weekdays 10–6, weekends 9–midnight. Hours and prices subject to change.*

If Disneyland specializes in a high-tech brand of fantasy, ❷ **Knott's Berry Farm,** located nearby in Buena Park, offers a dose of reality. The farm has been rooted in the community since 1934, when Cordelia Knott began serving chicken dinners on her wedding china to supplement the family's meager income. The dinners and the boysenberry pies proved more profitable than husband Walt's berry farm, so the family moved first into the restaurant business, and then into the entertainment business. The park with its Old West theme is now a 150-acre complex with 100-plus rides and attractions, 60 eating places, and 60 shops, including several that have been here for decades.

There are attractions both inside and outside the gates of the park. Mrs. Knott's Chicken Dinner Restaurant is the centerpiece of **Knott's California MarketPlace,** a collection of 32 shops and restaurants outside the gates. The rides, shows, and attractions are, of course, located inside the gates.

Like Disneyland, the park has themed areas. **Ghost Town** offers a delightful human-scale visit to the Old West. Many of the buildings were relocated here from their original mining-town sites. You can stroll down the street, stop and chat with the blacksmith, pan for gold, crack open a geode, ride in an authentic 1880s passenger train, or take the Gold Mine ride and descend into a replica of a working gold mine. A real treasure here is the antique **Dentzel carousel** with a menagerie of animals. **Camp Snoopy** is a kid-sized High Sierra wonderland where Snoopy and his Peanuts-gang friends hang out. Tall trees frame **Wild Water Wilderness,** where you can really ride white water in an inner tube in Big Foot Rapids. Themes aside, thrill rides are placed throughout the park. Teenagers, especially, love the rides found in **Roaring '20s:** the Boomerang roller coaster, X-K-1, a living version of a video game, and Kingdom of the Dinosaurs. More thrill rides including Montezooma's Revenge, a roller coaster that goes from 0 to 55 mph in less than 5 seconds, can be found in **Fiesta Village.** Throughout the park, costumed interpreters offer insight into the natural and human history of the attraction; visitors are encouraged to ask questions.

Time Out | Don't forget what made Knott's famous: Mrs. Knott's fried chicken dinners and boysenberry pies at **Mrs. Knott's Chicken Dinner Restaurant,** just outside the park in Knott's California MarketPlace.

Knott's also offers entertainment throughout the day with shows scheduled in Ghost Town, the Bird Cage Theater, and the Good Time Theater; occasionally stars appear here. *8039 Beach Blvd., Buena Park, tel. 714/220–5200. Admission: $25.95 adults, $15.95 children 3–11, $17.95 senior citizens. Open summer, Sun.–Fri. 9 AM–11 PM, Sat. 9 AM–midnight; winter, weekdays 10–6, Sat. 10–10, Sun. 10–7. Park closes during inclement weather. Times and prices subject to change.*

Visitors will find 70 years of movie magic immortalized at
❸ **Movieland Wax Museum** in 250 wax sculptures of Hollywood's greatest stars including Michael Jackson, Dudley Moore, John Wayne, Marilyn Monroe, and George Burns. Figures are displayed in a maze of realistic sets from movies such as *Gone with the Wind, Star Trek, The Wizard of Oz,* and *Home Alone.* The Chamber of Horrors is designed to scare the daylights out of you. *7711 Beach Blvd., 1 block north of Knott's, tel. 714/522–1155. Admission: $12.95 adults, $6.95 children; combination tickets including Ripley's Believe It or Not across street are available. Open summer, daily 9–8; winter, daily 10–7.*

❹ The **Anaheim Museum,** housed in a 1908 Carnegie Library building, illustrates the history of Anaheim including the original wine-producing colony. Changing exhibits include art collections, women's history, and hobbies. *241 S. Anaheim Blvd., tel. 714/778–3301. Suggested admission: $1.50; children free. Open Wed.–Fri. 10–4, Sat. noon–4.*

About 7 miles north of Anaheim, off Highway 57 (Yorba Linda
❺ Blvd. exit), the **Richard Nixon Library and Birthplace** is more museum than library. Displays illustrate the checkered career of the 37th president, the only one to resign from office. Interactive exhibits give visitors a chance to interview Nixon, press-conference style, and get pre-recorded replies on 300 topics. One room contains impressive life-size sculptures of world leaders and an array of gifts received from international heads of state. Visitors can listen to Nixon's Checkers speech or to the so-called smoking gun tape from the Watergate days, among other recorded material. In contrast to the high-tech exhibits across the lawn and palm tree-lined reflecting pond is the small farmhouse where Nixon was born in 1913. The restored structure contains the original furnishings, including a

cast iron stove, piano, Bible, and family photos. Within the main building is a small but interesting gift shop, containing presidential souvenir items. *18001 Yorba Linda Blvd., Yorba Linda, tel. 714/993–3393. Admission: $4.95 adults, $2.95 62 and over, children 11 and under free. Open Mon.–Sat. 10–5, Sun. 11–5.*

Garden Grove, a community just south of Anaheim and Buena Park, is the home of one of the most impressive churches in the ❻ country, the **Crystal Cathedral.** The domain of television evangelist Robert Schuller, this sparkling glass structure resembles a four-pointed star with more than 10,000 panes of glass covering a weblike steel truss to form translucent walls. The feeling as you enter is nothing less than mystical. In addition to tours of the cathedral, two pageants are offered yearly— "The Glory of Christmas" and "The Glory of Easter"–featuring live animals, flying angels, and other special effects. *12141 Lewis St., Garden Grove, tel. 714/971–4013. $2 donation. Guided tours Mon.–Sat. 9–3:30. Call for schedule. For reservations for Easter and Christmas productions, call 714/544–5679.*

❼ The **Bowers Museum of Cultural Art,** once a quaint cultural-arts gallery, is now the largest museum in Orange County, having tripled in size after a recent $12 million expansion and restoration of its original 1936 Spanish-style buildings. The museum houses a first-rate 85,000-piece collection of artworks by indigenous peoples from around the world. Permanent galleries illustrate sculpture, costumes, and artifacts from Oceania; sculpture from West and Central Africa; Pacific Northwest wood carvings; dazzling beadwork of the Plains cultures; and California basketry. The museum's trendy Topaz Cafe offers an ethnically eclectic menu. *2002 N. Main St., Santa Ana, tel. 714/567–3600. Admission: $4.50 adults, $3 students and senior citizens, $1.50 children. Open Tues.–Sun. 10–5, Thur. 10–9.*

Santa Ana, the county seat, is undergoing a dramatic restoration in its downtown area. Gleaming new government buildings meld with turn-of-the-century structures to give a sense of ❽ where the county came from and where it is going. The **Fiesta Marketplace** is a new downtown development, notable as a grass-roots effort involving businessmen and government. The Spanish-style, four-block project brings life to one of the traditionally most successful Hispanic marketplaces in Southern California.

To glimpse the pristine California landscape as it was before development brought houses and freeways to hillsides, visit the ❾ newly opened **Irvine Museum.** Located on the 12th floor of a circular marble-and-glass office building, the museum displays a collection of California impressionist landscape paintings dated 1890 to 1930. The collection was assembled by Joan Irvine Smith, granddaughter of James Irvine, who once owned one-quarter of what is now Orange County. *18881 Von Karman Dr., Irvine, tel. 714/476–0294. Admission free. Open Tues.–Sat. 11–5.*

Known for its forward-looking concept of community planning, ❿ Irvine is also a center for higher education. The **University of California at Irvine** was established on 1,000 acres of rolling ranch land donated by the Irvine family in the mid-1950s. The **Bren Events Center Fine Art Gallery** (tel. 714/856–5000; admission free; open Tues.–Sat. 10–5) on campus sponsors exhibitions of 20th-century art. Tree lovers will be enthralled by the campus; it's an arboretum with more than 11,000 trees from all over the world. *San Diego Fwy. (I–405) to Jamboree Rd., west to Campus Dr. S.*

It is no small irony that the Costa Mesa/South Coast Metro area is known first for its posh shopping mall and second for its performing arts center. A mega-shopping complex, **South Coast Plaza** (3333 S. Bristol St., Costa Mesa) along with its annexes, the Crystal Court and South Coast Village, attracts more than 20 million visitors per year, making it the busiest mall in Southern California. It's so big that a shuttle bus transports shoppers between the three complexes. This is Adventureland for the Gold Card set, built around boutiques with names like Polo/Ralph Lauren, Charles Jourdan, Tiffany, Chanel, and Courrèges. The adjacent theater/arts complex contains the acclaimed avant-garde **South Coast Repertory Theater** (655 Town Center Dr., tel. 714/957–4033) and **Orange County Performing Arts Center** (600 Town Center Dr., tel. 714/556–2787). This dramatic 3,000-seat facility for opera, ballet, and symphony hosts such notables as the Los Angeles Philharmonic, the Pacific Symphony, and the New York City Opera. **The California Scenario,** a 1.6-acre sculpture garden designed by Isamu Noguchi, surrounds the theater complex, which also houses restaurants and the South Coast Plaza Hotel.

Time Out   Take a spin around Arnold Schwarzenegger's **Planet Hollywood** (1641 W. Sunflower, across from South Coast Plaza, tel. 714/434–7827), a restaurant that recalls the 1930s and '40s with changing displays of movie memorabilia, giant TV screens showing clips of old movies, and loud rock music. The fare here has a '50s diner flare, with hamburgers topping the menu.

After you've sightseen yourself to exhaustion, pamper yourself at **Glen Ivy Hot Springs.** Thirty-five miles east of Anaheim, the spa is a day-use-only resort. It features an Olympic-size mineral water pool, seven outdoor whirlpool baths, a pool designed for tanning, champagne pools, and full service salon on 15 tropically landscaped acres. The highlight is California's only European-style clay bath. Certified massage therapists are on duty. *Hwy. 91 east to I–15 south. Continue 8 mi to Temescal Canyon Rd. exit, turn right and go 1 mi to Glen Ivy Rd. to end. Tel. 714/277–3529. Admission: $16.75 weekends and holidays; $14.75 weekdays. Open daily 10–6.*

The Coast

Coastal Orange County, dotted with charming beach towns, and punctuated with world-class resorts, offers the quintessential laid-back Southern California experience. You can catch a monster wave with the bronzed local kids, get a glimpse of some rich and famous lifestyles, and take a walk through this stretch of shoreline's natural treasures. Sites and stops on this tour are strung out along some 30 miles of the Pacific Coast Highway (known locally as PCH), and we'll take this route north to south. While there is bus service along the coast road, by car is really the best way to explore it.

If you're interested in wildlife, a walk through **Bolsa Chica Ecological Reserve** (tel. 714/897–7003) will reward you with a chance to see an amazingly restored 300-acre salt marsh, which is home to 315 species of birds, plus other animals and plants. You can see many of them along the 1.5-mile loop trail that meanders through the reserve. The walk is especially delightful in winter months, when you're likely to see great blue heron, snowy and great egrets, common loons, and other migrating birds. The salt marsh, located off PCH between Warner Avenue and Golden West Street, can be visited at any time, but a local support group, Amigos de Bolsa Chica, offers free guided tours from 9 to 10:30 AM on the first Saturday of the month, September through April.

⑭ Huntington Beach, with its 9 miles of white sand and sometimes towering waves, offers one of the hippest surf scenes in Southern California. Each year it hosts the Pro Surfing Championships competition. This beach is a favorite of Orange County residents and has ample parking, food concessions, fire pits, and lifeguards. For years, the town itself was little more than a string of small, tacky buildings across PCH from the beach containing surf shops, T-shirt emporiums, and hot dog stands. In the early '90s, however, work began on a face-lift aimed at transforming the town into a shining resort area, with the newly reconstructed 1,800-foot-long Huntington Pier as its centerpiece. The new Pierside Pavilion, across PCH from the pier, contains shops, a restaurant, nightclub, and theater complex. The **Museum of Surfing** (411 Olive St., tel. 714/960–3483; call for schedule) contains an extensive collection of surfing memorabilia.

Newport Beach has a dual personality: It's best known as the quintessential (upscale) beach town, with its island-dotted yacht harbor and a history of such illustrious residents as John Wayne, author Joseph Wambaugh, and Watergate scandal figure Bob Haldeman; and then there's inland Newport Beach, just southwest of John Wayne Airport, a business and commercial hub of the county with a major shopping center and a clutch of high-rise office buildings and hotels.

Even if you're not a boat captain, and you don't qualify as seaside high society, you can explore the charming avenues and **⑮** alleys surrounding the famed **Newport Harbor,** which shelters nearly 10,000 small boats. If you're here during the Christmas holidays, don't miss the Christmas boat parade—one of the best on the West Coast—with hundreds of brightly lit and decorated yachts cruising through the channels. You can see the parade from various restaurants overlooking the marina, but reserve a table early.

The waterside portion of Newport Beach consists of a U-**⑯** shaped harbor with the mainland along one leg and the **Balboa Peninsula** separating the marina from the ocean along the other. Set within the harbor are eight small islands, including Balboa and Lido, both well-known for their famous residents. The homes lining the shore may seem modest but remember that this is some of the most expensive real estate in the world.

You can reach the peninsula from PCH at Newport Boulevard, which will take you to Balboa Boulevard. Begin your exploration of the peninsula at the **Newport Pier,** which juts out into the ocean near 20th Street. Street parking is difficult here, so grab the first space you find and be prepared to walk. A stroll along Ocean Front reveals much of the character of this place. On weekday mornings head for the beach near the pier, where you're likely to encounter the dory fishermen hawking their predawn catches, as they've done for generations. On weekends the walk is alive with kids (of all ages) on skates, roller blades, skateboards, and bikes weaving among the strolling pedestrians and whizzing past fast-food joints, swimsuit shops, and seedy bars.

Continue your drive along Balboa Boulevard nearly to the end of the peninsula, where the charm is of quite a different character. On the bay side is the historic Victorian **Balboa Pavilion,** perched on the water's edge. Built in 1905 as a bath- and boathouse, it hosted big band dances in the 1940s. Today it houses a restaurant and shops and is a departure point for harbor and whale-watching cruises. Adjacent to the pavilion is the three-car ferry, which connects the peninsula to Balboa Island. Several blocks surrounding the pavilion support shops that are a little nicer than those at Newport Pier, restaurants, and a small Fun Zone with a Ferris wheel and arcade. On the ocean side of the peninsula the Balboa Pier juts into the surf, backed by a long, wide beach that seems to stretch to forever.

The attractions of inland Newport Beach are in striking contrast to the beach scene. **Fashion Island** is a trendy shopping mall centered in a circle of office and hotel buildings and anchored by department stores such as Robinsons-May and Broadway. Atrium Court, a Mediterranean-style complex, is popular with upscale shoppers, featuring shops such as Splash and Flash, with trendy swimwear; and Posh, a men's store. *Newport Center Dr. between Jamboree and MacArthur Blvds., off Pacific Coast Hwy.*

Time Out | **Farmer's Market at Atrium Court** (tel. 714/760–0403) is a grocery store and more, selling a vast array of exotic foods, prime meats, and glorious fresh produce arranged in color-coordinated patterns. Also on the ground floor of the Atrium Court is a gourmet food fair, with stands offering sushi, exotic coffees, a salsa bar, a Johnny Rocket's hamburger stand, plus the usual deli selections.

The **Newport Harbor Art Museum** is internationally known for its impressive collection of abstract expressionist works and cutting-edge contemporary works by California artists. Snacks are available in the Sculpture Garden Cafe. *850 San Clemente Dr., tel. 714/759–1122. Admission: $4 adults, $2 students and senior citizens, children free.. Open Tues.–Sun. 10–5.*

Just south of Newport Beach, **Corona del Mar** is a small jewel of a town with an exceptional beach. You can walk clear out onto the bay on a rough-and-tumble rock jetty. Much of the beach around here is backed by short cliffs that resemble scaled-down versions of the Northern California coastline. The town itself stretches only a few blocks along the Pacific Coast Highway, but some of the fanciest stores and ritziest restaurants in the county are located here. **Sherman Library and Gardens,** a lush botanical garden and library specializing in Southwest flora and fauna, offers diversion from sun and sand. You can wander among cactus gardens, rose gardens, a wheelchair-height touch-and-smell garden, and a tropical conservatory. *2647 E. Coast Hwy., Corona del Mar, tel. 714/673–2261. Admission: $2; free Mon. Gardens open daily 10:30–4.*

The drive south to Laguna Beach passes some of Southern California's most beautiful oceanfront; **Crystal Cove State Beach** stretches from Corona del Mar to Laguna, and its undersea park lures swimmers and divers. Each curve in the highway along here turns up a sparkling vista of crashing surf to one side and gently rolling golden brown hills sweeping inland to the other.

Laguna Beach has been called SoHo by the Sea, which is at least partly right. It is an artists' colony, which during the 1950s and 1960s attracted the beat, hip, and far-out, but it is also a colony of conservative wealth. The two camps coexist in relative harmony, with Art prevailing in the congested village, and Wealth entrenched in the canyons and on the hillsides surrounding the town.

Walk along PCH in town or side streets such as Forest or Ocean, and you'll pass gallery after gallery filled with art ranging from billowy seascapes to neon sculpture and kinetic structures. In addition, you'll find a wide selection of crafts, high fashion, beachwear, and jewelry shops. To get a sense of Laguna's beat-generation past, stop at **Farenheit 451** (540 S. Pacific Coast Hwy., tel. 714/494–5151) for a cup of coffee and stimulating conversation; this alternative bookstore, established in 1968, presents live entertainment every night and carries an eclectic selection of volumes not found in your everyday mall bookshop.

⓴ The **Laguna Beach Museum of Art,** near Heisler Park, has exhibits of historical and contemporary California art. *307 Cliff Dr., tel. 714/494–6531. Admission: $3. Open Tues.–Sun. 11–5.*

Time Out The patio at **Las Brisas** (tel. 714/494–5434) restaurant next door to the museum offers one of the loveliest views of the coastline available in Laguna Beach. Stop here for a snack and drink in the scene.

In front of the Pottery Shack on PCH is a bit of local nostalgia—a life-size **statue of Eiler Larsen,** the town greeter, who for years stood at the edge of town saying hello and goodbye to visitors. In recent years Number One Archer has assumed the role of greeter, waving to tourists from a spot at the corner of PCH and Forest.

Laguna's many arts festivals bring visitors here from all over the world. During July and August, the Sawdust Festival and Art-a-Fair, the Laguna Festival of the Arts, and the Pageant of the Masters take place. The **Pageant of the Masters** (tel. 714/494–1147) is Laguna's most impressive event, a blending of life and art. Live models and carefully orchestrated backgrounds are arranged in striking mimicry of famous paintings. Participants must hold a perfectly still pose for the length of their stay on stage. It is an impressive effort, requiring hours of training and rehearsal by the 400 or so residents who volunteer each year.

Going to Laguna without exploring its beaches would be a shame. To get away from the hubbub of Main Beach, go north to **Woods Cove,** off the Coast Highway at Diamond Street; it's especially quiet during the week. Big rock formations hide lurking crabs. As you climb the steps to leave, you'll see a stunning English-style mansion that was once the home of Bette

Davis. At the end of almost every street in Laguna, there is a little cove with its own beach.

㉑ The **Ritz-Carlton Laguna Niguel** is the classiest hotel for miles and has developed a worldwide following for its sweeping oceanside views, gleaming marble, and stunning antiques. Even if you're not a registered guest, you can enjoy the view and the elegant service by taking English tea, which is served each afternoon in the library. *33533 Ritz-Carlton Dr., Dana Point, tel. 714/240–2000.*

㉒ **Dana Point** is Orange County's newest aquatic playground, a small-boat marina tucked into a dramatic natural harbor surrounded by high bluffs. The harbor was first described more than 100 years ago by its namesake Richard Henry Dana in his book *Two Years Before the Mast.* The marina has docks for small boats and marine-oriented shops and restaurants. Recent development includes a hillside park with bike and walking trails, hotels, small shopping centers, and a collection of eateries. A monument to Dana stands in a gazebo at the top of the bluffs in front of the Blue Lantern Inn. There's a pleasant sheltered beach and park at the west end of the marina. Boating is the big thing here. **Dana Wharf Sportfishing** (tel. 714/496–5794) has charters year-round and runs whale-watching excursions in winter, and the community sponsors an annual whale festival in late February.

㉓ The **Orange County Marine Institute** offers a number of programs and excursions designed to entertain and educate about the ocean. Three tanks containing touchable sea creatures are available on weekends. Anchored near the institute is *The Pilgrim*, a full-size replica of the square-rigged vessel on which Richard Henry Dana sailed. Tours of *The Pilgrim* are offered Sunday from 11 to 2:30. A gallery and gift shop are open daily. *24200 Dana Point Harbor Dr., tel. 714/496–2274. Open daily 10–3:30.*

San Juan Capistrano is best known for its mission, and, of course, for the swallows that migrate here each year from their winter haven in Argentina. The arrival of the birds on St. Joseph's Day, March 19, launches a week of festivities. After summering in the arches of the old stone church, the swallows head home on St. John's Day, October 23.

㉔ Founded in 1776 by Father Junipero Serra, **Mission San Juan Capistrano** was the major Roman Catholic outpost between Los Angeles and San Diego. Scaffolding supports the original Great Stone Church, the victim of an 1812 earthquake, which is undergoing a preservation project. Many of the mission's adobe buildings have been restored to illustrate mission life, with exhibits of an olive millstone, tallow ovens, tanning vats, metalworking furnaces, and padres' living quarters. The impressive Serra Chapel is believed to be the oldest building still in use in California. The knowledgeable staff in the mission's visitor center can help you with a self-guided tour. *Camino Capistrano and Ortega Hwy., tel. 714/248–2048. Admission: $4 adults, $3 children 11 and under. Open daily 8:30–5.*

㉕ Near the mission is the postmodern **San Juan Capistrano Library,** built in 1983. Architect Michael Graves mixed classical design with the style of the mission to striking effect. Its courtyard has secluded places for reading, as well as a running water fountain. *31495 El Camino Real, tel. 714/493–3984. Open Mon.–Thur. 10–9, Fri.–Sat. 10–5.*

The **Decorative Arts Study Center,** just up the street from the mission, presents exhibits and lectures on interior design and decorating, gardens, plus an annual antiques show and story-telling festival in October. *31431 Camino Capistrano, tel. 714/496–2132. Open Tues.–Sat. 10–3.*

Galleria Capistrano, occupying the historic Egan House, is one of Southern California's leading galleries devoted to the art of Native Americans. Exhibits include first-rate paintings, prints, jewelry, and sculpture from Southwest and Northwest artists. *31892 Camino Capistrano, tel. 714/661–1781. Open Tues.–Sun. 11–6, Mon. noon–5.*

Time Out   The **Capistrano Depot** (26701 Verdugo St., tel. 714/496–8181) is not only the local Amtrak train station but also a restaurant. The eclectic menu runs from rack of lamb to southwestern fare to pasta. There's entertainment nightly and Dixieland jazz on Sunday. It's a perfect way to see San Juan if you are based in Los Angeles—a train ride, a meal, and then a little sightseeing.

The southernmost city in Orange County, **San Clemente,** is probably best remembered as the site of Richard Nixon's Western White House. Casa Pacifica was often in the news dur-ing Nixon's presidency. Situated on a massive 25-acre estate, the house, now a private residence, is visible from the beach; just look up at the cliffs.

Perhaps even more infamous than Nixon's house—and a good **26** deal more menacing as far as locals are concerned—is the **San Onofre Nuclear Power Plant,** a collection of space-age domes lending an eerie feeling to the nearby beach, where surfers ride the waves undaunted. The plant is scheduled to be shut down in the near future, but information on its operation is available at the San Onofre Nuclear Information Center, off the Coast Highway.

San Onofre State Beach, located just south of the nuclear plant, boasts some of the best surfing in California. Below the bluffs here are 3.5 miles of sandy beach, where you can also swim, fish, and watch wildlife.

For avid bicyclists, the next 20 miles south of San Clemente are prime terrain. **Camp Pendleton,** the country's largest Marine Corps base, welcomes cyclists to use some of its roads—just don't be surprised to see a troop helicopter taking off right beside you. Training involves off-shore landings; overland treks are also conducted on the installation's three mountain ranges, five lakes, and 250 miles of roads.

Off the Beaten Track

Lido Isle, an island in Newport Harbor, the location of many elegant homes, provides some insight into the upper-crust Or-ange County mindset. A number of grassy areas offer great harbor views; each is marked "Private Community Park." *Hwy. 55 to Pacific Coast Hwy. in Newport Beach. Turn left at signal on Via Lido and follow onto island.*

Old Towne Orange contains at least 1,200 buildings documented as historically relevant. A walking tour explores some of the most interesting of these, including the Ainsworth House, a museum dedicated to the city's early lifestyle; the 1901 Finley Home, location of the 1945 film *Fallen Angels;* and O'Hara's Irish Pub, a hangout for local reporters. A brochure describing all the stops is available. *City of Orange, 300 E. Chapman Ave., Room 12, Orange, tel. 714/744–7220.*

Little Saigon, an area of the city of Westminster between Ward Street on the east and Magnolia on the west, is home to 115,000 or so Vietnamese residents, the largest Vietnamese community outside Vietnam. Check out the jewelry and gift shops, Asian herbalists, and restaurants in colorful Little Saigon Plaza (Bolsa and Buishard), where Song Phung Restaurant offers an extensive menu of authentic dishes. The Dynasty Seafood Restaurant, in the Asian Garden Mall (Bolsa between Magnolia and Bushard), is considered the best place in Orange County for Chinese dim sum.

Shopping

Shopping is Orange County's favorite indoor sport, and it's got the shopping malls to prove it. Indeed Orange County is home to some of the biggest, most varied, classiest malls in the world. Even if the merchandise offered by Tiffany, Chanel, and Brooks Brothers is beyond your budget, you can always window shop. The following is just a small selection of the shopping possibilities in the county.

South Coast Plaza (Bristol and Sunflower Sts., Costa Mesa), the most amazing of all the malls and the largest in Orange County, is actually two enclosed shopping centers, complete with greenery and tumbling waterfalls bisecting the wide aisles, plus a collection of boutiques and restaurants across the street. A free tram makes frequent runs between the three sections. The older section is anchored by Nordstrom, Sears, and Bullocks; the newer Crystal Court across the street has the Broadway department store as its centerpiece. However, it's the variety of stories that makes this mall special. You'll find Gucci, Burberry's, Armani, F.A.O. Schwarz, Saks Fifth Avenue, and Mark Cross just up the aisle from Sears. Kids will want to browse through the Disney and Sesame Street stores. There's even an outpost of the Laguna Beach Museum of Art, just a few steps from McDonald's and Eddie Bauer. For literary buffs, there is a branch of the famous Rizzoli's International Bookstore. The mall is particularly festive during the holidays, when Santa's village fills the Carousel Court and a five-story Christmas tree soars to the top of the Crystal Court.

Fashion Island on Newport Center Drive in Newport Beach sits on the top of a hill, where shoppers can enjoy the ocean breeze. It is an open-air, single-level mall of more than 200 stores. Major department stores here include Neiman Marcus, Bullocks, and the Broadway. The enclosed **Atrium Court** is a Mediterranean-style plaza with three floors of boutiques and stores such as Sharper Image, Benetton, and Caswell-Massey.

Main Place, just off I–5 in Santa Ana, opened recently with major department stores such as Robinsons-May, Bullocks, and Nordstrom as its anchors. Although many of the 170 shops are upscale, the mall resembles a warehouse. It's busy and noisy.

If you can look past the inflatable palm trees, unimaginative T-shirts, and other tourist novelties, there is some good browsing to be done in **Laguna Beach.** There are dozens of art galleries, antiques shops, one-of-a-kind craft boutiques, and custom jewelry stores. Some of the best can be found along arty Forest Avenue, just a few steps off PCH. Thee Foxes Trot, at 264 Forest Avenue, features a delightful selection of handcrafted items from around the world; Georgeo's Art Glass and Jewelry, at 269 Forest Avenue, contains a large selection of etched and blown-glass bowls, vases, glassware, and jewelry; Rosovsky Gallery, at 263 Forest Avenue, showcases the work of three Russian artists; and Pacific Gallery, at 228 Forest Avenue, specializes in whimsical and lighthearted work by about 60 local artists.

Participant Sports

Bicycling Bicycles and roller skates are some of the most popular means of transportation along the beaches. A bike path spans the whole distance from Marina del Rey all the way to San Diego, with only some minor breaks. Most beaches have rental stands. In Laguna, try **Rainbow Bicycles** (tel. 714/494–5806) or, in Huntington Beach, **Team Bicycle Rentals** (tel. 714/969–5480).

Golf Golf is one of the most popular sports in Orange County, and owing to the climate, almost 365 days out of the year are perfect golf days. Here is a selection of golf courses:

Anaheim Hills Public Country Club (tel. 714/748–8900), **Costa Mesa Public Golf and Country Club** (tel. 714/540–7500), **H. G. Dad Miller** (Anaheim, tel. 714/991–5530), **Mile Square Golf Course** (Fountain Valley, tel. 714/545–3726), **Meadowlark Golf Course** (Huntington Beach, tel. 714/846–1364), **Rancho San Joaquin Golf Course** (Irvine, tel. 714/786–5522), **Costa del Sol Golf Course** (Mission Viejo, tel. 714/581–0940), **Newport Beach Golf Course** (tel. 714/852–8681), **San Clemente Municipal Golf Course** (tel. 714/492–3943), **San Juan Hills Country Club** (San Juan Capistrano, tel. 714/837–0361), **Aliso Creek Golf Course** (South Laguna, tel. 714/499–1919).

Running The **Santa Ana Riverbed Trail** hugs the Santa Ana River for 20.6 miles between Pacific Coast Highway at Huntington State Beach and Imperial Highway in Yorba Linda; there are entrances, as well as rest rooms and drinking fountains, at all crossings. The **Beach Trail** runs along the beach from Huntington Beach to Newport.

Snorkeling The fact that **Corona del Mar** is off-limits to boats—along with its two colorful reefs—makes it a great place for snorkeling. **Laguna Beach** is also a good spot for snorkeling and diving; the whole beach area of the city is a marine preserve.

Surfing There are 50 surf breaks along the Orange County coastline, with wave action ranging from beginner to expert. If you are not an expert, you can get a sense of the action on a boogie board at one of the beginners' beaches: **Doheny State Beach, San Clemente Pier,** and **San Onofre. Huntington Beach** is popular for surfers and spectators. "The Wedge" at **Newport Beach,** one of the most famous surfing spots in the world, is known for its steep, punishing shore break. Don't miss the spectacle of surfers, who appear tiny in the midst of the waves, flying through this treacherous place. San Clemente surfers usually take a primo spot right across from the San Onofre Nuclear Reactor. Rental stands are found at all beaches.

Tennis Most of the larger hotels have tennis courts. Here are some other choices; try the local Yellow Pages for further listings.

Anaheim **Tennisland Racquet Club** (1330 S. Walnut St., tel. 714/535–4851) has 10 courts, a teaching pro, and a practice court.

Huntington Beach **Edison Community Center** (21377 Magnolia St., tel. 714/960–8870) has four courts available on a first-come, first-served basis in the daytime. The **Murdy Community Center** (7000 Norma Dr., tel. 714/960–8895) has four courts, also first-come, first-served during the day. Both facilities accept reservations for play after 5; both charge $2 an hour.

Laguna Beach Six metered courts can be found at **Laguna Beach High School,** on Park Avenue. Two courts are available at the **Irvine Bowl,** Laguna Canyon Road, and six new courts are available at **Alta Laguna Park,** at the end of Alta Laguna Blvd., off Park Ave., on a first-come, first-served basis. For more information, call the City of Laguna Beach Recreation Department at 714/497–0716.

Newport Beach Call the recreation department at 714/644–3151 for information about court use at **Corona del Mar High School** (2101 E. Bluff Dr.). There are eight courts for public use.

San Clemente There are four courts at **San Luis Rey Park,** on Avenue San Luis Rey. They are offered on a first-come, first-served basis. Call the recreation department at 714/361–8200 for further information.

Water Sports Rental stands for surfboards, windsurfers, small power boats, and sailboats can be found near most of the piers. **Hobie Sports** has three locations for surfboard and boogie-board rentals—two in Dana Point (tel. 714/496–2366 and 714/496–1251) and one in Laguna (tel. 714/497–3304).

In the biggest boating town of all, Newport Beach, you can rent sailboats and small motorboats at **Balboa Boat Rentals** in the harbor (tel. 714/673–1320; open Fri.–Sun. 10–4). Sailboats rent for $25 an hour, and motorboats for $26 an hour, half price for each subsequent hour. You must have a driver's license, and some knowledge of boating is helpful; rented boats are not allowed out of the bay.

Parasailing is also rising as a water sport. At **Davey's Locker** in the Balboa Pavilion (tel. 714/673–1434; open summer, daily 9–5:30), you can parasail for 8 to 12 minutes during a 90-minute boat ride. Cost is $45 per person, with up to six persons per boat. The last excursion leaves at 4.

In Dana Point, power and sailboats can be rented at **Embarcadero Marina** (tel. 714/496–6177, open weekdays 8–5, weekends 7–5:30), near the launching ramp at Dana Point Harbor. Boat sizes vary—sailboats range from $15 to $30 an hour, motorboats are $20 an hour. Cash only is accepted. Parasailing is available from **Dana Wharf Sports Fishing** (tel. 714/496–5794) during the spring and summer. Call for hours and prices.

Spectator Sports

Orange County has some of the best, unplanned, casual spectator sports; besides the surfers, you are bound to catch a vigorous volleyball or basketball game at any beach on any given weekend. Professional sports in Orange County include the following:

Baseball The **California Angels** (tel. 714/634–2000) play at the Anaheim Stadium from April through October.

Football The **Los Angeles Rams** (tel. 714/937–6767) have called Anaheim Stadium their home since 1980. The season runs from August through December.

Hockey The **Mighty Ducks** (tel. 800/462–5394), the new NHL team owned by the Walt Disney Company, play on the Pond in Anaheim. The season runs from October through April.

Horse Racing The **Los Alamitos Race Course** (tel. 714/995–1234) has quarter horse racing and harness racing on a ⅝-mile track. Thoroughbred racing is part of the fare here as well.

Horse Shows Twice monthly at the **Orange County Fair Equestrian Center** (tel. 714/641–1328) show jumping is featured. Admission is free.

Beaches

All of the state, county, and city beaches in Orange County allow swimming. Make sure there is a staffed lifeguard stand nearby, and you are pretty safe. Also keep on the lookout for posted signs about undertow: It can be mighty nasty around here. Moving down the coast in order, here are some of the best beaches:

Huntington Beach State Beach (tel. 714/536–1454) runs for 9 miles along the Pacific Coast Highway (Beach Blvd. [Hwy. 39] from inland). There are changing rooms, concessions, barbecue pits, and vigilant lifeguards on the premises, and there is parking. **Bolsa Chica State Beach** (tel. 714/536–1454), just north of Huntington and across from the Bolsa Chica Ecological Reserve, has barbecue pits and is usually less crowded than its neighbor.

Lower Newport Bay provides an enclave sheltered from the ocean. This area, off Coast Highway on Jamboree, is a 740-acre preserve for ducks and geese. **Newport Dunes Resort** (tel. 714/729–3863), nearby, offers RV spaces, picnic facilities, changing rooms, water-sports rentals, and a place to launch boats.

Just south of Newport Beach, **Corona del Mar State Beach** (tel. 714/644–3044) has a tide pool and caves waiting to be explored. It also sports one of the best walks in the county—a beautiful rock pier jutting into the ocean. Facilities include barbecue pits, volleyball poles, food, rest rooms, and parking.

Located at the end of Broadway at Pacific Coast Highway, Laguna Beach's **Main Beach Park** has sand volleyball, two half-basketball courts, children's play equipment, picnic areas, rest rooms, showers, and road parking.

The county's best spot for scuba diving is in the **Marine Life Refuge** (tel. 714/494–6571), which runs from Seal Rock to Diver's Cove in Laguna. Farther south, in South Laguna, **Aliso County Park** (tel. 714/661–7013) is a recreation area with a pier for fishing, barbecue pits, parking, food, and rest rooms. Swim Beach, inside **Dana Point Harbor** (tel. 714/661–7013), also has a fishing pier, barbecues, food, parking, and rest rooms, as well as a shower.

Doheny State Park (tel. 714/496–6171), at the south end of Dana Point, one of the best surfing spots in Southern California, has an interpretive center devoted to the wildlife of the Doheny Marine Refuge, and there are food stands and shops nearby. Camping is permitted here; there are also picnic facilities and a pier for fishing. **San Clemente State Beach** (tel. 714/492–3156) is a favorite of locals and surfers. It has ample camping facilities, RV hookups, and food stands.

Dining and Lodging

Dining Orange County seems to prove that nothing raises the quality of restaurants quite so much as being in a high-rent district. Since the region became one of the most costly places to buy a home, the dining scene is vastly improved. Restaurant prices, however, are still not as high as in upscale neighborhoods of Los Angeles and San Francisco (perhaps high mortgage payments have made the natives dining-dollar wary). The growing number of luxury hotels, with dining rooms to match, has also broadened gastronomic choices.

Highly recommended restaurants are indicated by a star ★.

Category	Cost*
Very Expensive	over $35
Expensive	$25–$35
Moderate	$15–$25
Inexpensive	under $15

per person, excluding 8.25% tax, service, and drinks

Lodging Lodging to suit every budget and taste is available in Orange County; offerings range from the very expensive four-star Ritz-Carlton on the coast to the comfortable-but-plain chain motels around Disneyland. Those who haven't been to Orange County for a while will be pleasantly surprised to see that many hotels near Disneyland have recently undergone renovation and now have a bright new look. In addition to the choices listed here for the Anaheim area, there are a number of motels; but visitors should be careful to pick only familiar chain names. Central Orange County also supports a number of lodgings that normally cater to business travelers, but offer substantial discounts on weekends.

Prices listed here are based on summer rates. Winter rates, especially near Disneyland, tend to be somewhat less. It pays to shop around for promotional and weekend rates.

Highly recommended lodgings are indicated by a star ★.

Category	Cost*
Very Expensive	over $100
Expensive	$75–$100
Moderate	$50–$75
Inexpensive	under $50

All prices are for a double room.

Anaheim
Dining
JW's. You would never guess you were in a hotel—the dining room looks like a French country inn, complete with a fireplace. The food is well-prepared classic French, featuring roasted saddle of lamb, venison, and wild boar. *Marriott Hotel, 700 W. Convention Way, tel. 714/750–8000. Reservations required. Jacket required. AE, D, DC, MC, V. Valet parking. No lunch. Closed Sun. Very Expensive.*

Bessie Wall's. Citrus rancher John Wall built this house for his bride-to-be in 1927. It has been restored, and the rooms converted into dining areas decorated with Wall memorabilia. Bessie's favorite chicken-and-dumplings recipe is on the menu, which also features Southern California–Mexican dishes. *1074 N. Tustin Blvd., tel. 714/630–2812. Reservations advised. Jacket advised. AE, D, DC, MC, V. No Sat. lunch. Moderate.*

Overland Stage. A dining Disneyland of sorts, Overland Stage tries to recreate California's Wild West days. There's a stagecoach over the entrance, and all sorts of Western bric-a-brac within. The daily specials are intriguing: wild boar, buffalo, rattlesnake, bear, and elk. *1855 S. Harbor Blvd., tel. 714/750–1811. Reservations advised. Dress: casual. AE, D, DC, MC, V. No weekend lunch. Moderate.*

Lodging
Anaheim Hilton and Towers. This hotel is one of several choices convenient to the Anaheim Convention Center, which in fact is just a few steps from the front door. It is virtually a self-contained city—complete with its own post office. The lobby is dominated by a bright, airy atrium, and guest rooms are decorated in pinks and greens with light-wood furniture. Because it caters to conventioneers, it can be busy and noisy, with long lines at restaurants. *777 Convention Way, 92802, tel. 714/750–4321 or 800/222–9923. 1,600 rooms. Facilities: 4 restaurants, lounges, shops, duty-free shopping, outdoor pool, Jacuzzis, fitness center ($10 charge), sun deck, concierge, summer Vacation Station for kids. AE, D, DC, MC, V. Very Expensive.*

Anaheim Marriott. This hotel, comprised of two towers of 16 and 18 floors, is another good headquarters for Convention Center attendees and was recently renovated to achieve a more contemporary look. The expanded lobby's huge windows allow sunlight to stream in, highlighting the gleaming marble. Spacious rooms, decorated with pastels, have balconies. Discounted weekend packages available. *700 W. Convention Way, 92802, tel. 714/750–8000. 979 rooms, 54 suites. Facilities: 3 restaurants, 2 lounges, 2 heated pools, Jacuzzi, entertainment, fitness center; video games, concierge. AE, D, DC, MC, V. Very Expensive.*

★ **Disneyland Hotel.** This hotel, which is connected to the Magic Kingdom by monorail, carries the Disney theme in lobby, restaurants, entertainment, shops, and spacious guest rooms. Consisting of three towers surrounding lakes, streams, tumbling waterfalls, and lush landscaping, the once-tired hotel was recently renovated and now gleams with brass and marble. In Goofy's Kitchen, kids can breakfast with Donald, Mickey, or Chip and Dale. There are marina and park views, and rooms in the Bonita tower overlook the Fantasy Waters, a nighttime Disney-theme lighted fountain and music display. *1150 W. Cerritos Ave., 92802, tel. 714/778–6600 or 800/642–5391. 1,131 rooms. Facilities: 6 restaurants, 5 lounges, 3 pools, spa, white-sand beach, concierge floor, 10 tennis courts, fitness center, business center, entertainment. AE, DC, MC, V. Very Expensive.*

Hyatt Regency Alicante. This hotel, located a few blocks south of Disneyland and Convention Center, is a good choice for those seeking some distance from the park. Set beneath a 17-story high steel and glass atrium, the lobby has an indoor/outdoor feel, and abounds with tropical greenery, 60-foot high palm trees and fountains. The guest rooms are standard issue, but on a clear day those on the upper floors have mountain and city views. *Harbor at Chapman, Box 4669, 92803, tel. 714/750–1234 or 800/972–2929. 396 rooms, 18 suites. Facilities: 2 restaurants, lounge, pool, spa, fitness area, 2 lighted tennis courts, concierge floor, Camp Hyatt, shuttle service to area attractions. AE, D, DC, MC, V. Very Expensive.*

Pan Pacific Anaheim. Geared to business travelers, this hotel also has some appeal for families visiting Disneyland across the street. It's a short walk to the monorail. Spacious rooms come with sitting areas containing sofa beds. Lanai suites have private patios with direct access to recreation deck. The hotel's Keyaki restaurant features authentic Japanese cuisine. *1717 S. West St., 92802, tel. 714/999–0990 or 800/821–8976. 502 rooms, 13 suites. Facilities: 2 restaurants, pool, fitness facilities, Jacuzzi, video games. AE, DC, MC, V. Very Expensive.*

Sheraton-Anaheim Motor Hotel. This Tudor-style hotel was recently renovated and now has a contemporary, bright look while retaining its castle theme in large tapestries, faux stone walls, and frescoes in the public areas. The large guest rooms open onto interior gardens. A Disneyland shuttle, and multilanguage services are available. *1015 W. Ball Rd., 92802, tel. 714/778–1700 or 800/325–3535. 500 rooms. Facilities: dining room, deli, bar, heated pool, suites, game room, wheelchair units available. AE, D, DC, MC, V. Very Expensive.*

Anaheim Plaza Hotel. Soft pastel colors and plants fill the lobby of this low-rise hotel on 10 acres of tropical gardens near Disneyland. Wheelchair units and suites are available. *1700 S. Harbor Blvd., 92802, tel. 714/772–5900 or 800/228–1357. 298 rooms, 6 suites. Facilities: restaurant, heated pool, whirlpool. AE, DC, MC, V. Expensive.*

Grand Hotel. Lobby and rooms are decorated in a pleasant plum-teal green combination. The hotel is close to Disneyland, and some rooms have a good view of nighttime fireworks. Each room in the nine-story high rise has a balcony. *7 Freedman Way, 92802, tel. 714/772–7777. 242 rooms. Facilities: dining room, coffee shop, corporate lounge, pool, Jacuzzi, fitness facilities, weekend entertainment, shuttle service to area attractions, video games. AE, DC, MC, V. Expensive.*

Inn at the Park. This hotel, a longtime favorite of conventioneers, was recently redecorated. Rooms and public areas sport a fresh coat of pink and mauve paint. All rooms have balconies, and those in the tower offer good views of Disneyland's summer fireworks show. *1855 S. Harbor Blvd., 92802, tel. 714/750–*

Dining

Orange County Dining and Lodging

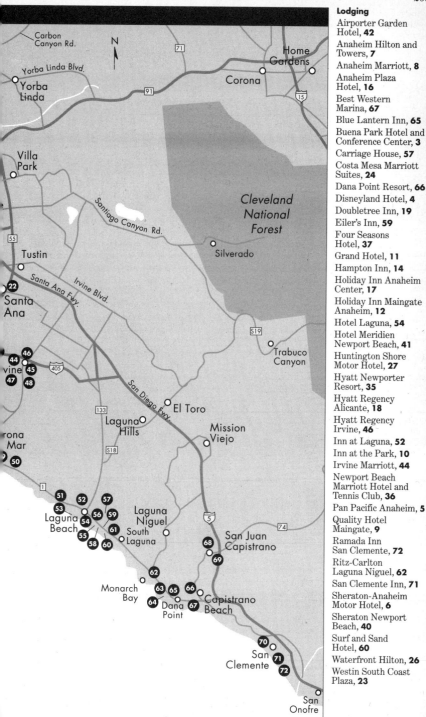

Lodging

Airporter Garden Hotel, **42**

Anaheim Hilton and Towers, **7**

Anaheim Marriott, **8**

Anaheim Plaza Hotel, **16**

Best Western Marina, **67**

Blue Lantern Inn, **65**

Buena Park Hotel and Conference Center, **3**

Carriage House, **57**

Costa Mesa Marriott Suites, **24**

Dana Point Resort, **66**

Disneyland Hotel, **4**

Doubletree Inn, **19**

Eiler's Inn, **59**

Four Seasons Hotel, **37**

Grand Hotel, **11**

Hampton Inn, **14**

Holiday Inn Anaheim Center, **17**

Holiday Inn Maingate Anaheim, **12**

Hotel Laguna, **54**

Hotel Meridien Newport Beach, **41**

Huntington Shore Motor Hotel, **27**

Hyatt Newporter Resort, **35**

Hyatt Regency Alicante, **18**

Hyatt Regency Irvine, **46**

Inn at Laguna, **52**

Inn at the Park, **10**

Irvine Marriott, **44**

Newport Beach Marriott Hotel and Tennis Club, **36**

Pan Pacific Anaheim, **5**

Quality Hotel Maingate, **9**

Ramada Inn San Clemente, **72**

Ritz-Carlton Laguna Niguel, **62**

San Clemente Inn, **71**

Sheraton-Anaheim Motor Hotel, **6**

Sheraton Newport Beach, **40**

Surf and Sand Hotel, **60**

Waterfront Hilton, **26**

Westin South Coast Plaza, **23**

1811. 497 rooms. Facilities: restaurant, coffee shop, lounge, heated pool, spa, exercise room, video games. AE, D, DC, MC, V. Expensive.

Holiday Inn Anaheim Center. This is a big pink Mediterranean-style building set at the edge of Disneyland at the Santa Ana Freeway. Designed for families visiting the Magic Kingdom, it has pleasant, if functional, rooms including some with separate sitting areas. Shuttle service is available to nearby attractions including Knott's Berry Farm, Movieland Wax Museum, and Medieval Times. *1221 S. Harbor Blvd., 92805, tel. 714/758–0900 or 800/545–7275. 252 rooms, 2 housekeeping suites. Facilities: restaurant, lounge, pool, spa, sauna, video games, disabled access. AE, D, DC, MC, V. Moderate.*

Holiday Inn Maingate Anaheim. Large glass chandeliers in the lobby set the tone at this establishment one block south of Disneyland. *1850 S. Harbor Blvd., 92802, tel. 714/750–2801 or 800/624-6855. 312 rooms, including 3 suites. Facilities: dining room, lounge, heated pool, video games. AE, D, DC, MC, V. Moderate.*

Quality Hotel/Maingate. A large, open, red-tile lobby is filled with mirrors, plants, and flowers; guest rooms are decorated in greens and yellows. The hotel is close to Disneyland and the convention center. *616 Convention Way, 92802, tel. 714/750–3131 or 800/231–6215. 284 rooms, including 12 suites. Facilities: 2 restaurants, lounge, heated pool, game room. AE, DC, MC, V. Moderate.*

Ramada Maingate/Anaheim. A clean, reliable, new member of the worldwide chain. Located across the street from Disneyland, with free shuttle service to the park. *1460 S. Harbor Blvd., 92802, tel. 714/772–6777 or 800/447–4048. 465 rooms. Facilities: restaurant, pool, Jacuzzi, game room. AE, MC, V. Moderate.*

Hampton Inn. Basic lodging at a basic price. *300 E. Katella Way, 92802, tel. 714/772–8713. 136 rooms. Facilities: pool, complimentary breakfast. AE, DC, MC, V. Inexpensive.*

Buena Park
Lodging

Buena Park Hotel and Convention Center. A spiral staircase leading to the mezzanine centers a lobby of marble, brass, and glass. Rooms are done in green and peach tones. *7675 Crescent Ave., 90620, tel. 714/995–1111 or 800/854–8792. 350 rooms. Facilities: restaurant, lounge, nightclub, coffee shop, heated pool, Jacuzzi. AE, DC, MC, V. Expensive.*

Corona del Mar
Dining
★

The Five Crowns. This surprisingly faithful replica of Ye Old Bell, England's oldest inn, has its barmaids and waitresses costumed in Elizabethan dress. There's a wide array of British ales and, of course, Guinness stout. The roast beef with Yorkshire pudding and the rack of lamb are very good, as are the fish dishes, and all are priced reasonably. *3801 E. Pacific Coast Hwy., tel. 714/760–0331. Reservations required. Jacket advised. AE, D, DC, MC, V. No lunch Mon.–Sat. Moderate–Expensive.*

Trees. The contemporary look, atmosphere, and menu of this upscale restaurant are among the most appealing in the county. The three dining rooms, with walls and table appointments done in shades of pink, surround a glassed-in atrium planted with towering ficus trees. Each room has its own fireplace. Satisfying cooking matches the setting: Maryland crab cakes, roast turkey dinners on Sunday; Chinese chicken salad, potstickers and spring rolls; veal sweetbreads in puff pastry. Don't pass up the apricot mousse dessert. There's also a piano bar. *440 Heliotrope Ave., tel. 714/673–0910. Reservations advised.*

Dress: casual. AE, D, DC, MC, V. No lunch. Moderate–Expensive.

Costa Mesa Dining

Mandarin Gourmet. Dollar for bite, owner Michael Chang provides what the critics and locals consider the best Chinese cuisine in the area. His specialties include: a crisp-yet-juicy Peking duck, cashew chicken, and, seemingly everyone's favorite, mu-shu pork. There is also a very good wine list. *1500 Adams Ave., tel. 714/540–1937. Reservations accepted. Dress: casual. AE, DC, MC, V. Moderate.*

Ruby's. This is one in a chain of 14 lunch spots in Orange County that recall 1940's diners. Everyone seems to order Ruby's hamburger "with the works." Following in popularity: smothered steak and satay chicken. The location at the Balboa Pier has a great view. *Crystal Court, 3333 Bear St., tel. 714/662–7829. Dress: casual. AE, D, MC, V. Inexpensive.*

Lodging

Costa Mesa Marriott Suites. This new all-suite hotel convenient to the airport is a good choice for business travelers. Well-lit rooms have traditional decor and offer dual-line phones, large work areas, refrigerators, and coffee makers. Weekend guests will find sharply reduced prices and a complimentary buffet breakfast. *500 Anton Blvd., 92626, tel. 714/957–1100 or 800/228–9290. 253 suites. Facilities: restaurant, lounge, pool, fitness facilities, business services. AE, DC, MC, V. Very Expensive.*

Westin South Coast Plaza. This recently renovated hotel is surrounded by the Performing Arts Center entertainment complex, chic restaurants, and the shopping wonders of the South Coast Plaza mall across the street. Even with the ballrooms brimming with conventioneers, the lobby and corridors are quiet. Rooms are decorated with soft colors and traditional furnishings. *686 Anton Blvd., 92626, tel. 714/540–2500 or 800/228–3000. 394 rooms. Facilities: café, 2 lounges, pool, shuffleboard, 4 lighted tennis courts, entertainment, concierge floor, wheelchair access. AE, D, DC, MC, V. Very Expensive.*

Dana Point Dining

Chart House. This is a popular member of a small chain of steak-and-seafood houses in Southern California. Mud pie is the dessert everyone asks for. This particular location has a sensational view of the harbor from most of the tables and booths. *34442 Green Lantern, tel. 714/493–1183. Reservations advised. Jacket advised. AE, DC, MC, V. No lunch. Moderate–Expensive.*

Watercolors. This light, cheerful dining room provides a clifftop view of the harbor and an equally enjoyable Continental/California menu, along with low-calorie choices. Try the baked breast of pheasant, roast rabbit, grilled swordfish, and either the Caesar or poached spinach salad. *Dana Point Resort, tel. 714/661–5000. Reservations advised. Dress: casual but neat. AE, D, DC, MC, V. Valet parking. Moderate–Expensive.*

Delaney's Restaurant. Fresh seafood from nearby San Diego's fishing fleet is what this place is all about. Your choice is prepared as simply as possible. If you have to wait for a table, pass the time at the clam and oyster bar. *25001 Dana Dr., tel. 714/496–6196. Reservations advised. Dress: casual. AE, D, MC, V. Moderate.*

Lodging

Blue Lantern Inn. This brand-new Cape Cod–style bed-and-breakfast is perched on top of the bluffs, and has stunning harbor and ocean views. Rooms are individually decorated with period furnishings, fireplaces, stocked refrigerators, and private Jacuzzis. Breakfast and afternoon refreshments are included in the price. *34343 St. of the Blue Lantern, 92629, tel. 714/661–1304. 29 rooms. Facilities: library, concierge, fitness facilities. AE, MC, V. Very Expensive.*

★ **Dana Point Resort.** This Cape Cod–style hillside resort is done in shades of seafoam green and peach. The lobby is filled with large palm trees and original artwork, and most rooms have ocean views. The ambience is casual yet elegant. The Capistrano Valley Symphony performs here in the summer, on the attractively landscaped grounds. *25135 Park Lantern, 92629, tel. 714/661–5000 or 800/533–9748. 350 rooms. Facilities: restaurant, jazz lounge, 3 pools, 3 spas, health club, concierge level, croquet, volleyball, basketball. AE, D, DC, MC, V. Very Expensive.*

★ **Ritz-Carlton Laguna Niguel.** This acclaimed hotel has earned itself world-class status for its gorgeous setting right on the edge of the Pacific, its sumptuous Mediterranean architecture and decor, and its reputation for flawless service. With colorful landscaping outside and an imposing marble columned and antiques-filled entry, it feels like an Italian country villa. Every possible amenity, and then some, is available to guests. Recently redecorated rooms still feature traditional furnishings, sumptuous fabrics, private balconies with ocean or garden views, marble bathrooms. Reduced-rate packages are sometimes available. *33533 Ritz-Carlton Dr., 92677, tel. 714/240–2000 or 800/241–3333. 393 rooms. Facilities: 3 restaurants, 3 lounges, club with entertainment, 2 pools, Jacuzzis, beach access, health club with steam room and massage service, 4 tennis courts, concierge, use of nearby 18-hole golf course. AE, D, DC, MC, V. Very Expensive.*

Best Western Marina Inn. Set right in the marina, this hotel is convenient to docks, restaurants, and shops. Rooms vary in size from basic to family units with kitchens and fireplaces. Many rooms in this three-level motel have balconies and harbor views. *24800 Dana Point Harbor Dr., 92629, tel. 714/496–1203 or 800/255–6843. 26 rooms, 10 suites. Facilities: pool, fitness facilities. AE, D, DC, MC, V. Moderate.*

Fullerton
Dining
★

The Cellar. The name tells the story here: a subterranean dining room with beamed ceiling and stone walls, wine racks, and casks. Appropriately, the list of wines from Europe and California is among the best in the West. The bill of fare is classic French cuisine that has been lightened for the California palate. *305 N. Harbor Blvd., tel. 714/525–5682. Reservations required. Jacket and tie advised. AE, DC, MC, V. No lunch. Closed Sun., Mon. Expensive–Very Expensive.*

Huntington Beach
Dining

Texas Loosey's Chili Parlor & Saloon. This place serves Tex-Mex cooking with the fixin's to make it even hotter, plus steaks, ribs, and burgers. Country-and-western music is played in the evenings. *14160 Beach Blvd., tel. 714/898–9797. Reservations accepted for parties of 6 or more. Dress: casual. AE, MC, V. Inexpensive.*

Lodging

Waterfront Hilton. This new oceanfront hotel rises 12 stories above the surf. The Mediterranean-style resort is decorated in soft mauves, beiges, and greens, and offers a panoramic ocean view from every guest room. *21100 Pacific Coast Hwy., 92648, tel. 714/960–7873 or 800/822–7873. 293 rooms. Facilities: 2 restaurants, lounge, 2 lighted tennis courts, pool, Jacuzzi, fitness center, concierge level, bike and beach-equipment rentals. AE, DC, MC, V. Very Expensive.*

★ **Huntington Shore Motor Hotel.** Just across from the ocean, some rooms at this small hotel have balconies and ocean views. The lobby is made cozy by a fireplace. The rooms are extra-large and decorated in earth tones. Complimentary Continental breakfast is offered. *21002 Pacific Coast Hwy., 92648, tel. 714/536–8861 or 800/554–6799. 50 rooms. Facilities: restaurant, heated pool, children's pool, kitchens in 6 rooms. AE, DC, MC, V. Expensive.*

Irvine
Dining

Chanteclair. This Franco-Italian country house is a lovely, tasteful retreat amid an island of modern high-rise office buildings. French Riviera-type cuisine is served, and the Chateaubriand for two and rack of lamb are recommended. *18912 MacArthur Blvd., tel. 714/752–8001. Reservations advised. Jacket required. AE, D, DC, MC, V. No Sat. lunch. Moderate–Expensive.*

Gulliver's. Jolly old England is the theme of this groaning board. Waitresses are addressed as "wenches" and busboys as "squires." Prime rib is the specialty. *18482 MacArthur Blvd., tel. 714/833–8411. Reservations advised. Jacket advised. AE, DC, MC, V. No weekend lunch. Moderate.*

Pavilion. Excellent Chinese food is offered in what resembles a formal eating hall of Chef Hu's native Taiwan. Specialties include steamed whole fish, ginger duck, and Hunan lamb. *14110 Culver Dr., 714/551–1688. Reservations advised. Dress: casual. AE, MC, V. Moderate.*

Prego. A much larger version of the Beverly Hills Prego, this one is located in an attractive approximation of a Tuscan villa and has an outdoor patio. A favorite of Orange County Yuppies, who rave about the watch-the-cooks-at-work open kitchen and the oak-burning pizza oven. Try the spit-roasted meats and chicken, or the charcoal-grilled fresh fish. Also try one of the reasonably priced California or Italian wines. *18420 Von Karman Ave., tel. 714/553–1333. Reservations advised. Dress: casual. AE, DC, MC, V. Valet parking. No weekend lunch. Moderate.*

Lodging

Hyatt Regency Irvine. Offering all the amenities of a first-class resort, this hotel is elegantly decorated in soft contemporary tones, and the marble lobby is flanked by glass-enclosed elevators. Special golf packages at nearby Tustin Ranch are available. The lower weekend rates are a great deal. *17900 Jamboree Rd., 92714, tel. 714/975–1234. 526 rooms, 10 suites. Facilities: 2 restaurants, 2 lounges, pool, Jacuzzi, 4 tennis courts, fitness facilities, entertainment, concierge, bike rentals, wheelchair access. AE, D, DC, MC, V. Very Expensive.*

Airporter Garden Hotel. This hotel, across the street from John Wayne Airport and convenient to most area offices, caters primarily to business travelers, with newly decorated rooms furnished with large work areas and two phones. One suite has a private swimming pool outside the bedroom door. Special rates are available for weekend guests. *18700 MacArthur Blvd., 92715, tel. 714/833–2770 or 800/854–3012. 195 rooms, 17 suites. Facilities: restaurant, café, 2 lounges, heated pool, fitness center, free shuttle bus, entertainment. AE, D, DC, MC, V. Expensive.*

Irvine Marriott. This contemporary looking hotel towers over Koll Business Center, making it a convenient spot for business travelers. Ask about special reduced-rate weekend packages. *1800 Von Karman, 92715, tel. 714/553–0100. 465 rooms, 24 suites. Facilities: 2 restaurants, sports bar, entertainment, indoor-outdoor pool, 4 tennis courts, health club, spa and massage services,* *concierge floors, business-service center. AE, D, DC, MC, V. Expensive.*

Laguna Beach
Dining

Ritz-Carlton. The dining room in this oceanside resort hotel serves rather pretentious pseudo-nouvelle cuisine, but its Cafe's lavish Sunday brunch is considered the best in Southern California. Be sure to make reservations several days in advance and ask for a table on the terrace, overlooking the swimming pool. *33533 Ritz-Carlton Dr., Niguel, tel. 714/240–2000. Reservations required. Dress: casual but neat. AE, DC, MC, V. Very Expensive.*

The Beach House. A Laguna tradition, the Beach House has a water view from every table. Fresh fish, lobster, and steamed clams are the drawing cards. *619 Sleepy Hollow La., tel. 714/494–9707. Reservations advised. Jacket advised. AE, MC, V. Moderate.*

Las Brisas. From its clifftop terrace, this longtime coastal favorite has a spectacular view of the rugged coastline, wonderful margaritas, addictive guacamole, and nouvelle-Mexican dishes. The first three compensate for the last. *361 Cliff Dr., tel. 714/497–5434. Reservations advised. Dress: casual. AE, DC, MC, V. Moderate.*

Partners Bistro. Beveled glass, antiques, and lace curtains adorn this neighborhood hangout. The menu features Continental fare such as fresh fish and tournedos of beef. *448 S. Coast Hwy., tel. 714/497–4441. Reservations advised. Dress: casual. AE, MC, V. Moderate.*

The White House. Bing Crosby and Cecil B. DeMille dined at this local hangout. The broad, mostly American menu has everything from bagels and lox to Mexican favorites. There's also a salad bar, for while you're making up your mind. *340 S. Coast Hwy., tel. 714/494–8088. No reservations. Dress: casual. AE, DC, MC, V. Moderate.*

The Cottage. The menu is heavy on vegetarian dishes, and the price is right. Specialties include fresh fish, Victoria Beach scallops, and chicken Alfredo. *308 N. Pacific Coast Hwy., tel. 714/494–3023. Weekend reservations advised. Dress: casual. AE, D, DC, MC, V. Inexpensive.*

Tortilla Flats. This hacienda-style restaurant specializes in first-rate chile rellenos, carne Tampiquena, soft-shell tacos, and beef or chicken fajitas. There's also a wide selection of Mexican tequilas and beers. Sunday brunch is served. *1740 S. Coast Hwy., tel. 714/494–6588. Dinner reservations advised. Dress: casual. AE, MC, V. Inexpensive.*

Lodging

Surf and Sand Hotel. This is the largest hotel in Laguna and is right on the beach. The rooms are decorated in soft sand colors, have wood shutters, and have private balconies. Weekend packages are available. *1555 S. Coast Hwy., 92651, tel. 714/497–4477 or 800/524–8621. 157 rooms, including 5 suites. Facilities: 2 restaurants, lounge, private beach, pool, concierge. AE, DC, MC, V. Very Expensive.*

Carriage House. This bed-and-breakfast has one- and two-bedroom suites surrounding a lushly landscaped courtyard, New Orleans–style. Complimentary family-style breakfast is offered daily. Fresh fruit and wine gifts welcome guests. *1322 Catalina St., 92651, tel. 714/494–8945. 6 suites with kitchens. No credit cards. 2-night minimum on weekends. Expensive–Very Expensive.*

★ **Inn at Laguna.** This new Southwest-style inn has one of the best locations in town. It's close to Main Beach and Las Brisas restaurant and bar, one of Laguna's most popular watering holes, yet far enough away to be secluded. Set on a bluff overlooking the ocean, the inn has luxurious amenities, and many rooms with views. *211 N. Coast Hwy., 92651, tel. 714/497–9722. 70 rooms. Facilities: VCRs in rooms, heated pool, Jacuzzi, complimentary Continental breakfast in rooms, free parking. AE, DC, MC, V. Expensive–Very Expensive.*

Eiler's Inn. A light-filled courtyard centers this European-style B&B. Rooms are on the small side, but each is unique and decorated with antiques. Breakfast is served outdoors, and in the afternoon there's wine and cheese, often to the accompaniment of live music. A sundeck in back has an ocean view. *741 S. Coast Hwy., 92651, tel. 714/494–3004. 12 rooms. AE, MC, V. Expensive.*

Hotel Laguna. This downtown landmark, the oldest hotel in Laguna, has recently been redone with four rooms now featuring canopy beds and reproduction Victorian furnishings. Lobby windows look out onto manicured gardens, and a patio restaurant overlooks the ocean. *425 S. Coast Hwy., 92651, tel. 714/494–1151. 65 rooms. Facilities: restaurant, lounge, entertainment, private beach. AE, DC, MC, V. Expensive.*

La Habra
Dining

Café El Cholo/Burro Alley. This is a sibling of the ever-popular El Cholo in Los Angeles, where people have been going for decades to enjoy the very best in Mexican cooking geared to American tastes. Green corn tamales served in season, Sonora-style enchilada, fajitas, and grilled chicken and beef are among the specialties. There is a cheery outdoor patio and maybe the best margaritas north of the border. *840 E. Whittier Blvd., tel. 714/525–1320. Dress: casual. AE, MC, V. Inexpensive.*

Newport Beach
Dining
★

Antoine's. This lovely, candle-lit dining room is made for romance and quiet conversation. It serves the best French cuisine of any hotel in Southern California; the fare is nouvelle, but is neither skimpy nor gimmicky. *4500 MacArthur Blvd., tel. 714/476–2001. Reservations advised. Jacket and tie required. No lunch Mon.–Sat. Very Expensive.*

★ **Pascal.** Although it's in a shopping center, you'll think that you're in St-Tropez once you step inside this bright and cheerful bistro. And, after one taste of Pascal Olhat's light Provençal cuisine, the best in Orange County, you'll swear you're in the south of France. Try the sea bass with thyme, the rack of lamb, and the lemon tart. *1000 Bristol St., tel. 714/752–0107. Reservations advised. Jacket advised. AE, DC, MC, V. Very Expensive.*

★ **The Ritz.** This is one of the most comfortable Southern California restaurants—the bar area has red leather booths, etched glass mirrors, and polished brass trim. Don't pass up the smorgasbord appetizer, the roast Bavarian duck, or the rack of lamb from the spit. This is one of those rare places that seems to please everyone. *880 Newport Center Dr., tel. 714/720–1800. Reservations advised. Jacket required. AE, DC, MC, V. No Sat. lunch. Closed Sun. Expensive.*

The Cannery. The building once was a cannery, and it has wonderful wharf-side views. The seafood entrées are good, and the sandwiches at lunch are satisfying, but the location and lazy atmosphere are the real draw. *3010 Lafayette Ave., tel. 714/675–*

*5777. Reservations advised. Dress: casual. AE, D, DC, MC, V.
Moderate.*

Le Biarritz. Newport Beach natives have a deep affection for
this restaurant, with its country French decor, hanging greenery, and skylit garden room. There's food to match the mood:
a veal-and-pheasant pâté, seafood crepes, boned duckling and
wild rice, sautéed pheasant with raspberries, and warm apple
tart for dessert. *414 N. Newport Blvd., tel. 714/645–6700. Reservations advised. Dress: casual. AE, D, DC, MC, V. No Sat. lunch.
Closed Sun. Moderate.*

Marrakesh. In a casbah setting straight out of a Hope-and-
Crosby road movie, diners become part of the scene—you eat
with your fingers while sitting on the floor or lolling on a has-
sock. Chicken b'stilla, rabbit couscous, and skewered pieces of
marinated lamb are the best of the Moroccan dishes. It's fun.
*1100 Pacific Coast Hwy., tel. 714/645–8384. Reservations ad-
vised. Dress: casual. AE, DC, MC, V. No lunch. Moderate.*

Crab Cooker. If you don't mind waiting in line, this shanty of a
place serves fresh fish grilled over mesquite at low-low prices.
The clam chowder and cole slaw are quite good, too. *2200 Newport Blvd., tel. 714/673–0100. No reservations. Dress: casual. No
credit cards. Inexpensive.*

★ **El Torito Grill.** Southwestern cooking incorporating south-of-
the-border specialties is the attraction here. The just-baked
tortillas with a green pepper salsa, the turkey molé enchilada,
and the blue-corn duck tamalitos are good choices. The bar
serves 20 different tequila brands and hand-shaken margaritas. *951 Newport Center Dr., tel. 714/640–2875. Reservations advised. Dress: casual. AE, D, DC, MC, V. Inexpensive.*

Lodging **Four Seasons Hotel.** This hotel lives up to its chain's reputation.
★ Marble and antiques fill the airy lobby; all rooms—decorated
with beiges, peaches, and southwestern tones—have spectacular views, private bars, original art on walls. Weekend golf
packages are available in conjunction with the nearby Pelican
Hill golf course, as well as fitness weekend packages. *690 Newport Center Dr., 92660, tel. 714/759–0808 or 800/332–3442. 285
rooms. Facilities: 2 restaurants, lounge, pool, whirlpool, sauna,
2 lighted tennis courts, health club with steam room and massage service, complimentary mountain bikes, concierge, business center, disabled access. AE, D, DC, MC, V. Very Expensive.*

Hotel Meridien Newport Beach. The eye-catching cantilevered
design is the trademark of this ultramodern hotel in Koll Center. The decor is Southern Californian, with striking pastel accents. Luxuriously appointed rooms have minibars and built-in
hair dryers. This is also the home of Antoine, one of the best
restaurants in Orange County. Special weekend theater and
Pageant of the Masters packages are available. *4500 MacArthur Blvd., 92660, tel. 714/476–2001. 435 rooms. Facilities: 2 restaurants, lounge, pool, tennis courts, health club with Jacuzzi,
complimentary bicycles, concierge. AE, D, DC, MC, V. Very Expensive.*

Hyatt Newporter Resort. The garden setting of this recently
redecorated and expanded resort imparts a get-away-from-it-
all feeling that's quite unexpected, given the hotel's proximity
to Newport Center and Fashion Island. There's plenty here to
lure you outdoors: colorfully landscaped grounds, Upper Newport Bay, and tennis at John Wayne Tennis Club next door.
Rooms, designed to take advantage of the garden setting, all
have private patios or balconies. Four pricey villas have private

swimming pools. *1107 Jamboree Rd., 92660, tel. 714/644–1700. 390 rooms, 20 suites. Facilities: 2 restaurants, 2 lounges, 3 pools, outdoor Jacuzzi, entertainment, 9-hole golf course, jogging paths, exercise room, concierge. AE, DC, MC, V. Very Expensive.*

Newport Beach Marriott Hotel and Tennis Club. Arriving guests' first view of the hotel's interior is the distinctive fountain surrounded by a high, plant-filled atrium. Rooms in two towers have balconies or patios, overlook lush gardens; many have a stunning Pacific view. The hotel is across the street from Fashion Island shopping center. *900 Newport Center Dr., 92660, tel. 714/640–4000 or 800/228–9290. 560 rooms, 15 suites. Facilities: 2 restaurants, 2 lounges, 2 pools, 2 outdoor Jacuzzis, health club, sauna, 8 lighted tennis courts, Jacuzzi, adjacent golf course, business center, concierge. AE, D, DC, MC, V. Expensive.*

Sheraton Newport Beach. Bamboo trees and palms decorate the lobby in this Southern California beach-style hotel. Vibrant teals, mauves, and peaches make up the color scheme. Complimentary morning paper, buffet breakfast, and cocktail parties are offered daily. *4545 MacArthur Blvd., 92660, tel. 714/833–0570. 338 rooms. Facilities: 3 restaurants, lounge, entertainment, pool, Jacuzzi, 2 tennis courts. AE, D, DC, MC, V. Expensive.*

Orange
Dining

The Hobbit. This is the place for a feast, if you make reservations two to three months in advance. The six- to eight- course French-Continental meal starts in the wine cellar at 7:30 and ends about three hours later. *2932 E. Chapman Ave., tel. 714/997–1972. Reservations required far in advance. Jacket and tie required. MC, V. One seating only. Closed Mon. Very Expensive.*

La Brasserie. It doesn't *look* like a typical brasserie, but the varied French cuisine befits the name over the door. One dining room in the multi-level house is done as an attractive, cozy library. There's also an inviting bar-lounge. *202 S. Main St., tel. 714/978–6161. Reservations advised. Dress: casual. AE, DC, MC, V. No Sat. lunch. Closed Sun. Moderate.*

Lodging

Doubletree Inn. This hotel has a dramatic lobby of marble and granite and silent waterfalls cascading down the walls. The recently renovated guest rooms are large and come equipped with a small conference table. Located near the shopping center called The City, UCI Medical Center, and Anaheim Stadium. Discount rates are available for summer weekends. *100 The City Dr., 92668, tel. 714/634–4500 or 800/222–8733. 435 rooms, 19 suites. Facilities: 2 restaurants, lounge, pool, spa, 2 tennis courts, fitness facilities, concierge floor, disabled access. AE, D, DC, MC, V. Expensive–Very Expensive.*

San Clemente
Dining

Etienne's. Smack-dab in the center of town, this restaurant is housed in a white stucco historical landmark. There is outdoor seating on a terra-cotta patio with fountains. Indoors, the decor is French château. Only the freshest fish is served; chateaubriand, frogs' legs, and other French favorites are on the menu, along with flaming desserts. *215 S. El Camino Real, tel. 714/492–7263. Reservations advised. Jacket advised. AE, D, DC, MC, V. No lunch. Closed Sun. Expensive.*

Lodging

San Clemente Inn. This time-share condo resort is located in the secluded southern part of San Clemente, adjacent to Calafia State Beach. Studio and one-bedroom units (accommodating up to six) are equipped with kitchens, and bars are available. *2600 Avenida del Presidente, 92672, tel. 714/492–6103.*

95 units. Facilities: restaurant, pool, Jacuzzi, sauna, tennis, exercise equipment, playground, barbecue pits. MC, V. Expensive.
Ramada Inn San Clemente. This Mission-style hotel is beautifully set on a lush hillside. The lobby has a dramatic vaulted ceiling. Rooms have private balconies or patios; many also have refrigerators. *35 Calle de Industrias, 92672, tel. 714/498–8800 or 800/272–6232. 110 rooms. Facilities: restaurant, lounge, pool, disabled access. AE, D, DC, MC, V. Moderate.*

San Juan Capistrano
Dining

El Adobe. President Nixon memorabilia fills the walls in this Early American–style eatery serving Mexican-American food. Mariachi bands play Wednesday–Sunday. *31891 Camino Capistrano, tel. 714/830–8620. Weekend reservations advised. Dress: casual. AE, D, MC, V. Moderate.*

L'Hirondelle. There are only 12 tables at this charming French inn. Duckling is the specialty and is prepared three different ways. *31631 Camino Capistrano, tel. 714/661–0425. Reservations required. MC, V. No Sun. dinner, no lunch Tues.–Sat. Closed Mon. Moderate.*

Santa Ana
Dining

Saddleback Inn. The decor here harks back to Orange County's hacienda days, blending Old Spain and California Mission styles. Slow-cooked barbecued roast beef is the house specialty; filet of sole amandine, barbecued baked chicken, and filet mignon with bordelaise sauce are other choices. *1660 E. 1st St., tel. 714/835–3311. No reservations. Dress: casual. AE, D, MC, V. Inexpensive–Moderate.*

The Arts and Nightlife

The Arts

The **Orange County Performing Arts Center** (600 Town Center Dr., tel. 714/556–2787), in Costa Mesa, is the hub of the arts circle, hosting a variety of touring companies year-round. Groups that regularly schedule performances here include New York City Opera, American Ballet Theater, Los Angeles Philharmonic Orchestra, as well as touring companies of popular musicals such as *Les Misérables*. Information about current offerings can be found in the Calendar section of the *Los Angeles Times*.

Concerts The **Irvine Meadows Amphitheater** (8808 Irvine Center Dr., tel. 714/855–4515) is a 15,000-seat open-air venue offering a variety of musical events from May through October.

The **Pacific Amphitheater** (Orange County Fairgrounds, Costa Mesa, tel. 714/740–2000) offers musical entertainment and stages plays from April through October.

Theater **South Coast Repertory Theater** (655 Town Center Dr., tel. 714/957–4033), near the Orange County Performing Arts Center in Costa Mesa, is an acclaimed regional theater complex with two stages presenting both traditional and innovative new works. A resident group of actors forms the nucleus for this facility's innovative productions.

La Mirada Theater for the Performing Arts (14900 La Mirada Blvd., tel. 714/994–6150) presents a wide selection of Broadway shows, concerts, and film series.

Nightlife

Bars   **Metropolis** (4255 Campus Dr., Irvine, tel. 714/725–0300) is the hottest nightclub ticket in Orange County, with iron-and-gilt decor, pool tables, a sushi bar, and nightly entertainment; admission is $5. **The Cannery** (3010 Layfayette Ave., tel. 714/675–5757) is a crowded Newport Beach bar that offers live entertainment. The **Studio Cafe** (100 Main St., Balboa Peninsula, tel. 714/675–7760) presents jazz musicians every night. **La Vie en Rose** (240 S. State College Blvd., Brea, tel. 714/529–8333), a sedate French restaurant, has a quiet bar with entertainment and dancing. **Randall's** (3 Hutton Centre, Santa Ana, tel. 714/556–7700) presents jazz groups nightly.

In Laguna Beach, the **Sandpiper** (1183 S. Pacific Coast Hwy., tel. 714/494–4694) is a tiny dancing joint that attracts an eclectic crowd. And Laguna's **White House** (340 S. Pacific Coast Hwy., tel. 714/494–8088) has nightly entertainment that runs the gamut from rock to motown, reggae to pop.

Comedy   **Irvine Improv** (4255 Campus Dr., Irvine, tel. 714/854–5455) and the **Brea Improv** (945 Birch St., Brea, tel. 714/529–7878) present up- and-coming and well-known comedians nightly.

Country   **Cowboy Boogie Co.** (1721 S. Manchester, Anaheim, tel. 714/956–1410) offers live country music Tuesday through Sunday night. The complex comprises three dance floors and four bars.

Dinner Theaters   Several night spots in Orange County serve up entertainment with dinner. **Tibbie's Music Hall** (4647 McArthur Blvd., Newport Beach, tel. 714/252–0834) offers comedy shows along with prime rib, fish, or chicken.

Elizabeth Howard's Curtain Call Theater (690 El Camino Real, Tustin, tel. 714/838–1540) presents a regular schedule of Broadway musicals.

Medieval Times Dinner and Tournament (7662 Beach Blvd., Buena Park, tel. 714/521–4740 or 800/899–6600) takes guests back to the days of knights and ladies. Knights on horseback compete in medieval games, sword fighting, and jousting. Dinner, all of which is eaten with your hands, includes appetizers, whole roasted chicken or spareribs, soup, pastry, and beverages such as mead.

Wild Bill's Wild West Extravaganza (7600 Beach Blvd., Buena Park, tel. 714/522–6414) is a two-hour action-packed Old West show featuring foot-stomping musical numbers, cowboys, Indians, dancing girls, specialty acts, and audience participation in sing-alongs.

Nightclubs   **Crackers** (Anaheim Plaza Hotel, 1700 S. Harbor Blvd., Anaheim, tel. 714/535–4386), is a zany restaurant and nightclub where waiters and waitresses double as on-stage musical performers. There's live entertainment seven days a week, which ranges from music of the '40s to the '90s. It's a casual place, but don't come in your beachwear.

Bill Medley's Music City (18774 Brookhurst St., Fountain Valley, tel. 714/963–2366) is a 1950s–1970s–style diner-nightclub offering dancing to classic rock. Dress casual but not for the beach.

11 Palm Springs

What do you get when you start with dramatic scenery, add endless sunshine, mix in deluxe resorts, and spice things up with a liberal dash of celebrities? Palm Springs desert resorts, a magnet for socialites, sun worshipers, and star gazers.

The fashionable resort community, once limited to the village of Palm Springs, has expanded into other Coachella Valley towns in recent years. Now you'll find resorts stretching all the way from the foot of 10,831-foot Mt. San Jacinto in the north to once-sleepy Indio in the south. Streets are named for the celebrities who live here in unmarked gated estates—Frank Sinatra, Dinah Shore, Betty Ford, Bob Hope. Although the social, sports, shopping, and entertainment scenes now center around Palm Desert, you'll also find resorts and attractions in Indian Wells, Rancho Mirage, Desert Hot Springs, La Quinta, Cathedral City, and Indio.

During the "season" (January–April) resident celebrities and wealthy winter visitors present a nearly nightly round of parties and balls in conjunction with an endless round of world-class golf and tennis tournaments to support their favorite charities. They play during the day, too. There are more than 80 golf courses in a 20-mile radius, more than 600 tennis courts, 35 miles of bicycle trails, horseback riding, 10,000 or so swimming pools, and even cross-country skiing atop Mt. San Jacinto. Shopping is a serious pursuit here with clutches of chic boutiques to be found along main streets and fashionable department stores such as Saks Fifth Avenue and I. Magnin in enclosed malls. The McCallum Theater in Palm Desert even presents top-name entertainment.

This is the spot for stargazing. Bob Hope, Frank Sinatra, Gerald and Betty Ford, and other luminaries can be spotted at charity events and restaurants and on the golf course. Carrie Fisher and Bette Midler have done stints at the Palms spa, and Donna Mills, Goldie Hawn, and Kurt Russell have been poolside stars at the Ingleside Inn. Year-round resident Dinah Shore can be seen at the Westin Mission Hills, finalizing details for her golf tournament, and Michael Jackson and Sylvester Stallone escape the crowds at La Quinta resort.

The desert became a Hollywood hideout in the 1920s, when La Quinta Hotel opened the Coachella Valley's first golf course. But it took a pair of tennis-player actors to put Palm Springs on the map in the 1930s; Charlie Farrell and Ralph Bellamy bought 200 acres of land for $30 an acre and opened the Palm Springs Racquet Club, which soon listed Ginger Rogers, Humphrey Bogart, and Clark Gable among its members. Today you can take a tour that points out the homes of celebrities of yesterday and today.

Developers have been careful not to overshadow the stunning beauty of the desert setting: City buildings are restricted to a height of 30 feet; flashing, moving, and neon signs are restricted, preserving an intimate village feeling; and 50% of the land consists of open spaces with palm trees and desert vegetation.

This beauty is particularly evident in the canyons surrounding Palm Springs. Lush Tahquitz Canyon, one of the five canyons that line the San Jacinto Mountains, was the setting for Shangri-La in an early movie version of *Lost Horizon*. The original inhabitants of these rock canyons were the Cahuilla Indians.

Their descendants came to be known as Agua Caliente—"hot water"—Indians, named after the hot mineral springs that flowed through their reservation. The Agua Caliente still own about 32,000 acres of Palm Springs desert, 6,700 of which lie within the city limits of Palm Springs. The Indians, while dedicated to preserving their historic homeland, will doubtless account for the next "boom" in the desert. Nearby tribes have already opened card and bingo parlors here; Agua Caliente have voted to construct a casino on land they own in town.

One brief comment on the weather: Although daytime temperatures average a pleasantly warm 88°F, you are still in the desert. And that means during the middle of the day in the summer it is going to be very hot—sometimes uncomfortably so. You'll be told that "it is a dry heat." And it is. But it is still desert hot: Plan activities in the morning and late afternoon, and wear a hat and plenty of sunscreen if you're out for a midday stroll. Anytime of the year be sure to drink plenty of water to prevent dehydration.

Essential Information

Important Addresses and Numbers

Tourist Information
Desert Resorts Bureau (tel. 619/770–9000) is at 69-930 Highway 111, Suite 201, Rancho Mirage, 92270.
Palm Springs Visitor Information Center (2781 N. Palm Canyon Dr., Palm Springs, 92262, tel. 800/347–7746) provides tourist information.

Emergencies
Dial 911 for police, fire, and ambulance in an emergency.

Doctors
Desert Hospital (tel. 619/323–6511).

Dentists
Dental emergency service is available from **R. Turnage, D.D.S.** (tel. 619/327–8448) 24 hours each day.

Arriving and Departing

By Plane
Major airlines serving **Palm Springs Regional Airport** include Alaska Airlines, American Airlines, American Eagle, America West, Delta, Skywest/Delta Connection, United Airlines, United Express, and USAir Express. The airport is about 2 miles east of the city's main downtown intersection; most hotels provide service to and from the airport. **Bermuda Dunes Airport** in Palm Desert is served by Pacific Coast Airlines (tel. 800/426–5400).

By Train
Amtrak (tel. 800/USA–RAIL) passenger trains serve the Indio area, 20 miles east of Palm Springs. From Indio, Greyhound/Trailways bus service is available to Palm Springs.

By Bus
Greyhound/Trailways Bus Lines stop in Palm Springs (311 N. Indian Canyon Dr., tel. 619/325–2053).

By Car
Palm Springs is about a two-hour drive east of Los Angeles and a three-hour drive northeast of San Diego. Highway 111 brings you right onto Palm Canyon Drive, the main thoroughfare in Palm Springs and connecting route to other desert communities. From Los Angeles take the San Bernardino Freeway (I–10E) to Highway 111. From San Diego, I–15N connects with the Pomona Freeway (I–60E), leading to the San Bernardino

Freeway (I–10E). If you're coming from the Riverside area, you might want to try the scenic Palms-to-Pines Highway (Hwy. 74). This 130-mile route begins in Hemet and connects directly with Highway 111; the trek from snowcapped peaks to open desert valley is breathtaking.

Getting Around

By Car The desert resort communities occupy about a 20-mile stretch between I–10 in the east and Palm Canyon Drive in the west. Although some areas such as Palm Canyon Drive in Palm Springs and El Paseo are walkable, having a car is the best way to get around.

By Bus **SunBus** serves the entire Coachella Valley from Desert Hot Springs to Coachella with regular routes. Call 619/343–3451 for route and schedule information. **Palm Desert/Indian Wells Resort Express Shuttle** (tel. 619/346–6111) has regular free service between major hotels and shopping centers Tuesday–Saturday.

By Taxi **Desert Cab** (tel. 619/325–2868) and **Desert City** (tel. 619/329–3334) serve the area.

Guided Tours

Orientation Tours **Gray Line Tours** (tel. 619/325–0974) offers several good general bus tours, from the hour-long Palm Springs Special highlight tour to the tour through Palm Springs, Cathedral City, Rancho Mirage, and Palm Desert. Prices are $12 for adults, $9 for children. Most departures are in the morning; call for reservations.

Special-Interest Tours In Palm Springs, special-interest tours mean one thing: celebrity homes. **Gray Line** and **Palm Springs Celebrity Tours** (tel. 619/325–2682) both cover this turf well. Prices range from $10 to $14 for adults. **Desert Off Road Adventures** (tel. 619/324–3378) takes to the wilds with jeep tours of Indian canyons, off-road in the Santa Rosa Mountains and into a mystery canyon. For a different perspective of the desert, try floating over the valley in a balloon. Trip lengths and prices vary; call **Fantasy Balloon Flights** (tel. 619/568–0997), **Sunrise Balloons** (tel. 800/548–9912) for information. Customized helicopter tours are also available from Sunrise Balloons. **Covered Wagon Tours** (tel. 619/347–2161) will take you on an old-time two-hour exploration of the desert with a cookout at the end of the journey.

Exploring Palm Springs

Numbers in the margin correspond to points of interest on the Palm Springs map.

Physically, Palm Springs proper is easy to understand. Palm Canyon Drive runs north–south through the heart of downtown; the intersection with Tahquitz Canyon Way is pretty much the center of the main drag. Heading south, Palm Canyon Drive splits: South Palm Canyon Drive leads you to the Indian Canyons and East Palm Canyon becomes Highway 11, taking you through the growing satellite resort areas of Cathedral City, Rancho Mirage, Palm Desert, La Quinta, and Indio. The Aerial Tramway is at the northern limits of Palm Springs.

Joshua Tree National Monument is about an hour's drive north.

Most Palm Springs desert resort attractions can be seen in anywhere from an hour or two to an entire day, depending upon your interests. Do you want to take the tram up Mt. San Jacinto, see the view, and come right back down, or spend the day hiking? Would you rather linger for a picnic lunch in one of the Indian Canyons, or double back for a snack and people-watching at sidewalk café along El Paseo? Your best bet is to think of the list of sights and activities as if it were an à la carte menu and pick and choose according to your appetite. To help you organize your outings, we will start in the north and work our way south and southeast. A separate tour of Joshua Tree follows.

Palm Springs and Environs

❶ Take the **Palm Springs Aerial Tramway** to get a stunning overview of the desert. The 2½-mile ascent brings you to an elevation of 8,516 feet in less than 20 minutes. On clear days, which are common, the view stretches some 75 miles from the peak of Mt. San Gorgonio to the north and the Salton Sea in the southeast. At the top you'll find several diversions. Mountain Station has an Alpine buffet restaurant, cocktail lounge, apparel and gift shops, picnic facilities. Mt. San Jacinto State Park offers 54 miles of hiking trails and camping and picnic areas; during winter the Nordic Ski Center has cross-country ski equipment for rent. *Tram cars depart at least every 30 min from 10 AM weekdays and 8 AM weekends. Cost: $14.95 adults, $9.95 children 3–12. Closed for 2–4 wks after Labor Day for maintenance. Call 619/325–1391 for information; 619/325–4227 for ski and weather conditions.*

Although not the fashionable shopping street it once was, **Palm Canyon Drive** offers some pleasant diversions for those wishing to take a stroll. Tucked in among the T-shirt and yogurt shops is **Desert Fashion Plaza,** an otherwise typical mall containing a pair of icons of the city's glamorous past, Saks Fifth Avenue and Gucci.

❷ Downtown Palm Springs is not without hidden historical treasures. The **Village Green Heritage Center** illustrates pioneer life in Palm Springs in three museums. McCallum Adobe, dating back to 1885, displays the collections of the Palm Springs Historical Society and McCallum family memorabilia. Miss Cornelia White's House, dating back to 1894, exhibits this pioneer family's memorabilia including an extensive collection of Bibles, clothing, tools, books, paintings, even the first telephone in Palm Springs. Roddy's General Store Museum dates from a later pioneer era, the 1930s and 1940s, and displays signs, packages, and products of the period. *221 and 223 S. Palm Canyon Dr., tel. 619/323–8297. Nominal admission. House open Wed. and Sun. noon–3, Thur.–Sat. 10–4; store open Thur.–Sun 10–4; summer hours flexible.*

❸ If further evidence is needed to prove that the desert is no barren wasteland, there is the dramatic **Palm Springs Desert Museum.** This surprisingly large facility contains galleries devoted to western and Indian art, changing exhibitions, sculpture gardens, plus natural science and history exhibits. It also houses the Annenberg Theater. *101 Museum Dr., just north of*

Palm Springs

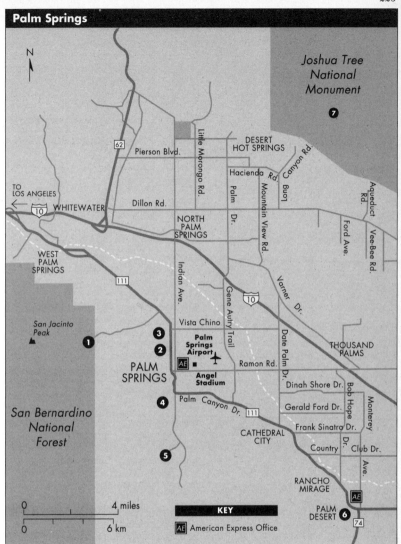

Joshua Tree National Monument

❼

N

62

Pierson Blvd.

DESERT HOT SPRINGS

Little Morongo Rd.

Hacienda Rd.

Palm Dr.

Long Canyon Rd.

Aqueduct Rd.

Vee-Bee Rd.

Ford Ave.

Mountain View Rd.

TO LOS ANGELES

10 WHITEWATER

Dillon Rd.

NORTH PALM SPRINGS

WEST PALM SPRINGS

111

Indian Ave.

Gene Autry Trail

Varner Dr.

10

Date Palm Dr.

THOUSAND PALMS

San Jacinto Peak ▲

❶

❸

Vista Chino

Palm Springs Airport

AE ■

❷

PALM SPRINGS

Ramon Rd.

Angel Stadium

Dinah Shore Dr.

❹

Palm Canyon Dr.

111

Gerald Ford Dr.

Bob Hope Dr.

Monterey

San Bernardino National Forest

❺

CATHEDRAL CITY

Frank Sinatra Dr.

Country Club Dr.

Dr.

Ave.

RANCHO MIRAGE

AE

| 0 | | 4 miles |
| 0 | | 6 km |

PALM DESERT ❻

74

KEY

AE American Express Office

Tahquitz Way, on south side of Desert Fashion Plaza, tel. 619/325–7186. Admission: $4 adults, $2 children under 17; free 1st Tues. of month. Open late Sept.–May, Tues.–Fri. 10–4, weekends 10–5.

❹ A short drive or distinctly long walk farther south on Palm Canyon is the **Moorten Botanical Garden.** More than 2,000 plant varieties cover the 4-acre site in settings that simulate the plants' original environments. Indian artifacts and rock, crystal, and wood forms are exhibited. *1701 S. Palm Canyon Dr., tel. 619/327–6555. Admission: $1.50 adults, 50¢ children. Open Mon.–Sat. 9–4:30, Sun. 10–4.*

❺ The **Indian Canyons,** 5 miles south of downtown Palm Springs, are the ancestral home of the Agua Caliente Band of Indians. The Indians selected these canyons for their lush oases, abundant water and wildlife. Even now visitors can see remnants of this life: rock art, house pits and foundations, irrigation ditches, bedrock mortars, pictographs, and stone houses and shelters built atop high cliff walls. Four canyons are open to visitors: Palm Canyon, noted for its lush stand of Washingtonia palms, the largest such stand in the world; Tahquitz, noted for waterfalls and pools; Murray, home of Peninsula big horn sheep and a herd of wild ponies; and Andreas, where a stand of fan palms contrasts with sharp rock formations. A Trading Post in Palm Canyon has hiking maps, refreshments, Indian art, jewelry, and weavings. *End of S. Palm Canyon Dr., tel. 619/325–5673. Admission: $3.50 adults, $1 children. Open Sept.–June daily 8–5.*

Elegant resorts, fine dining, world-class golf and tennis tournaments, and celebrity residents come together in **Rancho Mirage.** The city is home to the famed Eisenhower Medical Center and Betty Ford Center, as well as to such celebrities as Walter Annenberg, Gerald and Betty Ford, and Frank Sinatra. Bighorn sheep can frequently be sighted in a hillside preserve surrounding the Ritz-Carlton Hotel.

Some of the best desert people-watching, shopping, and dining can be found along trendy **El Paseo,** a 2-mile avenue just west of Highway 111 in Palm Desert. The flower-decked avenue is lined with apparel shops, specialty stores, art galleries, and restaurants.

❻ Bighorn sheep, coyotes, eagles, and other desert wildlife roam in naturalistic settings at the **Living Desert Reserve,** in Palm Desert. There is a 6-mile nature walk, a walk through an aviary, a coyote grotto, a desert reptile exhibit, and regularly scheduled animal shows. Eagle Canyon, a recently opened exhibit, is a huge wildlife-breeding center in a remote landscaped canyon. This is a particularly enjoyable learning experience for children. *47-900 Portola Ave., less than 2 mi south of Hwy. 111, tel. 619/346–5694. Admission: $6 adults, $3 children 3–15. Open daily 9–5, closed mid-June–Aug.*

Time Out The world-famous **Palm Springs Spa Hotel and Mineral Springs,** on an ancient hot spring, was recently purchased by the Agua Caliente Indians, who are renovating it. You can sample the spa experience for an hour or longer; visit the inhalation room with its soothing menthol vapors, the steam room, and the natural hot mineral spring and cooling room. Facials and massages are also available. *100 N. Indian Canyon Dr., Palm*

Springs, tel. 619/325–1461. Rates start at $25, facials $63.25.
Open daily 8:30–6.

Joshua Tree National Monument

7 Joshua Tree National Monument is about a one-hour drive
from Palm Springs, whether you take I–10 north to Highway
62, which swings east to the Oasis Visitor Center on the park's
northern edge, or I–10 south to the Cottonwood Visitor Center.
The northern part of the park is in the Mojave (or high) Desert
and has the Joshua trees. The southern part is Colorado (or
low) Desert; in spring this is one of the desert's best wildflower
viewing areas, covered with carpets of white, yellow, purple,
and red flowers stretching as far as the eye can see on the hillsides east of I–10. It's possible to take a loop drive in a single
long day; enter by way of the Oasis Visitor Center or at Cottonwood and follow the road from either across the park to the
other entrance. Pack a picnic and water, as facilities are limited
in the area.

On the northern route, you may want to consider stopping at
the **Big Morongo Wildlife Reserve Covington Park.** Once an Indian village, then a cattle ranch, and now a regional park, the
reserve is a serene natural oasis supporting a wide variety of
plants, birds, and animals. There is a shaded meadow for picnics and choice hiking trails. *From I–10 or Indian Ave., take
Hwy. 62 east to East Dr., tel. 619/363–7190. Admission free. Open
Wed.–Sun. 7:30–sunset.*

Joshua Tree is immense, complex, and ruggedly beautiful. Its
mountains of jagged rock, lush oases shaded by tall, elegant
fan palms, and natural cactus gardens mark the meeting place
of the Mojave and Colorado deserts. This is prime hiking, rock
climbing, and exploring country, where you can expect to see
such wildlife as coyotes and desert pack rats, and exotic plants
such as the red-tipped ocotillo, sharp barbed cholla cactus,
smoke trees, creamy white yucca. Extensive stands of Joshua
trees give the park its name. The trees were named by early
white settlers who felt their unusual forms resembled the bib-
lical Joshua raising his arms toward heaven. The **Oasis Visitor
Center** is probably the best place to start. The center has an
excellent selection of free and low-cost brochures, books, post-
ers, and maps as well as several educational exhibits. Rangers
are on hand to answer questions and offer advice. *Hwy. 62 to
town of Twentynine Palms, follow signs short distance south to
Visitor Center. Admission: $5 per car.*

Near the Visitor Center is the **Oasis of Mara.** Inhabited first
by Indians and later by prospectors and homesteaders, the
oasis now provides a home for birds, small mammals, and other
wildlife. Once inside the park, you will find nine campgrounds
with tables, fireplaces, and primitive rest rooms and several
picnic areas for day use. Sights range from the **Hidden Valley,**
a legendary cattle rustlers' hideout reached by a trail winding
through massive boulders; and the **Lost Horse Mine,** a remnant
of the gold-mining days; to **Keys View,** an outstanding scenic
point commanding a superb sweep of valley, mountain, and desert. Sunrise and sunset are magic times to be here, when the
light throws rocks and trees into high relief before (or after)
bathing the hills in brilliant shades of red, orange, and gold.

Palm Springs for Free

Big Morongo Wildlife Reserve Covington Park (*see above*) has walking trails and picnic areas.

Several date gardens are open to the public for touring. **Shields Date Gardens** (74-774 Hwy. 111, Palm Desert, tel. 619/347–0996) presents a continuous slide program on the history of the date.

Several communities hold **street fairs** on a regular basis with vendors offering everything from antiques and contemporary crafts to clothing, jewelry and produce. College of the Desert Alumni Association sponsors one of the biggest of these Saturday and Sunday mornings at its campus at Fred Waring Drive and Monterey Ave.

Off the Beaten Track

Dog-sled races in Palm Springs? Why not? Snow conditions permitting, the **Moosehead Championship Sled Dog Races** are held in January atop Mt. San Jacinto. Take the Aerial Tramway up. Call 619/325–1449 for information.

The **Eldorado Polo Club** (50-950 Madison Blvd., Indio, tel. 619/342–2223), known as the "Winter Polo Capital of the West," is home of world-class polo events. You can pack a picnic and watch practice matches free during the week; there's a $6 per person charge on weekends.

Hadley's Fruit Orchards (I-10 at Apache Trail, Cabazon, tel. 619/849–5255) contains a vast selection of dried California fruit, plus nuts, date shakes, wines. Taste samples before you buy.

Shopping

The Palm Springs area is full of toney boutiques and lively art galleries. The resort community also has several large air-conditioned indoor malls with major department stores and chic shops. El Paseo in nearby Palm Desert is the desert's fanciest shopping mecca, with its own collection of upscale and elegant galleries and shops. Most stores are open Monday–Saturday 10–5 or 6, and a fair number are open Sunday, typically noon–5.

Shopping Districts **Palm Canyon Drive** is Palm Springs's main shopping destination, although many of the major stores have moved to Palm Desert. What began as a dusty two-way dirt road is now a one-way, three-lane thoroughfare with parking on both sides. Its shopping core extends from Alejo Road on the north to Ramon Road on the south. Anchoring the center of the drive is the **Desert Fashion Plaza,** now a more functional than fashionable mall, which features **Saks Fifth Avenue, Gucci,** and **Sabina Children's Fashions.**

El Paseo (73-111 El Paseo, tel. 619/340–1414) is the trendiest shopping spot in the desert. French and Italian fashion boutiques, shoe salons, jewelry designers, children's boutiques, nearly 30 galleries, and restaurants are clustered around fountains and courtyards along this 2-mile Mediterranean-style avenue. Specialty shops include **Polo/Ralph Lauren** (73-111 El Paseo, tel. 619/340–1414), featuring Lauren's classic fashions and accessories for men and women, and **Cabale Cachet** (73-151

El Paseo, tel. 619/346–5805), a collection of European haute couture.

The **Palm Desert Town Center** (Hwy. 111 at Monterey Ave., tel. 619/346–2121) is an enclosed mall anchored by major department stores that include **Bullocks, I. Magnin, J. C. Penney,** and **The May Co.** There are 150 specialty shops, including **Avanti, Caché,** and **Miller Stockman,** as well as seven movie theaters, an Ice Capades Chalet, and fast-food outlets.

Rancho las Palmas (Highway 111 and Bob Hope Drive, Rancho Mirage) is an open-air center containing 15 home-furnishings stores, interior design studios, and restaurants.

Specialty Shops Although Palm Springs is known for glamour and high prices,
Discount the city does offer bargains if you know where to look. Several outlets can be found in the **Loehmann's Plaza** (2500 N. Palm Canyon Dr.), including **Mikasa Factory Store** (tel. 619/778–1080), **Dansk** (tel. 619/320–3304), and **Loehmann's** (tel. 619/322–0388). **Desert Hills Factory Stores** (48650 Seminole Rd., Cabazon, tel. 619/849–6641) is an outlet center with about 50 name-brand fashion shops selling at a discount.

Golf Equipment **John Riley Golf** (72-047 Hwy. 111, Rancho Mirage, tel. 619/341–6994) offers personally fitted golf clubs.
Nevada Bob's Discount Golf & Tennis (4721 E. Palm Canyon Dr., Palm Springs, tel. 619/324–0196) offers a large selection of golf and tennis equipment, clothing, and accessories.

Participant Sports

The "Desert Guide" from *Palm Springs Life* magazine, available at most hotels and the Convention and Visitors Bureau, contains a listing called "Courts and Courses." The Convention and Visitors Bureau also publishes a handy "Desert Golf Guide" describing courses open to the public, private/reciprocal courses and annual tournaments; a map will help with locations.

Bicycling There are more than 35 miles of bike trails, with six mapped-out city tours. Trail maps are available at the **Palm Springs Recreation Department** (401 S. Pavilion, tel. 619/323–8276) and bike-rental shops. You can rent a bike at **Palm Springs Cyclery** (611 S. Palm Canyon Dr., Palm Springs, tel. 619/325–9319).

Golf Palm Springs is known as the "Winter Golf Capital of the World." The area has more than 80 golf courses, a number of which are open to the public. Among these are the **Palm Springs Municipal Golf Course** (1885 Golf Club Dr., tel. 619/328–1005), **Fairchilds Bel-Aire Greens Country Club** (1001 S. El Cielo Rd., Palm Springs, tel. 619/327–0332), and **Field Golf Club** (19300 Palm Dr., North Palm Springs, tel. 619/251–5366), a Robert Trent Jones course nominated as one of the best new courses in the country. Don't be surprised to spot well-known politicians and Hollywood stars on the greens.

Hiking Nature trails abound in the **Indian Canyons, Mt. San Jacinto State Park and Wilderness,** and **Living Desert Reserve** (*see* Exploring, above). The Palm Springs Recreation Department (*see* above) has trail maps for $2.

Physical Fitness The **Clark Hatch Physical Fitness Center** (Hyatt Regency Suites Hotel, 285 N. Palm Canyon Dr., tel. 619/322–2778) is the latest in a worldwide chain of Hatch health clubs. The facilities are high-quality and low-key. Fees are $10 daily, $65 monthly.

Tennis Of the 600 or so tennis courts in the area, the following are open to the public: the **Palm Springs Tennis Center** (1300 Baristo Rd., tel. 619/320–0020), with nine lighted courts; **Ruth Hardy Park** (Tamarisk and Caballeros, no tel.), with eight lighted courts and no court fee; and **Demuth Park** (4375 Mesquite Ave., tel. 619/325–8265), with four lighted courts.

Spectator Sports

Golf More than 100 golf tournaments are presented in Palm Springs; the two most popular are the **Bob Hope Desert Classic** (Jan.) and the **Dinah Shore LPGA Championship** (Mar. or Apr.). Call the Convention and Visitors Bureau (*see* above) for exact dates and places.

Tennis The *Newsweek* **Champions Cup tournament** (Feb. or Mar.), held at Hyatt Grand Champions Resort in Indian Wells, attracts the likes of Boris Becker and Yannick Noah. For tickets, tel. 619/341–2757.

Dining and Lodging

Dining So many L.A. residents have second homes or condos "down in the Springs" that local restaurateurs try to outdo themselves to match the Big City's standards—and more and more are succeeding. Most of the restaurants listed below are on or near Highway 111 running from Palm Springs to Palm Desert.

Highly recommended restaurants are indicated by a star ★.

Category	Cost*
Very Expensive	over $50
Expensive	$30–$50
Moderate	$20–$30
Inexpensive	under $20

*per person, excluding 8.25% tax, service, and drinks

Lodging One of the reasons the Palm Springs desert resorts attract so many celebrities, entertainment-industry honchos, and other notables is its stock of luxurious hotels. There is a full array of resorts, inns, clubs, spas, lodges, and condos, from small and private to big and bustling. Room rates cover an enormous range—from $40 to $1,600 a night—and also vary widely from summer to winter season. It is not unusual for a hotel to drop its rates from 50% to 60% during the summer (June through early Sept.). For a growing number of off-season travelers, the chance to stay in a $180 room for $60 is an offer they just can't refuse. If you're seeking budget or moderate accommodations, you're more likely to find them in Palm Springs than in the newer resort areas. Also discounts are sometimes given for extended stays.

Don't even think of visiting here during winter and spring holiday seasons without advance reservations. The **Palm Springs Chamber of Commerce** (tel. 619/325–1577), **Desert Resorts Bureau** (tel. 619/770–9000), and **Palm Springs Tourism** (tel. 800/347–7746) can help you with hotel reservations and information. For a more comprehensive hotel guide complete with prices, pick up a copy of the Convention and Visitors Bureau **"Accommodations Guide"** (tel. 800/347–7746).

Highly recommended lodgings are indicated by a star ★.

Category	Cost*
Very Expensive	over $100
Expensive	$75–$100
Moderate	$50–$75
Inexpensive	under $50

*All prices are for 2 people in a double room.

Rentals　Condos, apartments, and even individual houses may be rented by the day, week, month, or for longer periods. Rates start at about $850 a week for a one-bedroom condo, $1,600 for two bedrooms, and $3,500 for three-bedroom house for a month. Contact **The Rental Connection** (Box 8567, Palm Springs 92263, tel. 619/320–7336 or 800/462–7256).

Cathedral City　**The Wilde Goose.** The award-winning restaurant is popular
Dining　with celebrities for its beef and lamb Wellington, and five varieties of duck. A specialty of the house is duck with apricot and triple sec sauce. The food and the service here are dependable. *67-938 Hwy. 111, tel. 619/328–5775. Reservations advised. Dress: casual. AE, D, DC, MC, V. No lunch. Moderate.*
Stuft Pizza. What would any listing be without at least one pizza parlor? This one is popular for its thick, Chicago-style crusts and generous heaps of fresh toppings. *67-555 Hwy. 111, tel. 619/321–2583. No reservations. Dress: casual. MC, V. Inexpensive.*

Lodging　**Doubletree Resort at Desert Princess.** This 345-acre luxury golf resort has attractively decorated rooms and condo units with balconies or terraces, refrigerators; some rooms have views. *67-967 Vista Chino, 92234, tel. 619/322–7000. 289 rooms, 100 condo suites. Facilities: 3 restaurants, lounge with entertainment, golf course, pool, Jacuzzi, 10 tennis courts, health club, and racquetball courts. AE, DC, MC, V. Very Expensive.*

Desert Hot Springs　**Two Bunch Palms.** Reputedly built by Al Capone as an escape
Lodging　from the pressures of gangsterdom in 1920s Chicago, this collection of white-walled villas on 250 acres is still something of a secret hideaway for Hollywood celebrities, who come for its laid-back privacy and state-of-the-art spa. There are one- and two-bedroom villas, plus some condo units with kitchens, living rooms, and private hot tubs. *67-425 Two Bunch Palms Trail, 92240, tel. 619/329–8791 or 800/472–4334. 44 villas. Facilities: restaurant, pool, mineral springs, tennis courts, spa. AE, MC, V. Very Expensive.*

Indian Wells **Sirocco.** This restaurant in the Stouffer Esmeralda Hotel fea-
Dining tures dishes of the Mediterranean shores: a splendid Spanish
★ paella, roast lamb encrusted with herbs and peppercorns, seafood pastas. This is probably the best hotel restaurant in Palm
Springs, both for its food and its gracious, impeccable service.
*44400 Indian Wells La., tel. 619/773–4444. Reservations advised
in winter. Jacket advised. AE, D, DC, MC, V. No lunch. Expensive.*

Lodging **Hyatt Grand Champions Resort.** This stark white resort on 34
acres of natural desert is home to the *Newsweek* Champions
Cup tennis tournament, which is played in the largest stadium
in the West. Nicely appointed rooms are suite-style and are
either split-level, one- or two-bedroom garden villas, or pent-
houses. All have balconies or terraces, living areas, and minibars. Some have fireplaces and private butler service. *44-600
Indian Wells La., 92210, tel. 619/341–1000 or 800/233–1234. 336
units. Facilities: 3 restaurants, lounge, 4 pools, Jacuzzis, 12 tennis courts, 2 golf courses, putting green, driving range, pro shop,
health club with sauna, Camp Hyatt. AE, DC, MC, V. Very Expensive.*
Stouffer Esmeralda Resort. The centerpiece of this luxurious
Mediterranean-style resort is an eight-story atrium lobby with
controlled fountain, surrounded by a dual grand staircase,
which flows through a rivulet in the lobby floor to cascading
pools and outside to lakes surrounding the property. Spacious,
well-appointed guest rooms are decorated in light wood with
green and blue accents; they have sitting areas, balconies, refreshment centers, two TV sets, and travertine-marble vani-
ties in bathrooms. One pool has a sandy beach. Golf and tennis
instruction are available. *44-400 Indian Wells La., 92210-9971,
tel. 619/773–4444 or 800/552–4386. 560 rooms, 44 suites. Facilities: 3 restaurants, lounge with entertainment, 3 pools, 2 outdoor
Jacuzzis, 2 golf courses, 7 tennis courts, health club, shops, gallery. AE, DC, MC, V. Very Expensive.*

La Quinta **Dolly Cunard's.** This restaurant in a converted French-style
Dining villa features a Franco-Italian menu. The warm atmosphere
★ and inventive cuisine, such as charred chili with four cheeses,
grilled duck breast with mangoes and raspberries, and fresh
peach in ravioli in a lemon and shallot sauce, have made it the
area's biggest hit. *73-045 Calle Cadiz, tel. 619/564–4443. Reservations advised. Jacket and tie required. AE, MC, V. No lunch.
Closed June–Sept. Expensive.*

Lodging **La Quinta Hotel Golf and Tennis Resort.** Opened in 1926, this
★ lush green oasis with red-roofed, blue-trimmed casitas is the
oldest resort in the desert. Rooms are in historic adobe casitas
separated by broad expanses of lawn and in newer, two-story
units surrounding individual swimming pools and brilliant gardens. Furnishings are simple; there are fireplaces, robes,
stocked refrigerators, and fruit-laden orange trees right outside the door. The atmosphere is discreet and sparely luxurious, and a premium is placed on privacy, which accounts for La
Quinta's continuing lure for the brightest Hollywood stars.
Frank Capra, for example, lived here for many years, and it's
said that Greta Garbo roamed the grounds bumming cigarettes
from guests. Contemporary stars such as Michael Jackson,
Clint Eastwood, and Natalie Cole still seek tranquility here.
*49-499 Eisenhower Dr., 92253, tel. 619/564–4111 or 800/854–1271.
640 rooms, including 22 suites. Facilities: 5 restaurants, lounge*

with entertainment, wine-tasting bar, 25 swimming pools, 35 outdoor Jacuzzis, 30 tennis courts, golf, beauty salon, children's program, shops, holiday events. AE, D, DC, MC, V. Very Expensive.

Palm Desert
Dining

Mama Gina's. Generally considered the best Italian restaurant in the Palm Springs area, this attractive, simply furnished trattoria was opened by the son of the original Mama Gina in Florence, Italy. There is an open kitchen where you can watch the chef from Tuscany prepare such specialties as deep-fried artichokes, fettuccine with porcini mushrooms, and prawns with artichoke and zucchini. The soups are robust. *73-705 El Paseo, tel. 619/568–9898. Reservations required. Dress: casual. AE, DC, MC, V. Expensive.*

The Rusty Pelican. A seafood restaurant in the desert? Why not? This restaurant has fresh seafood flown in from both coasts, then serves it up in a nautical atmosphere. The Oyster Bar shucks to order. There's live entertainment and dancing. *72-191 Hwy. 111, tel. 619/346–8065. Dress: casual. Reservations advised. AE, DC, MC, V. No Lunch. Moderate.*

Lodging

Marriott's Desert Springs Resort and Spa. Althouth this spectacular-looking hotel is popular with business groups, it is not a typical meeting facility. The hotel surrounds an indoor stair-stepped waterfall and waterway leading to 23 acres of lake with 3 miles of shoreline including a 12,000-square-foot beach; boats transport guests from one place to another. Rooms have a lake or mountain view, balconies or patios, oversize bathrooms, and minibars. The facility is famed for its full-service European Health Spa. *74855 Country Club Dr., 92260, tel. 619/341–2211. 891 rooms, 51 suites. Facilities: 5 restaurants, 4 lounges, entertainment, 3 pools, Jacuzzis, 21 tennis courts, 2 golf courses, putting green, croquet, lawn bowling, badminton, volleyball, jogging trails, barbecue grills, shops. AE, DC, MC, V. Very Expensive.*

Palm Springs
Dining

Le Vallauris. Formerly a private club, this stylish, rather romantic restaurant's cuisine ranges from classic to nouvelle French. There is a fine wine list. *385 W. Tahquitz-McCallum Way, tel. 619/325–5059. Reservations advised. Jacket advised. Valet parking. AE, MC, V. Expensive.*

Melvyn's Restaurant. "Lifestyles of the Rich and Famous" calls this Old World–style spot "one of the 10 best." It isn't, but the French-Continental cooking is above average. Snugly nestled in the gardens of the Ingleside Inn, it serves a weekend brunch that's a Palm Springs tradition. There is also a piano bar. *200 W. Ramon Rd., tel. 619/325–2323. Reservations advised. Jacket required. MC, V. Expensive.*

Lyon's English Grille. When was the last time you had real honest-to-goodness roast beef and Yorkshire pudding as only the Brits can make it? Lyon's has it, and other old-country favorites. Good value and good food make this a popular stop for the locals. *233 E. Palm Canyon Dr., tel. 619/327–1551. Reservations advised. Dress: casual. AE, DC, MC, V. No lunch. Closed summer. Moderate–Expensive.*

Bono. Owned by Palm Springs's former mayor Sonny Bono, this restaurant serves southern Italian dishes like those his mother used to make. It's a favorite feeding station for show-biz folk and the curious, and a good place for pasta, chicken, veal, and scampi dishes. Outdoor dining is available. *1700 N. Indian Canyon Dr., tel. 619/322–6200. Reservations advised.*

Dress: casual. Valet parking. AE, D, DC, MC, V. No lunch. Moderate.

Brussels Cafe. The best spot in town for people-watching is this sidewalk café in the heart of Palm Canyon Drive. Try the Belgian waffles or homemade pâté. Beers from around the world are featured, and there's entertainment nightly. *109 S. Palm Canyon Dr., tel. 619/320–4177. Reservations required. Dress: casual. AE, D, MC, V. Moderate.*

Cafe St. James. From the plant-filled balcony you can watch the passing parade below, and dine on Mediterranean-Italian cuisine, Indian curries, or vegetarian dishes. *254 N. Palm Canyon Dr., tel. 619/320–8041. Reservations advised. Dress: casual. AE, MC, V. No lunch. Closed Mon. Moderate.*

Flower Drum. Related to the highly popular Flower Drum in New York, this health-conscious Chinese restaurant features Hunan, Peking, Shanghai, Canton, and Szechuan cuisines in a setting meant to resemble a Chinese village. *424 S. Indian Canyon Dr., tel. 619/323–3020. Reservations advised. Dress: casual. AE, MC, V. Moderate.*

Las Casuelas Original. A longtime favorite among residents and visitors alike, this restaurant offers great (in size and taste) margaritas and average Mexican dishes: crab enchilada, carne asada, lobster Ensenada. It gets very, very crowded during the winter months. *368 N. Palm Canyon Dr., tel. 619/325–3213. Reservations advised. Dress: casual. AE, MC, V. Moderate.*

Riccio's. Tony Riccio, formerly of the Marquis and Martoni's, in Hollywood, serves the old-fashioned Italian food that comforts his steady patrons: fettuccine Alfredo, veal piccata, chicken Vesuvio, and a luscious Italian cheesecake. *2155 N. Palm Canyon Dr., tel. 619/325–2369. Reservations advised. Jacket required. No weekend lunch. Moderate.*

Di Amico's Steak House. Hearty eaters will enjoy this Early California–style restaurant. Prime Eastern corn-fed beef, liver steak vaquero, and Son-of-a-Gun stew are featured. *500 E. Palm Canyon Dr., tel. 619/325–9191. Reservations advised. Dress: casual. MC, V. Inexpensive.*

Elmer's Pancake and Steak House. Forget about Aunt Jemima—Elmer's offers 25 varieties of pancakes and waffles. There are steaks, chicken, and seafood on the dinner menu. A children's menu is also available. *1030 E. Palm Canyon Dr., tel. 619/327–8419. No reservations. Dress: casual. AE, D, DC, MC, V. Inexpensive.*

Louise's Pantry. A local landmark, in the center of downtown Palm Springs for almost 40 years, the 1940s-style Louise's features down-home cooking such as chicken and dumplings and short ribs of beef. You can get soup, salad, entrée, beverage, and dessert for under $15. There's usually a line to get in. *124 S. Palm Canyon Dr., tel. 619/325–5124. No reservations. Dress: casual. MC, V. Inexpensive.*

Lodging **Autry Resort Hotel.** This venerable resort has recently undergone a complete renovation. Rooms are in two buildings and bungalows on 13 landscaped acres. The place is decked out for a number of activities, including tennis instruction at the Reed Anderson Tennis School, and dining and entertainment are offered nightly. *4200 E. Palm Canyon Dr., 92262, tel. 619/328–1171 or 800/443–6328. 187 units. Facilities: restaurant, 3 pools, Jacuzzis, 6 lighted tennis courts, fitness center with sauna and massage. AE, DC, MC, V. Very Expensive.*

Hyatt Regency Suites. Located adjacent to the downtown Desert Fashion Plaza, this hotel's striking six-story asymmetrical lobby houses two restaurants, including the popular outdoor Cafe 285. There are one, two, and three-bedroom suites with city or golf course/mountain views. *285 N. Palm Canyon Dr., 92262, tel. 619/322–9000 or 800/233–1234. 194 suites. Facilities: 2 restaurants, lounge, pool, health club, golf privileges at Rancho Mirage Country Club. AE, DC, MC, V. Very Expensive.*

★ **La Mancha Private Pool Villas and Court Club.** Only four blocks from downtown Palm Springs, this Spanish-Moroccan Hollywood-style retreat blocks out the rest of the world with plenty of panache. Opulently appointed villas, surrounded by lushly landscaped gardens, have kitchens, fireplaces, and private pools; four have private tennis courts. *444 N. Avenida Caballeros, 92262, tel. 619/323–1773. 54 villas. Facilities: restaurant, 7 tennis courts, paddle-tennis court, pool, putting greens, health club with sauna, bicycles, croquet lawns, convertibles available for local transporation. AE, DC, MC, V. Very Expensive.*

Palm Springs Hilton Resort and Racquet Club. The cool, white marble elegance of this plant-filled resort hotel, just off Palm Canyon Drive, and its two superb restaurants make it a popular choice for visitors to the city. Rooms have private balconies and refrigerators. *400 E. Tahquitz Way, 92262, tel. 619/320–6868 or 800/522–6900. 189 rooms, 71 suites. Facilities: 2 restaurants, pool, 6 tennis courts, pro shop, health club, Jacuzzi. AE, DC, MC, V. Very Expensive.*

Palm Springs Marquis. Posh, desert-modern style with pastel color schemes, marble, and greenery mark this centrally located hotel. Villas have fireplaces, wet bars, and private patios. *150 S. Indian Canyon Dr., 92262, tel. 619/322–2121 or 800/223–1050. 264 rooms. Facilities: restaurant, café, 2 pools, tennis, fitness center, Jacuzzi, meeting and convention facilities. AE, DC, MC, V. Very Expensive.*

Spa Hotel and Mineral Springs. This hotel contains the hot mineral springs from which Palm Springs got its name. Always popular for its therapeutic springs, massages, and spa services, the hotel was under renovation in 1993. Rooms have private balconies and views. *100 N. Indian Canyon Dr., 92262, tel. 619/325–1461. 230 rooms. Facilities: restaurant, lounge, mineral springs, pool, 35 swirlpool tubs, fitness center, tennis. AE, DC, MC, V. Very Expensive.*

Sundance Villas. Beautifully decorated, spacious time-share villas include fireplace, wet bar, kitchen, and private patio for dining or sunning. Each villa has a private pool and Jacuzzi. This is not a place for the weak of pocketbook. *303 Cabrillo Rd., 92262, tel. 619/325–3888. 19 villas. Facilities: pool, tennis, Jacuzzi, sauna, golf. AE, MC, V. Very Expensive.*

Casa Cody. This very clean, Western-style bed-and-breakfast is just a few steps from the Palm Springs Desert Museum. Simply furnished spacious studios and one- and two-bedroom suites are individually decorated. Service is personal and gracious. *175 S. Cahuilla Rd., 92262, tel. 619/320–9346 or 800/231–2639. 17 units. Facilities: 2 pools, kitchens, gardens, complimentary Continental breakfast. AE, MC V. Expensive.*

★ **Ingleside Inn.** Like many desert lodgings, this hacienda-style inn attracts its share of Hollywood personalities, who appreciate good service and relative seclusion. Rooms are individually decorated, many with antiques. Those in the main building are dark and cool, even in summer. The adjacent Melvyn's Restaurant is locally popular. *200 W. Ramon Rd., 92262, tel. 619/325–0046. 29 rooms. Facilities: pool, Jacuzzi, sauna, tennis. AE, MC, V. Expensive.*

Racquet Club Resort Hotel. Built by Charlie Farrell and Ralph Bellamy in 1933, the Racquet Club marked the beginning of Palm Springs's glamour era. The grounds cover 25 acres, and it is said that Marilyn Monroe was "discovered" on the tennis courts here. *2743 N. Indian Canyon Dr., 92262, tel. 619/325–1281. 124 units. Facilities: restaurant, lounge, 4 pools, Jacuzzi, sauna, fitness center, 12 tennis courts. AE, DC, MC, V. Expensive.*

Courtyard by Marriott. This property represents part of the Marriott chain's effort to expand into comfortable, smaller hotels offering a good value. The concept works nicely. *1300 Tahquitz Canyon Way, 92262, tel. 619/322–6100. 149 rooms. Facilities: restaurant, pool, fitness center, Jacuzzi, tennis. AE, DC, MC, V. Moderate.*

Villa Royale. In this charming bed-and-breakfast, each room is individually decorated with a European theme. Some rooms have private Jacuzzis, fireplaces, kitchens. The grounds feature lush gardens. *1620 Indian Trail, 92264, tel. 619/327–2314. 34 rooms. Facilities: restaurant, lounge, 2 pools, Jacuzzi. AE, MC, V. Moderate.*

Mira Loma Hotel. The small scale and friendly atmosphere make this hotel popular with Europeans. Rooms and suites have eclectic decor, some Oriental, some 1940s Hollywood; all have refrigerators, patios, and fireplaces. Marilyn Monroe slept here. Really. *1420 N. Indian Canyon Dr., 92262, tel. 619/320–1178. 12 rooms. Facilities: pool. AE, MC, V. Inexpensive.*

Villa Rosa Inn. This is a cute pink-and-white inn with rooms surrounding a small flower-filled courtyard. There is no air-conditioning. *1577 S. Indian Trail, 92264, tel. 619/327–5915. 6 units. Facilities: pool, kitchens in rooms. AE, MC, V. Inexpensive.*

Westward Ho Hotel. This typical motel-style property is popular with tour groups. *701 E. Palm Canyon Dr., 92262, tel. 619/320–2700. 207 rooms. Facilities: coffee shop, lounge, pool, therapy pool. AE, MC, V. Inexpensive.*

Rancho Mirage
Dining

Dominick's. An old favorite of Frank Sinatra's and what's left of his "rat pack," the steaks, pasta, and veal dishes here are the order of the day. *70-030 Hwy. 111, tel. 619/324–1711. Reservations advised. Dress: casual. AE, DC, MC, V. No lunch. Closed Tues. Easter–Dec. Expensive.*

Wally's Desert Turtle. If price is no object, and you like plush, gilded decor, then this is where to come. You'll be surrounded by the golden names of Palm Springs and Hollywood society, and served old-fashioned French cooking: rack of lamb, imported Dover sole, braised sea bass, veal Oscar, chicken Normande, and dessert souffles. *71-775 Hwy. 111, tel. 619/568–9321. Reservations required. Jacket required. Valet parking. AE, MC, V. No lunch Sat.–Thur. Expensive.*

Lodging

Ritz-Carlton Rancho Mirage. This hotel is tucked into a hillside in the Santa Rosa Mountains with sweeping views of the valley below. Sheep from the surrounding bighorn preserve frequently visit the hotel grounds. The surroundings are elegant, with gleaming marble and brass, original artwork, deep plush carpeting, and remarkable comfort. All rooms are enormous and meticulously appointed with antiques, fabric wallcoverings, marble bathrooms, and often two phones and two TVs. Service is impeccable, anticipating your every need. *68-900 Frank Sinatra Dr., 92270, tel. 619/321–8282 or 800/241–3333. 221 rooms, 19 suites. Facilities: 3 restaurants, lounge with entertainment, pool, outdoor Jacuzzi, 10 tennis courts, croquet, 9-hole pitch-and-putt golf, basketball, volleyball, children's programs. AE, DC, MC, V. Very Expensive.*

Westin Mission Hills Resort. This sprawling Moroccan-style resort on 360 acres, home to the annual Nabisco Dinah Shore LPGA Classic, is surrounded by fairways and putting greens. Rooms are in two- story buildings enveloping patios and fountains scattered throughout the property. Nicely furnished, the rooms have soft desert colors, terra-cotta tile floors, shuttered windows, and private patios or baloncies; amenities include double sinks, in- room coffee makers, and refrigerators. Paths and creeks meander through the complex, encircling a lagoon-style swimming pool with a 60-foot water slide. *71333 Dinah Shore Dr., 92270, tel. 619/328–5955 or 800/228–3000. 512 rooms. Facilities: 7 restaurants, lounge with entertainment, 3 pools, outdoor Jacuzzis, 7 tennis courts, 2 18-hole golf courses, health club, shops, children's programs. AE, DC, MC, V. Very Expensive.*

The Arts and Nightlife

For complete listings of upcoming events, pick up a copy of *Palm Springs Life* magazine or *Palm Springs Life*'s "Desert Guide," a free monthly publication found in any hotel.

The Arts

The **McCallum Theatre** (73-000 Fred Waring Dr., Palm Desert, tel. 619/340–2787), site of the **Palm Springs International Film Festival** in January, is the principal cultural venue in the desert, offering a number of arts series November through May. Programs include film, classical music, opera, ballet, popular music, and theater.

The **Annenberg Theatre** (Palm Springs Desert Museum, 101 Museum Dr., north of Tahquitz Way, tel. 619/325–7186 or 619/325–4490) is the other film-festival venue. The 450-seat theater hosts film series, Sunday-afternoon chamber concerts, lectures, and symposia.

Concerts The **College of the Desert** (43-500 Monterey Ave., Palm Desert, tel. 619/346–8041) is where the annual **Joanna Hodges Piano Conference and Competition** is held.

Theater **Palm Springs Follies** is a "Ziegfeld Follies"–style review featuring retired professional showgirls, actresses, and musicians in skits and specialty acts at the **Plaza Theater** (128 S. Palm Canyon Dr., tel. 916/327–0225, admission $24–$37).

Valley Players Guild, a well-established community theater, performs at **Palm Springs Playhouse** (500 S. Indian Canyon Dr., tel. 619/320–9898).

Nightlife

Two good sources for finding current nightlife attractions are the *Desert Sun* (the local newspaper) and *Guide* magazine, a monthly publication distributed free at most downtown merchants' counters.

Live entertainment, ranging from soft dinner music to song-and-dance numbers, is frequently found in the city's hotels and restaurants. The piano bar at **Melvyn's Ingleside Inn** is popular.

Comedy Clubs **The Comedy Haven.** Stand-up comics and improv groups dished up with American/Italian fare. *Desert Fashion Plaza (enter parking lot from Tahquitz Way), tel. 619/320–7855.*

Discos Between the flashing lights of its top-40 disco and the retro-memorabilia in its new '50s–'60s room, **Cecil's** (1775 E. Palm Canyon Dr., tel. 619/320–4202) is bound to keep you dancing. There's dancing to live country music at the **Cactus Corral** (67–501 E. Palm Canyon Dr., Cathedral City, tel. 619/321–8558). **Pompeii** (67–399 Hwy. 111, Palm Springs, tel. 619/328–5800) is a large disco playing Top 40 music. You'll know you've found this lively joint when you see the fiery torches out front. **Zelda's** (169 N. Indian Canyon Dr., Palm Springs, tel. 619/325–2375) is another active spot featuring talent and fashion shows, hot-body competitions, and limbo contests.

Jazz **Peabody's Jazz Studio and Coffee Bar** (134 S. Palm Canyon Dr., Palm Springs, tel. 619/333–1877) presents jazz in a warm atmosphere. **Lincoln View Coffee House** (278-C N. Palm Canyon Dr., Palm Springs, tel. 619/327–6365) presents jams on Sunday afternoon and live jazz Friday and Saturday nights.

12 Santa Barbara

Although it's only 90 miles from the ever-growing sprawl of Los Angeles, Santa Barbara maintains a relaxed atmosphere and cozy scale. Wedged as it is between the Pacific and the Santa Ynez Mountains, it's never had much room for expansion, and the city's setting, climate, and architecture combine for a Mediterranean feel that permeates not only its look but its pace. The mountains assure a sunny climate and a Riviera-like setting, and there is an outdoors emphasis on everything here. The waterfront—with its beaches, pier, and harbor—and the Spanish-style downtown and the centers of business, and the number-one business here is tourism. Farther up in the hills are the exclusive residential areas of Montecito and Hope Ranch, home to movie stars and celebrities.

Essential Information

Important Addresses and Numbers

Tourist Information Free pamphlets on accommodations, dining, sports, and entertainment are available at the **Visitors Information Center** (1 Santa Barbara St. at Cabrillo Blvd., tel. 805/965–3021, open Mon.–Sat. 9–5, Sun. 10–4). Before arriving, contact **Santa Barbara Conference and Visitors Bureau** (510A State St., 93101, tel. 805/966–9222 or 800/927–4688 for mailing of publications).

Arriving and Departing

By Plane **American** and **American Eagle** (tel. 800/433–7300), **Sky-west/Delta** (tel. 800/453–9417), **United** and **United Express** (tel. 800/241–6522), and **US Air Express** (tel. 800/428–4322) fly into Santa Barbara Municipal Airport (tel. 805/683–4011) 8 miles from downtown at 500 Fowler Road.

Santa Barbara Airbus (tel. 805/964–7374) runs limousines to and from the airport and shuttles travelers between Santa Barbara and Los Angeles Airport. **Aero Airport Limousine** (tel. 805/965–2412) serves Los Angeles Airport (by reservation only). **Metropolitan Transit District** (tel. 805/963–3364) bus No. 11 runs from the airport to the downtown transit center.

By Car You can drive to Santa Barbara from Los Angeles in about two hours (along U.S. 101 and Highway 1). Once in Santa Barbara, you may run into some horrendous traffic. Downtown parking can be difficult but there are several large multi-story, inexpensive public parking lots, so you'll find something.

By Bus Local service is provided by the **Santa Barbara Metropolitan Transit District** (tel. 805/963–3364).

By Train **Amtrak** (tel. 800/USA–RAIL or 805/963–1015) runs the *Coast Starlight* train along the coast from Santa Barbara to San Luis Obispo, and inland for the rest of the route to the San Francisco Bay Area and Seattle.

Guided Tours

Santa Barbara Trolley Co. (tel. 805/965–0353) has five daily, regularly scheduled runs in Santa Barbara. Motorized San Francisco–style cable cars deliver visitors to major hotels, shopping areas, and attractions. Stop or not as you wish and pick up another trolley when you're ready to move on. All depart from and return to Stearns Wharf. The fare is $5 adults, $3 children and senior citizens.

Walking Tours Through History (tel. 805/967–9869). Longtime Santa Barbara resident Elias Chiacos takes small groups on walking tours of gardens and historic buildings. Morning and afternoon tours are available by reservation, beginning at the courthouse lobby.

Exploring Santa Barbara

Highlights for First-Time Visitors

The Botanic Gardens
The Courthouse
El Paseo
Santa Barbara Mission
Santa Barbara Museum of Art

Santa Barbara

Numbers in the margin correspond to points of interest on the Santa Barbara map.

Santa Barbara's attractions begin with the ocean, with most everything else along Cabrillo Boulevard. In the few miles between the beaches and the hills, you pass the downtown and then reach the old mission and, a little higher up, the botanic gardens. A few miles farther up the coast, but still very much a part of Santa Barbara, is the exclusive residential district of Hope Ranch. To the east is the district called Montecito, where Charlie Chaplin built the Montecito Inn to house his guests in the days when he made his movies in Santa Barbara before moving to Hollywood. Montecito is also where the exclusive San Ysidro Ranch is located.

Because the town is on a jog in the coastline, the ocean is to the south, and directions can be confusing. "Up" the coast is west, "down" toward Los Angeles is actually east, and the mountains are north.

Everything in town is so close that the 8-mile drive to the airport seems like a long trip. A car is handy, but not essential, if you're planning on staying pretty much in town. The beaches and downtown are easily explored by bicycle or on foot, and the Santa Barbara Trolley takes visitors to most of the major hotels and sights, which can also be reached on the local buses.

The Visitors Information Center publishes a free guide to a scenic drive that circles the town with a detour into the downtown. It passes the harbor, beaches, Hope Ranch, and the old mission, offers fine views on the way to Montecito, then returns you to the beaches. You can pick up the drive, marked with blue "Scenic Drive" signs, anywhere along the loop. A free guide to the downtown, the "Red Tile Walking Tour," is also available free from the tourist office. It hits historical spots in a 12-block area.

The town of Goleta, the home of the University of California at Santa Barbara, is located a few miles up the coast via U.S. 101.

If you start at the Pacific and move inland, one of the first spots **❶** to visit is **Stearns Wharf** on Cabrillo Boulevard at the foot of State Street. Originally built in 1872 and reconstructed in 1981 after a fire, the wharf extends the length of three city blocks into the Pacific. The view from here back toward the city gives you a sense of the town's size and general layout. You can drive out and park on the pier, then wander through the shops or stop for a meal at one of the wharf's restaurants or at the snack bar. The **Sea Center,** a recent addition to the pier, is a branch of the Museum of Natural History that specializes in exhibits of marine life. *211 Stearns Wharf, tel. 805/962–0885. Admission: $2 adults, $1.50 senior citizens, $1 children 3–17. Open daily 2–5.*

❷ The nearby **Santa Barbara Yacht Harbor** is sheltered by a man-made breakwater at the west end of Cabrillo Boulevard. You can take a ½-mile walk along the paved breakwater, check out the tackle and bait shops, or hire a boat from here.

❸ Planted in 1877, the **Moreton Bay Fig Tree,** at Chapala Street and Highway 101, is so huge it reportedly can provide shade for 10,000 people. In recent years, however, the tree has become a gathering place for an increasing number of homeless people.

Back along Cabrillo, sandy beaches stretch for miles. The sprawling reddish Spanish-style hotel across from the beach is **❹** the **Fess Parker Red Lion Resort.** Parker, the actor who played Davy Crockett and Daniel Boone on television, owned the oceanfront acreage for many years and spent several more trying to convince city fathers to allow him to develop a hotel. He finally did, and the hotel opened in 1987 as the largest in Santa Barbara.

❺ Just beyond the hotel is the area's most popular beach, **East Beach,** a wide swatch of sand at the east end of Cabrillo. Nearby **❻** is the **Andree Clark Bird Refuge,** a peaceful lagoon and gardens. *1400 E. Cabrillo Blvd. Admission free.*

❼ Adjoining the lagoon is the **Santa Barbara Zoo,** a small lushly landscaped home to big-game cats, elephants, and exotic birds. *500 Ninos Dr., tel. 805/962–6310. Admission: $5 adults, $3 senior citizens and children 2–12. Open daily in winter 10–5; daily in summer 9–6.*

Where Cabrillo Boulevard ends at the lagoon, Channel Drive **❽** picks up and, a short distance east, passes the **Biltmore Hotel,** now owned by the Four Seasons chain (*see* Lodging, *below*). For more than 60 years, Santa Barbara's high society and the visiting rich and famous have come here to indulge in quiet California-style elegance.

To reach the downtown area, return to Cabrillo Boulevard and **❾** then head inland along State Street. **The Courthouse,** in the center of downtown, has all the grandeur of a Moorish palace. As you wander the halls, admiring the brilliant hand-painted tiles and spiral staircase, you might just forget that you're in a courthouse until you spot a handcuffed group of offenders being marched by. This magnificent building was completed in 1929, as part of the rebuilding of Santa Barbara made necessary by a 1925 earthquake that destroyed much of downtown. At the time the city was also in the midst of a cultural awakening, and the trend was toward an architecture appropriate to the area's climate and history. The result is the harmonious

243

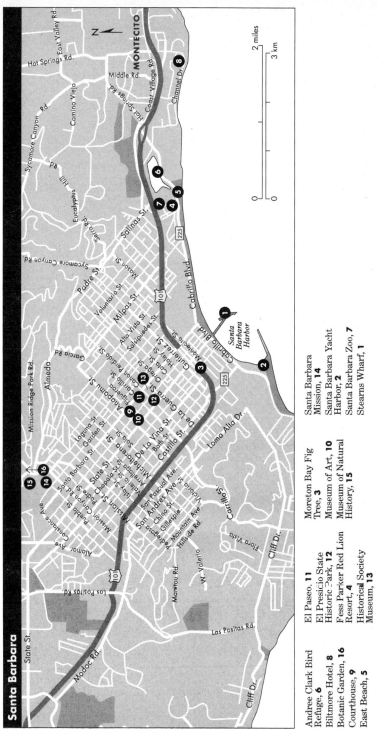

Santa Barbara

Andree Clark Bird
Refuge, **6**
Biltmore Hotel, **8**
Botanic Garden, **16**
Courthouse, **9**
East Beach, **5**

El Paseo, **11**
El Presicio State
Historic Park, **12**
Fess Parker Red Lion
Resort, **4**
Historical Society
Museum, **13**

Moreton Bay Fig
Tree, **3**
Museum of Art, **10**
Museum of Natural
History, **15**

Santa Barbara
Mission, **14**
Santa Barbara Yacht
Harbor, **2**
Santa Barbara Zoo, **7**
Stearns Wharf, **1**

Mediterranean-Spanish look of much of Santa Barbara's downtown area, especially its municipal buildings. An elevator to the Courthouse tower takes visitors to a lovely, arched observation area with a panoramic view of the city, and is a fine spot from which to take photos. In the supervisors' ceremonial chambers on the Courthouse's second floor are murals painted by an artist who did backdrops for Cecil B. DeMille's silent films. *1100 block of Anacapa St., tel. 805/962–6464. Open weekdays 8–5, weekends 9–5. Free 1-hour guided tours Mon.–Sat. 2 PM, Wed. and Fri., 10:30 AM and 2 PM.*

🔟 One block down Anapamu Street past the Spanish-style **Public Library** is the **Santa Barbara Museum of Art.** This fine small museum houses a permanent collection featuring ancient sculpture, Oriental art, a collection of German expressionist paintings, and a sampling of American artists such as Grandma Moses. *1130 State St., tel. 805/963–4364. Admission: $3 adults, $2.50 senior citizens, $1.50 children 6–16; admission free Thur. and first Sun. of each month. Open Tues.–Sat. 11–5 (until 9 PM Thur.), Sun. noon–5. Guided tours Tues.–Sat. 1 PM, Sun. noon.*

⑪ To the east you'll find **El Paseo,** a shopping arcade built around an old adobe home. There are several such arcades in this area
⑫ and also many small art galleries. A few blocks south is the **El Presidio State Historic Park.** Built in 1782, the presidio was one of four military strongholds established by the Spanish along the coast of California. The guardhouse, El Cuartel, is one of the two original adobe buildings that remain of the complex and is the oldest building owned by the state. *123 E. Cañon Perdido St., tel. 805/966–9719. Admission free. Open daily 10:30–4:30.*

⑬ A block away is the **Historical Society Museum,** with an array of items from the town's past, including a silver-clad riding saddle and a collection of fancy ladies' fans. *136 E. De la Guerra St., tel. 805/966–1601. Admission free. Open Tues.–Sat. 10–5, Sun. noon–5.*

A short distance from downtown (take State Street north and
⑭ make a right on Los Olivos) at the base of the hills is the **Santa Barbara Mission,** the gem of the chain of 21 missions established in California by Spanish missionaries in the late 1700s. One of the best preserved of the missions, it is still active as a Catholic church. *Laguna St., tel. 805/682–4713. Admission: adults $2, children under 16 free. Open daily 9–5.*

⑮ Continuing north a block you pass the **Museum of Natural History** (2559 Puesta del Sol, tel. 805/682–4711, admission: $3 adults, $2 students and senior citizens, $1 under 13; open Mon.–
⑯ Sat. 9–5, Sun. 10–5) and then the **Botanic Gardens,** 1½ miles north of the mission. The 60 acres of native plants are particularly beautiful in the spring. *1212 Mission Canyon Rd., tel. 805/682–4726. Admission $3 adults, $2 senior citizens, and $1 children 5–12. Open 8 AM–sunset. Guided tours 10:30 AM and 2 PM Thur., Sat., and Sun.*

Ojai

A half-hour drive east of Santa Barbara over the narrow and winding Highway 150 will put you in **Ojai,** a surprisingly rural town reminiscent of earlier days in California when agriculture was the uncontested king. You'll see acres of ripening orange and avocado groves that look like the picture-postcard images of Southern California from decades ago. In recent years the area has seen an influx of show-biz types, and other Angelinos who've opted for a life out of the fast lane. Moviemaker Frank Capra used the Ojai Valley as a backdrop for his 1936 classic, *Lost Horizon.* Be aware that the valley sizzles in the summer when temperatures routinely reach 90°.

The works of local artists can be seen in the Spanish-style shopping arcade along the main street. On Sunday they display their paintings and crafts at the outdoor exhibition in the Security Bank parking lot (205 W. Ojai Ave.). The **Art Center** (113 S. Montgomery, tel. 805/646–0117) features art exhibits, theater, and dance.

A stroll around town should include a stop at **Bart's Books** (302 W. Matilija, tel. 805/646–3755), an outdoor store sheltered by native oaks and overflowing with used books.

Nearby **Lake Casitas** on Highway 150 offers boating, fishing, and camping. It was the venue for the 1984 Summer Olympic rowing events.

One of the attractions in Ojai is a hot spring that makes use of natural mineral water from the nearby hills. The spa at **Wheeler Hot Springs** emerges like an oasis 7 miles north of town on Highway 33. Its tall palms and herb gardens are fed by an adjacent stream, and natural mineral waters fill the four redwood hot tubs and a large pool at the well-kept spa. Massage is also available. A restaurant on site offers dinner and live entertainment Thursday through Sunday, and Saturday and Sunday brunch. *16825 Maricopa Hwy., tel. 805/646–8131 or 800/227–9292. Open Mon.–Thur. 10–9, Fri.–Sun. 9 AM–10 PM. Reservations advised at least a week in advance for weekends, especially for spa.*

Off the Beaten Track

Channel Islands Hearty travelers should consider a day visit or overnight camping trip to one of the five Channel Islands that often appear in a haze off the Santa Barbara horizon. The most often visited is Anacapa Island, 11 miles off the coast. The islands' remoteness and unpredictable seas have protected them from development, and now provide a nature enthusiast's paradise—both underwater and on land. In 1980 the islands became the nation's 40th national park, and the water a mile around each is protected as a marine sanctuary.

On a good day, you'll be able to view seals, sea lions, and an array of bird life. From December through March, migrating whales can be seen close up. On land, tide pools alive with sea life are often accessible. Underwater, divers can view fish, giant squid, and coral. Off Anacapa Island, scuba divers can see the remains of a steamship that sank in 1853. Frenchy's Cove, on the west end of the island, has a swimming beach and fine snorkeling.

The waters of the channel are often rough, and can make for a rugged trip out to the islands. You can charter a boat and head out on your own, but most visitors head to Ventura Harbor, a 40-minute drive south from Santa Barbara, from where a park district concessionaire carries small groups to the islands for day hikes, barbecues, and primitive overnight camping.

Island Packers (1867 Spinnaker Dr., Ventura 93001, tel. 805/642–7688) provides day trips to the islands and overnight camping to three of them. Boats link up with National Park naturalists for hikes and nature programs. A limited number of visitors is allowed on each island and unpredictable weather can limit island landings. Reservations are essential in the summer.

Shopping

Antiques In Santa Barbara a dozen antiques and gift shops are clustered in restored Victorian buildings on Brinkerhoff Avenue, two blocks west of State Street at West Cota Street.

Arcade In all, 32 shops, art galleries, and studios share the courtyard and gardens of **El Paseo** (Cañon Perdido St., between State and Anacapa Sts., Santa Barbara), a shopping arcade rich in history. Lunch at the outdoor patio is a nice break from a downtown tour.

Beach Wear If you want to go home with the absolutely latest in California beach wear, stop by **Pacific Leisure** (808 State St., Santa Barbara, tel. 805/962–8828), which specializes in volleyball fashions, shorts, tops, and beach towels.

Sports and Fitness

Participant Sports

Bicycling Santa Barbara's waterfront boasts the level, two-lane Cabrillo Bike Lane. In just over 3 easy miles, you pass the zoo, a bird refuge, beaches, and the harbor. There are restaurants along the way, or you can stop for a picnic along the palm-lined path looking out on the Pacific. Rent bikes from **Beach Rentals** (8 W. Cabrillo Blvd., tel. 805/963–2524; open 8 AM to sunset in winter, and 8 AM–dusk in summer). It also has roller skates for hire. Bikes and quadricycles can be rented from the **Cycles 4 Rent** concession near the pool at Fess Parker's Red Lion Resort (633 E. Cabrillo, tel. 805/564–4333, ext. 444).

Boating **Sailing Center of Santa Barbara** (Santa Barbara Harbor, at the launchng ramp, tel. 805/962–2826 or 800/350–9090) offers sailing instruction, rents and charters sailboats, and organizes dinner cruises, sunset champagne cruises, and whale-watching expeditions.

Fishing Surface and deep-sea fishing are possible all year. Fully equipped boats leave the harbor area for full- and half-day trips, dinner cruises, island excursions, and whale-watching from **SEA Landing** (Cabrillo Blvd. at Bath and breakwater, tel. 805/963–3564).

Golf Play nine or 18 holes at the **Santa Barbara Golf Club** (Las Positas Rd. and McCaw Ave., tel. 805/687–7087). **Sandpiper Golf Course,** 15 miles west (7925 Hollister Ave., Goleta, tel. 805/968–1541), offers a challenging course that used to be a stop on the women's professional tour.

Horseback Riding The **San Ysidro Ranch** hotel (900 San Ysidro La., Montecito, tel. 805/969–5046) offers trail rides for parties of no more than six into the foothills by the hour. Reservations are required; on Saturday it's for hotel guests only.

Tennis Many Santa Barbara hotels have their own courts, but there are also excellent public courts. Day permits, for $3, are available at the courts. **Las Positas Municipal Courts** (1002 Las Positas Rd., Santa Barbara), has six lighted courts. Large complexes are also at the **Municipal Courts** (near Salinas Street and Hwy. 101), and **Pershing Park** (Castillo St. and Cabrillo Blvd.).

Volleyball The east end of **East Beach** has more than a dozen sandlots. There are some casual, pickup games, but if you get into one, be prepared—these folks play serious volleyball.

Spectator Sports

Polo The public is invited to watch the elegant game at the **Santa Barbara Polo Club**, 7 miles east in Carpinteria. *Take the Santa Claus La. exit from Hwy. 101, turn left under the freeway and then left again onto Via Real. The polo grounds are ½ mi farther, surrounded by high hedges. Tel. 805/684–6683. Apr.–Oct., Sun. Admission $6, children under 12 free.*

Beaches

Santa Barbara's beaches don't have the big surf of the beaches farther south, but they also don't have the crowds. A short walk from the parking lot can usually find you a solitary spot. Be aware that fog often hugs the coast until about noon in May and June.

East Beach. At the east end of Cabrillo Boulevard, this is *the* beach in Santa Barbara. There are lifeguards, volleyball courts, a jogging and bike trail, and the Cabrillo Bath House with a gym, showers, and changing rooms open to the public.

Arroyo Burro Beach. Located just west of the harbor on Cliff Drive at Las Positas Road, this state beach has a small grassy area with picnic tables and sandy beaches below the cliffs. The Brown Pelican Restaurant on the beach serves a delicious breakfast.

Goleta Beach Park. To the north of Santa Barbara, in Goleta, this is a favorite with the college students from the nearby University of California campus. The easy surf makes it perfect for beginning surfers and families with young children.

State Beaches. West of Santa Barbara on Highway 1 are **El Capitan, Refugio,** and **Gaviota** state beaches, each with campsites, picnic tables, and fire pits. East of the city is the state beach at **Carpinteria,** a sheltered, sunny and often crowded beach.

Dining

By Bruce David Colen

The variety of good food in Santa Barbara is astonishing for a town its size. Menu selections range from classic French to Cajun to fresh seafood, and the dining style from tie, jacket, and reservations necessary to shorts-and-T-shirt hip. A leisurely brunch or lunch will take the best advantage of the beach and harbor views afforded by many restaurants and cafés. At the Biltmore's acclaimed and expensive Sunday brunch, however, all attention is squarely on the spread of fresh fruits, seafood, and pastries. Served in the hotel's airy glass-roof courtyard, it is a perfect choice for special occasions.

But a tasty and satisfying meal certainly doesn't have to cost a fortune. If it is good, cheap food with an international flavor you are after, follow the locals to Milpas Avenue on the east edge of downtown. A recent count there found three Thai restaurants, a Hawaiian, a Greek, and a New Mexican food place. Freshly made tortillas are easily found in the markets on Milpas, particularly at La Super Rica, reputedly one of Julia Child's favorites for a quick, authentic Mexican snack.

Highly recommended restaurants are indicated by a star ★. Casual dress is acceptable, unless noted otherwise.

Category	Cost*
Very Expensive	over $50
Expensive	$30–$50
Moderate	$20–$30
Inexpensive	under $20

per person, without tax, service, or drinks

Santa Barbara
Expensive–Very Expensive

The Stonehouse. The restaurant is in a turn-of-the-century, granite farmhouse, part of the San Ysidro Ranch resort. The classic American regional menu offers such treats as dry aged New York steak with black-bean sauce and puree of sweet potato, or Mississippi catfish with orange-pecan crust, fresh shrimp, and corn hush puppies. The food is good, but the real drawing card is the pastoral setting. Be sure to have lunch—seafood salads, pastas, and sandwiches—on the treehouselike outdoor patio. At night, the candle-lit interior becomes even more romantic and the cuisine more serious, with game, roasts,chicken, steak, and fresh fish entrées. *900 San Ysidro La., tel. 805/969–5046. Reservations required. Jacket required. AE, D, MC, V.*

Expensive
★

Citronelle. This offspring of Michel Richard's famed Citrus in Los Angeles has brought Santa Barbara folk some of the best California-French cuisine they've ever had this close to home. The accent is on Riviera-style dishes: light, delicate but loaded with intriguing good tastes. The desserts here are unmatched anywhere in Southern California. There are splendid, sweeping views of the harbor from the second story dining room's picture windows. *901 East Cabrillo, tel. 805/963–0111. Reservations advised. AE, D, DC, MC, V.*

The Palace Cafe. A stylish and lively restaurant, the Palace has won acclaim for its Cajun and Creole dishes such as blackened redfish and jambalaya with dirty rice. Caribbean fare here includes Bahamian slipper lobster tails—tender lobster sautéed with garlic, mushrooms, and tomatoes, then flambéed in a Madeira sauce. Just in case the dishes aren't spicy enough for you, each table has a bottle of hot sauce. The Palace offers dinner only; be prepared for a wait. *8 E. Cota St., tel. 805/966–3133. Reservations accepted for 5:30 PM seating only on Fri. and Sat. AE, MC, V.*

Pane & Vino. This tiny trattoria, and its equally small sidewalk dining terrace, is in a tree-shaded, flower-decked shopping center in Montecito, just east of Santa Barbara. The cold anti-pasto is very good, as are grilled meats and fish, pastas, and salads. There's a nearby water trough and hitching post for the ride-by horsey set. *1482 E. Valley Rd., Montecito, tel. 805/969–9274. Reservations advised. No credit cards. Closed Sun.*

Moderate–Expensive **The Harbor Restaurant.** Still sparkling fresh from a complete renovation in 1989, this on-the-wharf spot is where locals like to take out-of-town guests. The upstairs, now a bar and grill, offers an extensive menu of fresh seafood, sandwiches, large salads, and a huge variety of appetizers. The spacious room boasts nautical decor and a complete new video system. Head downstairs for healthy portions of fresh seafood, prime rib, or steaks, and order one of the house's specialty drinks; every seat in the remodeled restaurant has a harbor view. *210 Stearns Wharf, tel. 805/963–3311. Reservations required. AE, MC, V.*

Moderate **Castagnola Bros. Seafood Restaurant.** At this unassuming spot just two blocks from the beach, wonderfully good, fresh broiled fish is served on paper plates. The homemade clam chowder is excellent, too. Newly expanded indoor space and the outdoor patio provide ample seating. *205 Santa Barbara St., tel. 805/962–8053. No reservations. AE, D, MC, V. Open daily 11–5.*

Joe's Cafe. The vinyl checked tablecloths and simple round stools at the hefty wooden counter tell the story: nothing fancy, but solid café fare in generous portions. Joe's is a popular hang-out and drinking spot, particularly for the younger crowd. *536 State St., tel. 805/966–4638. AE, D, MC, V. No lunch Sun.*

Inexpensive **East Beach Grill.** Watch the waves break and the action on the sand from a surprisingly pleasant outdoor café right on this busy beach. It's a step above a fast-food joint, with its friendly table service and pleasant shoreline view. You'll find basic breakfast fare served with real plates and cutlery, and hot dogs and burgers for lunch. *At the Cabrillo Bath House, East Beach, tel. 805/965–8805. No reservations. MC, V. Closes daily at 3 PM, at 5 PM during summer.*

★ **La Super-Rica.** This tiny, tacky food stand serves the best and hottest Mexican dishes between Los Angeles and San Francisco. Fans drive for miles to fill up on the soft tacos. *622 N. Milpas St., at Cota St., tel. 805/963–4940. No credit cards.*

Ojai
Moderate **Wheeler Hot Springs Restaurant.** The menu, California Mediterranean in spirit, changes weekly but always features herbs and vegetables grown in the spa's garden. It's in Ojai, 7 miles north of Santa Barbara on Highway 33. The restaurant serves brunch on Saturday and Sunday. *16825 Maricopa Hwy., tel. 805/646–8131. Reservations advised. AE, MC, V. No lunch. Closed Sun.–Mon.*

Lodging

Bargain lodging is hard to come by in Santa Barbara, where high-end resorts are the staple. Long patronized by for congestion-crazed Los Angeles residents, the resorts promise, and usually deliver, pampering and solitude in romantic settings. The beach area is most frequented and is certainly the most popular locale for lodging. Many places offer discounts in the winter season. Come summer weekends, when 90% of the town's 46,000 motel and hotel rooms are filled, reservations well in advance are strongly advised.

Highly recommended lodgings are indicated by a star ★.

Category	Cost*
Very Expensive	over $100
Expensive	$75–$100
Moderate	$50–$75
Inexpensive	under $50

for a double room, excluding tax

Santa Barbara
Very Expensive

Four Seasons Biltmore. Santa Barbara's grande dame got a $15 million sprucing-up by its new Four Seasons owners. The decor of muted pastels and bleached woods gives the cabanas a light, airy touch without sacrificing the hotel's reputation for understated elegance. It's a bit more formal than elsewhere in town, with lush gardens and palm trees galore. *1260 Channel Dr., 93108, tel. 805/969–2261 or 800/332–3442. 236 rooms. Facilities: 2 Olympic pools, whirlpool, croquet, shuffleboard, racquetball, health club, casino, putting green, tennis courts, 2 restaurants, bar. AE, DC, MC, V.*

San Ysidro Ranch. At this luxury "ranch" you can feel at home in jeans and cowboy boots, but be prepared to dress for dinner. A hideout for the Hollywood set, this romantic place hosted John and Jackie Kennedy on their honeymoon. Guest cottages, some with antique quilts and all with wood-burning stoves or fireplaces, are scattered among 14 acres of orange trees and flower beds. There are 500 acres more left in open space to roam at will on foot or horseback. The hotel welcomes children and pets. *900 San Ysidro La., Montecito, 93108, tel. 805/969–5046 or 800/368–6788. 45 rooms. Facilities: restaurant, pool, tennis courts, horseback riding, bocce ball, horseshoes. AE, MC, V. Minimum stay: 2 days on weekends, 3 days on holidays.*

Expensive–
Very Expensive
★

Fess Parker Red Lion Resort. This is a sprawling resort complex with a slightly Spanish flair. Two- and three-story stucco buildings are located directly across the street from the beach. A showplace for this chain of hotels, this is Santa Barbara's newest luxury resort. There is a huge and lavishly appointed lobby, the guest rooms are spacious, furnished with light-wood furniture, and decorated in pastel colors. All have either private patio or balcony, and many have ocean views. *633 E. Cabrillo Blvd., 93103, tel. 805/564–4333 or 800/879–2929. 359 rooms. Facilities: 2 restaurants, bar, pool, sauna, tennis courts, exercise room, Jacuzzi, lounge with dance floor, putting green, shuffleboard, basketball court, bikes to rent. AE, D, DC, MC, V.*

Santa Barbara Inn. This three-story motel, directly across the street from East Beach, has recently been spruced up, with a crisp new exterior and a sophisticated interior decor featuring light woods, teal accents, and subdued tones. Many rooms have ocean views, and the lower-priced rooms have mountain views but also look over the parking lot. The inn's restaurant, Citronelle, is presided over by French chef Michel Richard, who rustles up California cuisine and has become a favorite of local residents. *901 E. Cabrillo Blvd., 93103, tel. 805/966–2285 or 800/231–0431. 71 rooms. Facilities: restaurant, pool, whirlpool. AE, D, DC, MC, V.*

Expensive **Villa Rosa.** Inside this 60-year-old hotel, a red-tile roofed Spanish-style house of stucco and wood, the rooms and intimate lobby are decorated in an informal southwestern style. The Villa Rosa is just one block from the beach. Rates include Continental breakfast and wine and cheese in the afternoon. *15 Chapala St., 93101, tel. 805/966–0851. 18 rooms. Facilities: pool, spa. AE, MC, V.*

Moderate– **Ambassador by the Sea.** The wrought-iron trim and mosaic til-
Expensive ing on this Spanish-style building near the harbor and Stearns Wharf make this seem the quintessential California beach motel. The rooms have verandas, and there are sundecks that overlook the ocean and the bike path. *202 W. Cabrillo Blvd., 93101, tel. 805/965–4577. 32 units. Facilities: pool, 2 units with kitchenettes. AE, D, DC, MC, V.*

Old Yacht Club Inn. Built in 1912 as a private home in the California Craftsman style, this inn near the beach was one of Santa Barbara's first bed-and-breakfasts. The rooms feature turn-of-the-century furnishings and Oriental rugs. Guests receive complimentary full breakfast and evening wine, along with the use of bikes and beach chairs. No smoking. *431 Corona del Mar Dr., 93103, tel. 805/962–1277 or 800/676–1676, 800/549–1676 in CA. 9 rooms. Facilities: dining room open Sat. for guests only. AE, D, MC, V.*

Moderate **Pacific Crest Inn.** A block from East Beach on a quiet residential street, this motel has clean and comfortable rooms, without the austerity of some budget operations. Kitchens are available in some rooms. *433 Corona del Mar Dr., 93103, tel. 805/966–3103. 26 rooms. Facilities: pool, coin laundry. AE, D, DC, MC, V. Minimum stay: 2 nights on weekends, 3 on holidays.*

Inexpensive **Motel 6.** The low price and location near the beach are the pluses for this no-frills place. Reserve well in advance all year. *443 Corona del Mar Dr., 93103, tel. 805/564–1392. 52 units. Facilities: heated pool. AE, D, DC, MC, V.*

Ojai **Ojai Valley Inn and Country Club.** Reopened in 1988 after a $40
Very Expensive million renovation, the hotel is set in landscaped grounds lush
★ with flowers. The peaceful setting comes with hillside views in nearly all directions. Some of the nicer rooms are in the original adobe building, which has been totally remodeled, but that preserved such luxurious features as huge bathrooms and the original tiles. Suites in the cabanas are more expensive than other rooms. The decor is southwestern style, and works by local artists are featured throughout the resort. *Country Club Rd., 93023, tel. 805/646–5511 or 800/422–OJAI. 212 units. Facilities: 2 restaurants, bar, golf course, lighted tennis courts, 2 pools, men's and women's sauna and steam room, bicycles. AE, D, DC, MC, V.*

Expensive **Oaks at Ojai.** This is a well-known, comfortable health spa with a solid fitness program that includes lodging, three nutritionally balanced, low-calorie meals (surprisingly good), complete use of spa facilities, and 16 optional fitness classes. *122 E. Ojai Ave., 93023, tel. 805/646–5573 or 800/753–6257. 88 rooms. Facilities: dining room, spa with pool, Jacuzzis, sauna, weight room. D, MC, V.*

Moderate– **Best Western Casa Ojai.** On the main street of town, across from
Expensive the Soule Park Golf Course, this spacious modern hotel is topped with a red-tiled Spanish-style roof. Rooms are decorated in blue and white, with tropical-print bedspreads; the

larger deluxe rooms have refrigerators and separate sitting areas. *1302 E. Ojai Ave. 93023, tel. 805/646–8175 or 800/528–1234. 45 rooms. Facilities: pool, Jacuzzi. AE, D, DC, MC, V.*

The Arts and Nightlife

The Arts

Santa Barbara prides itself on being a top-notch cultural center. It supports a professional symphony and chamber orchestra and an impressive art museum. The proximity to the University of California at Santa Barbara assures an endless stream of visiting artists and performers.

The enormous Moorish-style **Arlington Theater** on State Street is home to the Santa Barbara Symphony. The **Lobero,** a state landmark, at the corner of Anacapa and Cañon Perdido streets, shares its stage with community theater groups and touring professionals.

The **Santa Barbara International Film Festival** (1216 State St. 201, 93101, tel. 805/963–0023), held each March, pulls in the Hollywood crowd, with premieres and screenings of American and international films.

Nightlife

Most of the major hotels offer nightly entertainment during the summer season and live weekend entertainment all year. To see what's scheduled at the hotels and many small clubs and restaurants, pick up a copy of the free weekly *Santa Barbara Independent* newspaper for an extensive rundown.

Dancing **Zelo** (630 State St., Santa Barbara, tel. 805/966–5792). This high-energy restaurant doubles as a progressive rock and punk dance club featuring offbeat videos and innovative lighting.

13 Los Angeles for Children

By Mary Jane Horton

L.A. resident Mary Jane Horton contributes to several national magazines and is the mother of two.

Some cities have one famous attraction for kids; Los Angeles and its sprawling environs has them from one end to the other: amusement parks, children's museums, zoos, train rides, children's theater every weekend, nature walks, pony rides, art classes, and much more. Add this to the natural environment—beaches, surrounding mountains, and warm weather almost year-round—and you have a city tailor-made for children. Almost tailor-made, that is. A kid will need a willing adult along, because unlike many big cities, Los Angeles is not a place where kids can get around on their own.

Curiously, although Los Angeles offers a endless array of options for children in their own domain, the city does not welcome kids into the adult domain. Don't go to the trendiest of Beverly Hills restaurants and ask for a high chair. Do go to the many restaurants that cater to children with high chairs, booster seats, and their own menus. The most expensive and poshest of hotels, however, are used to children—many even offer camps and other programs to help keep them busy.

See Traveling with Children in Chapter 1 for information on planning your trip to the Los Angeles area.

Exploring

Activities for kids are spread throughout the Los Angeles basin, but there are certain areas with especially strong offerings: the city proper, Anaheim, and the beach towns.

The *Los Angeles Times* provides ideas for the upcoming week in two regular Saturday columns: "54 Hours" and "Family Spots," both in the View section. *L.A. Parent,* a free monthly tabloid found at toy stores and children's clothing stores, has a monthly calendar section.

Los Angeles

Downtown The **Los Angeles Children's Museum** (*see* Tour 1 in Chapter 3) has lots of hands-on exhibits.

The **Museum of Contemporary Art** (*see* Tour 1 in Chapter 3) is great for older kids and for infants in strollers or carriers; it is not a place to let a two-year-old go crazy. The museum offers kids a booklet, *Together at MOCA: A Guide for Families,* published in several different languages.

Exposition Park Adjoining the USC campus, on Figueroa Street at Exposition Boulevard, this park was built for the 1932 Olympics and features two major museums. The **California Museum of Science and Industry,** beloved by preschool and school-age children, has just undergone a $43 million renovation. Especially popular is the Mitsubishi IMAX Theater—five stories and six-channel stereo. The **Natural History Museum of Los Angeles County** is an immense museum with lots to fascinate youngsters; be sure to visit the hands-on exhibits in the Ralph M. Parsons Discovery Center. *See* Sightseeing Checklists in Chapter 3.

Griffith Park The largest city park in the United States (*see* Sightseeing Checklists in Chapter 3), Griffith Park has several prime attractions for kids.

The **Observatory** has loads of exhibits to interest junior astonomers; film buffs may recognize it from *Rebel Without a Cause*. **Pony Rides** (Crystal Springs Dr., entrance near I–5 and Los Feliz Blvd., tel. 213/664–3266) are safe even for two-year-olds, who are routinely strapped on and paraded around on the slowest of old nags. The ponies come in three versions: slow, medium, and fast; the slow ones are the best, since the faster ones can be jarring. A ride costs $1.25 for two rounds. To round out an eventful morning (the lines are long in late afternoon), there are **stagecoach rides** ($1.25) and a **miniature train ride** ($1.75 adults, $1.25 children) that makes a figure eight near the pony rides. *Open summer, weekdays 10–5:30, weekends 10–6:30; fall-spring, Tues.–Fri. 10–4:30, weekends 10–5.*

Just up the road from the pony rides, a 1926-vintage **merry-go-round** offers melodic rides for families. The broad lawn nearby was the scene of some of the most colorful love-ins of the 1960s.

At **Travel Town,** 15 vintage railroad cars welcome the onslaught of climbing and screaming children. The collection includes a narrow-gauge sugar train from Hawaii, a steam engine, and an old L.A. trolley; there's also old planes, such as World War II bombers, an old fire engine, milk wagon, buggies, and classic cars. *5200 Zoo Dr., tel. 213/662–5874. Admission free. Open weekdays 10–4, weekends 10–5.*

Los Angeles Zoo, one of the major zoos in the United States, is noted for its breeding of endangered species, including white tigers. The 113-acre compound holds more than 2,000 mammals, birds, amphibians, and reptiles. Animals are grouped according to the geographical areas where they are naturally found—Africa, Australia, Eurasia, North America, and South America. Don't miss Adventure Island; the new children's zoo with its interactive exhibits; a walk-through bird exhibit with more than 50 different species; and a koala area, where the furry creatures live amid eucalyptus trees. Seeing the zoo calls for a lot of walking, seemingly all uphill, so strollers or backpacks are recommended for families with young children. The new Safari Shuttle ($4 adults, $1 children under 10 and senior citizens) takes visitors comfortably to the far corners of the zoo. *Tel. 213/666–4090. Admission: $7 adults, $5 senior citizens, $3 children 2–12, under 2 free. Open daily 10–5.*

Westside Kitschy as they can be, many **Hollywood** attractions (*see* Tour 2 in Chapter 3) are just the ticket for starstruck youngsters. Younger kids, however, may get spooked by the lifelike effigies in the Hollywood Wax Museum. If you have dinosaur-lovers in your family, go a short distance east on Wilshire Boulevard to visit **La Brea Tar Pits** and **George C. Page Museum of La Brea Discoveries** (*see* Tour 2 in Chapter 3).

The **Junior Arts Center** offers refreshingly low-priced arts-and-crafts classes year-round. Every Sunday, the center's patio is set up with worktables and art supplies for a two-hour free workshop where parents and children work together on special projects supervised by local artists. There are also gallery exhibits with strong kid appeal. *Barnsdall Park, 4800 Hollywood Blvd., Hollywood, tel. 213/485–4474. Open Tues.–Sat. 12:30–5.*

Santa Monica and **Angel's Attic,** a collection of antique dolls and dollhouses in a
the Beach Towns Queen Anne Victorian, is a popular venue for kids aged about seven years and up; the fact that they can't touch the display

makes it a bit difficult for younger children. A new display is a specially commissioned 1:12 replica of the central portion of Versailles. *516 Colorado Ave., Santa Monica, tel. 310/394–8331. Admission: $4 adults, $2 children under 12, $3 senior citizens. Open Thur.–Sun. 12:30–4:30.*

The **Santa Monica Pier** (*see* Tour 5 in Chapter 3) is a great place for kids to mingle with beach-going crowds; younger ones will love a ride on the vintage **merry-go-round.**

"Mothers' Beach" is the local nickname for Marina Beach (Admiralty Way and Via Marina, Marina del Rey), an apt reflection of its popularity with local families. Nestled in between the sleek sloops and singles condos and bars, this tiny crescent of man-made beach offers a wonderfully protected environment for very young children.

Palos Verdes, San Pedro, and Long Beach San Pedro's **Cabrillo Museum** and **Ports 'O Call Village** make an amusing outing for children; even better is the *Queen Mary,* the fabulous ocean liner docked in Long Beach. (*See* Tour 6 in Chapter 3.)

Long Beach Children's Museum, in its new expanded quarters in a Long Beach mall, features the regulation-issue children's-museum exhibits such as The Art Cafe and Granny's Attic. All exhibits welcome curious minds and eager hands. *445 Long Beach Blvd. at Long Beach Plaza, Long Beach, tel. 310/495–1163. Admission: $3.95, under 1 free. Open Thur.–Sat. 11–4, Sun. noon–4.*

Highland Park, Pasadena, and San Marino Among the attractions in these towns (*see* Tour 7 in Chapter 3), **Kidspace** is a logical stop for families; **Heritage Square** is interesting to school-age chidren.

San Fernando Valley Three entertainment-industry locales here are naturals for families: **Burbank Studios, NBC Studios,** and the ever-popular **Universal Studios Tour** (*see* The San Fernando Valley in Chapter 3). Be careful not to bring younger chiildren on the Universal Tour—they may be scared of the very things that their older siblings love: the realistic special-effects simulations of earthquakes and the like. The 45-minute tram-ride may be too much for younger kids, but there's plenty else for them to do here.

Other Places of Interest **Gene Autry Western Heritage Museum** (*see* Other Places of Interest in Chapter 3) has a new hands-on area for children. They can rummage through a re-created attic dolls, clothes, toys, pretend to use an old-fashioned washing machine, and dress up like cowboys. Kids from about one year old to preteens will enjoy this new facility.

Lomita Railroad Museum, hidden away in a typical suburban neighborhood, is housed in a replica of a turn-of-the-century Massachusetts train station. Beyond the gate, discover one of the largest collections of railroad memorabilia in the West. Climb aboard a real steam engine and take a look at the immaculate interior of the car itself. *2137 250th St., Lomita, tel. 310/326–6255. Admission: $1. Open Wed.–Sun. 10–5.*

Paramount Ranch was once wild terrain where grizzly bears ran wild; fledgeling Paramount Pictures bought the land in 1927 and shot many westerns here. In 1980 it became part of the Santa Monica Mountains National Recreation Area. Paramount's old western sets, still used to shoot television shows and movies, are open to the public. The 436-acre site also includes many hiking trails. Ranger-led tours of the area are offered monthly. *Cornell Rd., Agoura Hills; 101 Fwy. to Kanan Rd. exit, south on Kanan Rd. to Cornell, turn right, ranch is 2½ mi on right, tel. 818/597–9192. Admission free. Open daily sunrise–sunset.*

Raging Waters, Los Angeles's major water park, is situated in Bonelli Regional Park, using 44 acres for swimming pools, lagoons, water slides, and other water-related activities. There are slides for all ages and levels of daring, including the new Endless River ride. For nonwater-types there are sunny "beaches" and special pools for the tiniest visitors. Bring your own towels. Picnicking spots available as well as fast-food stands. *111 Raging Waters Dr., San Dimas, tel. 714/592–6453. Admission: $18.95 adults, $9.95 children 42″–48″ tall. Open Apr.–May, weekends 10–6; late June–Mar., weekdays 10–9, weekends 9–10.*

Six Flags Magic Mountain, the only real amusement park actually in Los Angeles County, offers 260 acres of rides, shows, and entertainments. The roster of major rides is headlined by Viper, the world's largest looping roller coaster. The first drop is 18 stories high, and three vertical loops turn you upside down seven times. There's also the Roaring Rapids, a simulated white-water wilderness adventure complete with whirlpools, waves, and real rapids; the Colossus, the largest dual-track wood roller coaster ever built, which speeds at more than 62 miles per hour; and the Revolution, a steelcoaster with a 360-degree, 90-foot vertical loop. On the Z-Force ride, passengers ride upside down; the new Yosemite Sam Sierra Falls is a two-person raft ride with a 760-foot twisting water slide. Children's World is a minipark with scaled-down rides, such as the Red Baron's Airplane and the Little Sailor Ride. Other attractions at the park include a puppet theater, crafts demonstrations, celebrity musical revues, Dixieland jazz, rock concerts, and the Aqua Theater high-diving shows. *26101 Magic Mountain Pkwy., off I–5, Valencia, tel. 818/992–0884. Admission: $26 adults, $17 senior citizens, $15 children 4 ft tall and under. Open May 8–Labor Day, daily 10–10 (later on weekends); rest of year, weekends and holidays 10–10.*

Orange County

Without a doubt, **Disneyland,** followed by **Knott's Berry Farm,** are the main attractions for children in Orange County (*see* Exploring Orange County in Chapter 10), but there's plenty else here to round out a family vacation.

Disneyland The news at Disneyland is **Mickey's Toontown,** perfect to wind down kids ages 3–8 after a long day. All the Disney characters live in this wonderful play area, with Goofy's Bounce House, Chip 'N Dale's Treehouse Slide, Go Coaster, Donald Duck's Boat, and Mickey's and Minnie's houses next door to one another. Other places in the park for the younger set are: **Fantasyland, Tom Sawyer's World,** and **Big Thunder Ranch** in Frontierland. For kids 6 and older, look for all the mountain rides—**Splash Mountain, Thunder Mountain, Space Mountain,** and the **Matterhorn,** all thrilling rollercoasters.

Knott's Berry Farm This famous theme park has plenty of thrill rides to attract older kids; the littler ones will be happier riding the antique **carousel** and exploring **Ghost Town** and **Camp Snoopy.**

Inland Orange County **Bowers Museum** (*see* Exploring Orange County in Chapter 10), which has been in Santa Ana since the 1930s, was recently expanded to five times its size. Children especially like the exhibits on Native Americans and there is a great interactive video for schoool-age kids in the Central America Room.

The **Children's Museum at La Habra** is housed in a 1923-vintage Union Pacific railroad depot, with old railroad cars resting nearby. This museum combines permanent and special exhibitions all designed to stimulate young minds—the painless way. In Grandma's Attic, children can try on old clothes and parade in front of a mirror. There's a real beehive (behind glass) and dozens of stuffed animals. *301 S. Euclid St., La Habra, tel. 310/905–9793. Admission: $3 adults, $2.50 children 2–16, $2.50 senior citizens. Open Mon.–Sat. 10–4.*

Golf-n-Stuff offers unusual family golfing fun, conveniently near Disneyland. Colored lights sparkle on the miniature golf courses' geyser fountains amid windmills, castles, and waterfalls. *1656 S. Harbor Blvd., tel. 714/994–2110. Admission: $5 adults and children 6 and up, 5 and under free; special family rates. Open Sun.–Thur. 10–10, Fri.–Sat. 10 AM–midnight.*

Hobby City Doll and Toy Museum houses antique dolls and toys from around the world in a replica of the White House. It is one of the world's largest hobby, crafts, and collector centers. *1238 S. Beach Blvd., Anaheim, tel. 714/527–2323. Open daily 10–6.*

Movieland Wax Museum (*see* Exploring Orange County in Chapter 10) is kitschy but fun, although it may be frightening to younger kids.

Wild Rivers is Orange County's newest water theme park. It has more than 40 rides and attractions. Among them: a wave pool, several daring slides, a river inner-tube ride, and several places at which to eat and shop. *8800 Irvine Center Dr., Laguna Hills, off I-405 at Irvine Center Dr., tel. 714/768–9453. Admission: $16.95 adults, $12.95 children 3–9, 2 and under free; discounts after 4. Open mid-May–Sept. Call for hours.*

The Coast **Bolsa Chica Egological Reserve** is great for young nature-lovers; the **Huntington Beach International Surfing Museum** is a good introduction to this quintessential West Coast sport; and the **Balboa Island Fun Zone** is a charming small set of rides, including a Ferris wheel, near the Balboa Pavilion. (*see* Exploring Orange County in Chapter 10.)

Palm Springs

Balloon flights are a popular way for families to see the desert. Several companies offer the rides: **American Balloon Charters** (tel. 619/327–8544); **Desert Balloon Charters** (tel. 619/346–8575); **Dream Flights** (tel. 800/933–5628); **Sunrise Balloons** (tel. 800/548–9912).

Bubba Bear's Pizza Theater is more than a restaurant—it's an entertainment area for kids of all ages, perfect if you get caught in the desert in the rain. Older kids will enjoy the video games and pinball arcade, and for the younger ones there are mechanical rides, a ball pit, a slide, and a climbing apparatus. *72–20 Dinah Shore Dr., Rancho Mirage, tel. 619/770–1333. Open daily 10 AM–11 PM except major holidays.*

Children's Museum of the Desert offers hands-on fun in an art recycling workshop, bakery, garden/science lab, dentist's office, and radio station. *42–501 Rancho Mirage La., Rancho Mirage, tel. 619/346–2900. Admission: $2. Open Thur. 3–7, Fri.–Sat. 9–3.*

The Dinosaur Gardens are a must-see. Claude Bell designed and built the 150-foot-long brontosaurus and matching Tyrannosaurus rex right off the main highway. The dinosaurs starred in the movie *Pee-wee's Big Adventure. 5800 Seminole Dr., Cabazon, off I–10 just before Hwy. 111, 18 mi northwest of Palm Springs, no tel. Open Wed.–Mon. 9–5.*

At the **Oasis Water Resort,** tubing, water slides, "Squirt City," and other watery delights will entertain a wide range of age groups. *1500 Gene Autry Trail, between Hwy. 111 and Ramon Rd., tel. 619/325–7873. Admission prices and hours vary by season.*

At the **Palm Springs Swim Center,** an Olympic-size pool has a separate children-only section. Swimming instruction is available for all ages. *405 S. Pavilion, at intersection of Sunrise Way and Ramon Rd., tel. 619/323–8278. Admission prices and hours vary by season.*

Other fun activities for kids around the desert resorts include the **Aerial Tramway, the Living Desert, Village Green Heritage Center,** and **Indian Canyons** (*see* Exploring Palm Springs in Chapter 11).

Riverside and San Bernadino Counties

Orange Empire Railway Museum is an outdoor museum the size of a town, where children can see—and ride on—many old trains and trolleys: diesel-operated locomotives, electric- and steam-powered locomotives, and cars from Los Angeles's old Red Line. *2201 S. A St., Perris, tel. 714/657–2605. Admission free; all-day ticket $5 adults, $3 children 11 and under. Open winter, weekends and holidays (except Christmas and New Year's Day), 11–4; summer, weekends and holidays 11–5.*

A Special Place, Children's Hands On Museum, allows handicapped and nonhandicapped children to participate side by side. Exhibits include: School Days, which helps kids learn history while sitting at old school desks or shovelling coal into a potbellied stove; a Shadow Room; a Drama Area for dress up; and a Disability Awareness area equipped with wheelchairs, crutches, Braille material, and other items used by physically challenged children. *1003 E. Highland Ave., San Bernadino, tel. 714/881–1201. Admission: $2. Open Tues.–Fri. 9–1, Sat. 11–3.*

Other attractions in Riverside include the **Castle Park** amusement park and, for older children who enjoy history, the restored Victorian mansion **Heritage House** (*see* Riverside in Chapter 9).

If you're making the trip to Lake Arrowhead, be sure to take your family to **Santa's Village** (*see* Big Bear/Lake Arrowhead in Chapter 9).

Santa Barbara

Children's Museum of Santa Barbara will keep children, the youngest to early teens, occupied for hours. Among the hands on exhibits are: a real fire truck along with boots, hats, coats and other clothes to try on; a new police exhibit that features real police calls on the twoway radio; a doctor's office complete with charts, examining table, scales; a dental office with a real dentist's chair; and a computer with games. *LaCumbre Plaza Shopping Center, 121 S. Hope Ave., tel. 805/682–0845. Admission: $2 adults, $1 children 2 and older, under 2 free. Open Mon. and Wed.–Fri. 11–5, Tues. and weekends 11–1.*

Sea Center on Stearns Wharf interests everyone from infants, who are lulled by the sight of fish in water, to teen agers and adults. This educational center is a joint project of the Santa Barbara Museum of Natural History and the Channel Islands National Marine Sanctuary. Exhibits depict marine life from the Santa Barbara coastline to the Channel Islands: aquariums, life-size models of whales and dolphins, undersea dioramas, interactive computer/video displays, and remains of shipwrecks. The Touch Tank lets you handle marine invertabrates, fish, and marine plants collected from nearby waters. *211 Stearns Wharf, tel. 805/962–0885. Admission: $2 adults, $1.50 senior citizens, $1 children 3–17, under 3 free. Sea Center open daily 2–5, Touch Tank open Tues.–Sun. noon- -4.*

At the **Santa Barbara Zoo,** youngsters particularly enjoy the scenic railroad and barnyard petting zoo. For children who quickly tire of the beach, there's an elaborate jungle gym play area at Santa Barbara's **East Beach,** next to the Cabrillo Bath House. Outside of Santa Barbara's **Museum of Natural History** is the skeleton of a blue whale, the world's largest creature. Kids are dwarfed by the bones and invited to touch them (they just can't climb on them). (*See* Exploring Santa Barbara in Chapter 12.)

Shopping

With world-renowned stores like FAO Schwarz for toys and Oilily for bright Scandinavian clothing, Los Angeles is like a labyrinth chockful of goodies of all kind. There are bookstores geared to children with story hours; lots of unusual toy stores; and several Disney and Warner Bros. stores to remind children and their parents that they are, after all, in the movie capital of the world.

Santa Monica Montana Avenue in Santa Monica is a treasure trove of colorful clothing and toy stores. If you start at First Street and crisscross, you'll be sure not to miss anything. Look for: **Sara** (1324 Montana Ave. tel. 310/393–2842), which specializes in unusual children's clothes from around the world; **And Apple Pie** (1211 Montana Blvd., tel. 310/393–4588), a tiny store with a big selection of the everpopular Flapdoodles line, Fitigues, and sweaters from Ball of Cotton, all for newborns and toddlers; and **Imagine** (1324 Montana Ave., tel. 310/395–9553) for custom-designed furniture and bedding as well as a large assortment of European wood toys and gifts.

Beyond Montana, **Malina's Children's Store** (2654C Main St., tel. 310/392–2611; 116088 San Vicente Blvd., tel. 310/820–2806) has the newest of European fashions for boys and girls in sizes newborn–6X, as well as Malina's own custom designs.

Santa Monica Place Mall (315 Broadway, tel. 310/394–5451) has quite a wide array of children's stores including: **Cotton Kids** for pure cotton clothing; **Footprints for Kids,** a children's shoe store; **Gymboree,** for activewear and toys; **Imaginarium,** one of the area's best chain toy stores; **Kidz in Motion,** for kids' clothing and haircuts; **Limited Too,** the children's line of the well-priced clothing chain; **Toys International,** with toys from around the world; **Sanrio Surprises,** selling Hello Kitty gifts and stationery; **Supertoons,** cartoon memorabilia and T-shirts; and **Warner Bros.,** with even more cartoon items.

Colors of the Wind (2900 Main St., tel. 310/399–8044) offers just about any kind of kite you can imagine.

Fred Segal Baby (500 S. Broadway, tel. 310/451–5200) sells a great selection of unusual American and European clothing.

Beverly Hills Area In Beverly Hills the stores that cater to children have the trendiest clothes and toys, and the highest price tags. Cotton separates and French designer clothes fill the shelves at **Agnes 'B** (100 N. Robertson Blvd., tel. 310/271–9643). **Auntie Barbara's Kids** (245 S. Beverly Dr., tel. 310/276–2864) is full of unusual American and European clothing. **Baby Guess** (461 N. Robertson Blvd., tel. 310/274–0515) has a big selection of playwear and lots of denim for children 3 months and up. A recently enlarged **FAO Schwarz** toy store is at the Beverly Center (8500 Beverly Blvd, at La Cienega Blvd.). **Harry Harris Shoes for Children** (409 N. Canon Dr., tel. 310/274–8481) offers a wide selection of European leather shoes and sports footwear for kids. **Imaginarium** (Century City Shopping Center, 10250 Santa Monica Blvd., tel. 310/785–0227) encourages children to play in the store with its nonviolent and educational playthings. **Oilily** (9520 Brighton Way, tel. 310/859–9145) stocks women's and children's wear splashed with bright primary colors in designs from the Netherlands. **Pixie Town** (400 N. Beverly Dr., tel. 213/272–6415) has impeccably designed clothing from newborn to size 14.

Books of Wonder (439 N. Beverly Dr., tel. 310/247–8025), sister store of the well-known New York children's bookstore, offers the best in classic and new books for all ages as well as old and rare collectible items. Each Sunday free storytelling hours at 11:30 feature well-known children's authors reading from their own books.

Hollywood Area **Sarah Patterson** (725 N. La Cienega Blvd., tel. 310/652–8159) sells imported European clothing and does haircuts in a submarine set-up. **Funny Papers** (1953½ N. Hillhurst Ave., tel. 213/666–4006) is a whimsical and cheery store filled with cards, wind-up toys, T-shirts, and other gift items. **Comic Connection** (1608 N. Hillhurst Ave., tel. 213/665–7715) always has the hottest comic books. **Every Picture Tells a Story** (836 N. La Brea Ave., tel. 213/962–5420) is an intriguing gallery exhibiting original artwork from children's books. **American Rag Cie Youth** (136 S. La Brea Ave., tel. 213/965–1404) specializes in vintage clothing for kids; they also have toys and gift items. **Flicka** (204 N. Larchmont Blvd., tel. 213/466–5822) has cowboy-themed clothing and other unusual items for infants and older children.

Happily Ever After Children's Bookstore (2640 Griffith Park Blvd., tel. 213/668–1996) has a wide selection of children's books, audio and video cassettes, and parenting books; storytelling is offered on the first and third Wednesdays of each month at 11.

Pasadena and the San Fernando Valley The valleys are a great place to shop because there are so many families with children living there. For the many malls in the area, *see* Chapter 4.

The Chocolate Giraffe (121 N. Maryland Ave., Glendale, tel. 818/243–5437; 16954 Ventura Blvd., Encino, tel. 818/907–5437; 516 S. Lake Ave., Pasadena, tel. 818/796–5437) carries brands such as Flapdoodles, Jean Bourget, and Polo as well as accessories, books, tapes, and gift items. **Karin & John** (110 W. Bellevue, No. 15, Pasadena, tel. 818/792–9515) is an outlet store with Fix of Sweden and Mixi of Denmark separates for infants and older children. **Pages Books for Children and Young Adults** (18399 Ventura Blvd., Tarzana, tel. 818/342–6657) has books for young children through the high school years. **Splash** (12109 Ventura Blvd., Studio City, tel. 818/762–6123) is the place to shop if you like to dress your child (newborn to toddler) in the latest chic fashions.

Orange County The largest concentration of child-related stores is at **South Coast Plaza,** in Costa Mesa (*see* Shopping in Chapter 10), which includes: **FAO Schwartz; The Disney Store; Sesame Street General store; Bergestrom's Children's Store,** with baby toys and equipment and clothing for all ages; **Toys International; Benneton 0–2–3; Gymboree;** and **Barneys New York/Chelsea Passage,** for very fashionable baby clothes.

Santa Barbara **This Little Piggy Wears Cotton** (Paseo Nuevo on State St., tel. 805/564–6982) specializes in natural clothing for infants to size-14 children.

Pinky Blue (1253 Coast Village Rd., Montecito, tel. 805/969–1094) carries clothing and accessories for babies and older children. It is known for its French imports and custom-made baby gifts.

Parks, Playgrounds, and Beaches

Parks

Los Angeles is a land of wide-open spaces—much of it covered with freeways, housing developments, and minimalls, it's true, but there are also many beautiful parks and recreation areas with special places for kids.

The main park in the city of Los Angeles is undoubtedly 4,000-acre **Griffith Park** (*see* Exploring, *above*), which offers tennis courts, bike lanes, horse trails, and hiking trails as well as the attractions covered above. It's a thrill to hike up the hill with vistas of the city in the background (although younger children should probably ride in a backpack or a stroller); one good trail starts right from the Observatory parking lot. For children there are several play areas around the park. Near the carousel is an especially good one with bars and rings, and bouncy animals for the younger kids.

Will Rogers State Historic Park in Pacific Palisades (*see* Tour 5 in Chapter 3) is a wonderful place for children, with broad lawns, walking trails, and even polo games on Saturdays and Sundays (call 310/454–8212 for polo information).

El Dorado Regional Park and Nature Center (*see* Tour 6 in Chapter 3) has stocked lakes for fishing, and **El Dorado West City Park** has a duck pond as well as skating and bicycling paths.

William S. Hart County Park (*see* Sightseeing Checklists in Chapter 3) is a real cowboy ranch, once owned by cowboy actor William S. Hart; there are hiking trails, barbeque pits, picnic tables, and a small museum on the grounds. Guided tours are given of Hart's house, which is filled with Western art and memorabilia.

Eaton Canyon Park and Nature Center (*see* Sightseeing Checklists in Chapter 3) offers children tours of the natural habitat of this area.

In the **Angeles National Forest,** above Pasadena, you can go to the top of Mount Wilson for spectacular views of Los Angeles. The Chilao Visitors Center, 13 miles north of Mount Wilson, offers nature walks and exhibits about the forest.

Playgrounds

Since so many Angeleno families have their own backyards to play in, playgrounds are not as prevalent as in more crowded cities. But here are some worth visiting, if you are nearby with kids who need to climb, slide, and swing.

Griffith Park has a small playground near the carousel (*see* Exploring, *above*); there is also one across from the Griffith Park Boulevard entrance, and one just past the golf course. A free map of the park is available at the Visitors Center, 4730 Crystal Drive.

In Beverly Hills, **Roxbury Park** (*see* Sightseeing Checklists in Chapter 3) has innovative wooden playing structures—one for younger kids and one for older kids.

The playground in **Lacy Park** (3300 Monterey Rd., San Marino) has a big steel spaceship that rises into the sky and a red fire truck for kids to climb on.

On the ocean, just below **Palisades Park** in Santa Monica (*see* Tour 5 in Chapter 3), is a playground right on the sand, with a view of the Pacific in the background; walk down the stairs at Arizona Avenue.

In Laguna Beach, there is a great seaside playground on **Main Beach,** and a more secluded one on **Cress Street.**

Beaches

Young families seem to frequent the beaches in Santa Monica, in South Bay towns such as Redondo Beach, and in Malibu. Teenagers flock to Huntington Beach, which is the center of

Orange County surfing activities. For write-ups on these beaches, *see* Beaches in Chapter 5.

Best Bets **Santa Monica State Beach** is definitely popular with families: a wide expanse of sand with all kinds of facilities including a pier, volleyball courts, and playground equipment.

Mother's Beach (Marina Beach) in Marina del Rey is good for young kids because of the lack of waves.

Will Rogers State Beach in Pacific Palisades is a nice family beach with areas for swimming and two separate areas for surfing.

Paradise Cove in Malibu is a secluded family beach with a pier and equipment rentals.

Newport Dunes Aquatic Park (Jamboree Rd. and Pacific Coast Highway, Newport Beach) is a lifeguarded lagoon perfect for younger children. Different types of boats are available for rent.

In Laguna, **Main Beach,** in the center of town, has the non-stop action; for a more private seaside romp, try **Wood's Cove** (*see* Exploring Orange County in Chapter 10), which is surrounded by high cliffs and has lots of rocks to climb on.

Dana Point (*see* Exploring Orange County in Chapter 10) is very popular with kids—there's a sheltered beach for swimming, tide pools, and a pier with boat rentals and whale-watching tours.

Dining

L.A. restaurants are receptive to families—all but the trendiest. Most have some booster seats and high chairs, but there often aren't enough to go around. Certain places welcome children with open arms, providing special activities and menus; we've listed the best of them below. For addresses, phone numbers, and other pertinent facts, *see* Chapter 6 and Dining in Chapters 10, 11, and 12.

Los Angeles **Art's Deli** is *the* typical Jewish deli in the Valley. Sandwiches are piled high; after all, Art's corny motto is "Every Sandwich is a Work of Art." **The California Pizza Kitchen** in Beverly Hills really welcomes kids; crayons on the table keep kids busy while they wait for the pizza. Teenagers will get a kick out of the unusual types of pizzas. **Ed Debevic's** in Beverly Hills is a raucous place with outrageous D.J.s, loud music, and waiters and waitresses in 1950s outfits who sit at your table when you order. The food is no-nonsense and great for kids. **The Hard Rock Cafe,** near the Beverly Center, deserves its reputation; it is a great place to starwatch. This haunt for local teenagers will give kids from other places an inside look at teen culture in Los Angeles. **The Pacific Dining Car** is a downtown Los Angeles landmark, located in a 1920's railroad car, which is a big draw for kids. The prices here are steep, and it's mostly business people during the week, but on weekends you will find families here. **R.J.'s the Rib Joint** in Beverly Hills is the epitome of Beverly Hills casual; younger kids will like all of the activity, and older kids will have fun filling their plates to the brim at the huge salad bar. **Victoria Station** is the perfect pit-stop while visiting Universal Studios. It's a re-creation of the London railroad station; Junior Conductor dinners cater to children under 12.

Orange County Children will revel at the Western memorabilia at **Overland Stage** in Anaheim, but you might have trouble convincing them to eat such specials as wild boar. Luckily, more tame food is also available. **Ruby's** has a great location at the end of the Balboa Pier; order from the outside window or go inside and drink in the ambiance of a 1940s diner. The view is a big pull for children and adults at **The Beach House** in Laguna Beach. You really feel as if you are eating right on the beach, and the waiters and waitresses are well accustomed to serving children.

Palm Springs **Elmer's Pancake and Steak House** is a Palm Springs tradition. Kids love to pick from the many different kinds of pancakes.

Santa Barbara **Castagnola Bros. Seafood Restaurant** is a child-friendly restaurant on the pier in Barbara. Fresh fish is served, casually, on paper plates.

Lodging

All hotels in Los Angeles and its environs are happy to welcome children. As a matter of fact, it sometimes seems that the more expensive the hotel, the more attentive it is to children. Areas near child-oriented attractions—Disneyland, Universal Studios, the beaches—are especially geared to handle lots of children.

For baby-sitting, try your hotel concierge first; he or she can usually set something up with at least 24 hours notice. Rates vary, but run around $7–$10. Many hotels use the **Babysitters Guild** (tel. 213/658–8792); **Sitters Unlimited** has franchises throughout the area (Huntington Beach and Long Beach, tel. 310/596–0550; Orange County, tel. 714/559–5360). All of the major chains—including Sheraton, Hilton, and Marriott- – have local hotels that participate in their corporate children's programs. In addition, many smaller chains and single properties have programs to entertain your child for a few hours or an entire day. Most children's programs go full force only in summer, but the hotels usually continue them during the winter on weekends and during school vacations. The following are some of the more popular children's programs; *see* Chapter 7 and Lodging in Chapters 10 and 12.

Los Angeles The **Ritz-Carlton** hotels in Laguna Niquel, Marina del Rey, and Pasadena all have some children's activities. For instance, the **Ritz-Carlton Marina del Rey** has three programs for children over 5 years old; a children's dinner theater; the Ritz Kids Day Camp for supervised activity; and a fire-station tour with lunch. At the **Century Plaza Hotel and Tower,** the "Little Stars" program offers special family rates and surprises for children 3–12: Century Plaza teddy bears, cookies and milk, balloons, and a hotel T-shirt. Free amenities for infants include "no tears" shampoo, baby oil, stuffed animals, high chairs, bottles, baby blankets, and even bottle warmers.

Orange County At the **Dana Point Resort,** Camp Cowabunga for ages 5–12 (cost: $30 per day, $15 per half day) lets kids swim, make kites, and handle sealife at nearby tidepools. Watercolors, the resort's restaurant, provides special coloring-book menus and crayons.

Santa Barbara The venerable **Four Seasons Biltmore Santa Barbara** calls its complimentary children's program "Kids for All Seasons." For ages 5 and up, there's a different theme each week—such as Dick Tracy, Teenage Mutant Ninja Turtles, or Little Mermaid Beach Party—with activities such as pool games, arts and crafts, sandcastle building, cooking lessons, and treasure hunts. At **Ojai Valley Inn and Country Club,** kids 3 years and older can attend Camp Ojai, a fun-filled day of supervised arts and crafts, games and races, and swimming.

The Arts

Los Angeles has quite a large selection of arty activities for kids, from children's theater to concerts and great museums. *L.A. Parent* is a great guide for up-to-date theater, concert, and movie listings; all listings of performances include a mention of the appropriate ages.

Bob Baker Marionette Theater (1345 W. 1st St., tel. 213/250–9995) has been a staple on the kid scene in Los Angeles for 30 years, with performances at 10:30 every weekday morning and 2:30 on weekend afternoons. Kids sit on a carpeted floor and get a close-up view of the intricate marionettes; ice cream and juice are served afterward. Reservations are required; tickets cost $10 per person, $8 senior citizens.

The Santa Monica Playhouse (1211 4th St., tel. 310/394–9779) offers children's productions of plays such as "Barnyard Madness with the Three Little Pigs" and "Beauty and the Beast." Tickets cost $7; performances are on weekends at 1 and 3.

The **Director's Guild** (7920 Sunset Blvd., Hollywood, tel. 213/461–9622) has a special **Saturday Matinees for Children** program, performing old stand-bys like "The Adventures of Tom Sawyer."

Storybook Theater (333 Cahuenga Blvd., Hollywood, tel. 818/761–2203) mounts original plays and musical theater for children aged 2–9.

Wonderworld Puppet Theater (tel. 310/532–1741) presents Saturday-morning puppet shows for an audience of short attention spans and curious young minds. After the adventure-filled performance, the curtains come down and children can see how it was done. Call for locations and schedule; tickets are $4–$5.

The Orange County Performing Arts Center (*see* The Arts and Nightlife in Chapter 10) has many children's plays. In late winter, the annual **Imagination Celebration** (with events around the county) is a fun arts festival for children, with public performances, exhibits, and hands-on workshops.

Laguna Moulton Playhouse (606 Laguna Canyon Rd., tel. 714/494–0743), also in Orange County, has a special children's theater with changing fare.

Index

Personal Itinerary

Departure *Date*

Time

Transportation

Arrival *Date*   *Time*

Departure *Date*   *Time*

Transportation

Accommodations

Arrival *Date*   *Time*

Departure *Date*   *Time*

Transportation

Accommodations

Arrival *Date*   *Time*

Departure *Date*   *Time*

Transportation

Accommodations

Personal Itinerary

Arrival	*Date*	*Time*
Departure	*Date*	*Time*
Transportation		
Accommodations		

Arrival	*Date*	*Time*
Departure	*Date*	*Time*
Transportation		
Accommodations		

Arrival	*Date*	*Time*
Departure	*Date*	*Time*
Transportation		
Accommodations		

Arrival	*Date*	*Time*
Departure	*Date*	*Time*
Transportation		
Accommodations		

Personal Itinerary

Arrival *Date*   *Time*

Departure *Date*   *Time*

Transportation

Accommodations

Arrival *Date*   *Time*

Departure *Date*   *Time*

Transportation

Accommodations

Arrival *Date*   *Time*

Departure *Date*   *Time*

Transportation

Accommodations

Arrival *Date*   *Time*

Departure *Date*   *Time*

Transportation

Accommodations

Fodor's Travel Guides

Available at bookstores everywhere, or call 1–800–533–6478, 24 hours a day.

U.S. Guides

Alaska

Arizona

Boston

California

Cape Cod, Martha's Vineyard, Nantucket

The Carolinas & the Georgia Coast

Chicago

Colorado

Florida

Hawaii

Las Vegas, Reno, Tahoe

Los Angeles

Maine, Vermont, New Hampshire

Maui

Miami & the Keys

New England

New Orleans

New York City

Pacific North Coast

Philadelphia & the Pennsylvania Dutch Country

The Rockies

San Diego

San Francisco

Santa Fe, Taos, Albuquerque

Seattle & Vancouver

The South

The U.S. & British Virgin Islands

The Upper Great Lakes Region

USA

Vacations in New York State

Vacations on the Jersey Shore

Virginia & Maryland

Waikiki

Walt Disney World and the Orlando Area

Washington, D.C.

Foreign Guides

Acapulco, Ixtapa, Zihuatanejo

Australia & New Zealand

Austria

The Bahamas

Baja & Mexico's Pacific Coast Resorts

Barbados

Berlin

Bermuda

Brazil

Brittany & Normandy

Budapest

Canada

Cancun, Cozumel, Yucatan Peninsula

Caribbean

China

Costa Rica, Belize, Guatemala

The Czech Republic & Slovakia

Eastern Europe

Egypt

Euro Disney

Europe

Europe's Great Cities

Florence & Tuscany

France

Germany

Great Britain

Greece

The Himalayan Countries

Hong Kong

India

Ireland

Israel

Italy

Japan

Kenya & Tanzania

Korea

London

Madrid & Barcelona

Mexico

Montreal & Quebec City

Morocco

Moscow & St. Petersburg

The Netherlands, Belgium & Luxembourg

New Zealand

Norway

Nova Scotia, Prince Edward Island & New Brunswick

Paris

Portugal

Provence & the Riviera

Rome

Russia & the Baltic Countries

Scandinavia

Scotland

Singapore

South America

Southeast Asia

Spain

Sweden

Switzerland

Thailand

Tokyo

Toronto

Turkey

Vienna & the Danube Valley

Yugoslavia

Special Series

Fodor's Affordables
Caribbean
Europe
Florida
France
Germany
Great Britain
London
Italy
Paris

Fodor's Bed & Breakfast and Country Inns Guides
Canada's Great Country Inns
California
Cottages, B&Bs and Country Inns of England and Wales
Mid-Atlantic Region
New England
The Pacific Northwest
The South
The Southwest
The Upper Great Lakes Region
The West Coast

The Berkeley Guides
California
Central America
Eastern Europe
France
Germany

Great Britain & Ireland
Mexico
Pacific Northwest & Alaska
San Francisco

Fodor's Exploring Guides
Australia
Britain
California
The Caribbean
Florida
France
Germany
Ireland
Italy
London
New York City
Paris
Rome
Singapore & Malaysia
Spain
Thailand

Fodor's Flashmaps
New York
Washington, D.C.

Fodor's Pocket Guides
Bahamas
Barbados
Jamaica
London

New York City
Paris
Puerto Rico
San Francisco
Washington, D.C.

Fodor's Sports
Cycling
Hiking
Running
Sailing
The Insider's Guide to the Best Canadian Skiing
Skiing in the USA & Canada

Fodor's Three-In-Ones (guidebook, language cassette, and phrase book)
France
Germany
Italy
Mexico
Spain

Fodor's Special-Interest Guides
Accessible USA
Cruises and Ports of Call
Euro Disney
Halliday's New England Food Explorer

Healthy Escapes
London Companion
Shadow Traffic's New York Shortcuts and Traffic Tips
Sunday in New York
Walt Disney World and the Orlando Area
Walt Disney World for Adults

Fodor's Touring Guides
Touring Europe
Touring USA: Eastern Edition

Fodor's Vacation Planners
Great American Vacations
National Parks of the East
National Parks of the West

The Wall Street Journal Guides to Business Travel
Europe
International Cities
Pacific Rim
USA & Canada

WHEREVER YOU TRAVEL, ℋELP IS NEVER FAR AWAY.

**From planning your trip to replacing
lost Cards, American Express® Travel Service
Offices* are always there to help.**

LOS ANGELES
*The Hilton Center
901 W. 7th St.*
213-627-4800

*8493 W. 3rd St.
at La Cienega Blvd..*
310-659-1682

*327 N. Beverly Drive
Beverly Hills*
310-274-8277

*351 S. State College Blvd.
Brea*
714-671-6967

*650 Anton Blvd.
Costa Mesa*
714-540-3611

*Chase Travel Service
316 E. Broadway
Glendale*
818-246-1661

*251 S. Lake Ave.
Pasadena*
818-449-2281

*Conejo Travel
575 Thousand Oaks Blvd.
Thousand Oaks*
805-497-3961

*267 Del Amo Fashion Center
Torrance*
310-542-8631

LONG BEACH
301 E. Ocean Blvd.
310-432-2029

PALM SPRINGS
*Anderson Travel
700 East Tahquitz Canyon Way
Palm Springs*
619-325-2001

*Anderson Travel
72785 Highway 111
Palm Desert*
619-346-8017

For the office nearest you, call 1-800-YES-AMEX.

INTRODUCING

AT LAST, YOUR OWN PERSONALIZED LIST OF WHAT'S GOING ON IN THE CITIES YOU'RE VISITING.

KEYED TO THE DAYS WHEN YOU'RE THERE, CUSTOMIZED FOR YOUR INTERESTS, AND SENT TO YOU BEFORE YOU LEAVE HOME.

EXCLUSIVE FOR PURCHASERS OF FODOR'S GUIDES...

Introducing a revolutionary way to get customized, time-sensitive travel information just before your trip.

Now you can obtain detailed information about what's going on in each city you'll be visiting <u>before</u> you leave home—up-to-the-minute, objective information about the events and activities that interest you most.

This is a special offer for purchasers of Fodor's guides – a customized Travel Update to fit your specific interests and your itinerary.

Travel Updates contain the kind of time-sensitive insider information you can get only from local contacts – or from city magazines and newspapers once you arrive. But now you can have the same information before you leave for your trip.

The choice is yours: current art exhibits, theater, music festivals and special concerts, sporting events, antiques and flower shows, shopping, fitness, and more.

The information comes from hundreds of correspondents and thousands of sources worldwide. Updated continuously, it's like having your own personal concierge or friend in the city.

You specify the cities and when you'll be there. We'll do the rest — personalizing the information for you the way no guidebook can.

It's the perfect extension to your Fodor's guide and the best way to make the most of your valuable travel time.

Your Itinerary:
Customized reports available for 160 destinations

99
Regen
The a
in this
domain c
tion as Jo
worthwhile.
the performa.
Tickets are usu
venue. Alterna
mances are cance
given. For more in
Open-Air Theatre, In
NW1 4NP Open Air
Tel: 935-5756. Ends: 9-1
International Air Tattoo
Held biennially, the v
military air displ
tions

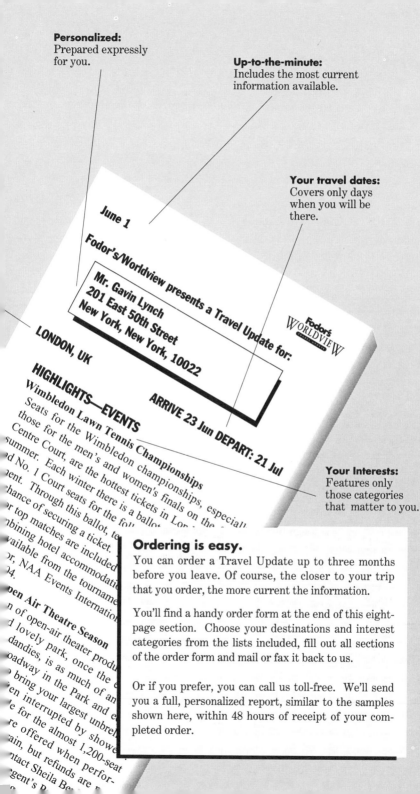

Personalized:
Prepared expressly
for you.

Up-to-the-minute:
Includes the most current
information available.

Your travel dates:
Covers only days
when you will be
there.

June 1

Fodor's/Worldview presents a Travel Update for:

Mr. Gavin Lynch
201 East 50th Street
New York, New York, 10022

LONDON, UK

ARRIVE 23 Jun DEPART: 21 Jul

Fodor's
WORLDVIEW

Your Interests:
Features only
those categories
that matter to you.

HIGHLIGHTS—EVENTS

Wimbledon Lawn Tennis Championships

Seats for the Wimbledon championships
those for the men's and women's finals on the
Centre Court, are the hottest tickets in Lon
summer. Each winter there is a ballo
d No. 1 Court seats for the foll
ent. Through this ballot, t
hance of securing a ticket.
r top matches are included
bining hotel accommodati
or, NAA Events Internation
04.

Open Air Theatre Season

n of open-air theater produ
d lovely park, once the e
dandies, is as much of an
oadway in the Park and e
bring your largest unbre
en interrupted by showe
e for the almost 1,200-seat
re offered when perfor-
ain, but refunds are
ntact Sheila Be
gent's P

Ordering is easy.

You can order a Travel Update up to three months
before you leave. Of course, the closer to your trip
that you order, the more current the information.

You'll find a handy order form at the end of this eight-
page section. Choose your destinations and interest
categories from the lists included, fill out all sections
of the order form and mail or fax it back to us.

Or if you prefer, you can call us toll-free. We'll send
you a full, personalized report, similar to the samples
shown here, within 48 hours of receipt of your completed order.

**Special concerts—
who's performing
what and where**

**One-of-a-kind,
one-time-only events**

**Special interest,
in-depth listings**

Children — Events
Angel Canal Festival
The festivities include a children's funfair,
entertainers, a boat rally and displays on the
water. Regent's Canal. Islington. N1. Tube:
Angel. Tel: 267 9100. 11:30am-5:30pm. 7/04.
Blackheath Summer Kite Festival
Stunt kite displays with parachuting teddy
bears and trade stands. Free admission. SE3.
BR: Blackheath. 10am. 6/27.
Megabugs
Children will delight in this infestation of
giant robotic insects, including a praying
mantic 60 times life size. Mon-Sat 10am-
6pm; Sun 11am-6pm. Admission 4.50
pounds. Natural History Museum, Cromwell
Road. SW7. Tube: South Kensington. Tel:
938 9123. Ends 10/01.
Childminders
This establishment employs only women,
providing nurses and qualified nannies to

Music — Jazz & Blues
Tito Puente's Golden Men of Latin Jazz
The father of mambo and Cuban rumba king
comes to town. Royal Festival Hall. South Bank.
SE1. Tube: Waterloo. Tel: 928 8800. 8pm. 7/15.
Georgie Fame and The New York Band
Riding a popular tide with his latest album, the
smoky-voiced Fame and his keyboard are on a
tour yet again. The Grand. Clapham Junction.
SW11. BR: Clapham Junction. Tel: 738 9000.
7:30pm. 7/07.
Jacques Loussier Play Bach Trio
The French jazz classicist and colleagues.
Kenwood Lakeside. Hampstead Lane.
Kenwood. NW3. Tube: Golders Green, then bus
210. Tel: 413 1443. 7pm. 7/10.
Tony Bennett and Ronnie Scott
Royal Festival Hall. South Bank. SE1. Tube:
Waterloo. Tel: 928 8800. 8pm. 7/11.
Santana
Royal Festival Hall. South Bank. SE1. Tube:
Waterloo. Tel: 928 8800. 8pm. 7/12.
Count Basie Orchestra and Nancy Wilson Trio
Royal Festival Hall. South Bank. SE1. Tube:
Waterloo. Tel: 928 8800. 8pm. 7/14.
King Pleasure and the Biscuit Boys
Royal Festival Hall. South Bank. SE1. Tube:
Waterloo. Tel: 928 8800. 6:30 and 9pm. 7/16.
Al Green and the London Community Gospel Choir
Royal Festival Hall. South Bank. SE1. Tube:
Waterloo. Tel: 928 8800. 8pm. 7/13.
BB King and Linda Hopkins
Mother of the blues and successor to Bessi
Hopkins meets up with "Blues Boy"

Music — Classical
Marylebone Sinfonia
Kenneth Gowen conducts music by Puc
and Rossini. Queen Elizabeth Hall. So
Bank. SE1. Tube: Waterloo. Tel: 928 88
7:45pm. 7/16.
London Philharmonic
Franz Welser-Moest and George Benja
conduct selections by Alexander Go
Messiaen, and some of Benjamin's own
positions. Queen Elizabeth Hall. South
SE1. Tube: Waterloo. Tel: 928 8800. 8pr
London Pro Arte Orchestra and Forest C
Murray Stewart conducts selection
Rossini, Haydn and Jonathan Willcocks
Queen Elizabeth Hall. South Bank.
Tube: Waterloo. Tel: 928 8800. 7:45pm
Kensington Symphony Orchestra

Here's what you get . . .

Detailed information about what's going on — precisely when you'll be there.

Reviews by local critics

Show openings during your visit

Exhibitions & Shows—Antique & Flower

Westminster Antiques Fair

Over 50 stands with pre-1830 furniture and other Victorian and earlier items. Thu-Fri 11am-8pm; Sat-Sun 11am-6pm. Admission 4 pounds, children free. Old Royal Horticultural Hall. Vincent Square. SW1. Tel: 0444/48 25 14. 6-24 thru 6/27.

Royal Horticultural Society Flower Show

The show includes displays of carnations, summer fruit and vegetables. Tue 11am-7pm; Wed 10am-5pm. Admission Tue 4 pounds, Wed 2 pounds. Royal Horticultural Halls. Greycoat Street and Vincent Square. SW1. Tube: Victoria. 7/20 thru 7/21.

...mpton Court Palace International Flower Show

Major international garden and flower show ...king place in conjunction with the British ...

Theater — Musical

Sunset Boulevard

In June, the four Andrew Lloyd Webber musicals which dominated London's stages in the 1980s (Cats, Starlight Express, Phantom of the Opera and Aspects of Love) are joined by the composer's latest work, a show rumored to have his best music to date. The 1950 Billy Wilder film about a helpless young writer who is drawn into the world of a possessive, aging silent screen star offers rich opportunities for Webber's evolving style. Soaring, aching melodies, lush technical effects and psychological thrills are all expected. Patti Lupone stars. Mon-Sat at 8pm; matinee Thu-Sat at 3pm. In-person sales only at the box office; credit card bookings, Tel: 344 0055. Admission 15-32.50 pounds. Adelphi Theatre. The Strand. WC2. Tube: Charing Cross. Tel: 836 7611. Starts: 6/21

Leonardo A Portrait of Love

A new musical about the great Renaissance arti... and inventor comes in for a London premier... tested by a brief run at Oxford's Old Fire Stati... ...autumn. The work explores the relations... ... Vinci and the woman '...

Spectator Sports — Other Sports

Greyhound Racing: Wembley Stadium

This dog track offers good views of greyhound racing held on Mon, Wed and Fri. No credit cards. Stadium Way. Wembley. HA9. Tube: Wembley Park. Tel: 902 8833.

Benson & Hedges Cricket Cup Final

Lord's Cricket Ground. St. John's Wood Road. NW8. Tube: St. John's Wood. Tel: 289 1611. 11am. 7/10.

Business-Fax & Overnight Mail

Post Office, Trafalgar Square Branch

Offers a network of fax services, the Intelpost system, throughout the country and abroad. Mon-Sat 8am-8pm, Sun 9am-5pm. William IV S...

Albuquerque • Atlanta • Atlantic City • N...
Baltimore • Boston • Chicago • Cincinnati
Cleveland • Dallas/Ft.Worth • Denver • D...
• Houston • Kansas City • Las Vegas • Los
Angeles • Memphis • Miami • Milwaukee •
New Orleans • New York City • Orlando •
Springs • Philadelphia • Phoenix • Pittsburg
Portland • Salt Lake • San Antonio • San Di...
• San Franc... • Seattle • St. Louis • Tamp...
Oslo • Was... ...lu • Island...
Hawaii • Kauai • Maui • Abacos • Bimini
Ber... a Columbus... • Hamilton... ...lar
Antigua & B... ...uilla
...Gorda • Barbados • Dominica • Gren...
...cia • St. Vincent • Trinidad &Tobago
...ymans • Puerto Plata • Santo Doming...
... Aruba • Bonaire • Curacao • St. Ma...
...ec City • Montreal • Ottawa • Toron...
...Vancouver • Guadeloupe • Martiniqu...
...helemy • St. Martin • Kingston • Ixta...
...o Bay • Negril • Ocho Rios • Ponce
...n • Grand Turk • Providenciales • S...
...St. John • St. Thomas • Acapulco •
...& Isla Mujeres • Cozumel • Guadal...
...a • Los Cabos • Manzanillo • Mazatl...
...City • Monterrey • Oaxaca • Puerto
...do • Puerto Vallarta • Ver...

Fodor's
WORLDVIEW
TRAVEL UPDATE

Interest Categories

For <u>your</u> personalized Travel Update, choose the categories you're most interested in from this list. Every Travel Update automatically provides you with *Event Highlights* – the best of what's happening during the dates of your trip.

1.	**Business Services**	Fax & Overnight Mail, Computer Rentals, Photocopying, Secretarial , Messenger, Translation Services

Dining

2.	**All Day Dining**	Breakfast & Brunch, Cafes & Tea Rooms, Late-Night Dining
3.	**Local Cuisine**	In Every Price Range—from Budget Restaurants to the Special Splurge
4.	**European Cuisine**	Continental, French, Italian
5.	**Asian Cuisine**	Chinese, Far Eastern, Japanese, Indian
6.	**Americas Cuisine**	American, Mexican & Latin
7.	**Nightlife**	Bars, Dance Clubs, Comedy Clubs, Pubs & Beer Halls
8.	**Entertainment**	Theater—Drama, Musicals, Dance, Ticket Agencies
9.	**Music**	Classical, Traditional & Ethnic, Jazz & Blues, Pop, Rock
10.	**Children's Activities**	Events, Attractions
11.	**Tours**	Local Tours, Day Trips, Overnight Excursions, Cruises
12.	**Exhibitions, Festivals & Shows**	Antiques & Flower, History & Cultural, Art Exhibitions, Fairs & Craft Shows, Music & Art Festivals
13.	**Shopping**	Districts & Malls, Markets, Regional Specialities
14.	**Fitness**	Bicycling, Health Clubs, Hiking, Jogging
15.	**Recreational Sports**	Boating/Sailing, Fishing, Ice Skating, Skiing, Snorkeling/Scuba, Swimming
16.	**Spectator Sports**	Auto Racing, Baseball, Basketball, Football, Horse Racing, Ice Hockey, Soccer

Please note that interest category content will vary by season, destination, and length of stay.

Destinations

The Fodor's/Worldview Travel Update covers more than 160 destinations worldwide. Choose the destinations that match your itinerary from this list. (Choose bulleted destinations only.)

United States (Mainland)
- Albuquerque
- Atlanta
- Atlantic City
- Baltimore
- Boston
- Chicago
- Cincinnati
- Cleveland
- Dallas/Ft. Worth
- Denver
- Detroit
- Houston
- Kansas City
- Las Vegas
- Los Angeles
- Memphis
- Miami
- Milwaukee
- Minneapolis/St. Paul
- New Orleans
- New York City
- Orlando
- Palm Springs
- Philadelphia
- Phoenix
- Pittsburgh
- Portland
- St. Louis
- Salt Lake City
- San Antonio
- San Diego
- San Francisco
- Seattle
- Tampa
- Washington, DC

Alaska
- Anchorage/Fairbanks/Juneau

Hawaii
- Honolulu
- Island of Hawaii
- Kauai
- Maui

Canada
- Quebec City
- Montreal
- Ottawa
- Toronto
- Vancouver

Bahamas
- Abacos
- Eleuthera/Harbour Island
- Exumas
- Freeport
- Nassau & Paradise Island

Bermuda
- Bermuda Countryside
- Hamilton

British Leeward Islands
- Anguilla
- Antigua & Barbuda
- Montserrat
- St. Kitts & Nevis

British Virgin Islands
- Tortola & Virgin Gorda

British Windward Islands
- Barbados
- Dominica
- Grenada
- St. Lucia
- St. Vincent
- Trinidad & Tobago

Cayman Islands
- The Caymans

Dominican Republic
- Puerto Plata
- Santo Domingo

Dutch Leeward Islands
- Aruba
- Bonaire
- Curacao

Dutch Windward Islands
- St. Maarten

French West Indies
- Guadeloupe
- Martinique
- St. Barthelemy
- St. Martin

Jamaica
- Kingston
- Montego Bay
- Negril
- Ocho Rios

Puerto Rico
- Ponce
- San Juan

Turks & Caicos
- Grand Turk
- Providenciales

U.S. Virgin Islands
- St. Croix
- St. John
- St. Thomas

Mexico
- Acapulco
- Cancun & Isla Mujeres
- Cozumel
- Guadalajara
- Ixtapa & Zihuatanejo
- Los Cabos
- Manzanillo
- Mazatlan
- Mexico City
- Monterrey
- Oaxaca
- Puerto Escondido
- Puerto Vallarta
- Veracruz

Europe
- Amsterdam
- Athens
- Barcelona
- Berlin
- Brussels
- Budapest
- Copenhagen
- Dublin
- Edinburgh
- Florence
- Frankfurt
- French Riviera
- Geneva
- Glasgow
- Interlaken
- Istanbul
- Lausanne
- Lisbon
- London
- Madrid
- Milan
- Moscow
- Munich
- Oslo
- Paris
- Prague
- Provence
- Rome
- Salzburg
- St. Petersburg
- Stockholm
- Venice
- Vienna
- Zurich

Pacific Rim Australia & New Zealand
- Auckland
- Melbourne
- Sydney

China
- Beijing
- Guangzhou
- Shanghai

Japan
- Kyoto
- Nagoya
- Osaka
- Tokyo
- Yokohama

Other
- Bangkok
- Hong Kong & Macau
- Manila
- Seoul
- Singapore
- Taipei

Fodor's
WORLDVIEW Order Form

THIS TRAVEL UPDATE IS FOR (Please print):

Name _____

Address _____

City	State	ZIP

Country	Tel # ( ) -

Title of this Fodor's guide: _____

Store and location where guide was purchased: _____

INDICATE YOUR DESTINATIONS/DATES: Write in below the destinations you want to order. Then fill in your arrival and departure dates for each destination.

		Month	Day		Month	Day
(Sample) LONDON	From:	6	/ 21	To:	6	/ 30
1	From:	/		To:	/	
2	From:	/		To:	/	
3	From:	/		To:	/	

You can order up to three destinations per Travel Update. Only destinations listed on the previous page are applicable. Maximum amount of time covered by a Travel Update cannot exceed 30 days.

CHOOSE YOUR INTERESTS: Select up to eight categories from the list of interest categories shown on the previous page and circle the numbers below:

1   2   3   4   5   6   7   8   9   10   11   12   13   14   15   16

CHOOSE HOW YOU WANT YOUR TRAVEL UPDATE DELIVERED (Check one):

❏ Please mail my Travel Update to the address above **OR**

❏ Fax it to me at **Fax #** ( ) -

DELIVERY CHARGE (Check one)

	Within U.S. & Canada	Outside U.S. & Canada
First Class Mail	❏ $2.50	❏ $5.00
Fax	❏ $5.00	❏ $10.00
Priority Delivery	❏ $15.00	❏ $27.00

All orders will be sent within 48 hours of receipt of a completed order form.

ADD UP YOUR ORDER HERE. *SPECIAL OFFER FOR FODOR'S PURCHASERS ONLY!*

	Suggested Retail Price	Your Price	This Order
First destination ordered	$13.95	$ 7.95	$ 7.95
Second destination (if applicable)	$ 9.95	$ 4.95	+
Third destination (if applicable)	$ 9.95	$ 4.95	+
Plus delivery charge from above			+
		TOTAL:	$

METHOD OF PAYMENT (Check one):   ❏ AmEx   ❏ MC   ❏ Visa   ❏ Discover
❏ Personal Check   ❏ Money Order

Make check or money order payable to: Fodor's Worldview Travel Update

Credit Card # _____ **Expiration Date:** _____

Authorized Signature _____

SEND THIS COMPLETED FORM TO:
Fodor's Worldview Travel Update, 114 Sansome Street, Suite 700, San Francisco, CA 94104

OR CALL OR FAX US 24-HOURS A DAY
Telephone **1-800-799-9609** • Fax **1-800-799-9619** (From within the U.S. & Canada)
(Outside the U.S. & Canada: Telephone 415-616-9988 • Fax 415-616-9989)

(Please have this guide in front of you when you call so we can verify purchase.)

Offer valid until 12/31/94.